Recipes Remembered

A Celebration of Survival

Recipes Remembered

A Celebration of Survival

The remarkable stories and authentic
recipes of Holocaust survivors

June Feiss Hersh

RUDER FINN PRESS

in association with the
Museum of Jewish Heritage–A Living Memorial to the Holocaust

MUSEUM
OF JEWISH
HERITAGE | A LIVING
MEMORIAL
TO THE
HOLOCAUST

Softcover Edition Published in 2012 By Eat Well - Do Good

ISBN 10: 0-615-66321-4

ISBN 13: 978-0-615-66321-0

Printed in the USA

Design: Ruder Finn Design, NYC

Editorial Director: Susan Slack

Creative Director: Lisa Gabbay

Art Director: Sal Catania

Design Director: Jennifer Sanders

Production Director: Valerie Thompson

Digital Imaging Specialist: Steve Moss

ISBN 10: 0-9834863-0-1

ISBN 13: 978-0-9834863-0-5

4th Printing, February 2012

Printed in the USA

This book is dedicated to
those who are here, and those who are not.
I am forever humbled and honored to share
your stories and recipes.

Inge Auerbacher, Arlette Levy Baker, Murray Berger and Fruma Gulkowich Berger, Nadzia Goldstein Bergson and Milton Bergson, Sonia and Zus Bielski, Edith Hamburger Blumenthal and Siggi Blumenthal, Luna and Haim Cohen, Michael and Florence Edelstein, Ruth and Julius Eggener, Mike and Frania Faywlowicz, Joan Ferencz, George and Ethel Feuerstein, Regina Schmidt Finer, Raymond Fishler, Mila Ginzburg Fishman, Stephen and Hela Fisk, Ida Frankfurter, Robert and Nella Frendel, Paula Gerson, Judith Kosczianska Ginsburg and Marvin Mordechai "Motke" Ginsburg, Angie and Moritz "Moshe" Goldfeier, Natalie Gomberg, Elly Berkovits Gross, Henny Durmashkin Gurko and Simon Gurko, Reni Hanau, Celina Hecht, Peri Hirsch, Judita Hruza, The Jacobs family, Cecile and Simon Jeruchim, Lilly Schwarcz Kaplan, Ellen and Ernest Katz, Luna Kaufman, Celia Kener, Solomon and Koula Koen Kofinas, Ruth Kohn, Rae and Joseph Kushner, George Lang, Freda Lederer, Miriam Lesorgen, Stella Levi, Dina and Jacob Liverant, Greta Margolis, Lily Mazur Margules and Edward Margules, Miriam Margulies, Mary Fenyes Mayer, Marsha Meyer, Rachel Angelou Mosios, Katherine Wassermann Noir and Robert (Bela Schwartz) Noir, Kurt and Gisela Obernbreit, Ruth and Vittorio Orvieto, Sonya and Aaron Oshman, David and Mary May Prussin, Helen and Henry Ptashnik, Wolfgang "Wolfie" Rauner, Irma and Martin Reich, Melly Resnicow, Sara "Hannah" Rigler, Gita Karelitz Roback & Godel Roback, Sol and Sally Rosenkranz, Maks and Gita Rothman, Ada Ehrlich Rubin and Leo Rubin, Evelyn Pike Rubin, The Rubach family, Helena Pradelski Sabat and Benjamin Sabat, Olga Paverman Schaerf and Henry Schaerf, Doris Schechter, Ruth Schloss, Cantor Gershon Sirota, Ruth Baumwald Stromer and Moty Stromer, Fira Stukelman, Florence Tabrys, Ruth Goldman Tobias, The Turiel Family, Berta Kiesler Vaisman, Jules Wallerstein, Dr. Ruth Westheimer, Chana Wiesenfeld, Matilda Winkler, Hanna Kleiner Wechsler, Rachela Introligator Weisstuch and Victor Weisstuch, Eva Young, Abraham and Millie Zuckerman

Acknowledgments

When a thought becomes an idea and that idea takes flight, it takes more than good intentions to see it through. For more than eighteen months, I lived this book and because of the nature of the project, it became all-consuming. It was truly a labor of love, which I could not have delivered without the help, support and encouragement of so many people.

Always there to listen, facilitate, bolster, listen, taste, cheerlead, clean-up and did I say, listen, was my husband, Ron, a true *mentsh*. When I didn't think I could write another story, or prepare another recipe - you did. Thank you for your unfailing, unending, unconditional love and support. In the ultimate role reversal, my children Allison, Dan and Jennifer (proofreader extraordinaire) became like parents; boastful, honest, tactful, meddling, and encouraging. The respect you have shown this project and the patience you have shown me tell me so much about your character and for that I could not be more proud, thankful or blessed. To my parents, Dorothy and Murray, who always told me that I could not fail, thank you for having that confidence in me. A shout out to my Dad who has never met a meal he didn't like-you tasted just about everything I made with a clear palate and objective honesty. To my Mom, a true survivor of a different kind, thank you for always making me feel that whatever I do is the very best. When I needed to hear, "you're doing great", I knew who to turn to, my sister Andrea. Thank you for introducing me to everyone, and I mean everyone, as your sister, the published author. To my brother-in-law, Robert, my resident rugelach maven, thank you for devouring every cookie I made, and knowing enough about each to give me precise feedback. To my front line tasters, Adam, Susan, Stacy, Erik, Seth and Aunt Fay the "kreplach queen", you took your seats at holiday gatherings, never completely sure what I would be serving, thank you for greeting each dish with honesty and an open mind. And to the newest tasters, Freya Rose, Eloise Rose and Jack Dylan, I hope you develop a love for these beautiful culinary traditions. To Barbra, Barbara, Carol, Debbi, Ellen, Helen, Judy, Paulette, Sally and all my friends and family who listened as I endlessly talked about the book, you always made me feel you were truly interested, I cannot thank you enough. I owe you hours of selfless conversation.

Thank you to Carla Glasser, who on faith alone guided me and held my hand along the way. Andy Smith, thank you for being my personal guardian angel and bringing this project to Ruder Finn Press. To all the professional chefs, authors and restaurateurs who graciously and generously donated their recipes, thank you for letting me play in your cyber-kitchen this past year; I had a ball. Thank you to David Marwell, Felica Kobylanski, Abby Spilka, Sheri Adler, Erica Blumenfeld, Bonnie Gurewitsch, and the entire Museum staff who helped me with initiating the project and provided assistance throughout. Thank you Rubenstein Associates and most notably Jane Rubinstein for your enthusiasm and dedication to promoting this book. A special thank you to David Finn, a true visionary, who saw the merit in this book and committed the resources of his firm, Ruder Finn, to developing the work, and for the incredible wisdom of placing Susan Slack as Editor. A big thank you to the entire team at Ruder Finn Press who brought the book to life; Lisa Gabbay, Sal Catania, Diana Yeo, Ruben Mercado, Jeff Gillam, Steve Moss and Jennifer Sanders.

TABLE OF CONTENTS

Preface

There is no doubt that memories of food and the social context of food—preparing it and partaking of it—are among the most potent that humans have. One need not read Proust to understand the capacity for food to unlock powerful memories and to transport us through time. Whatever explanation we seek—brain chemistry or something less clinical—we have all experienced how an aroma or a particular flavor can take us to another place. This meaningful and warmly written book—*Recipes Remembered: A Celebration of Survival*—is perfect proof of this phenomenon. Here we see how individuals whose lives were disrupted or torn apart by the events of World War II and the Holocaust retain intense memories of the food they enjoyed in happier times. It is as if food were the grain of sand around which pearls of memory were formed, enduring as tokens of a lost world and time.

We are so very pleased that June Hersh approached us with the proposal to write this book, and we were eager to cooperate in any way we could. Of course, June deserves all of the credit for the delicious and diligent work that is reflected here, but I would like to think that her experience in our Museum inspired her to approach the complex and tragic history of the Holocaust through the individual stories of those who lived it. Indeed, our visitors encounter the messages of our Museum through the personal narratives of the people who were lost and of those who survived to build new lives. Rather than having an impersonal voice guide our visitors through our Museum, they are led from one personal story to another. They relate to the history we teach by relating to the people who recount it. In this same way, June has sought out engaging individuals, whose stories and memories connect us to a different time and whose examples of determination and survival are both deeply compelling and inspirational.

Of course, just as recollections of food populate the prewar memories of the people whose stories are told in these pages, memories of the absence of food often plague those who experienced the hardships of war and persecution. In this sense, the memories—and recipes—revealed in this book have a special significance. Not only do they link to happier times, but they are, in a way, also antidotes to the poisonous periods of anguish and deprivation. One of the most powerful stories of our time remains how those who endured the worst —unceasing hatred, unpredictable violence, unimaginable trauma—found the best in themselves and mustered the fortitude and resolve to choose life and to rebuild their lives. Surely in this precarious and uniquely personal journey, they were strengthened along the way by warm memories of the kind that animate this book.

David G. Marwell, Ph.D.
Director
Museum of Jewish Heritage
A Living Memorial to the Holocaust

Introduction

While at its heart this is a book of recipes, in its soul it is a book of stories; life-affirming and uplifting stories about a community of remarkable people who have nourished and nurtured their families for decades. Plucked from their homes, our contributors were children of the Holocaust, thrown from comfort to chaos. Many survived death camps, displacement or years of hiding while others were sent to safety, arriving in unfamiliar places. We consider all these contributors survivors as they survived the unimaginable and their lives were forever changed. Prior to the war, they had enjoyed memorable meals and family gatherings. They learned about secret ingredients and timeless traditions. They came from cities with regional specialties, indigenous spices, local flavors and distinctive techniques. Through it all, one important constant was the food they remembered. With this cookbook, we celebrate the survival of these miraculous people and their *RECIPES REMEMBERED.*

I embarked on this project not fully knowing what to expect. I am not the child of survivors, and had little interaction with this community. What I did have was an association with the Museum of Jewish Heritage - A Living Memorial to the Holocaust. The Museum stands at the crossroads of lower Manhattan with unparalleled and fitting views of the Statue of Liberty and Ellis Island. It is dedicated to honoring the memory of those who died by embracing the traditions they established, examining their steadfast faith, exploring their pre-war lives and affirming their legacy. I knew the Museum's philosophy fell comfortably in place with the goals I had for this book and that they were the perfect institution to benefit from the proceeds. Very soon after presenting the concept to the Museum, I began my work. I knew it was important to personally speak to every contributor. Soon I found myself not simply conducting interviews or making appointments, but making friends. They became "my" survivors, my connection to the past and my reason to optimistically embrace the future. There were late night emails and early morning phone calls. I worried when one took a fall on the ice and rejoiced when another's memoir was published. I was invited to shop the markets of Brighton Beach, Brooklyn and to join an eighty-year-old survivor on Facebook! I listened to memories told through European accents that have defied decades of assimilation. I came to understand their psyches and how their minds' eye saw the past and remembered their own personal truths. "Second Gens" (children of survivors) shared stories of their parents' struggles and triumphs and together we marveled at their resilience and strength. The stories are all unique, all inspiring and all miraculous. But be mindful and understand that their stories reflect their own perspective and are an authentic retelling of their singular history.

My first interview was with Regina Finer, the mother of Museum supporter, Evelyn Goldfeier. Evelyn explained to me that every question you ask a survivor is answered one or two hours later. You will hear about the cat's cough, a second cousin who was looking for Mr. Right, an unforgettable trip to Israel, a visit to the dentist and then, your question will be answered. I was forewarned to be patient, but dogged. If I let the interview get away from me, I might never get it back. I sat down with Regina, ready to listen and poised to ask numerous questions. I left my watch behind.

Me: So Regina, tell me about a food that you remember enjoying as a child, something you still make today.

Regina: Kluskies, potato dumplings.

Me: Do you have the recipe?

Regina: I don't need a recipe to make them.

Me: Well can you describe to me how you go about it, so I can share your " recipe" with others?

Regina: Well, you take some potatoes.

Me: *How many?*

Regina: *How many? I never counted.*

Evelyn: *Mom, when you make dumplings do you buy a bag of potatoes?*

Regina: *Of course I buy a bag; the price is much better when you buy a bag.*

Evelyn: *And when you make your dumplings, do you use the entire bag?*

Regina: *What, you think I would waste potatoes?*

Evelyn: *And can you carry the entire bag of potatoes?*

Regina: *Who else is going to carry them for me?*

Evelyn to me: *Start with five pounds of potatoes.*

After taking copious notes, and more importantly taking in the essence of what Regina was describing, I had a very clear understanding of her personal life history and a basic concept of her recipe. I realized that like Regina, many of these cooks prepare from instinct and memory, from taste and smell or by *shitteryne*; Yiddish for without a recipe, a little of this and a little of that. How much is a glass of oil or an eggshell of matzo meal? Is *a bisel* a teaspoon or a pinch? And what about those recipes written in shorthand or scribbled as illegible notes stained with cooking oil and sauce? How could I write a cookbook based on recipes that were loose formulas? It was then I knew I would test and re-test every recipe and write each precisely so that I could provide you with detailed introductions, recipe context, clear directions, consistent format and exact measurements. All have been reviewed and approved by the contributor. There are those recipes that will appeal to your inner chef and other recipes that are simple and straightforward. What they all have in common is the journey they have made, how they relate to the story that is being told and the survivor they honor.

And while I was searching for authentic and timeless recipes, many of these cooks had found short cuts and tricks. One wonderful contributor to the book took me into her confidence. When I

asked for her matzo ball recipe she quipped " I used to make matzo balls that you could throw against the wall, until I learned a better way to make them." She went on to share her prized, secret recipe, walking me into her kitchen pantry as we spoke." First you take 2 teaspoons of oil, add 2 eggs and then 1 box of Streit's Matzo Ball Mix." Maybe cooking traditional food doesn't have to be a *Gantseh Megillah*! In many recipes, we leave that decision to you.

I further discovered that Jewish food is hard to define. I began to question, what really makes a food Jewish? To a *Sephardic* survivor it is stuffed onions and chicken with okra that graced her holiday table, for a German survivor it is arroz con pollo and fried plantains that she learned to prepare as a refugee in the Dominican Republic and for a Polish survivor it is the coveted Shabbos dinner with chopped liver, matzo ball soup and roast chicken. The answer to my question was more accurately, what isn't Jewish food? I know you will be comforted by the traditional recipes that we long associate with our heritage, but I also know you will be inspired by the new interpretations and less familiar recipes that are presented in the book.

Another thing I learned was the true definition of the two words I heard over and over, "The Best." Every contributor swore their gefilte fish or noodle *kugel* was the best. How could that be? And then it hit me, the best had less to do with the ingredients and preparation and more to do with the association and tradition. The best soup I ever tasted was at my grandmother's table, surrounded by family, being shushed by my father, and encouraged to misbehave by his. The soup might have been a little salty and the matzo balls sat like spheres of cardboard in my stomach, but I would have sworn that soup was perfection. Every recipe in this book represents someone's best, and there's a legion of loyal tasters who would swear to that. When you replicate a dish from this book, be faithful to the recipe, but be sure to include a piece of yourself in every preparation. Make it your own, make a food memory, make a new tradition and make it the best your family ever tasted.

And then there were the recipes remembered that the survivor could not recreate, a technique that was watched but not learned, a flavor that was lost but not forgotten.

That's when I brought in our professional chefs, cookbook authors and restaurateurs. The professional's recipes were designed to complement the survivor's recollections, and without exception these professionals graciously stepped in. Many of their recipes are exactly as the survivors described, while others are inspired by a contributor's recollections. They are designed to round out a meal, reflect a region's cuisine, enhance your cooking experience and honor the survivor's food memories.

What memories cannot be conveyed in a word can be seen in a photo; pictures of teenagers frolicking on a lakeside dock, children playing in their front yards, families gathering for life cycle events. Moments captured, preserved and now shared in black and white so that these true expressions of better times would be a legacy for years to come. While the survivors contributed personal and cherished family photos, the Museum contributed photos of artifacts that relate to cooking. A pot smuggled out of a ghetto or a noodle maker used to prepare for the Shabbos meal; these images are stark and real, authentic and speechless. We might not know the story behind each, but the fact that it survived till today, speaks volumes. Give voice to the photos; imagine the stories they could tell.

I spent hundreds of hours listening, learning, laughing and crying. I heard incredible stories of defiance, resolve, bravery and luck. I came home with recipes to test, savor, share and enjoy. The survivor community has so much to teach and we still have so much to learn. Devour their words and savor their message.

Navigating the Book

Chapters

If you are looking for appetizers in the front of the book and desserts at the end, you will certainly be confused; that's why we designed a good index. The book is organized by region, because the country where each contributor was born very much determined their experiences before and during the war as well as their food memories. Each chapter has an introduction to give you a taste of what's to come and a list of the stories and recipes that can be found in that chapter.

Kosher

Time for true confessions, I am not kosher. When I first considered the framework for this book I debated many things, but one that was non-negotiable was the book needed to be kosher. I felt that out of respect for those who were contributing recipes and especially to honor those who were not here to do so, the book would be kosher. Cooking kosher made me mindful of my ingredients and proved to be more an eye opener than a challenge. Every measure has been taken to assure that the recipes are in harmony with the rules of *Kashrut*. In some instances we offer substitutions or alternative preparations. If you are Kosher you know the rules better than anyone. So use your good judgment, and when in doubt, leave it out.

Servings

I must admit, that as I was raising my children I would look at the information on the back of a box of pasta where they list the serving size and mockingly scoff, those aren't Jewish portions! One of the hardest tasks in writing this book was assigning servings to the recipes. Some of the dishes in the book can serve as stand-alone main courses or double as dessert, so how do you accurately measure servings? Wherever possible I listed the yield, but in many cases, that depends on how big a piece of *kugel* you cut, or soup you ladle. My servings are generous, so my best advice, use the servings as a guide, not a guilt-trip.

Start to Finish

I don't always take the time I should to read a recipe from start to finish. Admit it, sometimes you're a skimmer too. So you get really excited about preparing a wonderful new recipe for your family, only to find out 30 minutes before dinner that the meat has to marinate in the fridge overnight. I've tried to take the guesswork out of recipe reading. While prep times vary for each individual, the cooking times are consistent, and overnight preps cannot be rushed. "Start to Finish" assumes you do not have a clean up crew who follows behind you washing the bowl that you will need for the next step. These are realistic guidelines for how long a preparation should take. And when a dish needs to rest, chill, freeze or just linger; you'll know that before starting.

Feedback

Want a good variation for serving blintzes, or learn about another herb that complements a dish? Want to know how to elevate a dessert from a weeknight treat to a Saturday night showstopper? Curious how to make a roux or the best way to clean mushrooms? My Feedback provides tasty bites designed to complement the recipe, provide variations or serving suggestions as well as share with you the interesting tidbits and information I've learned along the way.

Glossary

Most cookbooks use a glossary for fancy cooking terms or pretentious words for everyday foods. Not this book. Our glossary is dedicated to the language of many of our contributors, Yiddish. We have tried to place all Yiddish words and phrases in italics and have provided a glossary for you to refer to, at the end of the book. Yiddish, written from the Hebrew alphabet, relies heavily on idiomatic interpretation and the Americanized phonetic spellings can vary greatly. For anyone who has celebrated Chanukah, Hannukah, Hanukah, you know there are many variations in spelling Yiddish words. We have used several reliable sources for our spelling, including Yiddish Practical Dictionary, David C. Gross (Hippocrene Books, Inc. New York, NY, 2007) and "The Gantseh Megillah", an online resource, so try not to make a *gantseh megillah* if our spelling differs from yours.

Spell Check

Yes, my computer has spell check and yes, I employed it regularly while typing the manuscript. If you see your hometown spelled with an extra "z" or feel a vowel is misplaced in the name of a dish, understand that there are many acceptable spellings for a number of these words. We consulted several well-regarded authorities as well as Museum documents for our historic references and spelling decisions.

The Professionals

Gracious, generous and quick to help, that describes the professionals who stepped in to provide their personal recipes to honor the food memories of many of our survivors. While I enjoyed each and every dish they contributed, I was not presumptuous enough to make changes to any of them. They are presented as the professional provided them to me. These are highly regarded chefs, authors and restaurateurs who know their stuff and have proven track records for serving up delicious food with their own signature style and flare.

JFH

There are some recipes that required little or no changes, some that I wrote based on what the contributor provided, while others have been gently tweaked or faithfully re-interpreted. Those that I created to supplement a recipe are noted with JFH

Some Helpful Information To Make You a Baleboste...

Baking 101

Let me start by saying, baking is a science, cooking an art. In cooking an extra pinch of this or a dollop of that will really not change the outcome. Flavor a dish as you please, and feel free to adjust the recipe to meet your palate. However, baking does not allow that same flexibility. While you don't need to trade-in your apron for a lab coat, follow the recipe with greater precision and you will be rewarded with a better result.

Baking Cakes, Cookies and Pies: Baking can be intimidating, but remember, if you wanted cookies, pies and cakes that were fast, easy and looked and tasted store bought, you would have gone to the store. Here are some tips to help.

- There are many factors that can affect the measurements for flour; humidity, type of flour, size of the eggs etc. Always start with a little less flour than recommended in the recipe and slowly add the balance as directed. Use your sense of touch when determining how much flour to use.

- Use room temperature eggs, they combine and whip better than cold eggs. You can warm an egg that's come right from the fridge by placing it in a bowl with warm water for a minute or so. Unless otherwise specified, all recipes call for large eggs.

- Unless otherwise directed, add eggs to a preparation, one at a time to be sure you have thoroughly incorporated the egg into the mixture. It is also a good idea to crack the eggs into a bowl first, to insure that eggshells don't make their way into the preparation.

- When combining flour with other dry ingredients, it's good to sift or whisk the ingredients together so they are evenly distributed. A simple kitchen strainer makes a great sifter.

- For pastry and crusts, use cold ingredients such as cold butter and ice water.

- When you prepare cookie dough, let it rest in the fridge to help the ingredients bind and settle. Some recipes recommend chilling the dough overnight. Be sure to wrap the dough tightly in plastic wrap or wax paper. It is easier to roll if you flatten the dough into a disc before chilling.

- Be sure your work surface is clean and dry. The absolute best way to flour a work surface is to fill a basic dredging shaker with all-purpose flour and sprinkle it as you go.

- When rolling out chilled dough, if the dough cracks it is too cold, let it rest several minutes longer.

- Always roll the dough starting in the center and working out in all directions to keep the shape even. Lift and turn the dough a quarter turn after each roll.

- When you roll out and then cut the dough, you will inevitably have scraps. Gather the scraps and form a new ball of dough; you might need to briefly chill it in the fridge then roll out and repeat the cutting process.

- Use the right size rolling pin for the job. An over-sized pin is unwieldy when rolling a piece of *kreplach* dough, but is just the right size for a large crust. I like to have a small pastry rolling pin as well as a large one on hand. And remember to flour the rolling pin.

- A small metal cookie spatula is an indispensable tool for lifting and moving the rolled cut dough onto a cookie sheet.

- Cookie cutters, in varying sizes and shapes, are great to have on hand, however, most of our contributors used the rim of a glass.

- Every oven varies, and each has hot and cold spots. When baking with more than one sheet, rotate the trays so they bake evenly. You might want to turn the baking pan around halfway through the suggested cooking time.

- Unless otherwise directed, the oven racks should be set in the middle of the oven.

- Do not put your next batch of uncooked dough on a warm baking pan. Use a new pan or cool the pan down with cold water.

- When you need to test the doneness of your cake a natural wood toothpick works great for those baked in a shallow pan, a bamboo skewer is a better choice for testing cakes made in deeper spring form pans, where a toothpick cannot reach into the center.

- When adding heavy ingredients to a light batter, such as chocolate chips or berries, toss them in a bit of flour to help prevent them from sinking to the bottom of the finished cake.

Baking Dishes and Baking Pans

Pyrex dishes come in a variety of sizes, we mainly utilize the two listed below.

- *11x7x2-inch:* Holds up to 6 cups (an 8 x 8-inch square pan holds the same amount)

- *9x13x2-inch:* Holds up to 10 cups (a 9 x 9-inch square pan holds the same amount)

- *Tube Pan:* The funnel-like piece that rises from the center of this type of pan accomplishes two things. It helps the center of a cake cook as the funnel piece retains the heat and distributes it to the middle of the cake, and it also makes a lovely visual presentation. Usually the bottom is separate, or spring form for an easy release. Spring form pans are often used in Eastern European baking as they are great for light batters that are whipped with egg whites or cream. The mechanism opens to allow easy removal of the finished cake. They come in several sizes, but standard for our recipes is 9 x 3-inch, which holds 11 cups of batter.

- *Bundt Cake Pan:* Serves a similar function as the tube pan. Be sure to grease the entire Bundt pan to help your cake remove easily. Also understand that when you present the finished cake, the top becomes the bottom.

- *Jellyroll Pan:* Great for sheet cakes that don't rise very much as the sides are a mere 1-inch. The pan we use most often measures about 15½ x 10½ -inch and holds 10 cups of batter.

- *Round Cake Pans:* Always good to have two 8-inch and 9-inch on hand.

- *Baking Sheets:* A double wall, non-stick sheet will prevent burning, a Silpat (non-stick silicone mat) or parchment paper will prevent sticking (there is reusable parchment which is more cost effective and better for the environment), and having two pans on hand will prevent waiting in between batches.

If you need to substitute one pan for another, you will need to adjust the cooking times. A helpful website for reference is http://whatscookingamerica.net.

Boiling Salted Water

Throughout the book you'll see I suggest boiling almost every food in salted water. Why? First, it is a good chance to get a little extra seasoning into the food. Secondly, the salt doesn't actually cause the water to boil more quickly, but it does bring the temperature of the water up, so the foods boil better. Unless otherwise directed, salt the water and bring the water to boil over a high heat. When adding salt use about 1 ½ to 2 teaspoons of salt per quart (4 cups) of water. If you are watching your sodium intake, leave it out.

Butter

Unless otherwise specified, all recipes call for unsalted butter.

- When a recipe calls for room temperature butter, DO NOT microwave the butter to speed the process. You will not get the result you want. Let the butter sit out for at least 20 minutes. Butter can actually sit out of the fridge overnight. You should be able to indent a thumbprint into the butter when ready to use, you want it soft not melted.

- When combining butter with sugar or eggs, do not rush the step, it is important for the butter to become creamy and fluffy.

- If the recipe calls for cold butter, do not take the butter out of the fridge until ready to use.

- Butter freezes well, so keep an extra pound on hand in the freezer.

- A stick of butter is 8 tablespoons, equals 4 ounces (¼ lb) and measures ½ cup.

- When baking with butter, the result is generally lighter than when baking with oil. When you incorporate butter in a recipe, it entraps air bubbles as it bakes, creating a lighter finish. Do not substitute butter for oil in all cases. If you do the ratio is 1 cup butter = 7/8 cup oil. You will need to test the recipe and possibly adjust the other ingredients if making the change. If *pareve* is not an issue, you can substitute an equal amount of butter for the margarine suggested in a recipe.

- Burnt butter tastes bitter (say that ten times fast), so when baking cookies and crusts with butter be sure to keep a watchful eye.

- There are many varieties of butter on the market, and a new trend toward " European" butter. The main difference is European butter has a higher butterfat content, and therefore less water and milk solids. This should result in a lighter, richer baked product.

Cook and Stir

This is our way of saying sauté, and is a basic instruction in many recipes. The best order is to heat the specified pan, add the oil to the hot pan and then cook and stir the ingredients. The heated pan will bring the oil up to the perfect sautéing temperature. If using butter, always add butter to a cold pan to prevent it from burning on contact. If using butter and oil, add the oil first then whisk in the butter.

Equipment

For simple cakes and cookies, you might only need a trusty spoon and a bowl, after all, that's what most of our contributors used in the first place. But for preparations that have thick dough, require kneading, or should be combined at high speeds; you might need some additional muscle.

Standing mixer: Saved my rotator cuff and took the work out of what I prepared. The basic mixer comes with three attachments, a dough hook for bread, a flat paddle for most mixing and blending, and a whisk attachment for beating egg whites and heavy cream. If you have the space and a good 20% off coupon, invest in a standing mixer.

Food processor: Accomplishes most baking tasks using the standard metal blade. While the processor has a smaller capacity, it can usually do the job. It is good for most baking needs and very good for prep tasks such as grating, shredding and chopping.

Hand mixer: With at least 6 speeds is affordable, convenient and gets most blending, mixing and whipping jobs done. You will need to exhibit some dexterity, as it is hard to hold the mixer and add the ingredients. Place a potholder or towel under the mixing bowl to prevent it from spinning, and when adding flour to a preparation, wrap a towel around the bowl so the flour does not fly out.

Fork Tender and Cooked Through

These two instructions are used throughout the book, and they mean just what they say. To test for doneness in meat and vegetables, take a fork and pierce the food. If the fork removes easily and the food provides no resistance, it is cooked fork tender. Cooked through, which generally refers to chicken, is when the meat is pierced and the juices run clear.

Pots and Pans

Most home cooks have a basic assortment of pots and pans. Here are some of the basics to help you better determine which pan we reference for each preparation.

- *Sauce pans:* Small: 1½ quarts, Medium: 2 quart, Large: 3 to 4 quart = small soup pot, X-Large: 6 quart and greater = large soup pot.

- *Sauté Pans:* Have a high sidewall, usually 2 to 3 inches. They are great for preparations that have bulky ingredients.

- *Skillets:* Are your everyday fry pans, and are used for most preparations. Large: 12-inch, Medium: 10-inch, Small: 8-inch.

- *Dutch Ovens:* Or heavy lidded cast iron Le Creuset or Magna-Lite style pots work great on the stove but can also go into the oven and are perfect for braising.

Your Pantry: Some Basic Items To Have On Hand

Baking Powder and Baking Soda

Baking powder is a dry chemical leavening agent that adds volume to baked goods. Baking powder contains baking soda, and works by releasing carbon dioxide into your batter, which causes it to rise. Buy double acting baking powder; it contains agents that cause the powder to react first with your wet ingredients, then again while baking, giving rise to a lighter result. It's good to have baking soda on hand as well, but we call for it less often. Baking soda remains fresh only 6 months after opening, so record the date on your box to preserve freshness. Additionally, the baking soda developed for your fridge should not be substituted for general baking soda, it has additives you would not want to bake with.

Good Ingredients

Seems obvious, but we all make choices when marketing, and sometimes that imitation flavored vanilla seems like it will do the trick. Save somewhere else. Pure vanilla and almond extract, pure honey and high quality chocolate really do make a difference. If you are going to the trouble of making it from scratch, use the best ingredients you can.

Flour

There are many types of flour on the market, if you want to buy just one, make it all-purpose flour. Bread flour has higher gluten content, so it is preferred for baking bread.

Fresh Herbs

Are always best, but not always available. If substituting dried herbs for fresh, cut the amount by one third, as dried herbs are more concentrated. An easy guide is: 1 tablespoon of fresh = 1 teaspoon of dried. And remember, even dried herbs have a shelf life so if you've had that oregano since your first child was born and that child is being Bat Mitzvahed-time for a new bottle.

Parsley is called for in many of the recipes, it is a go-to food enhancer, imparting a fresh flavor when added. There are generally two types of parsley sold in the market, Italian flat-leaf and curly. For decoration, curly is great, but for flavor I recommend flat-leaf. When buying, rub a leaf in between your fingers. If you do not get a pungent whiff, the parsley is not fresh. This will also insure you are buying parsley, not cilantro, which looks very similar but has a completely different aroma. If you do not have fresh parsley available, do not substitute dried, it is not worth the effort. When you get the herbs home, trim then submerge the stems in a glass with a couple of inches of cold water to preserve freshness. When cooking soft herbs like parsley and basil, less cooking time is better, unlike woodsy herbs, such as rosemary, which benefit from longer cooking times.

Instant Seasoning and Bouillon

I have always shunned bouillon cubes or seasoning packets, feeling they are an easy way to cheat and compensate for flavor. However, many of the contributors to this book incorporate a form of instant seasoning in their dishes to elevate the flavor. Bouillon cubes, called *würful* in German, have their roots in Eastern Europe. Today we have powdered varieties, which are easy to blend into soups and stews. While I don't applaud the unnatural enhancers they rely on, they do come in handy as flavor boosters. The three varieties the contributors to this book have recommended are Telma, Osem and G. Washington's. They can usually be found in the soup or kosher food section of your market.

Oil

Ok, so you probably don't have (or want) chicken fat on hand. No problem, most of our cooks specified vegetable or canola oil anyway. You can lighten some of the baked goods by using light olive oil in place of vegetable oil. Peanut oil is great for deep-frying, but is costly, so you can substitute a neutral oil like vegetable, canola or corn. Save the extra virgin olive oil for the final drizzle where the flavor can really be tasted.

Salt and Pepper

Like Lucy and Ethel, these seasonings are almost always together and get into just about everything. Unless otherwise specified in a recipe, use kosher salt and freshly ground black pepper. Kosher salt has a clean salty taste, and is less pungent than table salt. Additionally, it features larger crystals than table salt, making it easier to measure and pinch. However, for all baking recipes, unless otherwise specified, use table salt. Its finer crystals distribute more evenly and dissolve more easily. There are many varieties of coarse salt available today. Try experimenting with unrefined sea salt, which has a pure, clean, ocean flavor. Other artisan salts like Fleur de Sel and Grey Salt impart their own nuance, so be mindful because the amount you add to a recipe will vary with the type of salt you choose. As for the pepper, it is best if you freshly grind it, but you can shake it straight from the can. Be sure, if you grind it, to adjust for coarseness. White pepper is almost never specified, but can be used in light sauces where the black pepper is seen as a distraction in the finished dish.

Sour Salt

Also known as citric acid, is a natural product found in citrus fruit. It is crystallized and provides an intense sour flavor. It is great to keep on hand if you do not have fresh lemons available. Use it sparingly; it packs a pucker.

Sugar

There are several types of sugar.

- *Granulated white sugar:* Basic household sugar. It is what is called for when a type is not specified.

- *Brown sugar:* Is granulated sugar with a hint of molasses; it is sweeter than white sugar and imparts almost a caramel taste and helps food develop a golden color.

- *Superfine:* Also known as baker's sugar or castor sugar, is granulated sugar that is more finely ground. It is not an even substitute for granulated sugar, but is often preferred in lighter preparations like meringue or angel food cake.

- *Confectioner's sugar:* Is very fine powdery sugar. This often-overlooked ingredient is very popular in Eastern European baking. It is a simple and easy way to dress up just about anything. Sprinkle confectioner's sugar on cookies and cakes to make them look festive and fresh. It melts easily, so don't sprinkle it on warm baked goods, it will disappear completely. The absolute best method for storing and sprinkling confectioner's sugar is to fill a dredging shaker with the sweet stuff and sprinkle away.

Sugar and Cinnamon

Could there be a better coupling? Mix 1 cup of granulated sugar with 4 teaspoons of cinnamon (more if you prefer a very cinnamony flavor) to make a simple topping for almost anything you bake. Use a simple saltshaker to easily sprinkle this confection.

Vinegar

To achieve the sweet and sour that you'll find in so many of the recipes, our contributors used lemon juice, or vinegar. If you want to stock just one vinegar, make it distilled white; it is the one used most often. Some of the German dishes call for apple cider vinegar, which is purported to have health benefits, and a sweet tart taste. Balsamic vinegar, which appears in one or two dishes, has a smooth, deep, bold flavor.

Yeast

Yeast can be purchased in small packets or in a jar; keep closed tightly and refrigerated after opening. Packaged yeast can hold for months in a cool cupboard. 2 ¼ teaspoons equals one ¼-ounce packet. If it does not bubble within ten minutes after combining it with a warm liquid (about 110 to 115 degrees), it is not fresh. A yeast thermometer is helpful but not essential to test the water temperature.

Poland

It seems fitting to start the book with the stories and recipes from our Polish survivors. Not only do they represent the largest group of contributors, but also their food represents many of the iconic Jewish classics. And while we have packed this chapter with surprises and culinary twists and turns, the familiar dishes such as challah, chopped liver, gefilte fish, matzo ball soup, noodle *kugel*, and brisket all appear in this section. We thought we'd ease you through the journey that is Jewish cooking by beginning with the dishes with which we all identify. There is an ancient Eastern European story, the parable of stone soup, which resonates with the cooking style of our Polish community. The story has many versions; here is one that captures the essence of Polish cooking.

In a small shtetl in Poland, the people were struggling and food was scarce. A soldier marched into the tiny village, hungry and tired and asked for something to eat. The townspeople told him of their plight and he reassured them that he could make a delicious soup from a stone. He dropped a stone into a pot of boiling water, and a crowd began to gather. They were skeptical, but the soldier assured them of a rich broth; so they waited with great anticipation to taste the soup. He encouraged the villagers to contribute small offerings from their gardens and farms. Soon the villagers began tossing in bits of cabbage, carrots, mushrooms, onions and potatoes. Some threw in pieces of beef, turkey and chicken as the soldier encouraged them and told them how delicious the soup would taste. By the time the entire village gathered to watch, the pot was filled with every vegetable grown in that small town and every cut of meat the butcher could find. Hand rolled dumplings and homemade noodles filled the pot and the aroma was splendid. The finished soup had an intense color and flavor and the villagers and the soldier enjoyed a wonderful meal.

Like stone soup, Polish cuisine is a creative mix of available, affordable ingredients. A little of this and a bit of that, lovingly tossed together to make a nourishing, satisfying meal. If it grew in the ground and you could pickle, salt or preserve it, even better. Meals would start with *forshpeiz* and always end with something delectably delicious, like apple cake; made more sweet when prepared by a Galicianer or less so when baked by a Litvak with an under-developed sweet tooth.

After the devastating effects of the war, many of the survivors from Poland immigrated to Israel (Palestine) or America and brought with them comforting preparations that have become a mainstay in our treasury of Jewish recipes. You will find an array of foods both savory and sweet, familiar and unfamiliar, contributed by people from this region. We proudly present new interpretations and timeless traditional recipes remembered from these resilient survivors.

RECIPES

Regina Finer: *Kluskies*–Classic Potato Dumplings

Angie Goldfeier: Chicken Savoy Soup

Judith Kosczianska Ginsburg: Brisket

The Ginsburg Family: Corned Beef

Rae Kushner: Potato Chip *Kugel*

Nadzia Goldstein Bergson: Home Baked Challah

Ada Ehrlich Rubin: Chocolate Chip Cake

Frania Faywlowicz: Meat and Potato *Cholent*

Frania Faywlowicz: Passover Noodles

Rhoda Fishler: Meringue Nut Cookie

Hela Fisk: Plum Cake

Natalie Gomberg: *Mohn*–Poppy Seed Cookies

Henny Durmashkin Gurko: Roasted Chicken

and Vegetables

Celina Hecht: Fresh Yellow Pepper Soup

Celina Hecht: Herb and Vegetable Veal Roast

The Jacobs Family: Baba's Cheesecake

Celia Kener: *Holishkes*–Shortcut Unstuffed Cabbage

Celia Kener: Citrus Rice Pudding

Miriam Lesorgen: *Kreplach*

Karen Banschick: BBQ Brisket

Dina Liverant: *Kutletela*–Small Chicken Burger

Lily Margulies: *Tsimmes*–Chicken with Prunes

Helen Ptashnik: Braised Red Cabbage and Apples

Gita Roback: Slow Simmered Sunday Sauce

Sally Rosenkranz: Honey Cake

Ruth Stromer: Honey and Lemon Stuffed Cabbage

Florence Tabrys: Sweet and Creamy Cheese Blintzes

Florence Tabrys: Polish Apple Cake

Ruth Tobias: *Peperonata*–Bell Peppers

Sabina Goldman: Bursting with Blueberries Tart

Ruth Tobias: Orange Flavored Sponge Cake

Hanna Wechsler: Strawberry Filled *Naleshniki*–Blintzes

Eva Young: Creamy Cheese Noodle *Kugel*

Millie Zuckerman: Sugar Cookies

PROFESSIONAL CONTRIBUTORS

Jennifer Abadi: *Chibiz* (Syrian Pita or Pocket Bread)

Mark Bittman: Simplest Whole Roast Chicken, Six Ways

Eric and Bruce Bromberg: Martha's Excellent Matzoh Ball Soup

Capsuto Freres: Basil Cured *Gravlax*

Susie Fishbein: Mandarin Chicken Salad

Susie Fishbein: Sesame Beef and Broccoli over Ramen Noodles

Ina Garten: Chopped Liver

JFH: Homemade Egg Noodles

JFH: Roasted Brussels Sprouts with Mushrooms, Leeks and Shallots

JFH: Gribenes and Schmaltz–Chicken Skin Cracklings and Rendered Fat

JFH: Orange Honey Ginger Soy Dipping Sauce

JFH: Next Day Brisket Stuffed Meatloaf

JFH: Sour Cream Strudel with Loukoum Filling

JFH: Candied Orange Peel

JFH: Strawberry Sauce

JFH: Chilled Cherry Soup

Judy Bart Kancigor: Louis Selmanowitz's Chopped Herring

Faye Levy: Apple Challah Bread Pudding with Vanilla Custard Sauce

Faye Levy: My Mother's Chicken and Barley Cholent

Gil Marks: Bialys (Polish Onion Rolls)

Gil Marks: *Chremslach* (*Ashkenazi* Sweet Matza Meal Pancakes)

Sara Moulton: Esther's Chicken Fricassee

Jeff Nathan: Duck with Apple and White Raisin Sauce

Jeff Nathan: Herb Scented Chicken Paillard with Wild Mushrooms

Joan Nathan: Classic Gefilte Fish

Valerie Romanoff: Beet Horseradish

Arthur Schwartz: "Kosher" Dill Pickles

Arthur Schwartz: *P'tcha* (Jellied Calf's Feet with Garlic)

Michael Solomonov: Beets with *Tehina*

Michael Solomonov: Prepared *Tehina*

Michael Solomonov: *Tehina*-Hummus

Mark Strausman: Gnocchi

Mark Strausman: *Involtini di Manzo* (Beef Braciole)

Mark Strausman: *Spaghetti al Rustico di Cipole* (Spaghetti with Onion and Tomato Sauce)

Mark Strausman: *Sugo di Crema e Funghi* (Mushroom Cream Sauce)

Mark Strausman: *Sugo al Funghetto di Bosco* (Wild Mushroom Sauce)

David Waltuck: Blintzes of Fresh and Smoked Salmon with Caviar Cream

Regina Schmidt Finer

In her own words

Regina was the first person I interviewed for this book. She set the bar for everyone to come. Her humor and positive outlook immediately put me at ease. Regina left me smiling when she asked if I thought we might make it on to a national talk show to tell her story and demonstrate her cooking, she felt that would be a great outcome.

I was a teenager when I was taken from my home, just outside of Warsaw, Poland. That was the last time I saw my parents. I was sent to the Warsaw ghetto along with my younger brother and sister, and my aunt who was two years older than me. For many months, we hid in a bunker in the ghetto and avoided being transported to a camp. Eventually, like all the others in the ghetto, we were discovered and sent to Majdanek. I went there with my sister and aunt; my brother was left behind, hidden in a kitchen cabinet. I fear he did not survive.

In the camp, my sister and I were separated. I remember seeing her on that first day and she seemed angry that we were apart; I felt terrible. On the second day there, I looked, but couldn't find her. I never saw her again. My aunt and I were moved to many camps including Auschwitz. Although my aunt was older than me, I felt I was the stronger one, and knew I had to protect her. The day of our last move, we were placed on different lines. I appealed to a guard to put us on the same line, I didn't care where it was going; I just wanted us to be together. Luckily she was moved to my line, the one that survived.

We were marched on foot through the woods of Germany, heading to our next and final destination. We knew that this would be our last chance to escape. When it became dark, we escaped into the woods. We stole boys' clothing from a laundry line and found shelter at a farmer's home. He and his wife sheltered us for several months, until the Russian army liberated us.

My aunt and I returned to Poland, to find our home and family gone. My aunt wasn't well, and a very kind gentleman offered us a place to stay; he later became her husband. I traveled to a displacement camp where I met and married my husband. We eventually came to America where we raised our children.

Through it all, there were so many memories of my childhood that helped me get through the difficult times. So many of my memories revolved around traditions and food. I remember how our family and neighbors would gather in my mother's home for Shabbos. It was a competition to see who was the biggest *baleboste*—that was determined by who baked the best challah and made the best noodles for the *kugel*. Holidays were especially joyous, the house would be freshly painted and the kitchen was cleaned spotless. The holidays meant: Get dressed, go to Shul, come home and eat! My mother would call me to help her, "Rivkala, help me chop, help me bake the cookies, help me make the gefilte fish." In those days, the fish would be stuffed into the head of a carp! I now make that same recipe for my family, but I leave the fish head out of it. I love to make potato dumplings, Polish cakes and *kugel*.

There is a feeling of community that binds us all. Everyone should treat everyone else with respect, and respect his or her religion. And most of all, the message I pass on to my three children, three grandchildren and two great grandchildren is, remember to be a *mentsh*.

Top left: Arriving in America, 1950

Regina Finer's Kluskies—Classic Potato Dumplings

Think of this recipe as the little black dress of potato dishes. It goes with everything and you can keep it basic or dress it up. Their firm but spongy consistency makes them perfect to soak up rich gravy or float happily in a bowl of soup. Regina likes to sauté some onions and spoon them over the dumplings for a variation of this popular side dish. When preparing the dumplings Regina suggests you have a *shmatteh* handy to wring out the excess water from the grated potatoes. If you don't have a *shmatteh*, no worries, a dishtowel or cheesecloth will do just fine.

Yields: About 30 dumplings; Start to Finish: Under 30 minutes

6 russet potatoes (about 2 pounds), peeled then grated

¾ cup of all-purpose flour, sifted

¼ cup matzo meal

1 egg, beaten

½ onion, grated (about ⅓ cup)

1½ teaspoons kosher salt

6 turns of grated black pepper

Bring a large pot of salted water to boil.

Grate the potatoes using a box grater or food processor fitted with the metal blade. Process in 3 batches and use the pulse feature to break up any chunks that do not finely grate. Place the grated potatoes in a towel and wring out the excess water. The potatoes go into the towel resembling applesauce and come out with the texture of Play-Doh.

Stir in the flour, matzo meal, beaten egg, onion, salt and pepper and mix thoroughly. Nothing works better then your hands, so get in there and knead the dough. You'll know it's ready when it is no longer sticky, adding a little extra matzo meal as needed. Roll the mixture in your hands and form small dumplings about the size of a walnut.

Drop the dumplings into the pot of salted boiling water. Do not over crowd the pot, as the dumplings will stick together; shake the pot while boiling to free those that cling to the bottom. Boil until they float to the top, about 5 minutes. Remove with a slotted spoon and allow them to drain. Serve while they are still nice and hot.

Homemade Egg Noodles

Regina says you could tell a *baleboste* by who made the best homemade noodles. While we know it is so easy to open a box, there is something incredibly satisfying about making your own. Here is a basic egg noodle recipe that can be turned into noodles or serve as the foundation for pierogis or *kreplach*. The dough can be used right away, or kept in the fridge for several days. If you have a pasta machine or attachment to your standing mixer, it makes the rolling and cutting much easier. Either way, you will have Regina's never ending respect.

Yields: 1 pound of noodles, about 6 to 8 servings; Start to Finish: Under 1 hour

2 cups all-purpose flour

3 eggs

½ teaspoon table salt

Water

Scoop the flour out onto a clean, dry counter and create a well in the center. Crack the eggs into the center of the well and lightly beat with a fork, season with salt. Slowly begin bringing the flour into the well, using the fork or your hands. (You can do this step in a food processor, using the pulse feature to incorporate, but do not over process the ingredients.) Once the ingredients are combined, begin kneading the dough, by hand, on a lightly floured surface, this should take about 10 minutes, adding a drop or two of water or a pinch of flour as needed. The dough will go from crumbly to smooth and elastic with a pale yellow color. When ready, push it in like the "Pillsbury Dough Boy" it should bounce back. Wrap the dough tightly in plastic wrap and let it rest for 30 minutes.

Take the dough and divide it into manageable pieces that you can easily roll. If you have a pasta attachment, use it to stretch and roll the dough. Otherwise, roll each piece of dough out on a lightly floured board, using a large rolling pin. Do not tug at the dough, it will resist and pull back. Use the rolling pin, turning the dough after each roll to prevent it from sticking to the board and to create an even sheet. Roll the dough to about ⅛-inch thick, you should be able to see your hands through the pasta. Let the pasta sit for a few minutes before cutting.

Cut the pasta into ribbons, thick or thin, depending on their usage, using a pizza wheel or sharp knife. A good trick is to fold the pasta into a sheet about 3 inches wide to make cutting easier. Toss the cut noodles with a little flour or cornmeal and let the cut noodles rest on a lined pan or drying rack while you bring a large pot of salted water to boil. If making pierogis or *kreplach* use a 3-inch cookie cutter to cut the dough into rounds, and then fill according to your recipe. Let the pierogi or *kreplach* rest while you boil the water.

Fresh pasta cooks quickly, just 3 to 5 minutes. When done, quickly toss with your sauce or gravy and enjoy. If you are not using the pasta immediately, you can roll the uncooked strands into loose balls, cover and refrigerate up to a day on an aluminum foil-lined pan. To preserve the pasta for several days, allow it to dry out completely (if you don't it will get moldy) then seal in a Ziploc bag and freeze (no need to thaw before cooking).

JFH

Angie and Moritz "Moshe" Goldfeier

As told by Angie and excerpted from Museum material

Walking into Angie's home in Manhattan is like stepping into a beautiful china shop in Eastern Europe. The only difference, this shop is run by a gracious woman with a terrific sense of humor and a flair for conversation and cooking. Her table displayed delicious desserts, and I nibbled marble sponge cake throughout our conversation.

Angie Goldfeier: in her own words
When the war began and affected Poland, I was only nine years old. Within three years both of my parents were taken from our home. At first I lived with strangers and then I moved into the ghetto on the outskirts of town. Toward the end of 1942, my older sister Regina and I were moved from the ghetto and sent to the first of several camps we were in. I credit my sister, and a lot of luck, with my survival. When liberated from Bergen- Belsen, we returned to Poland to find our remaining family members. We found one sister, and learned that our two brothers had survived and were living in Germany. For the next three years, I lived in Germany, with my sister at my side. When I came to the United States I felt uncomfortable at first. While my husband attended to business in Germany, I moved to Florida to be with my sister; this helped me accept my new life. I am very grateful to this country because sixty-five years ago, I would never dream I would be where I am today.

Moshe's story based on Museum material
Moshe was born in 1927 in Brzeziny, Poland in a traditional home where he was one of four children. His mother attended to the cooking and cleaning and made holidays memorable and special. His grandfather was a Rabbi and he gave him a strong Jewish identity. In 1939 when Moritz was twelve, the family learned of the German invasion of Poland. Fearing for their lives, his father and cousin fled to the Soviet Union and Moshe's mother ultimately was held accountable for those actions. Friends and relatives stepped in to care for the children. Within months, a ghetto was formed. However, Moshe's mother was able to find a teacher willing to give Moshe Jewish lessons, she then secretly gathered a Minyan in a tailor shop and even obtained a Torah; all so he could celebrate becoming a Bar Mitzvah.

In May of 1942, after losing his younger brother, the ghetto was liquidated and the inhabitants were moved to a ghetto in Lodz. They worked and lived there until the summer of 1944, when this ghetto was liquidated as well. The two remaining brothers, mother and sister were sent to Auschwitz. Moshe's mother and sister did not survive, but he and his brother Berek did and were transferred to a labor camp where they remained until they were liberated. After being liberated the two brothers headed to Germany in hopes of finding other family members. It was there Moshe met and married Angie. Moshe learned that his father survived and had immigrated to Israel. They reconnected and saw each other every year. Sixty-one years later, he and Angie are the proud parents of 2 children, 5 grandchildren and 6 great grandchildren.

Top left: Angie and Moshe

Angie Goldfeier's Chicken Savoy Soup

Chicken soup was a staple in every Polish home. It would be prepared for Shabbos and stretched to last throughout the week. Every cook had her own variation. Angie's is really a departure from the usual, and the results are rich and satisfying. She combines three different meats to create the stock, includes lots of root vegetables and herbs, and the crowning glory is the head of Savoy cabbage that flavors the broth and anchors the taste. Angie has a special way to prepare the flanken to prevent *shmuts* from, as she says, "ruining your soup." At the end, she adds one packet of chicken flavor seasoning to help bring all the flavors together.

Yields: About 12 servings; Start to Finish: Under 4 hours (for best results, refrigerate overnight)

1 pound beef flanken, boiled and rinsed

1 (3 ½ to 4 pound) chicken, quartered and rinsed

2 turkey wings, rinsed

1 head Savoy cabbage (about 1½ pounds), halved

4 carrots, rinsed, cut into chunks (about 2 cups)

2 turnips, washed and halved

2 parsnips, washed and cut into large chunks

4 celery ribs, rinsed, cut into large chunks (about 2 cups)

Kosher salt and pepper

½ cup chopped fresh dill leaves

1 (G. Washington's Golden Seasoning) packet or 1 to 2 chicken flavor bouillon cubes

Bring a medium pot of water to boil and add the beef flanken. Boil for 30 minutes, skimming off and discarding the foam that rises to the surface. While the beef cooks, put the chicken, turkey wings, cabbage, carrots, turnips, parsnips, and celery in an extra-large soup pot. Fill the pot with enough cold water to cover all the meat and vegetables. Bring the water to boil, skimming and discarding any foam that rises to the surface.

Remove the flanken from the pot and rinse it quickly under cold, running water. Pat the meat dry and add to the soup pot, adding more water if needed to cover the meat. Season with salt and pepper and simmer, covered, for 2 to 3 hours, until the soup taste has fully developed.

Strain the broth, discarding everything except the cabbage. Slice the cabbage and reserve; you will add it back to the soup when it is time to serve. If time allows, cool the soup in the refrigerator overnight so the fat will rise to the top and solidify, making it easy to remove. Before serving, add the cabbage, dill and 1 seasoning packet or bouillon cube to the soup. Heat until the soup and cabbage are nice and hot. The soup gets better everyday, and can be used in other recipes such as preparing Brussels sprouts (recipe follows).

Roasted Brussels Sprouts with Mushrooms, Leeks and Shallots

After brewing a large pot of Angie's chicken Savoy cabbage soup you will realize that unless you are feeding the entire *meshpokha*, it will take days to finish every drop. But, it is just too good to waste a single ladleful. The broth develops a savory cabbage flavor as it sits, and makes a wonderful braising liquid for Brussels sprouts. The meaty Cremini mushrooms and sweet shallots help balance the cabbage to create a wonderful side dish.

Yields: 4 to 6 servings; Start to Finish: Under 45 minutes

½ pound Cremini, Shitake or assorted wild mushrooms, chopped

2 large shallots, chopped

1 leek, white part only, chopped and thoroughly rinsed

3 tablespoons olive oil

1 tablespoon balsamic vinegar

1 pound Brussels sprouts, trimmed and halved lengthwise (if possible, buy them on the stalk and clip them fresh. Smaller sprouts are the sweetest)

¾ cup Angie's Chicken Savoy Broth, plus more if needed

½ teaspoon kosher salt

½ teaspoon pepper

Preheat the oven to 350 degrees.

Heat 2 tablespoons of the olive oil in a large ovenproof skillet, cook and stir the mushrooms, shallots and leeks, over medium heat, until the mushrooms are soft and the shallots and leeks are translucent, about 10 minutes. Stir in the balsamic vinegar; the mushrooms will soak up the vinegar quickly and turn a rich brown color. Place the Brussels sprouts cut-side down in the mushroom mixture, and pour in ½ cup broth. Drizzle the remaining tablespoon of olive oil over the sprouts and season with salt and pepper.

Put the ovenproof skillet directly in the preheated oven and roast at 350 degrees for 10 minutes. After that time, turn the sprouts over, add the remaining ¼ cup of broth and continue to roast until the sprouts are fork tender and lightly browned, about 10 minutes.

Feedback

Leeks have a sweet mild oniony flavor, and are notorious for hiding grit in their layers. To best clean a leek, cut it down the middle lengthwise, and then chop. Soak the chopped leeks in a bowl filled with cold water; the dirt will fall to the bottom of the bowl. Rinse then pat dry before adding to your recipe.

JFH

Sonia and Zus Bielski

As told by their sons Zvi and Jay Bielski

I spoke to Zvi and Jay shortly after the movie *Defiance* was released. The movie is based on the story of the Bielski partisans, led by their father Zus, and their two uncles, Tuvia and Asael. The Bielski brothers were single-handedly responsible for saving over 1200 people who lived in the dense forests of Poland for much of the war. These 1200 people now account for over 20,000 people who would not be here today had it not been for the heroic actions of the Bielski brothers. Several other contributors to this book were part of the Bielski partisans, and owe their lives to these brave men. Written words cannot convey the passion and the pride these sons have for their family.

Zvi Bielski

I remember when I was a soldier in the Israeli army, and I was with friends at the Yad Vashem Memorial. I was fooling around with my buddies, when one of them called out to me, "Bielski, we gotta go." A couple walked over to me and asked, "You Bielski? We know the Bielskis, are you related?" When I told them I was the son of Zus

Bielski, they literally fell to their knees and cried uncontrollably. I can feel it in my bones even now. They began to tell me stories about how my family saved their family and how they would not be here today were it not for my father and his brothers. I felt very honored.

At the time of the war, they were just a small group, my Dad and uncles and a few other families, hiding in the forest that my father and uncles knew so well. They would send people into the ghetto to smuggle others out. They would bribe the guards; even get them drunk to enable those inside to escape under the fence. They were devoted to saving as many Jewish lives as possible. One man came to my Dad and said, "I have a cousin, maybe we should get her out too." My father brazenly asked, "is she cute?" That woman, named Sonia, was my mother. They sneaked her out, her parents had to force her to go. She hid during the day and traveled at night. When she arrived at the camp, she was so frightened; she was only seventeen at the time. When my mother joined the group, she was happy to find a woman whom she had known from home. The woman was Chaya, my uncle Asael's girlfriend. My Mom jokingly asked Chaya if there was another commander, another brother, for her. It was then that she was introduced to my father, who was a strong, tall, good-looking guy (my parents were together for 55 years!). Days later he arranged for my grandparents to escape the ghetto.

My father was always my hero; he was like a giant to me. I look back on my childhood and remember the impact of my father's story. I was

Top left: Zus Bielski

a 2nd or 3rd grader and I remember when the Beatles came to the U.S. All my classmates felt the Beatles were their heroes. I tapped a classmate on the shoulder and said that if she really wanted to hear a story and meet a hero,

she should meet my Dad. That was my family history. Resistance in the purest sense is what they did. Resistance takes many forms, as even today we are still defying the Nazis by retelling these stories.

Jay Bielski *(a recollection of Sonia's cooking):*
In 1970, we moved into our first American house, it was in Brooklyn, New York. Alex (Zus) and Sonia loved that house. It was the first house since before the war that we could all call our own. There it was, a giant kitchen with a fan to blow out the heat; they were so proud. We were living the American dream. We lived ten minutes from Tuvia, Lilka, and their three kids. Some weekends it was Sonia's turn to cook for Lilka's family. She had a giant pot in which she made *chaunt* (*cholent*)—that's beans, beef, potatoes, carrots, celery, onions, garlic and whatever was fresh in the season. In addition, the centerpiece would be the *kishke*. The *kishke* was made from a cow's intestines, which were thoroughly cleaned and stuffed with mincemeat, sometimes rice and vegetables and flour. People would drop by to

socialize and recall the partisan days, have some chaunt, drink some vodka, and tell the developing stories of their lives. They spoke of the new births, Bar Mitzvahs, weddings, deaths, birthdays and graduations of various kinds. What was left unsaid was that they were there in Zus' and Sonia's house, with Tuvia's family, as well as Aaron, the youngest Bielski partisan. The whole thing was a miracle that they were alive.

Taeba Seltzer Bielski, who gave her infant daughter Lola to be raised by Polish peasants later retrieved by Zus with a gun, during the war, was there. Lola was now grown up and married with kids. It was a group cook-off, just like in the woods of Belarus. They made veal ribs with pockets and *tsimmes* (prunes, carrots and potatoes). Those two main dishes were done for weekends, which inevitably featured Bielski partisans from all over the metropolitan area. They would come over and stay late to play cards, gin rummy mostly for the ladies. Some would smoke and they gambled while the men played poker. Mostly they drank shots that they didn't have to duck from! We can't forget the butcher on 17th and M in Brooklyn. His name was Abie Kotler, and he was the chief butcher from the Bielski partisans. He would be the one to get the cow's intestines or the chicken feet (used for another great dish), which tasted like kosher shrimp, cooked over a slow fire with a tomato base with onions, garlic, carrots, and celery. It was succulent! Everyone would just be sucking and sucking trying not to make too many unpleasant noises; these were cultured partisans, don't forget! The women were educated back then, from good families and fortunately they met up with some unruly Jewish men folks who had the audacity to be defiant against ever-changing enemies: Nazis, Belorussians, Poles and the Cossacks, all out to destroy them.

And so in the end there are 20-30,000 living Jews because of Tuvia, Zus, Asael and Aaron who all long to eat the foods of their Macabees, the defiant Bielskis. I still cook for this Bielski clan, which includes three children, six grandchildren and one great grandchild. They still can get a touch of partisan food on a regular basis. it's just difficult to get cow's intestines to stuff these days so aluminum foil will have to do!

Top left: Sonia Bielski

Susie Fishbein

Professional contributor

Zvi laughed when I asked him what recipe his mother Sonia would like to contribute to the book. "If you were to ask her what she made for dinner on Sunday nights, she would have to say, 'reservations.' She loved to go to Chinatown for great Chinese food." In her honor, Susie Fishbein, best selling author of the *Kosher by Design* series of books, provided two wonderful recipes that Sonia just might have ordered on a typical Sunday night.

Mandarin Chicken Salad

Excerpted from Kosher by Design Entertains(Artscroll/Shaar Press, 2005)

This is a winner of a salad. It is a healthy full meal in a bowl. It works well as a main dish, in a picnic basket, or on a buffet.

Yields: 4-6 salad sized servings; 8 eggroll wrapper cup sized servings

4 boneless, skinless chicken breasts

Salt

Freshly ground black pepper

1 tablespoon olive oil

4 tablespoons seasoned rice wine vinegar

3 tablespoons roasted or toasted sesame oil

1 tablespoon soy sauce

1 (11-ounce) can Mandarin oranges, reserve juice

1 small red onion, cut in half and thinly sliced

1 head Romaine lettuce

1 cup thin chow mein noodles

Black sesame seeds

White sesame seeds

Eggroll wrapper cups (optional) (see next page)

Season both sides of each chicken breast with salt and pepper. Place the olive oil into a skillet over medium-high heat. Add the chicken and sear 5-6 minutes per side until golden brown on both sides. Reduce the heat if necessary to finish cooking the inside without burning the outside. Remove from skillet and slice on the diagonal. Set aside.

In a small bowl whisk the rice wine vinegar, sesame oil, soy sauce and ½ cup reserved mandarin orange juice. Season with salt and pepper. Place the onions into a large bowl. Pour ½ the dressing over the onions and let the onions sit in the dressing for a few minutes. This will mellow their flavor and soften them just a little. Reserve the remaining dressing.

Break off the leaves of the Romaine lettuce. Cut off the stem and stack the leaves. Cut on each side of the center rib and discard the rib. Chop the leaves into bite-sized pieces.

Add the Romaine and Mandarin oranges into the bowl of onions and dressing. Add the chow mein noodles.

Toss the chicken with the reserved dressing, coating each slice of chicken. Toss the dressed chicken slices with the greens. Garnish with black and white sesame seeds.

Eggroll wrapper cups
Preheat oven to 350 degrees. Invert 8 oven-proof ramekins or custard cups on a cookie sheet. Spray the inside of the cups with non-stick cooking spray. Drape an eggroll wrapper over the outside of each cup. Bake for 10 minutes until golden. Allow to cool for 5 minutes, remove eggroll wrapper from cup. Store in a heavy duty Ziploc bag at room temperature for up to two days.

Sesame Beef and Broccoli over Ramen Noodles

Excerpted from Kosher by Design Entertains (Artscroll/Shaar Press, 2005)

Yields: 6 servings

¼ cup reduced sodium soy sauce

3 tablespoons rice wine vinegar

2 tablespoons hoisin sauce

2 tablespoons dark brown sugar

1 tablespoon chopped fresh ginger or
¼ teaspoon ground ginger

2 teaspoons roasted or toasted sesame oil

2 teaspoons cornstarch

¼ teaspoon crushed red pepper flakes

2 pounds pepper steak sliced into long,
thin strips

2 (3-ounce) packages beef or oriental-flavored ramen noodles, reserve 1 spice packet, discard the other

4 scallions, sliced

1 teaspoon roasted or toasted sesame oil

1 tablespoon Canola oil

3 cloves minced garlic

12 ounces broccoli florets, cut into small pieces

Sesame seeds

In a Ziploc bag or non-reactive bowl, combine the soy sauce, vinegar, hoisin sauce, brown sugar, ginger, sesame oil, cornstarch, and pepper flakes. Add the meat and marinate for 30 minutes in the refrigerator.

Place 4 cups water into a medium pot. Bring to a boil and add the 2 packages ramen noodles with one of the spice packets. Add the scallions and 1 teaspoon sesame oil. Remove from the heat, let stand, covered. Set aside.

In a large skillet or wok, heat the Canola oil to medium heat. Remove the meat from the marinade, reserving marinade, and add the meat to the skillet. Cook for 3 minutes. Add in the minced garlic. Add the broccoli and sauté for 6-8 minutes. Add the marinade into the pan and stir until thickened. Toss to combine.

Serve over the ramen noodles. You can drain them or serve them in the broth.

Sprinkle with sesame seeds.

Murray Berger and Fruma Gulkowich Berger

As told by their son Ralph Berger

The Museum's amazing exhibit entitled *"Daring to Resist"* has among its artifacts a simple fork and spoon. These innocuous utensils would seem commonplace were it not for the fact that they were used by Ralph's mother, Fruma, while hiding in the woods of Poland as part of the "Bielski Brigade." Ralph shared with me some of his recollections of his parents and their life in America.

My father was from Wsielub, Russia and my Mom was from Korelicze, Poland. They met as fighters in the Bielski Brigade after they had escaped from the Novogrudok Ghetto. My father was an original member of the group, one of the 15 men who elected Tuvia Bielski as Commander of the Brigade. My Mom escaped after the ghetto *Aktion* on August 7, 1942 in which over 4,000 innocent Jews were killed. My mother and her sister-in-law, Judy Gulkowich, escaped by hiding in a cesspool for six days, without any food. My uncle, Ben Zion Gulkowich, rescued them. Soon thereafter, all three escaped into the woods and joined the Bielski partisans. My father would always say with a sly smile, "I found my wife in the woods." For nearly 2½ years my parents were fighters in the Bielski Brigade, which they spoke openly about after the war. The spoon and fork displayed in the Museum exhibit were the only possessions my mother had left from her parents' home. She escaped from the ghetto with them, cooked with them while in the Brigade, carried them across Europe and displaced persons camps, and then used them to prepare delicious meals for family and friends for the next fifty years.

My brother, Al, and I were born here in America and were raised in a traditional household. Every Friday night, it was chicken soup with matzo balls or noodles, chicken, potato *kugel* or noodle pudding, *tsimmes*, and some kind of *babka* or "*zemmel*," a kind of Danish. My Mom was a great cook, making everything from scratch. Her gefilte fish was really second to none. She and my Dad would go from one fish store to another before the holidays to find the best fish. Growing up, the holidays were bittersweet. The food would be delicious, but our celebrations were different from those of the kids with American-born parents. We didn't have grandparents and lots of aunts and uncles and cousins surrounding the table and sharing in the holiday. For my family, you also could not have a celebration without great food. I remember lots and lots of food on the table at the *Kiddush* in my parents' home following my Bar Mitzvah. Shortly after most of the company had left and the table was cleared, Tuvia Bielski, who lived across the street with his family, came in to tell us that he had just become a grandfather. Immediately, the food came back out. I can still picture Tuvia, my Dad and my Uncle Ben doing shots and eating gefilte fish.

One of my favorite dishes was *gribenes*, chicken cracklings. Even when I was in college and law school, I would bring *gribenes* back with me from my visits home and everyone would go crazy for it. I am spoiled by my mother's cooking, as even now I judge the traditional Jewish foods by what she would make and they usually just don't compare. My parents were married for 48 years and had two children and two grandchildren.

Gribenes and Shmaltz
Chicken Skin Cracklings and Rendered Fat

Ralph is certainly not the only child of Eastern Europeans who remembers the intense aroma or rich flavor of *gribenes*, a Jewish delicacy that has humble roots. Out of necessity, the Jewish homemaker would render her own chicken, duck or goose fat and the by-product, crisp cracklings, would be *shmeered* on thick slices of challah bread, sprinkled with salt and devoured. For the most authentic chopped liver, delicious pierogi filling or to fry just about anything, try using the *shmaltz* (rendered fat). It will take your kitchen back in time and fill your senses with a sense of tradition.

Collect the fat from the excess skin of chicken, duck or goose. It might take time to do so, simply clip the fat and store it in the freezer in a tightly sealed bag until you have enough to render. Be careful not to clip any meat with the fat. When you have collected about 2 cups, you can render the fat and create *gribenes* from the combination of skin and onions. You might also ask your butcher to collect the trimmings for you.

Yields: About 2 cups shmaltz; Start to Finish: Under 1½ hours

2 cups chicken, goose or duck fat, cut into small pieces or strips

1 medium onion, sliced

Place the cut fat and about ½ cup of water (enough to cover the fat) in a heavy skillet, or cast iron pan, and cook over low heat until the fat begins to liquefy and the water begins to evaporate. Stir the onions into the pan and continue cooking, over very low heat until the skin and onions are very brown, but not burnt. Remove the bits of skin and onions with a slotted spoon, and allow them to drain on a paper towel. Pour the fat into a jar that has a tight fitting lid and refrigerate for up to 3 months, or freeze for up to a year. Spread the cracklings on a slice of bread and sprinkle with kosher salt, or use them to flavor a multitude of dishes.

JFH

Eric and Bruce Bromberg

Professional contributors

No doubt, Ralph would love to have a steaming bowl of his Mom's chicken soup, just as he did every Friday night growing up. While Fruma is not here to provide that recipe, we have the real deal provided to us by Eric and Bruce Bromberg, chef/owners of the Blue Ribbon restaurants. Grandma Martha's chicken and matzoh ball soup is a mainstay on their brasserie menu.

Martha's Excellent Matzoh Ball Soup

Contributed by Eric and Bruce Bromberg, chef/owners of Blue Ribbon restaurant, New York City.

Our Grandmother Martha's influence is everywhere in our restaurants but perhaps no more prevalent anywhere than in this dish that defined her grace and profound understanding of all that is good in so many ways. Martha brought the matzoh balls and was often touted with delight at our family gatherings and holidays. It was said with resolve and relief as if it meant that everything was going to be just fine. It was a constant, something we could all always count on. It meant that even if the brisket was overcooked and the blintzes dry, the *kugel* too sweet and the chopped liver bland, the *harosset* overly alcoholic and the wine barely passable that everything would fall into irrelevance once you bit into those ethereal cloudlike matzoh balls and sipped her deceptively simple and transcending broth laden with dill, carrots and its luminescent golden puddles of *shmaltz* that danced and dipped on the turbulent surface.

There was a specific method to the recipe, a temperature for the eggs and other ingredients that were treated with love and reverence, a specific urn for transportation to a relative's house, a specific linen that shrouded that urn and even a wicker basket reserved for that occasion, and that occasion only, to transport the contents as if they were as precious as the sanctity of our beliefs or even baby Moses on his journey down the river Nile. Perhaps this is just a recipe, but for us and hopefully in its own way will be so much more for you as well. It is a way of life, a return to simpler things, simple things that if done just so can transform life and lead to so much more.

(Continued)

For the Broth:

1 whole hen (3-4 pounds)

4 ribs of celery with leaves (cleaned and chopped)

3 carrots (2-cleaned and chopped)

1 onion (chopped)

2 leeks (cleaned and chopped)

3 cloves garlic (whole)

4 sprigs flat parsley

3 sprigs dill

½ teaspoon black peppercorns

2 dried bay leaves

1 tablespoon kosher salt

Garnish:

Carrot rounds (blanched till soft)

Chopped dill

Salt and pepper

For the Matzoh Balls:

1 cup matzo meal

4 eggs

1 ounce rendered chicken fat (*shmaltz*)

½ ounce kosher salt

½ teaspoon double acting baking powder

2 ounces seltzer

Procedure Broth

Rub chicken with kosher salt inside and out. Let stand 15 minutes. Rinse WELL under cold water. Pat dry with paper towel. Put chicken in a large pot of cold water covering chicken by 3 inches. Bring to boil. Impurities will rise to the top, then skim off and discard. Add everything. Bring back to boil, skim and then reduce to a simmer. Let simmer. After 45 minutes (or until chicken is cooked) remove chicken. Take meat off of bone (save meat for another meal), put bones back in pot. Cook for 1 hour more. Strain though a sieve and cheesecloth and let cool in refrigerator. When cool, fat will rise to the top and solidify, making it easy to remove.

Procedure Matzoh Balls

In large mixing bowl add all ingredients except seltzer, mix well. Add seltzer water and let mixture sit covered and refrigerated for 1 hour. Fill a large diameter pot ¾ full with water and bring to a simmer (190 to 200 degrees). With wet hands roll out 1-ounce balls. Lower balls into water. Cook until tender approximately 45 to 60 minutes (test with toothpick or do the famous chef Eric cut in half). Balls should be light and fluffy in the center. Let matzoh balls cool.

For Soup

Slice carrot into rounds. Chop 2 sprigs of dill. Bring broth to a boil with carrots and dill and matzo balls. Season to taste. Serve when matzoh balls are warm in center.

Judith Koszcianska Ginsburg and Marvin Mordechai "Motke" Ginsburg

As told by Judith, and her daughter, Fran

Judith described in great detail her experiences during the war. Judith was part of the Bielski Partisans, and her husband, Motke, was an active resistance fighter throughout the war. Their story is inspiring, and her recipes, which were collected in a Ginsburg Family cookbook, are delicious.

Judith

I was born in a town called Lida; it was in Poland, but is now called Belarus. When I was 16 I was sent to the ghetto with my sister, her husband and their children. The rest of my family had perished. On May 8, 1942 our ghetto was liquidated and we were marched to the train station, it was a 3km walk. My sister told me to run (she could not because she had the children with her) saying, "One of us should survive." There was a young German soldier marching with us, and I don't know why, but he talked to me. He said, "I don't know where you are going, but it will be bad." I turned to the soldier and said, "I'm going to run, if you shoot me, shoot me." I don't know where I got the courage. A friend of mine was walking with her mother, and her mother told us both to run. We tore off our patches and did just that. We jumped over fence after fence, and finally fell into a garden. We waited till we heard the trains leave, staying very quiet until it was pitch dark. We were wet, hungry and crying. This part of the city was unfamiliar to us, but we did know German guards surrounded it. We encountered a stranger who

told us to go with God. I know someone was watching over us that day, God was with us.

We knocked on a door and while the woman of the house shooed us away, the husband invited us in. He gave us a jug of cold milk and said, "God sent you to my house." He promised that if we stayed the night he would take us to the partisans. Fearing that this seemed too good to be true, we left during the night and wandered toward the area where we heard the partisans were hiding. The Russian partisans were looking for recruits and we joined them. We had to carry guns and go out on actions during the day and defend the camp at night. My friend stayed with them, but after several months, I left that group and joined the Bielskis. The way they are shown in the movie *Defiance* is very accurate. Tuvia, the leader of our group, saved us all and took care of us. Every Jew meant so much to him. Survival there was like a movie. Some local farmers shared food with us, if they didn't we took the food from them. When you have no choice, you go along with anything you need to do to survive. You learn to put on an act that you're not afraid. I fought with the partisans until we were liberated, after about 1½ years. Over 1200 people survived because of Tuvia and his protection.

After the war, I returned to my hometown where I got married to one of the Ginsburg brothers. Though considered heroes among the Russian partisans, they were not Communists and feared conscription. We fled Russia to Poland, Poland to Germany arriving in Foehrenwald DP Camp. I gave birth to a son and daughter there. I believe our son was the first Jewish child born in that camp. We named him after my husband's younger brother who was murdered after the

Top left: The Ginsburg family in Foehrenwald DP camp

liberation...another reason we ran. I wanted to bring young children into the world. There was survivor's guilt, why did I survive, why me? Every survivor feels this way. I knew we had to bring in new generations to build up, that's why my children and family are the most important things.

Fran

My father, Motke, and his younger brother, Tzalke, were young, strong and heroic, risking their lives to save others in the ghetto. He and his brother joined *Iskra*, a Russian partisan group. They went back to help hundreds escape from the ghetto in Iwje (Iwye), their small hometown. They were valiant fighters who blew up many German transport trains and were responsible for significant acts of sabotage.

After the Russians liberated the territory, my father was awarded The Order of Lenin. His family settled in Lida, as there was little left of his *shtetl* after the war. He shared a big house with his brother, sisters and father. One day, my father's sister saw my hungry mother returning to town and thought it would be nice to bring her home for dinner. The rest is history. My parents were married 61 years and have four children, ten grandchildren and seven great grandchildren.

My father had family members in Troy, New York, who sponsored their trip to America. One was a kosher butcher, one a turkey farmer. My father became a cattle dealer and dairy farmer, so meat and food were always plentiful in our house. I remember that food was extremely important and had special emphasis because of the times my parents didn't have it. We lived almost communally with my aunt, uncle and cousins; all the holiday cooking was done together. I have vivid childhood memories of my mother and aunt standing at opposite ends in the kitchen stuffing a huge *kishke* or cooking *taiglach* (fried dough) in a giant vat of honey. We even kashered our own meat. Our freezer was always filled with amazing baked goods. Even now my mom bakes her own challah and famous rugelach. Our food memories were seasonal, in the summer my father would come with a bushel of this or a sack of that, which could easily result in a night of making pickles. Even if we didn't have money we always had food.

Top left: Judith and Marvin Ginsburg in Foehrenwald DP camp, with son, Howard

Judith Ginsburg's Brisket

Every family has a method for preparing brisket. There's the ubiquitous onion soup mix or splash of Coca-Cola. Judith's version has no gimmicks, just lots of fresh garlic and vegetables. There are two options when buying the brisket. First cut, commonly referred to as flat brisket, is a lean carefully trimmed cut. It's a little less juicy and requires less cooking time. The alternative is the whole brisket, which includes the deckle, the top layer. It needs to cook longer to be tender, but the layer of fat lends lots of flavor to the dish. The choice is yours. The sauce is created afterward and the brisket can be eaten right away, or sleep in the sweet and sour gravy to be devoured the next day.

Yields: 8 servings; Start to Finish: Under 4 ½ hours

1 (5 to 6 pound) brisket

Kosher salt and pepper

2 tablespoons paprika

2 tablespoons garlic powder

1 pound carrots (about 5 to 6), peeled and cut into chunks

6 medium onions (about 2 pounds), cut into large chunks

8 to 10 cloves garlic (look for heavy closed bulbs), coarsely chopped

For the sauce:

1 (14.5-ounce) can condensed tomato soup

1 cup ketchup

2 tablespoons brown sugar

1 tablespoon white vinegar

Preheat the oven to 350 degrees.

Rub the brisket generously with salt, pepper, paprika and garlic powder. Place it in a covered roasting pan with the carrots, onions, garlic and ½ cup of water. Cover and roast until fork tender, about 4 hours, checking on the brisket every hour to see if additional water is needed to prevent the meat from scorching.

When the meat is done, remove it from the roasting pan and thinly slice it against the grain. To make the sauce, stir into the pan ½ cup water, the can of soup, ketchup, brown sugar and vinegar. Place the brisket slices back into the sauce. You can heat the sliced beef and sauce and serve at once, or let the brisket soak up the big flavors, overnight in the fridge. It will be worth the wait.

Feedback

Eastern European cooks have relied on ketchup as a recipe enhancer for many years. It is a great combination of sweet and sour. Concentrated tomatoes blend with vinegar and sugar and assorted spices, making it a terrific flavor balance in many of our recipes. If you want to bring sweet and sour in a tomato-based recipe, try adding ketchup.

The Ginsburg Family Corned Beef

Corned beef and brisket are the same cut of meat, the difference is that corned beef is brined (cured with large kernels called corned salt), giving it its distinctive taste. The key to home prepared corned beef is to baby the beef before cooking, and be patient while it slowly simmers. It takes a little extra time and attention, but the end result is well worth it. Be warned, your house will smell like your local deli—not such a bad thing!

Yields: Depends on the weight of the beef, about ½ pound per person; Start to Finish: Step One: 12 to 24 hours to soak the beef and change the water; Step Two: based on weight, 50 minutes per pound

1 pre-packaged corned beef

4 celery ribs, cut into bite-sized pieces (about 1½ to 2 cups)

1 medium onion, sliced

3 sprigs fresh parsley

3 sprigs fresh thyme

5 bay leaves

5 garlic cloves, coarsely chopped

3 tablespoons kosher salt

5 black peppercorns

Step One: Remove the meat from the package and rinse under cold water. Cover the beef in a cold-water bath, in the fridge, for at least 12 hours or up to 1 day. This will remove the intense saltiness and soften the meat. Change the water every 2 to 6 hours, more in the beginning, less as the day goes on. When ready to cook, remove the corned beef from the fridge, rinse and pat dry.

Step Two: Place the beef in a large Dutch oven with all the remaining ingredients. Cover the meat with fresh cold water and bring to a boil. Lower the heat to a slow simmer and cook until a knife inserted in the center comes out easily, about 50 minutes per pound. The cooking is to tenderize the meat, as the corning process actually cures and "cooks" it. Allow the meat to cool in the liquid before carving into thin slices, against the grain.

If serving with vegetables or potatoes, simmer them in a separate pot, as the corned beef water tends to get fatty. If you reheat the corned beef, be sure to add water to the pot or dish; the beef dries out easily.

Feedback

The third version of this cut of meat is pastrami. It is seasoned with salt, garlic, pepper and spices. It is then smoked and steamed. It requires nothing more than a good piece of rye bread, tangy mustard and a crisp pickle (recipe follows). May we suggest you leave the pastrami to the experts? Go out and buy a good pastrami sandwich to enjoy while the house fills with the aroma of roasted brisket or simmering corned beef.

Arthur Schwartz

Professional contributor

Prepare the corned beef, buy the rye bread and mustard, and Arthur Schwartz, "the Food Maven," will instruct you on how to make the pickles, just as the Ginsburgs might have when they would turn a bushel of cucumbers into this iconic Jewish food.

"Kosher" Dill Pickles

Excerpted from Arthur Schwartz's Jewish Home Cooking (Ten Speed Press, 2008)

My paternal grandfather, Bernard (Barney) Schwartz, was a professional pickle man at one point in his life. From a pushcart, he sold pickles, along with coleslaw, potato salad, and Manhattan clam chowder, to bars and grills in Manhattan. Later in life he continued to make all of these for his family and friends. I have great memories of making pickles with him. By the way, there is nothing intrinsically kosher about pickles, but people call them "kosher" because they are a famous item of Jewish delicatessens. The combination of pickles with a pastrami, corned beef, or salami sandwich is unbeatable. Because this style of pickle is naturally fermented, things can go wrong. A bitter cucumber will also make a bitter pickle. Taste a raw cucumber from your batch: it should have a cool refreshing flavor. Use small to medium Kirby cucumbers, the best for pickling. Large cucumbers will, of course, take longer to pickle than small cucumbers, so try not to mix sizes in one jar, unless you want the variety of pickle strength that will result.

Makes 3 quarts

4 quarts water

¾ cup kosher salt

20 (3-to 4-inch) Kirby cucumbers, scrubbed

12 to 16 whole cloves garlic, unpeeled, lightly crushed

2 tablespoon mixed pickling spices

6 bay leaves

1 large bunch dill, preferably going to seed, with tough stems, washed

To make the brine, bring the water to boil in a large pot over high heat. Add the salt and stir until dissolved. Set aside to cool to room temperature.

To prepare the jars, either run them through a hot cycle of the dishwasher or fill them with boiling water and pour out the water.

Pack the jars tightly with cucumbers, which prevents the cucumbers from floating to the top when the brine is added. As you pack the jars with cucumbers, distribute the garlic, pickling spices, and bay leaves equally among the jars and around the cucumbers.

(Continued)

For each jar, pour enough brine to cover the cucumbers. Add sprigs of dill and dill seed, pushing them in wherever you can. If you have dill with woody stems, jam them into the shoulders of the jars to help keep the cucumbers in place.

Cover the jars loosely with their lids or with pieces of cheesecloth secured with rubber bands. Store in a cool, dark place. After 3 days, the cucumbers may be pickled enough to your taste. After 4-5 days, they should definitely taste like green pickles. For really sour pickles, let them ferment for about 6 days.

Once the pickles are at the stage you like, refrigerate them. They will get more sour as time goes by, but at a much slower pace.

Rae and Joseph Kushner

Based on my conversation with Jared Kushner

Jared, the owner of *The New York Observer* and husband of Ivanka Trump, is a young and modern businessman who maintains the ancient daily ritual of laying *Tefillin*. He explained that when he learned that some prisoners in Auschwitz, amidst the chaos and devastation, still practiced this daily covenant, he could not do any less. He is equally committed to remembering and honoring his grandparents, Rae and Joseph Kushner, who survived the Holocaust.

Jared's grandmother, Rae, grew up in a middle class home in Novogrudok, Poland. When the family was forced into the ghetto, they were part of a courageous group who dug a tunnel to freedom. Rae, her sister and father worked tirelessly digging a tunnel that would lead them outside the ghetto. After many months, Jared's grandmother, aunt and great grandfather successfully escaped the ghetto. Despite the fact that most of the young people were among the first to emerge, Jared proudly explained that Rae and her sister chose to remain in the rear with their father. Miraculously, they escaped into the woods where they spent the balance of the war. At times they hid to evade capture, while at other times they aligned themselves with the Bielski Brigade. Jared's grandfather, Joseph

Kushner, also survived the war by hiding in the woods, sometimes working with the partisans, and other times on his own. Rae and Joseph met in the woods and were married in a group ceremony in Budapest. After the war, like so many others, they went to a DP camp in Italy. Together they came to America settling first in Brooklyn and then moving to New Jersey. Joseph rose from a standard carpenter to a homebuilder and eventually became a successful real estate developer.

When I asked Jared what he learned from his grandparents (he was only 4 when his grandfather died), Jared said, "I learned that life brings adversity, but you choose how you can respond to it." Jared's love for his grandmother was evident as he described her: "my grandmother always had a smile on her face. She saw horrible things in her life yet somehow remained an incredible optimist who espoused that she felt very blessed. She was always able to get us excited." He continued by saying, "I think it's important to be proud of being Jewish. My family's survival is a miracle and it is the job of my generation to make sure we make the opportunity of life that we were given count." Together Rae and Joseph had four children, fifteen grandchildren and twenty-eight great grandchildren! *Kaynahorah.*

Top left: Rae and Joseph Kushner

Rae Kushner's Potato Chip *Kugel*

This is not so much a recipe as a preparation, but that doesn't diminish the memory of noodles and eggs crisping up in a pan and being served every Shabbos. Jared remembers his grandmother sneaking him into the kitchen to snack on these noodles before dinner was served. They were never eaten sweet, as Rae's daughter Linda explains, "we were Litvaks," so leave the sugar and cinnamon in the cabinet. Be sure to fry the noodles till they are so crisp that they begin to resemble potato chips.

Yields: 8 servings; Start to Finish: Under 30 minutes

1 (12–ounce) bag no yolk noodles

1 tablespoon vegetable oil

2 eggs, beaten

Salt and pepper

Boil the noodles according to package directions. If using leftover noodles, rinse them in warm water to bring them back to life. Heat the oil in a 12-inch skillet. Combine the cooked noodles and beaten egg, season with salt and pepper and pour into the heated pan. Cook, over medium heat, until the underside is golden brown. Flip (use a large spatula or use the two-dish method: slide the noodles onto a plate, cover that plate with a second plate and flip, revealing the cooked side on top. Slide back into the pan). Continue browning the second side until very crisp. To serve, cut into eighths. To reheat, wrap in foil, make a slit for the steam to escape and place in the oven on the warming temperature. Serve as a side dish or *nosh*.

Mark Bittman

Professional contributor

Friday night dinner was and still is a time for the Kushner family to come together. It features time-honored food, none more universal for Shabbos dinner than roast chicken. Mark Bittman, the man who knows how to cook everything, shares with us a number of preparations for this ever-present Friday night centerpiece.

Simplest Whole Roast Chicken, Six Ways

Excerpted from How To Cook Everything (Wiley 2008)

Yields: 4 servings; Starrt to Finish: About 1 hour

We justifiably associate roast chicken with elegance, but it can also be super weeknight food, cooked in just about an hour. This method works because the high heat provided by the heated skillet cooks the thighs faster than the breasts, which are exposed only to the heat of the oven. It gives you nice browning without drying out the breast meat, and it's easily varied. If at any point during the cooking the pan juices begin to smoke, just add a little water or wine (white or red, your choice) to the pan. This will reduce browning, however, so don't do it unless you must. I suggest serving the pan juices with the chicken (you can call it "sauce naturel" if you like).

1 whole chicken, 3 to 4 pounds, trimmed of excess fat	**A few sprigs fresh tarragon, rosemary or thyme (optional)**
3 tablespoons extra virgin olive oil	**5 or 6 cloves garlic, peeled (optional)**
Salt and freshly ground black pepper	**Chopped fresh herbs for garnish**

Heat the oven to 450 degrees. Five minutes after turning on the oven, put a cast-iron or other heavy ovenproof skillet on a rack set low in the oven. Rub the chicken with the olive oil, sprinkle it with salt and pepper, and put the herb sprigs on it if you're using them.

When both oven and pan are hot, 10 or 15 minutes later, carefully put the chicken, breast side up, in the hot skillet; if you're using garlic, scatter it around the bird. Roast, undisturbed, for 40 to 50 minutes or until an instant-read thermometer inserted in the meaty part of the thigh registers 155-165 degrees.

Tip the pan to let the juices from the bird's cavity flow into the pan (if they are red, cook for another 5 minutes). Transfer the bird to a platter and let it rest; if you like, pour the pan juices into a clear measuring cup, then pour or spoon off some of the fat. Reheat the juices if necessary, quarter the bird, garnish, and serve with the pan juices.

(Continued)

Herb-Roasted Chicken

A little more elegant. Start the cooking without the olive oil. About halfway through, spoon a mixture of ¼ cup olive oil and 2 tablespoons chopped fresh parsley, chervil, basil, or dill over the chicken. Garnish with more chopped herbs.

Lemon-Roasted Chicken

Brush the chicken with olive oil before roasting; cut a lemon in half and put it in the chicken's cavity. Roast, more or less undisturbed, until done; squeeze the juice from the cooked lemon over the chicken and carve.

Roast Chicken with Paprika

With good paprika, quite delicious. Combine the olive oil with about 1 tablespoon sweet paprika or smoked pimentón.

Roast Chicken with Soy Sauce

Chinese-style roast chicken, made easy. Replace the olive oil with peanut or neutral oil, like grape seed or corn. Halfway through the cooking, spoon or brush over the chicken a mixture of ¼ cup soy sauce, 2 tablespoons honey, 1 teaspoon minced garlic, 1 teaspoon grated or minced fresh ginger (or 1 teaspoon ground ginger), and ¼ cup minced scallion.

Roast Chicken with Cumin, Honey, and Orange Juice

Sweet and exotic. Halfway through the cooking, spoon or brush over the chicken a mixture of 2 tablespoons freshly squeezed orange juice, 2 tablespoons honey, 1 teaspoon minced garlic, 2 teaspoons ground cumin, and salt and pepper to taste.

5 More Ways to Flavor Simplest Whole Roast Chicken

There are many ways to flavor a roast chicken. Here are some simple ideas to get you started:

1. Lemon: Use 3 tablespoons freshly squeezed lemon juice in addition to or in place of olive oil.

2. Lime: Use 3 tablespoons freshly squeezed lime juice in a soy sauce mix (as in the Roast Chicken with Soy Sauce variation) or with some minced jalapeño or Serrano chiles or hot red pepper flakes, chopped fresh cilantro leaves to taste, and a tablespoon or two of peanut oil.

3. Honey-Mustard: Combine 2 tablespoons to ⅓ cup mustard with 2 tablespoons honey and rub the chicken with this mixture during the final stages of roasting.

4. Wine: Put ½ cup white wine and 2 cloves crushed garlic in the bottom of the roasting pan; baste with this in addition to or in place of the olive oil mixture.

5. Curry: In place of the olive oil, use neutral oil, like grape seed or corn, or butter. Combine ½ cup coconut milk and 2 tablespoons curry powder and baste the chicken with this mixture during the final stages of roasting.

Sonya and Aaron Oshman

In Sonya's words

Listening to Sonya retell her story in vivid detail was like an unimaginable history lesson. She survived so many remarkable events and was an active character in her story of resistance and refusal to give up. Her message to anyone who will listen is, "Hope lives when people remember. You must spread the message that hate is a failure and love a success."

I was born in Novogrudok, Poland and was the second oldest in a family of five children. I had two wonderful parents who were successful business owners and very influential people. My father was a good friend of the Governor, who lived across the street. I went to the best school and continued my studies at the *Gymnasium* (secondary school) and dreamed of becoming a doctor. In 1937, when Poland was divided, we resided on the east side, which Russia controlled.

Among other changes, we now had to learn to speak Russian. For several years, the Germans, much like Napoleon did in the 1800s, began invading our territory. It was in 1942 when we found ourselves ghettoized and under Nazi control. I was given the job of cleaning the streets of rubble caused by the constant bombing of our town. It soon became clear that our ghetto was being liquidated and one by one people were disappearing and not returning. I was part of a group of about 250 people who decided we had to do something to save ourselves. I was lucky to still have one brother, Shaul, with me and began to make the acquaintance of Aaron Oshman, the man I would later marry. We would work during the day at our regular jobs, then at night, tired and exhausted, we would dig a tunnel to the outside. We had no real tools, so we used only forks and spoons. Fortunately, we had a carpenter in our group who would sneak lumber back into the ghetto in the sleeves of his coat and use it to shore up the tunnel as we dug. On the rainy evening of September 23rd, we decided to make our escape. The night would be long, the sky was dark and an electrician in our group cut the wires that lit the area.

One by one we crawled like mice through the tunnel, praying that the wood beams would support the dirt above us and prevent the tunnel from caving in. When we crawled out the end of what I believe was an almost 300 meter tunnel, we scrambled to safety. Most of our group survived. I escaped with my brother at my side; Aaron and his brother were safely in front of us. When we reached the end, we weren't sure which way to go. I knew that to the right was the ghetto and to the left was a large cornfield situated beside a road. I ran across that road and for weeks, hid in the fields. One day, I spotted a little

Top left: Sonya Oshman

the forest where we had heard the Bielski partisans were hiding. The land around the forest had soft earth, which was like quicksand. The Nazis avoided the area fearing that they would fall into the dirt and never get out. The Bielskis knew the land well, so they felt relatively safe in these familiar woods. The farmer took me to the partisans where I remained until I was liberated. During those years Aaron and I were able to sneak into his hometown where a Rabbi married us. He was my husband for over 57 years.

After liberation, Aaron and I knew we wanted to go to Israel and that we needed to get to Italy for that trip. There were no trains or planes for us to travel on, so we walked the entire way. First we crossed from Poland to Romania. When we were in Romania, I noticed a gold, broken ladies watch lying in the street. I wasn't sure I should pick it up, but luckily for us, I did. From Romania we walked to Switzerland, crossing the Alps that were in our path. As we crossed the border from Switzerland into Italy, Russian soldiers tried to hold us back. I took out the watch and said in the Russian I had learned years earlier, that the soldier should give this watch to his wife. His eyes lit up and he allowed us to cross into Italy. On foot we had made it from Poland to Romania, Romania to Switzerland, Switzerland to Italy and then hopefully on to Israel. In Italy I gave birth to my first son and because I was ill, gave up my dream of going to Israel. We remained in the DP camp for five years. After that time, Aaron, my now five year old son, Matthew, and I passed through Ellis Island and landed in America. We were housed on 34th Street, where the wonderful HIAS set us up on the 10th floor of a place I use to call Hotel De Vance (Yiddish for bedbug). Through it all, I am a very happy person. I thank God every day when I get up. From this sorrow that I went through, God compensated me with two wonderful children and four beautiful grandchildren.

house, much like the one in *Little House on the Prairie*. It was lit by a kerosene lamp and I could see an elderly man who resembled Santa Claus, sewing. I knocked on his window and he said in Polish, "Come in my child, don't worry, I will save your life." He had heard about our daring escape and quickly hid me in the potato cellar below the main floor of the house. Aaron was hidden as well, in another area. Every night, for weeks, the old man would bring me a little bread, some potatoes and water. He was a poor man, but shared what he had with me. His house was near

Top left: Aaron and Sonya Oshman seated, with Matthew. Saul standing behind them.

Mark Strausman

Professional contributor

While in the DP camp in Italy, Sonya recalled, "I shared facilities with other refugees. I cooked a lot of spaghetti and tomato sauce, sprinkled with plenty of Parmesan cheese, what could be bad?" Italian cooking maestro, Mark Strausman, shares his recipe to honor all the nights that classic spaghetti and tomato sauce nourished Sonya's growing family.

Spaghetti al Rustico di Cipole–Spaghetti with Onion and Tomato Sauce

Excerpted from two meatballs in the italian kitchen
(Artisan, a division of Workman Publishing Company, Inc., 2007)

This is my favorite everyday pasta dish, and after twenty-five years of serving it to American customers, I can tell you that they like it too. There's nothing easier to make at home, since you probably have all the ingredients in the house. It's a perfect example of the way Italian food can be very simple and very delicious at the same time. You'll notice that I sauté the onions in a little bit of butter, rather than olive oil. Over the years, I've found that if I cook the onions slowly in just a small amount of butter, the result is a very creamy sauce without any need to add cream.

Makes about 2 cups sauce; Serves 4 to 6

2 tablespoons (28 grams) butter

1 medium red onion, thinly sliced

2 cups (480 ml) canned Italian plum tomatoes, preferably San Marzano, with their juice, pureed in a food processor or food mill

2 tablespoons plus 1 teaspoon kosher salt

1 pound (454 grams) spaghetti or linguine (see tip)

¼ cup (1 ounce/28 grams) freshly grated Parmigiano-Reggiano cheese

1 tablespoon (15 ml) extra-virgin olive oil

Place the butter in a 10-to-12-inch skillet over medium heat. Add the onion and cook, stirring frequently, until soft, about 5 minutes. Add the tomatoes and 1 teaspoon of the salt. When the mixture starts to bubble, reduce the heat to very low and cook at a bare simmer for 5 minutes. Remove from the heat and set aside.

While the sauce is cooking, fill a 10-quart stockpot with 7 quarts (6.5 liters) of water and bring to a boil over high heat. Add the remaining 2 tablespoons kosher salt. Add the pasta, stir and cook until al dente.

Reserve ½ cup of the pasta cooking water, and drain the pasta. Add the pasta to the skillet with the sauce. If the pasta looks dry, add the reserved cooking water 1 tablespoon at a time, tossing to combine between additions. While still tossing the pasta and sauce, slowly sprinkle on the cheese, and toss until all the cheese is incorporated. The dish should look creamy and moist. Serve immediately, drizzling each portion with a little bit of olive oil.

Tip: Look for #11 spaghetti—it's just the right thickness.

Nadzia Goldstein Bergson and Milton Bergson

As told by their children Jaffa Feldman and Simon Bergson

Both Jaffa and Simon recall that not until her later years did their mother, Nadzia, really talk about her experiences during the Holocaust. Had she, they might have learned more about Nadzia's role in the Sonderkommando Revolt that took place in Auschwitz, in October of 1944. This was the only organized uprising ever recorded at Auschwitz, involving the smuggling of gunpowder to help create the explosives used to destroy a crematorium at the camp. Nadzia was one of those brave women who worked in the clothing department at Auschwitz, and aided in the endeavor. While we don't know the extent of her involvement, we do know these women, many from the same city in Poland, would sew "trapdoors" in the lining and hems of their clothing to transfer the gunpowder. One of the collaborators, Rosa Robota, was a friend of Nadzia's and was regarded as a principal organizer of the plan. Their plot not only resulted in the death of five or six SS guards and a commander, but their courageous actions unnerved the Germans, which might have resulted in saving a number of inmates.

Jaffa

My Mom was born and raised in Ciechanow, Poland, which was a relatively large town. She was the oldest of three children from a middle class family. She had a younger brother and sister, but was the only family member to survive the war. My Mom was young, healthy and strong and it certainly helped her survive three long years in Auschwitz. She talked little about the war, opening up more in her last years. She was very proud of her role in smuggling gunpowder through what she described as a women's underground. I know that was an outstanding memory for my mother.

I had a lovely childhood, my parents were very social and hardworking. I never knew we were poor in the beginning. Our holidays were very traditional, very European. Even though we were not very observant, on Friday nights my mother would make the chicken soup and flanken and always enough food so we didn't need to cook the entire weekend.

Simon

My Dad was also from Ciechanow, and was nine years older than my mother. My Dad was in three camps, Auschwitz being the third and last. When he arrived at Auschwitz he was experienced with how to handle life in the camp, he had learned the ropes. So, when they asked for volunteers to work as glazers, my father volunteered. On weekdays he worked in the kitchen, and was able to gather extra food, and on Sundays he would go to the women's camp, to fix their broken windows. Once there, he would also share what he had squirreled away. He would ask for the barracks that housed the girls from Ciechanow. He wanted to speak with people from his hometown, spend time with them and share stories. He was able to find that barrack and took an instant liking to my mother.

Top left: Nadzia and Milton Bergson

When Auschwitz was being liquidated, they were marched from the camp. After the march he and my mother took a train together to their hometown. They discovered that they were each the only surviving member of their family. Like so many, they married. They spent the next four years waiting to immigrate to America. My sister, Jaffa, was born in their hometown; I was born in a DP camp in Austria.

My parents would both say that they had two birthdays, their biological birthday and then the date of their liberation. I learned so much, especially from my father. He spoke openly about the war, both positive and negative. My father had a philosophy about America, and it's one that I find to be so true,

"The harder you work, the luckier you get!" My parents were married for over 40 years when my Dad died suddenly from a heart attack. They had three children, eight grandchildren and five great grandchildren.

Top left: Nadzia and Milton (standing on the right), in their hometown, Ciechanow, 1945

Nadzia Goldstein Bergson's Home Baked Challah

There is nothing as satisfying as baking your own challah. It is a feast for all the senses: the tactile sensation of kneading the dough, the welcoming aroma in your home, and the satisfying visual of braided bread with its golden, eggy crust. The recipe handwritten years ago by Nadzia is an authentic reminder that makes preparing this challah so meaningful. We've filled in some of the blanks, but Nadzia's recipe is the foundation. Her original notes were to make two loaves, which commemorates the double portion of manna that fell in the desert on Fridays when we wandered for 40 years after the exodus from Egypt. It is also traditional to cast off a small piece of challah into the oven as a nod to the ancient custom of providing a bit of challah as a tithe to the priests in the Temple in Jerusalem. For the home baker, two loaves can be hard to manage, so this recipe creates one large loaf. There are many braiding techniques, six strands being the most traditional, round for the New Year, and this version which has three strands, a good place for the home baker to start.

Yields: 1 large loaf; Start to Finish: Under 4 hours

1¼ cups warm water (yeast thermometer should read between 105 to 115 degrees)

1½ teaspoons active dry yeast

½ cup sugar

2 tablespoons vegetable oil

1 egg

4 cups bread flour

1 teaspoon salt

Egg wash glaze:

1 egg plus 1 tablespoon water, beaten

In the bowl of a standing mixer, combine the yeast, water and sugar and allow the yeast to bubble, about 10 minutes. Add the oil and egg, beat on low speed with the flat paddle until combined. Slowly begin adding the flour and mix until all 4 cups have been incorporated. You can then turn the mixer to medium and mix for several minutes. Replace the beater with the dough hook and knead for 10 minutes longer, adding more flour if needed to create a smooth, firm, elastic, non-sticky dough. Turn the dough out onto a lightly floured surface and knead for a minute or two so you can judge if the dough is right. This is more about feel than exact measure. Pour a drop of oil into a bowl and then place the dough in the bowl rolling it around so all sides are covered with oil; this will help prevent a crust from forming while the dough rises. Cover the bowl with plastic wrap and then drape with a towel. Let it rise in a warm place for at least 1 hour, or until it has doubled in size. If baking the dough at a later time, you can refrigerate the dough overnight and proceed to the next step.

Turn the dough out onto a lightly floured surface and punch down several times, so that all the air is released from the dough. Return the dough to the greased bowl and cover in the same manner as before. Let the dough rise an additional hour.

Lightly flour a work surface, and turn the dough out. Punch down the dough and separate into three equal parts. Roll the dough sections in your hands to form three ropes, each about 12 inches long. Squeeze out the air as you roll and gently pull on the ends so the strand is thicker in the middle and narrower at the ends (picture a piece of taffy in its wrapper, with the ends pinched and the center fat).

Place the three ropes on a lightly greased baking sheet. Pinch the ends together at one end and begin braiding the bread just like you would a ponytail, by moving the far right piece over the middle piece, taking the far left piece and bringing it over the middle piece. When done braiding, pinch the remaining ends together, and then tuck them underneath to create a neat finish. Cover with a plastic wrap and a towel and let the dough rise one more time, about 30 minutes. Preheat the oven to 350 degrees.

Prepare the egg wash and using a pastry brush, coat the challah. Bake at 350 degrees for 40 minutes, or until the top is nicely golden brown. When you tap the bread you should hear a hollow sound. Let the bread cool completely before slicing.

Feedback
1 cup of raisins can be mixed in for a sweet holiday version, and poppy or sesame seeds can be sprinkled on top right before baking. Keep in mind, making the bread more savory than sweet makes it less versatile the next day when using the leftovers for French toast or bread pudding.

Faye Levy

Professional contributor

Speaking of bread pudding, cookbook author and columnist for the *Jerusalem Post*, Faye Levy, has an excellent idea for what to do with that leftover challah, and it is way more interesting than French toast!

Apple Challah Bread Pudding

Excerpted from 1,000 Jewish Recipes (Hungry Minds, Inc., 2000)

Makes 6 servings

Bread pudding made with challah is a scrumptious dessert. This one is studded with apples and flavored with cinnamon and vanilla. It rises slightly and, like a soufflé, sinks when cool. For special occasions you might like to accompany the pudding with vanilla custard sauce (recipe follows).

4 ounces (¼ of a 1-pound challah), day-old or stale

1¼ cups milk

1 pound sweet apples such as Golden Delicious

6 tablespoons sugar

2 large eggs, separated

1 teaspoon vanilla extract

1½ teaspoons ground cinnamon

2 tablespoons butter, cut into small pieces

Preheat oven to 375 degrees. Generously butter a 5-cup baking dish. Remove crust and cut challah into chunks. Put it in a large bowl. Bring the milk to a simmer in a small saucepan. Pour it over the bread and let it stand about 5 minutes to soften.

Peel, halve and core apples. Slice them very thin.

Mash challah with a fork. Add 4 tablespoons sugar, egg yolks, and 1 teaspoon cinnamon and mix well. Add apples and mix well.

Whip egg whites until they form soft peaks. Gradually beat in remaining 2 tablespoons sugar and beat until stiff and shiny. Gently fold whites, in 2 batches, into bread mixture. Transfer mixture to baking dish. Sprinkle with remaining ½ teaspoon cinnamon and scatter butter pieces on top. Bake about 50 minutes or until a thin knife inserted in the pudding comes out dry.

The pudding is best served warm. Although it sinks when cool, it still tastes good.

Vanilla Custard Sauce

This luscious vanilla bean sauce turns even a simple dessert into a fancy finale like those served at the finest restaurants. It is perfect with challah bread pudding, sweet noodle *kugels*, and cakes that are not frosted. If you want to make it *pareve,* you can substitute a nondairy rice milk, soy milk or multigrain drink. You can discard the vanilla bean after using it—or you can rinse, dry, and reuse it.

Makes 6 to 8 servings

1½ cups milk or nondairy milk

1 vanilla bean, split lengthwise

5 large egg yolks

¼ cup sugar

Bring milk and vanilla bean to a boil in a medium, heavy saucepan. Remove from heat. Cover and let stand 15 minutes. Reheat to a boil. Remove the vanilla bean.

Whisk egg yolks slightly in a large bowl. Add sugar; whisk until smooth. Gradually whisk in hot milk. Return mixture to saucepan, whisking. Cook over medium-low heat, stirring mixture and scraping bottom of pan constantly with a wooden spoon, about 5 minutes or until mixture thickens slightly and reaches 170 degrees to 175 degrees on an instant-read or candy thermometer. To check whether the sauce is thick enough without a thermometer, remove pan from heat. Dip a metal spoon in sauce and draw your finger across back of spoon. Your finger should leave a clear path in the mixture that clings to the spoon. If it does not, cook 30 seconds more and check again. Do not overcook sauce or it will curdle.

Immediately strain sauce into bowl. Stir about 30 seconds to cool; cool completely. Refrigerate at least 30 minutes before serving, or up to 2 days.

Ada Ehrlich Rubin and Leo Rubin

As told by their granddaughter, Jolie Feldman

Ada's story is intrinsically linked to Nadzia Bergson's story, not only because these two courageous women survived Auschwitz together, but because of what transpired decades later. Her granddaughter Jolie told me the beautiful story of a true *bashert*.

My grandmother, Ada Ehrlich Rubin, was born in Poland and was sent to Auschwitz during the war. There she met and befriended Nadzia Bergson. Luckily, they both survived the war and years later bumped into each other walking down the street in New York City. Both were now married and had families of their own. My grandmother married my grandfather, Leo, also a survivor, who came to this country with nothing and worked what felt like a million jobs to make a life. He and my grandmother lived well in America, as did Nadzia and her husband. They became reacquainted and the two families spent much time together, sharing the holidays and *simchas*. Because both had suffered such losses during the war, they regarded each other as family. My grandparents eventually moved to Florida, and although they stayed in touch with the Bergsons, they certainly were not as close as they were when they lived in New York.

Years later, although I was a native Californian, I made the decision to head east and study broadcast journalism at Syracuse's Newhouse School. My roommate was dating a really nice guy, and one day in 1995, he brought his good friend, Jason, over to meet me. We hit it off. Jason was a student at nearby Ithaca College. We certainly knew we had made a connection, but we didn't realize how deep it ran. It was not until Jason told his parents about me that we learned that we were the grandchildren of those same two women who survived Auschwitz more than fifty years earlier. We were married in 2000, and happily, both grandmothers lived to see us as a couple. My grandmother, Ada, passed away knowing Jason and I were to be married. She could not have been happier, and it gave her and Nadzia the chance to reconnect once again.

While my grandparents didn't speak much of the war, in her later years my grandmother did write down some of her recollections. My grandparents were wonderful people who tried to give us everything they could, even when they couldn't. They were married over 50 years and had one child, two grandchildren and two great grandchildren (my twin sons), who are named in memory of their great grandmothers—these two amazing women.

Above: Ada's original recipe notes

Ada Ehrlich's Chocolate Chip Cake

This recipe was interpreted from handwritten notes that Ada wrote in her later years, making it even more special. The egg whites are whipped into a cloud-like state to create this airy cake studded with sweet grated chocolate. Ada prepared the cake to be *pareve,* but we've offered a variation, using butter and milk. Either way, it's simply satisfying.

*Yields: 10 to 12 servings; Start to Finish: Under **1½** hours*

7 eggs, separated

1½ cups sugar

½ cup oil or ½ cup melted butter

2 tablespoons vanilla extract

¾ cup water or ¾ cup milk

2 cups all-purpose flour

3 teaspoons (1 tablespoon) baking powder

½ tablespoon cream of tartar

6 ounces semi-sweet or bittersweet chocolate, grated

Preheat the oven to 350 degrees and lightly grease a 9 x 3-inch spring form pan.

Beat the egg yolks and sugar, in a large bowl, on medium speed, until light and creamy, about 3 minutes. Add the oil (or butter), vanilla and water (or milk) and combine. Sift the flour and baking powder together then add to the egg mixture, on low speed. Beat until the flour is incorporated, then increase to medium speed for several minutes.

In a separate bowl, beat the egg whites with the cream of tartar until they form stiff peaks. Gently fold the egg whites into the batter. Pour the batter into the prepared baking pan. Grate the chocolate on the largest hole of a box grater (hold the chocolate in place with a towel so the heat from your hands does not melt it) or in a nut or coffee grinder. Sprinkle the chocolate with a light dusting of flour (this will prevent it from sinking into the batter) and then drop the chocolate, by handfuls, on top of the cake batter and blend the chocolate into the batter by dragging a knife in swirling motions through the cake.

Bake for 1¼ hours, or until the top of the cake is lightly browned and slightly crusty. A bamboo skewer inserted into the cake's center should come out clean.

Cool the cake before un-molding. You might need to run a knife around the edge to release it from the rim. Serve as is or with a drizzle of chocolate ganache (see page 233).

Feedback
Many of the recipes in this book rely on separating and whipping egg whites. It is a great way to stretch an ingredient, add volume and create light and fluffy desserts. When whipping egg whites, or incorporating eggs into a batter, be sure the eggs are at room temperature, they will fluff better and produce a lighter finished product. Adding cream of tartar helps stabilize the egg whites and some would say, prevent that massive exhale that some cakes experience when removed from the oven. If you have cream of tartar, throw a pinch in, it couldn't hurt.

And what about those white yucky strands of egg white that anchor the yolk in place. Many people believe they are not edible and should be removed from the egg. Not so, they are called chalazae and are actually the sign of a very fresh egg, just be sure to beat the eggs completely so the strands are no longer visible.

Mike and Frania Faywlowicz

As told by their daughter Toby Schafer

There is a romantic element to the story of Toby Schafer's parents that makes you almost forget you are listening to a true wartime story and feel you are peering into a beautiful Hollywood love story.

Both my parents were from the same town of Piotrkó Trybunalski, Poland. My father was the youngest of ten children and two years older than my mother. My father worked as an apprentice tailor for my mother's father. When the Germans forced them into the ghetto, my father, who worked outside the ghetto as a tradesman, was able to sneak in food. He always had a soft spot for my mother, so he would sneak food to her as well. He worked in a glass factory near the train station, where he watched the train carrying his parents and siblings, fatefully pull away.

When my parents were liberated, they both went back to their hometown where they found nothing was left and anti-Semitism was prevalent. They went to the DP camp in Foehrenwald, and there they planned to be married. My father wanted to sew something special for his bride-to-be. He didn't have access to a fabric store, so he stole a United States military issued blanket to make her a pair of pants. Two days before their wedding, my parents were bicycling around town, my mother sporting her new pants. The police arrested her for having stolen goods! In spite of that, two days later they were married in Foehrenwald—we believe it was the first wedding to take place in that camp. My mother proudly wore her U.S. Army blanket pants and medical gauze served as her veil. Many brides married after her used her veil for their ceremony.

In 1950, my parents were sponsored by a relative and moved to Montreal, a community with a large number of survivors. They lived well, and I remember them speaking often about the Holocaust. My mother cooked very European. Like most children, I wanted to eat out and my Dad would say, "if you want to eat out, go out on the porch." Nothing was as good as something that was made at home. When we moved to an apartment in Coney Island, I remember one dinner there as the best meal of my life. I don't know why it stands out; it was rye bread with *shmaltz*, dried salami and a little salt on the bread. I remember sitting in this new home and feeling very safe. I always wanted to make things better for my parents because of all they had gone through. In our home it was always family first. My parents had two children, four grandchildren, and three great grandchildren.

Since completing the book, I sadly learned that Frania passed away. We extend our sincerest condolences to her devoted family. May her memory be a blessing.

Top left: Frania (center), wearing the pants Mike (on the right) made for her, January, 1947. Miks's oldest brother is pictured on the left

Frania Faywlowicz' Meat and Potato *Cholent*

Cholent is considered a special dish by observant Jews who needed to prepare Saturday's midday meal, before Friday at sundown. The combination of ingredients are as varied as the families who prepared them, but traditionally included meat, potatoes, beans and barley. The common factor is the slow baking, up to 24 hours, at a very low temperature. The stew would be assembled at home and then the pot would be brought to a local bakery Friday before Shabbos began, to bake overnight. Almost a ritual itself was retrieving the pot from the bakery and eating the dish Saturday afternoon.

Frania's version has two textures of potato, melding into beef flanken and creating a satisfying, comforting, full-bodied meal. If the aroma from your kitchen could be bottled, it would be called *haimish*. Frania recalls everyone coming over to enjoy this dish; not because its brownish color is divine, but the taste seems almost sanctified.

Yields: 4 to 6 servings; Start to Finish: 15 minutes prep, then slow roasted for up to 15 hours

2 russet potatoes, peeled and very thinly sliced, plus 1 russet potato, peeled and grated

2 teaspoons kosher salt

Fresh cracked black pepper, to taste

2 pounds beef flanken

Preheat the oven to 225 degrees and line the bottom of a heavy lidded pot with wax paper.

Slice 2 of the potatoes paper-thin. If you have a mandolin or professional vegetable slicer, now would be the time to use it. Cover the wax paper with half the sliced potatoes. Sprinkle the potatoes with 1 teaspoon of salt and a few turns of cracked black pepper. Lay the flanken on top of the potatoes and surround the flanken with the grated potato. Season with the remaining salt and additional pepper. Pour 2 cups of water into the pot, and then spread the remaining sliced potatoes on top. Cover with a piece of wax paper, which seals the ingredients and helps retain moisture while the dish bakes. Cover the pot and bake at 225 degrees, overnight. Do not stir the dish or disturb the ingredients while baking.

Take the *cholent* out of the oven, remove the wax paper and dab a paper towel on top of the sauce to absorb any oil that has collected on the surface. Be sure when serving that you do not scoop up the wax paper from the bottom of the pot.

Feedback

Did you know that the trendy short rib, that appears on every menu today, is really good old-fashioned flanken, cut in a different direction? You can substitute one cut for the other and the final result will be very similar. The short rib, which is cut parallel to the bone, looks meatier with one hefty chunk of meat, while flanken, which is cross-cut, has several smaller bones.

Faye Levy

Professional contributor

Frania's *Cholent* has the traditional elements of slow cooked meat and potatoes. But for many, it's not *cholent* without beans and barley. Faye Levy presents her mother's version, which adds several additional flavors to make a hearty stew lover out of anyone.

My Mother's Chicken and Barley *Cholent*

Excerpted from Faye Levy's 1,000 Jewish Recipes (Hungry Minds, Inc., 2000)

My mother has lived in Jerusalem for many years. Like many cooks in Israel, over time her way of making *cholent* has changed to a hybrid of *Ashkenazi* and *Sephardic* styles. Sometimes she adds a touch of cumin to the basic *Ashkenazi* seasoning mixture of salt, pepper, and paprika. She has also adopted the *Sephardic* custom of putting eggs on top so they brown "because Israelis like it that way."

To make good *cholent*, she feels it's important to include both white and brown beans and barley. Generally she makes her *cholent* with chicken but occasionally she uses beef. Often she browns the onion so it will add more flavor. When I asked her if you could cook the *cholent* ahead for 2 or 3 hours or until everything is tender, refrigerate it, and reheat it in a low oven, she answered, "Why would you want to do that? *Cholent* tastes much better when it cooks very slowly all night."

If you like, remove the skin from the chicken before cooking the *cholent*. The chicken will stay moist because of all the liquid in the pot. However, leaving the skin on and removing it before serving will give you a richer tasting *cholent* because some of the fat from the chicken skin will blend in.

Makes 6 to 8 servings

4 pounds chicken pieces, excess fat removed

1 to 2 tablespoons vegetable oil

2 large onions, cut into thick slices

1 teaspoon paprika

½ teaspoon ground cumin (optional)

¼ teaspoon freshly ground pepper

¾ cup navy beans or other white beans, sorted and rinsed

¾ cup brown beans or red kidney beans, sorted and rinsed

1 cup barley, sorted and rinsed

6 to 8 fairly small boiling potatoes

½ teaspoon salt

6 to 8 large eggs in shells, rinsed

Preheat oven to 200 degrees (or lowest number setting that isn't "keep warm"). Remove chicken skin, if you like. Heat oil in a large stew pan or Dutch oven. Add onions and sauté over medium-high heat, stirring often, about 5 minutes, until onions begin to brown; they don't need to soften. Remove from heat. Add chicken to stew pan or Dutch oven and sprinkle with paprika, cumin if using, and pepper. Mix well.

Add the beans and barley to the casserole. Peel potatoes, if you like. Add to pan and sprinkle with salt. Add enough water to cover ingredients by 2 inches. Bring to a boil. Cover and cook over very low heat 20 to 30 minutes. Set eggs gently on top of stew and push them slightly into liquid. Cover tightly and bake mixture, without stirring, overnight. Serve hot.

Frania Faywlowicz' Passover Noodles

Toby recalls her mother preparing *forshpeiz* every day, but on Friday nights, they would have soup that turned into something else as the week progressed. First it was chicken soup, and then she added potatoes and called it potato soup. She might add *lokshen* (noodles) or matzo balls. It was the same soup every night, but with new added ingredients. One of Toby's favorite add-ins were the homemade noodles her mother would make at Passover.

Yields: 4 servings of soup noodles; Start to Finish: Under 30 minutes

2 eggs

1 teaspoon Osem (or chicken flavor seasoning)

¾ cup water

½ cup matzo meal

Oil for frying

Beat the eggs and the Osem together in a small bowl. Stir in the water and then the matzo meal. The mixture will be thin; it will thicken as it rests. After 15 minutes, heat a large skillet with ¼-inch of oil to fry the pancakes. Stir the pancake mixture, it should be a little thicker than pancake batter, add more water if it is too thick. If you add too much water, simply balance it by adding more matzo meal.

Drop generous tablespoons of batter into the hot skillet, the pancakes should be about 2 ½ inches to 3 inches in diameter. The batter should yield about 20 pancakes. Fry them for a couple of minutes on the first side, and just a minute on the second.

Remove the pancakes to a waiting paper towel. Continue frying until all the mixture is used. Stack the pancakes 4 high and cut them into thin ribbons. Stir them into heated chicken soup for a lovely Passover noodle.

Gil Marks

Professional contributor

Frania's Passover noodles, ribbons of fried matzo meal, have their roots in an age-old tradition of preparing matzo meal pancakes and serving them in various creative ways. As Gil Marks, Rabbi, food historian and cookbook author explains, *chremslach* is another delicious way to re-invent the humble matzo meal pancake.

Chremslach–Ashkenazi Sweet Matza Meal Pancakes

Excerpted from The Encyclopedia of Jewish Food (Wiley, 2010)

In his cookbook, *De re conquinaria libri decem* (Cuisine in Ten Books), the Roman epicure Apicius included a recipe for preparing the popular Roman dish vermiculos (Latin for "little worms"): "Cook the finest flour in milk to make a stiff paste. Spread it on a dish, cut it into pieces, then, when fried in fine oil, cover with pepper and honey." Eventually, Italian Jews adopted the dish and it spread to the Jews to the north. In the twelfth century, numerous Franco-German rabbis mentioned the custom of eating fried strips of dough in honey called *vermesel* or *verimslish* at the start of the Friday evening meal. At some point, the name for boiled strips of dough (noodles) became *frimsel* in Western Yiddish, and the name for fritters in honey changed to *gremsel*. By the late fifteenth century, chicken soup with noodles replaced fried dough strips in honey as the first course for Friday evening dinner. When the fritters reached Eastern Europe, the name mutated into chremsel.

Each Passover I prepare all sorts of fancy desserts for my family and friends, often experimenting with adaptations of sophisticated modern fare. Yet every year I repeat one particular dish, *chremslach* (bite-size matzo meal pancakes in honey). The recipe I use is scribbled in my grandmother's handwriting on a yellowed, wine-splattered index card. I scrupulously follow the directions, making certain that the pancakes are "the size of a quarter" and "not too brown." Inevitably my father sneaks a sample of the nearly finished product with the excuse of "quality control," remarking on how they take him back to his childhood and the ones his mother used to make. The mere sampling of a piece of pancake, its lineage dating back through much of Jewish history, transcends time, linking generations.

Yields: About sixteen 3-inch or thirty six 1-inch pancakes

1 cup matzo meal	**4 large eggs, lightly beaten**
¼ to ½ cup finely chopped almonds, hazelnuts, or walnuts	**1 cup sweet wine, or 1 cup water and 2 tablespoons sugar**
1 teaspoon ground cinnamon	**Vegetable oil for frying**
About ½ teaspoon salt	**1 pound (1⅓ cups) honey**

Combine the matzo meal, nuts, cinnamon, and salt. Combine the eggs and wine. Stir into the matzo meal mixture and let stand for at least 30 minutes.

Heat about ⅛ inch oil in a large skillet over medium heat. Drop the batter by teaspoonfuls or tablespoonfuls and fry until lightly browned on the bottom, about 1 minute. Turn and fry until browned, about 30 seconds. Drain on paper towels.

Pour off the oil and add the honey to the skillet. Bring to a boil, stirring frequently (the honey may boil up). Add the pancakes and toss to coat. Store in the honey syrup.

Raymond Fishler

As told by his wife Rhoda

Raymond spent much of the war in Plaszow, which was initially a forced-labor camp and ultimately a concentration camp in Cracow. Plaszow gained worldwide attention when it was the focus of the Steven Spielberg film, *Schindler's List*. Raymond's wife, Rhoda, likened his emotions at seeing the film to "a cork being unleashed." She elaborated on his experiences.

Raymond was born near Cracow, Poland, one of six children. There were four boys and two girls; he and his father were the only family members to survive. When the war came to their hometown, the family became scattered. Raymond was just fourteen at the time. A non-Jewish family hid Raymond, until he ran away to the Cracow ghetto, where he volunteered to work at the airport. In 1943, he was taken from the airport to Plaszow where he met up with a sister, one brother and his father. His brother and sister perished. While Raymond managed a sewing factory at Plaszow, he met many of the "Schindler Jews." He also had many encounters with Amon Göth, the sadistic commandant.

As the war was drawing to a close, the camp was liquidated, with many of the prisoners being transported to Auschwitz. Raymond and his father were among the fortunate because when their train pulled into Auschwitz, it was turned away. They were put on another transport and went from camp to camp, fortunately being turned away each time. Two days before the war ended, he and his father escaped and hid in a barn in the Bavarian woods. There were 50 other men in the barn. Amazingly, they turned out to be German Air Force deserters who were hiding from the authorities. He viewed the airmen with restrained emotion as he felt "they were a different breed from the SS." He also realized they were frightened and feared capture as they began to ask Raymond more and more questions about the war. He said it was very bizarre. When the troops came through the woods, Raymond realized they looked different than the soldiers he was accustomed to seeing. That's when he knew the war had ended. He and his father wanted to go back home, but they were told there was nothing to go back to. Raymond immigrated to the United States, while his father remained in Europe.

Being married to a survivor is a unique experience. I try to maintain the traditions that he grew up with. My cooking style is very much like what he had in his home, which was very traditional Jewish cooking. I enjoy cooking everything. My mother would make two specific cookies, one for Passover, one for Rosh Hashanah. They have become traditional in our home, which was always filled with the flavors of the holidays, much to the delight of our two children and four grandchildren.

Top left: Raymond Fishler in DP camp in Altöting, Germany, 1947

Rhoda Fishler's Meringue Nut Cookie

This delectably light and moist confection has a mere three ingredients, and is a favorite at Rhoda's Passover table.

Yields: About 3 dozen cookies; Start to Finish: Under 30 minutes

2 cups (about ½ pound) finely chopped walnuts

¾ cup sugar

4 egg whites, beaten

Preheat the oven to 350 degrees and lightly grease a cookie sheet or line it with a piece of parchment paper or non-stick silicone mat.

Chop the walnuts in a food processor, nut grinder or by hand with a serrated knife in a rocking motion. Combine the sugar and the walnuts. In a separate bowl, beat the egg whites until stiff but not dry. Gently stir the nuts into the beaten egg whites. Drop by generous teaspoonfuls on the lined baking sheet, about 1-inch apart as they spread while baking. Bake at 350 degrees for 20 minutes or until lightly brown. They should still be a bit sticky and soft in the center. Do not overcook, or they will become crunchy and hard to bite.

Variation: Stir in 1 tablespoon cocoa powder, with the walnuts and sugar, for a chocolaty version.

Feedback
Sometimes, when separating eggs, you are left with remaining yolks or whites. No worries, they won't go to waste. They can be kept in the fridge for up to 5 days, in an airtight storage container, or they can be frozen by placing them in a covered ice cube tray, for ease of use at a later date.

Stephen and Hela Fisk

As told by their daughter Pearl Fisk

The evolution of Hela Fisk's name is really so illustrative of the way so many survivors reinvented themselves throughout their lives. Her daughter Pearl explains.

My mother, one of six children, was born in Wolysk, Poland, a small town of about 20,000 people. She was married prior to World War II in an arranged match, and at age 20 had a son Yankel (Jacob). After the German occupation of Poland, my Mom and her family were forced into the Ludmir ghetto. On the day the Germans "liquidated" the ghetto, my mother was out of the ghetto searching for water for her son. She knew the area and its townspeople well, and spoke Polish and Ukrainian. When she returned to the ghetto and saw what the Germans had done, she realized her son, spouse and extended family had perished. She hid on an existing rooftop, cried all night and asked, "why?" The following morning, she escaped from the ghetto and a non-Jewish Polish woman hid her in a hole in her barn for six weeks as German soldiers and Ukrainian collaborators scoured the area for Jews. When it became too dangerous for my mother to continue hiding in the barn, she left and was turned in to the Germans by nearby townspeople who recognized her and confirmed she was a Jew. She was sent to slave labor at Budzyn and remained in slave labor until she was liberated at the end of the war.

In 1945, after liberation, my mother returned to her home village searching for her family, and remains of her family life. She soon learned she was the sole survivor. One brother survived in Russia but was killed at the end of the war. As a person without a home, without anything, my mother entered the first of several DP camps. My mother met my father in one of these camps and they began dating. They each suffered similar losses. My father, who was from Slomniki/Cracow, Poland, was a survivor of Auschwitz. They both waited to go to America.

On Thanksgiving, 1952, my parents finally left Germany and arrived in New York City on an American transport ship, the "General Eisenhower." As they disembarked the ship, they said their goodbyes and promised to keep in touch. My mother was met by an HIAS representative and taken to the train station for a train to Boston. A relative who had left Poland after World War I, and resided in Ipswich, Massachusetts, met my mother at the train. My father remained in New York City.

Top left: Hela, outside DP camp, Germany, 1946

My mother was not happy in Ipswich, as no one understood what she had lived through and witnessed. Within two weeks, and with only $25.00 in her pocket, she returned to New York and rented a room in a tenement in the Bronx. Soon after, my mother found a job in the garment district and called my father. They met for coffee the next day and married in 1953. My twin sister and I were born in January, 1954–21 years after the birth of my mother's first child. Our parents celebrated our birth—yet mourned the children and extended family they lost in the Holocaust. Rose and I are named for our maternal grandmothers who perished. Our parents were only married 14 years when our father died, on February 13, 1967, after a long illness. Our mother died 38 years later to the date. Together they had my sister and me and five grandchildren. The foods in our home were traditional Jewish Eastern European. We never ate out, kept kosher and celebrated Shabbos and the Jewish holidays. Our mother worked full time yet always cooked all our meals. She was a wonderful baker and our home always smelled of her baking and cooking. My sister and I recall the first time our Mom saw a pineapple and the look on her face when she learned that *lokshen* (pasta) could come out of a box!

- My Mom's given name was Ruchel; it was changed to Helinka when she began using false papers in the ghetto .

- Helinka became Hela in either the concentration or DP camp.

- At the time my mother married my Dad, she was known as Hela Aiken. I'm not sure if this was her maiden name or her first married name as she spoke very little of her first husband and son who perished in the ghetto in 1942.

- In 1952, my parents arrived in New York City.

- My parents married in 1953, and my mother became Hela Finkelstein.

- Years later (1959-1960) when becoming citizens, the Judge could not pronounce Finkelstein so he asked my father if a new American name would be OK.

- Thus, Finkelstein became Fisk, and my mother became Hela Fisk.

Hela Fisk's Plum Cake

Pearl remembers her mother baking this quintessential batter version of Polish plum cake, for Shabbos and "always for company, delicious hot or cold!!!" Serve it hot for a luscious dessert or bake it the night before and enjoy the subtle sweet goodness of the plums with the acidic orange juice for a delicious breakfast. Make this from May to October when plums are at their peak.

Yields: 10 to 12 servings; Start to Finish: Under 1½ hours

For the Filling:

2 pounds dark, sweet plums, pit removed, cut into thin slices

¼ cup sugar (increase the sugar to ½ cup if the plums are tart or add a touch of honey) mixed with 2 teaspoons cinnamon

For the Batter:

4 eggs

1½ cups sugar

1 cup vegetable oil

½ cup orange juice

2 teaspoons vanilla extract

3 cups all-purpose flour

3 teaspoons baking powder

1 teaspoon salt

Topping:

2 tablespoons sugar mixed with ¼ teaspoon ground cinnamon

Preheat the oven to 350 degrees and grease a 9 x 3-inch spring form or tube pan

To make the filling, toss the plums with the sugar and cinnamon.

Prepare the batter in a large bowl. Beat the eggs, sugar, oil, orange juice and vanilla, several minutes, on medium speed, until light and fluffy. In another bowl, sift together the flour, baking powder and salt. On low speed, slowly add it to the egg mixture. Increase the speed to medium and beat for several minutes, until all the ingredients are well combined and the batter is smooth.

Pour a third of the batter (about 1 to 1¼ cups) into the prepared pan and top with a third of the plums, Repeat 2 more times, ending with a layer of plums on top. Sprinkle with the sugar and cinnamon topping. Bake at 350 degrees for 1¼ hours or until a bamboo skewer inserted in the middle of the cake comes out clean. Let the cake cool completely before removing from pan. If the cake does not release easily, loosen it by running a knife around the edges.

Variation: To use a rectangular 13 x 9 x 2-inch baking dish, make only 2 layers and reduce baking time to 45 to 60 minutes.

Paula Gerson

As told by her daughter-in-law Joan Nathan

Anyone who knows Jewish cooking knows Joan Nathan. She is a best-selling cookbook author and award-winning television personality. What you might not know is that her mother-in-law, Paula (Peshka), is a Holocaust survivor. Joan shared her mother-in-law's story as well as her famous recipe for gefilte fish.

Paula (Peshka) Gerson was my mother-in-law. She was from Zamosc, Poland, and was a wonderful seamstress before and during the war. When the war broke out, she went to Siberia, with her husband and infant. Her expertise with her sewing machine (which she carried with her) saved her and her family. When the war was over, they went to Uzbekistan where my husband, Allan, was born. From there they entered a DP camp in Germany. Using an assumed name they came illegally to the United States.

I felt that it was *bashert* that we were connected. Paula had an amazing memory for life before the Holocaust, and I love to hear stories about that life. Every year before Passover we would make gefilte fish together, with me taking notes and she, carefully, cooking, remembering every gesture from her childhood. At one point each year, she would put carrots in the eyes of the head of one of the fish and raisins in the nose. Then she would sigh. We all knew why she sighed. She was remembering her mother who did exactly the same thing. Her mother died in the Belzec Death Camp. My husband was one of three children, and there are five grandchildren in the family.

Top left: The gefilte fish recipe came with Joan's husband's family from the DP camp.

Joan Nathan

Excerpted from Jewish Cooking in America (Alfred A. Knopf, 1998)

Until I married into this "start-from-scratch" gefilte fish family, we graced our Passover table with the jarred variety. What a difference homemade makes! Now gefilte fish-making has become a welcome twice-yearly ritual in our house—at Rosh Hashanah and Passover. At our Passover seder, we all wait with baited breath for my husband's opinion. "Peshka, your gefilte fish is better than ever!" gets a broad grin from his Jewish mother. The gefilte fish recipe we use today came with my husband's family from the DP camps.

Gefilte fish is one of those recipes where touch and taste are essential ingredients. A basic recipe goes this way: "You put in this and add that." If you don't want to taste the raw fish, add a bit more seasoning than you normally would. What makes this recipe Galicianer (southern Polish) is the addition of sugar. For some reason the further south in Poland, the more sugar would be added. A Lithuanian Jew would never sweeten with sugar but might add beets to the stock. I have added ground carrot and parsnip to the fish, something that is done in the Ukraine, because I like the slightly sweet taste and rougher texture. If you want a darker broth, do not peel the onions and leave them whole.

Classic Gefilte Fish

Yields: About 26 patties

7 to 7½ pounds whole carp, whitefish, and pike, filleted and ground*

4 quarts cold water or to just cover

3 teaspoons salt or to taste

3 onions, peeled

4 medium carrots, peeled

2 tablespoons sugar or to taste

1 small parsnip, chopped (optional)

3 to 4 large eggs

Freshly ground pepper to taste

½ cup cold water (approximately)

⅓ cup matzo meal (approximately)

*Ask your fishmonger to grind the fish. Ask him to reserve the tails, fins, heads, and bones. Be sure he gives you the bones and trimmings. The more whitefish you add, the softer your gefilte fish will be.

Place the reserved bones, skin, and fish heads in a wide, very large saucepan with a cover. Add the water and 2 teaspoons of the salt and bring to a boil. Remove the foam that accumulates.

Slice 1 onion in rounds and add along with 3 of the carrots. Add the sugar and bring to a boil. Cover and simmer for about 20 minutes while the fish mixture is prepared.

Place the ground fish in a bowl. In a food processor finely chop the remaining onions, the remaining carrot, and the parsnip; or mince them by hand. Add the chopped vegetables to the ground fish.

Add the eggs, one at a time, the remaining teaspoon of salt, pepper, and the cold water, and mix thoroughly. Stir in enough matzo meal to make a light soft mixture that will hold its shape. Wet your hands with cold water, and scooping up about ¼ cup of fish form the mixture into oval shapes, about 3 inches long. Take the last fish head and stuff the cavity with the ground fish mixture.

Remove from the saucepan the onions, skins, head and bones and return the stock to a simmer. Gently place the fish patties in the simmering fish stock. Cover loosely and simmer for 20 to 30 minutes. Taste the liquid while the fish is cooking and add seasoning to taste. Shake the pot periodically so the fish patties won't stick. When gefilte fish is cooked, remove from the water and allow to cool for at least 15 minutes.

Using a slotted spoon carefully remove the gefilte fish and arrange on a platter. Strain some of the stock over the fish, saving the rest in a bowl.

Slice the cooked carrots into rounds cut on a diagonal about ¼-inch thick. Place a carrot round on top of each gefilte fish patty. Put the fish head in the center and decorate the eyes with carrots. Chill until ready to serve. Serve with a sprig of parsley.

The Rubach Family

As told by JoJo Rubach

JoJo credits the women in his life for teaching him to be strong and fearless.

My paternal grandmother, Genia, grew up in Wloclawek, Poland. She married my grandfather, Joseph, who in 1939 was taken into the army and never returned to his family. My grandmother, along with her two children, Leon, (my father) and his brother, Marc, survived the war by hiding with relatives and strangers. During the last years of the war, a kind woman, Sophia Tomashevsky, saved my father, grandmother and uncle. In the ultimate coming full circle, my daughter, Tessa, and my wife, Elle, went to Cracow, Poland and attended the ceremony when Sophia was inducted into the "Righteous Among the Nations."

My mother, Eva, who was from Budapest, Hungary, is also a survivor. My maternal grandmother was very resourceful and smart. She anticipated the problems coming to Hungary and urged my grandfather to change the family name from Israel to Iranyi. This definitely allowed them to stay under the radar and survive the war.

The importance of family and how a family sticks together is what got them through everything, and that's something I've learned from them. While visiting Israel with my entire family, including my parents, we gathered at the kibbutz where my great-aunt settled after she immigrated to Israel. There were 40 people there and at the end of lunch, my uncle raised a glass and toasted, *"L'chayim Meshpokha Rubacha."* I couldn't help but feel this is the true meaning of generation to generation, as one generation of survivors toasted another. My parents were married 46 years and had two children and five grandchildren.

Top left: The Rubach family celebrating in Israel

For 45 years, the Rubach family has an annual tradition of preparing Genia's gefilte fish. It is really a team effort, with JoJo (a non-gefilte fish eater) at the helm. The important aspect of this laborious endeavor is the team effort and the respect they are paying to their family's heritage. To celebrate Team Rubach and their ritual of preparing gefilte fish, we have included a homemade horseradish to complement their family tradition.

It was the week before Passover, and I went to my friend Valerie Romanoff's house to pick up a jar of her coveted homemade horseradish. She greeted me at the door, wearing swimming goggles! The horseradish was spectacular, and added the perfect pungent note to our holiday dinner.

Beet Horseradish

According to Valerie, "at our family's holiday dinners, Grandpa Jerry carries on a tradition that came from his grandparents in Russia; he eats the broth of the chicken soup first and saves the matzo ball for last. Then, when the bowl is dry, he heaps fresh red horseradish all over the matzo ball and eats it this way. Later, he puts more horseradish on the pot roast. Having homemade horseradish with fresh beets adds a zing to our holidays, as it is so fresh and pungent. I always make an extra jar of this special horseradish for him to take home. "

1 (6-inch piece) of horseradish root, peeled and chopped into 1-inch pieces

4 to 6 medium beets (fresh or canned)

½ cup white vinegar

1 pair swimming goggles (optional)

Put the chopped horseradish in a food processor fitted with the steel blade and grind until the root is in teeny pieces. If using canned beets, drain them, and then cut them into small pieces. Start by adding 3 of them to the food processor. If using fresh beets, boil them until tender, and then peel them before adding to the horseradish. The more beets you add, the deeper the color of the horseradish. Stir in the vinegar. The vinegar holds the mixture together, so add a small amount at a time, stopping when you reach a desired consistency.

It is important to remember that every time you take the lid off the food processor to check the mixture, the fumes are intense and can burn your eyes and throat. I started wearing swim goggles and it really helps. I wouldn't make horseradish without them anymore.

Natalie Gomberg

Based on our conversation

Natalie is the sole survivor of her family, which included her parents and five siblings.

Having been interned in several concentration and labor camps, Natalie was liberated by a Russian Jewish officer. Following her liberation she went to Leipzig, to look for family members who might have survived. Her search led her to the men's camp in Buchenwald, where she was told she might find more information. Eventually, Natalie was among 350 Jewish children who were transferred from Germany to Switzerland for rehabilitation. Interestingly, a Jewish captain in the American army, named Herschel Schachter, was responsible for that transfer. Natalie was hoping that when she reached Switzerland, she would be able to continue her search for family members, as Geneva was a central and important location for listing survivors. She stayed in Switzerland for nearly three years at which point, in 1947, she received a special visa to come to America, sent by her Canadian relatives. Once here, Natalie worked for 30 years as a social worker. For many years, she has been an active member of the Museum's Speakers Bureau, where she talks about her experiences during the Holocaust in an effort to inform and educate. Her son, three grandchildren, and one great grandchild, as well as her husband of 61 years, are certainly grateful that her strength and will prevailed.

Top left: Natalie Gomberg

Natalie Gomberg's *Mohn*–Poppy Seed Cookies

In her hometown of Opatow-Kielce, Poland, Natalie undoubtedly had lots of *Mohn* cookies and cakes. Natalie's uncomplicated cookie features a hint of lemon, which plays nicely with the mildly sweet crunchy poppy seeds. You can roll these out very thin and make crispy wafer-like cookies, or press the dough in your hands for a bigger bite.

Yields: 2 dozen (thick) cookies or 4 dozen (wafer-like) cookies; Start to Finish: Under 30 minutes

½ cup vegetable oil

½ cup sugar

2 eggs

1 teaspoon fresh lemon juice

1 teaspoon salt

2 teaspoons baking powder

2½ cups all-purpose flour

¼ cup poppy seeds

In a medium bowl, beat the oil, sugar, eggs and lemon juice until all the ingredients are well blended. In a separate bowl, combine the salt, baking powder and flour. Slowly add the flour mixture to the oil mixture and blend completely. Stir in the poppy seeds. The dough will be very thick and sticky.

Chill the dough while you preheat the oven to 350 degrees and lightly grease a large baking pan.

When the oven is ready, roll the dough out on a generously floured board to ¼–inch thick, and cut with a cookie cutter for a wafer-like cookie. For a thicker cookie, form small balls, about the size of a golf ball, 1½–inch diameter, and slightly flatten with your hands (a little oil on your hands will help). Place on the prepared pan. Both versions will bake at 350 degrees for 10 to 15 minutes or until the edges are lightly browned.

Feedback
For a more lemony version, add additional lemon juice or the zested peel of 1 lemon.

Henny Durmashkin Gurko and Simon Gurko

As told by their daughter Rita Lerner; Recipe provided by their daughter Vivian Reisman

Rita remembers her mother as a very positive person. She talks effusively about a house filled with love and music.

My mother was from Vilna, Poland and came from a loving, musical family. She had a sister, Fanny, who played the piano and a brother, Wolf, who was the first Jewish conductor of the Vilna Philharmonic. My mother was the singer in the family. My grandfather was the head of the Vilna Choir and he worked in the synagogue. When the Nazis came into Vilna, my grandfather was taken away and perished. The rest of the family went into the Vilna ghetto. Since the start of the war my uncle no longer conducted the orchestra, but helped out backstage. While in the ghetto, he was given a special pass, that allowed him to go in and out of the ghetto so he could continue working. Amazingly, during that time, he took apart a piano and sneaked it piece by piece into the ghetto, where he faithfully rebuilt it. He formed a choir in the ghetto and the Nazis would come and listen to them. (Tragically he perished only one hour before liberation.) When the ghetto was liquidated, my mother, her sister and my grandmother went by train to several camps and then eventually were sent to Dachau. There they were part of the concentration camp orchestra. After they were liberated, they continued to perform and called themselves the ex-concentration camp orchestra. Imagine the sight as a group of devastated survivors entertained other survivors who now resided in the DP camps.

Shortly after liberation, Leonard Bernstein came to Germany to conduct the Munich Symphony Orchestra. In lieu of his fee, he asked for special permission to perform with my mother's group. My mother and aunt performed with him in three different DP camps. He was very kind and offered to help them in any way he could, should they come to the United States. My Mom came to America on a boat, where she met my father, Simon a Polish survivor who spent the war in Siberia. After the war, my father, heroically, was part of the *Brihah*, which in Hebrew means "flight" or "escape." This valiant group smuggled many Jews out of Europe and into Israel.

My mother always sang in the house. She sang every year at the Vilna commemoration. Music was very much in our house growing up. My mother was always in the kitchen cooking and singing. She really made the house fun. She was a wonderful cook, making many traditional Polish dishes. When she made *cholent*, just the smell in the room was delicious. We ate chicken every Friday night; her baked chicken was our favorite. My parents were married 23 years; they had three children and six grandchildren.

Top left: Henny Gurko

Henny Durmashkin Gurko's Roasted Chicken and Vegetables

What could be more comforting and satisfying than well-seasoned roasted chicken nestled on a bed of fresh vegetables? Vivian recalls that Henny used lots of onions as well as chunks of carrots, celery and sweet potatoes, which made the chicken intensely flavorful and succulent.

Yields: 4 servings; Start to Finish: Under 2 hours

2 large onions, thinly sliced

1 pound of carrots (5 to 6), peeled and cut into 2-inch pieces

4 celery ribs, cut into 2-inch pieces (about 2 cups)

4 sweet potatoes, peeled and cut into 2-inch pieces

Kosher salt and pepper

1 (3½ to 4 pound) chicken, cut into eighths

2 tablespoons sweet paprika

2 tablespoons garlic powder

1 tablespoon onion powder

Preheat the oven to 350 degrees.

Place the onions, carrots, celery and sweet potatoes on the bottom of a large roasting pan. Lightly season them with salt and pepper. Pour enough cold water into the pan to just barely cover the vegetables. Season the chicken on all sides with salt, pepper, paprika, garlic powder and onion powder. Place the chicken pieces in the pan on top of the vegetables.

Bake at 350 degrees, skin side down, for 45 minutes. Turn the chicken pieces over and continue baking an additional 45 minutes or until the chicken is completely cooked through and the potatoes are tender. Occasionally baste the chicken to keep it moist, adding more water if necessary to create a nice sauce and prevent the vegetables from scorching.

Sara Moulton

Professional contributor

In many Eastern European homes, roasted chicken was a given for Friday night dinner. Henny's version was a nice departure bringing in new elements and flavors. Another popular variation on chicken, was fricassee, which for the frugal homemaker, was a terrific way to utilize the parts of the chicken that were collected every Shabbos and saved. Today we might consider these parts throwaway, but you'll discover this dish has tremendous flavor and history. Sara Moulton, who had been the executive chef of *Gourmet* magazine, and is a beloved television personality and cookbook author, shares her mother-in-law's recipe for this ultimate *shtetl* preparation.

Esther's Chicken Fricassee

Excerpted from Sara Moulton Cooks at Home (Broadway Books, 2002)

Esther Adler, my mother-in-law, gave birth to three sons in less than three years (yikes!) and a daughter three years later. All four kids had hearty appetites, and all four turned out to be fairly strapping individuals. I'll confess that I've often wondered how in the world she managed to feed them. This recipe is one answer.

Esther's wonderful chicken fricassee was a relatively rare treat. She served it only about once a month, because that's how long it took to assemble the parts. Every Friday night she'd cook two chickens, roasting one and making soup out of the other, while putting aside the packet of giblets that accompanied each bird. After four weeks of this routine she'd finally have enough giblets to make fricassee (as well as enough livers to make chopped liver). She'd put a big basket of fresh challah nearby, and they'd sop up the gravy. Truthfully, it is almost a meal in itself.

Serves 6

2 tablespoons vegetable oil

2 medium onions, finely chopped

4 chicken necks, trimmed and cut crosswise into 4 or 5 pieces

1 pound chicken gizzards, trimmed

6 chicken wings

Kosher salt and freshly ground black pepper to taste

1 pound ground beef

½ cup matzo meal

1 large egg

2 ½ teaspoons kosher salt

1 teaspoon sweet paprika

½ cup all-purpose flour

½ teaspoon freshly ground black pepper

Heat the oil in a large casserole over medium heat. Add the onions and cook, stirring often, until softened, about 5 minutes. Add the necks, gizzards and wings. Season with salt and pepper. Reduce the heat to low and cover. Cook, stirring often, until the chicken has lost all traces of pink, about 30 minutes.

Meanwhile, combine the ground beef, matzo meal, egg and 1½ teaspoons of the salt in a large bowl. Pour in ½ cup cold water, mix well, and form into small meatballs about the size of a walnut. You should have about 3 dozen.

Bring 2 cups of water to boil and pour it into the chicken parts mixture. Increase the heat to medium-high and bring to a simmer. Add the paprika and season with salt and pepper.

Mix the flour with the remaining teaspoon of salt and ½ teaspoon pepper in a large bowl. Add the meatballs and roll until coated on all sides. Shake off the excess flour.

Drop the meatballs into the simmering liquid in the casserole. Reduce the heat to low, cover and cook until the chicken is falling off the bones and the broth is slightly thickened and concentrated, about 2 hours.

Celina Hecht

In her own words

I spoke to Celina at the start of this project and I was so excited because she talked about food with such passion, yet as a child living a secret life in Poland, food was unimportant to her. As we spoke further, I realized that Celina is a passionate woman and whether we discussed her family, her life history or her cooking style, she exuded enthusiasm and zeal.

I was born in Warsaw, Poland, in 1933. I lived there with my parents and my twin sister and grandparents, the whole family, until the German invasion of Warsaw. My father escaped from Warsaw, and thereafter my mother, sister and I escaped to Bialystok where my mother's parents lived. By then, the Russian army had occupied Bialystok. The Russians took away our father in a transport to Russia. We remained in Bialystok, where we attended the Russian elementary school. Then in September, 1941, the Germans started the war against Russia, the Germans occupied Bialystok, and the ghetto was formed.

We lived in the Bialystok ghetto for a year and a half. After her great efforts, my mother encountered a Polish peasant woman, at the marketplace, outside the ghetto walls, who was willing to listen to my mother's pleas to save her two children. Miraculously, it was this peasant woman, a widow, Mrs. Kaczynska, who agreed to take us into her farm. Previously, my mother obtained blank church forms of birth certificates, which were filled out as if my sister and I were Polish Catholics.

Mrs. Kaczynska had her own two young sons. We were taken in as if we were Mrs. Kaczynska's nieces. At Mrs. Kaczynska's poor village home everyone treated us in every respect as if we were part of the family. We attended church. In our minds we transformed ourselves as genuine, fervent believing Catholics. Our mother had dresses made for our communion. Mrs. Kaczynska, during her visits to Bialystok, kept in touch with our mother. This continued until 1943 when the ghetto of Bialystock was liquidated. After that time there was no trace of my mother.

In the summer of 1944, the Red Army finally expelled the Germans. Then, Mrs. Kaczynska went to Bialystok to find Jewish survivors, specifically with the intention of finding our family. She did find an aunt, with whom we reunited shortly thereafter. Then through various organizations, our father was able to contact us from Russia. Finally, in 1946, our father caught up with us in Germany. It was then that our father took over. Eventually he was able to get papers for all of us to come to the U.S.A, where we settled in New York. I was married in 1962 to a survivor as well. We have two sons and five grandchildren, all of whom, without bragging, do like my cooking.

Top left: Celina Hecht, 1952

Celina Hecht's Fresh Yellow Pepper Soup

Celina's food memories are distinctly Eastern European, but her cooking style is eclectic. As she explains, "A number of years ago, we were in Florence, Italy. We stayed in a lovely hotel near the *Sephardic* temple. We ventured into a restaurant that had no menu. The only fare was what the cook prepared for that particular evening. As a first course, there was a delicious yellow pepper soup. I could not resist asking how this delicious soup was prepared." The recipe below is Celina's interpretation of that memorable soup.

Yields: 6 to 8 servings; Start to Finish: Under 1 hour

3 tablespoons olive oil

2 medium onions, chopped (about 1½ cups)

1½ pounds yellow peppers, cored, seeded and rough chopped

1 celery rib, chopped (about ½ cup)

1 carrot, peeled and chopped (about ½ cup)

2 large or 3 medium potatoes, peeled and diced (about 3 cups)

5 to 6 cups of chicken broth

2 bay leaves

Kosher salt and pepper

Seasoned croutons, for garnish (optional).

Heat the olive oil in a large soup pot, cook and stir the onions, over medium heat, until lightly browned, about 10 minutes. Stir in the peppers, celery, carrot, potatoes and enough broth to cover the vegetables, (about 2 cups). Cover and cook on low heat for 25 to 30 minutes, until the vegetables are soft.

When finished cooking, puree the soup in batches. Return the pureed soup to the pot and add the remaining 3 to 4 cups of broth, depending on your desired consistency. Toss in the bay leaves and season to taste with salt and pepper. Cook for an additional 15 minutes until heated through. Remove the bay leaves and serve with seasoned croutons on top.

Celina Hecht's Herb and Vegetable Veal Roast

Celina's veal roast enjoys the company of fresh herbs, colorful vegetables and crisp white wine as it roasts to perfection. The same preparation would match well with a lamb shoulder or lamb shanks.

Yields: 4 to 6 servings; Start to Finish: Under 2 hours (can be refrigerated overnight for more intense flavor)

1 carrot, peeled and chopped (about ½ cup)

1 medium onion, chopped (about ¾ cup)

1 medium celery root, peeled and chopped

5 fresh sage leaves

1 sprig fresh rosemary, leaves only

¼ cup olive or vegetable oil

1 (3½ pound) veal breast or shoulder, rolled and tied

1 teaspoon Dijon mustard

2 plum tomatoes, peeled, seeded and chopped

1½ cups dry white wine (broth can be substituted)

Kosher salt and pepper

Preheat the oven to 325 degrees.

Season the veal with kosher salt and fresh cracked pepper.

In a food processor, using the metal blade, pulse the carrot, onion, celery root, sage and rosemary until they are very finely chopped. Heat the olive oil in a heavy ovenproof pot or Dutch oven, cook and stir the vegetables, over medium heat, until they are lightly browned, about 10 minutes. Push them to the side, and add the meat to the pot. Brown the meat about 3 minutes on each side. When the meat is browned, stir in the mustard, tomatoes, wine (or broth) and season to taste with salt and pepper. Roast, covered, at 325 degrees for 1¼–1½ hours, checking at 30 minute intervals to baste the roast and add additional water or broth as needed.

When the meat is fork tender, remove it from the pot and thinly slice. Place the meat back into the sauce and season to taste with salt and pepper. Serve at once, or for more intense flavor, cover and refrigerate overnight and then reheat at 300 degrees until warmed through.

Jeff Nathan

Professional contributor

While living on Mrs. Kaczynska's farm, Celina recalled the many times she would forage through the woods and hunt for wild mushrooms, usually Chanterelles. She still enjoys mushrooms today as she identifies them with this warm memory. Jeff Nathan, acclaimed chef, cookbook author and television personality, pairs wild mushrooms in this delicious dish to honor Celina's memories.

Herb Scented Chicken Paillard with Wild Mushrooms

Excerpted from Jeff Nathan's Family Suppers (Clarkson Potter, 2005)

Makes 4 to 6 servings

This creamy, saucy dish (without any cream, of course) is made to be spooned onto a big bed of egg noodles. Use as many different mushrooms as you can to give the most interesting flavor. Put it at the top of your list of Favorite Family Comfort Foods.

⅓ cup vegetable oil, such as canola

10 thin-sliced chicken cutlets

Freshly ground black pepper to taste

¾ cup sliced shallots (about 3 large shallots)

6 garlic cloves, finely chopped

1 cup dry white wine, such as Chardonnay

2 cups chicken broth

1½ pounds assorted fresh mushrooms, cut into quarters

¼ cup all-purpose flour

3 tablespoons chopped fresh herbs, such as parsley, rosemary, and basil

Kosher salt to taste

Heat the oil in a large skillet over medium-high heat. Season the chicken with pepper. In batches, add the chicken to the skillet and cook, turning once, until lightly browned on both sides, about 4 minutes. Transfer the browned chicken to a plate.

Return all of the browned chicken to the skillet. Add the shallots and garlic, being sure they touch the bottom of the skillet, and cook for 1 minute. Add the mushrooms and cook until they give off their liquid and are beginning to brown, about 10 minutes. Sprinkle with the flour and stir well. Cook, stirring often, for 1 minute, adjusting the heat as needed to ensure that the flour doesn't brown. Add the broth and wine, stirring to release the browned bits in the pan. Bring to a simmer.

Reduce the heat to medium-low and simmer until the chicken is cooked through, about 15 minutes. Stir in the herbs and season the sauce with salt and pepper. Serve hot.

Gil Marks

Professional contributor

As you read in Celina's story, she spent much of her childhood in and around Bialystok. Gil Marks' recipe and detailed excerpt is a tribute to that region and assuredly will bring back food memories not only to Celina, but to all our Polish survivors.

Bialys–Polish Onion Rolls

Excerpted from The Encyclopedia of Jewish Food (Wiley, 2010)

Residents of the northeastern Polish town of Bialystock, which at its height before World War II boasted a Jewish community of more than 50,000, enjoyed an indigenous round onion-topped flat roll that they referred to as *kuchen*, but outsiders commonly called, after its home, a *Bialystoker kuchen* or simply "bialy." *Bialystoker kuchen* is a variation of the widespread *Ashkenazi* onion flatbread *tzibele pletzl*, originating in the early nineteenth century corresponding to the emergence of technology and agricultural methods in Europe to produce inexpensive white flour. By the end of the century, nearly every street in the Jewish sections of Bialystock contained a small *kuchen* bakery. These breads were once part of every weekday meal, and sometimes constituting the entire meal, complementing both dairy (delicious with a *shmeer* of butter) and meat. During World War II, the once dynamic Jewish community of Bialystock was liquidated by the Nazis, with Jews as well as bialys actually disappearing from the city. Today, residents of Bialystock no longer have any recognition of the *kuchen* or the role it once played. However, towards the end of the twentieth century, an increasing number of bagel stores in America, many owned by non-Jews, began offering bialys as well. At the end of the 1990s, an entrepreneur opened a shop in Bialystock, ironically named "New York Bagels," which also offered bialys, reclaiming part of the city's heritage. Consequently, the bialy endures as an image of nostalgia and a symbol of the tenacity and determination of a displaced people and culture that survives.

Makes 12 small rolls

Dough:

1 (¼ ounce) package (2¼ teaspoons) active dry yeast or 1 (0.6-ounce) cake fresh yeast

1¼ cups water (105 to 115 degrees (40 to 46 C) for dry yeast; 80 to 85 degrees (26 to 30 C) for fresh yeast)

2 tablespoons sugar

About 4 cups (20 ounces) high-gluten flour

2 teaspoons table salt or 4 teaspoons kosher salt

Topping:

⅓ cup minced onions

1 tablespoon vegetable oil

1½ teaspoons poppy seeds

½ teaspoon kosher salt

To make the dough
Dissolve the yeast in ¼ cup water. Stir in 1 teaspoon sugar and let stand until foamy, 5 to 10 minutes. Add the remaining water, remaining sugar, salt, and 2 cups flour. Gradually add enough of the remaining flour to make a soft dough.

On a lightly oiled or floured surface, knead until smooth and elastic, about 10 minutes. Place in an oiled bowl, turning to coat. Cover and let rise until doubled in bulk, about 1½ hours.

Punch down the dough and knead briefly. Return to the bowl, cover, and let rise a second time until doubled in bulk, about 1 hour.

Punch down the dough and knead briefly. Divide into 12 equal pieces, roll into balls, cover, and let stand for 10 minutes. On a lightly floured surface, roll each ball into a 3½-inch round about ½-inch thick. Place on ungreased baking sheets dusted with rye flour or cornmeal, cover, and let rise until puffy, about 30 minutes.

To make the topping
Combine the onions, oil, poppy seeds, and salt.

Using your thumb or a glass with a 1–to 1½-inch bottom, press down the center of the dough rounds, leaving a 1-inch rim. Sprinkle about 1 teaspoon onion mixture into each indentation. Cover and let rise until puffy, about 30 minutes.

Preheat the oven to 425 degrees.

Bake the bialys until lightly browned, switching the pans halfway through baking, about 12 minutes. If the onions are not browned, place under a broiler for about 1 minute. Transfer to wire racks and let cool slightly or completely. For softer rolls, place cooled bialys in a plastic bag.

The Jacobs Family

As told by Charles' daughter Lisa Jacobs

You cannot mistake the love and reverence Lisa has for her father, Charles, her Aunt Rose and beloved grandmother, Baba. Although they are no longer here, their presence is felt in the value she places on family and traditions, certainly an influence that was imbued in her by these three special people in her life.

My Dad, Charles, was the youngest of eight children born to a baker in Slomniki, Poland. He was the bravest and most humble person I've ever known. For all my life, my father's past was something "he put in a box on a shelf" except for one time. It was a Hanukah family gathering in 1997. My Dad and his sister, Rose, and brother, Marvin, opened up, and each knew a bit of the story and the other could fill in the rest. That was the first and last time my father's life during the war was brought into focus. His family was not wealthy, and their lives centered on their bakery. Like in many towns, on Friday night, it bustled with people carrying their various pots of *cholent* to slow bake for the night. Before they were sent to the camps, my grandfather, who perished in Plaszow, defied the Nazis by selling white bread on the Black Market. The family was warned that the Nazis were coming and were advised to leave. They were so worried, but with all the children where would they go?

Aunt Rose remembers the Nazis coming to their house with big shotguns in the early morning. My Dad hid in a neighbor's house under a bed. Someone told on him. The Ukrainian soldier who found him dragged him out and put a gun to his head. Uncle Marvin said that probably he was not killed because the Ukrainian did not have any bullets left. My Dad said that the Ukrainian marched him through a field. They walked for miles, with a gun pointed at my father's back the entire time. My Dad said that the field looked just "Like that painting with the girl sitting in the field," referring to "Christina's World" by Andrew Wyeth. He was about nine at the time. Dad said that after they had walked for about 2 miles, the soldier told him to "Go back now. Run." He said that he ran back and that he was very scared. He walked very quietly back into his house and there was a light on. He was amazed to find his mother, Baba, sitting in the kitchen and that everything was calm and "normal."

Eventually, my father was sent to Plaszow labor camp. One night, some men helped him escape through a hole in the wall of the Plaszow ghetto. The next morning he returned. All the men were asking him, "What are you doing back here." My father said he had no place to go and he was more afraid of being caught by the Nazis than being in the camp. After being in several more camps, the Americans liberated my Dad on April 29, 1945. He was on a train leaving Dachau heading nowhere and literally wrapped in newspapers. I have photos of him with American soldiers, sitting in their jeep and wearing an American army cap.

My Aunt Rose was the second oldest daughter. She had an influential boyfriend who worked on the Black Market and obtained false papers for her stating that she was gentile. Rose recounted how her boyfriend had come to her house late one evening and told her she had to pick a non-Jewish last name, something she

Top left: The Jacobs family, with all eight children

could remember. Aunt Rose said she was so frightened that she couldn't think of a last name that she could easily remember and then she saw a box of tea. That's how Rose Jakubowicz became Rose Wissotzky – it's the Lipton tea of Poland. Despite her new identity, she still became a prisoner in Auschwitz, although she received better treatment because they thought she was not Jewish. After she was liberated, she was walking with a group of non-Jewish girls who she had befriended in the camp. A man from Slomniki recognized her as Rose Jakubowicz. Rose said that she was embarrassed in front of her friends because she did not want them to

know the truth, that she was really Jewish, yet she was anxious to talk to the man and find out if he knew anything about her family. She told her friends to go ahead and that she would catch up with them later. She ran to speak to the man who told her that my Dad was alive and living in a DP camp in Frankfurt. Rose and my Dad were the first two siblings to reunite after the war. Although my father was the youngest, he was very resourceful. He gave Rose a watch and told her to use it to get the rest of the family out of Poland and bring them to Germany. After some time passed, Rose returned with Baba, and Uncle Marvin, and the watch! They remained in the DP camp until they immigrated to New York in 1948.

In my father's family, there are barely any family heirlooms to pass down. Everything they had was either taken, lost or stolen. That is why this recipe is so precious and so dear to me. It's really a family treasure. I feel that my love for baking is a special gift from my Dad's side of the family. Every time I bake I am really honoring my wonderful father, my Aunt Rose, my grandmother, as well as my grandfather, aunts and uncles who died in the war. I love to bake and baking is a way of preserving their memory.

My Dad had two children and two grandchildren.

Top left: Charles Jacobs and Aunt Rose in Frankfurt, circa 1947

Baba's Dough

Warmly described by Lisa

"This is the simple, traditional, perfect cookie dough that I associate with my wonderful Baba and it was one of Aunt Rose's signature confections. Aunt Rose was an exceptional baker but not only that. She'd look as though she could be dining at the Ritz instead of baking in her kitchen. There she was in her jewelry, silk blouse, heels and she never got a speck of anything anywhere. There were never any measuring cups in sight and whenever I would ask her, Baba how much, she'd laugh and then she'd just say in Yiddish, *Nacht, shitteryne*, "throw it in." Miraculously, Aunt Rose's hands were clean throughout the entire process. Dough never stuck to her fingers. Both Baba and Aunt Rose would make it with oil so no one would have to think about whether or not the cookies were *pareve*. I prefer to make them with butter (Pulgra brand) as they are even more scrumptious. This dough is a multi-tasker; as it makes the most delicious cookies, as well as crust for apple and blueberry pie."

Baba's Cheesecake

Baba's cookie dough is the foundation for this light ricotta cheesecake. Lisa has carried on the timeless "ritual" of making this dough completely by hand.

Yields: 10 to 12 servings; Start to Finish: Under 2 ½ hours

For the crust:
Baba's All-Purpose Cookie Dough
1½ - 2 cups all-purpose flour
1 egg
½ cup sugar
1 teaspoon vanilla
1 teaspoon baking powder
1 stick (½ cup) cold butter, cut into tiny pieces

Filling:
3 cups farmer's cheese
4 tablespoons (½ stick) butter
¾ cup sugar
4 eggs, beaten
1 tablespoon all-purpose flour
1 tablespoon sour cream

Preheat the oven to 250 degrees.

To prepare the dough by hand, create a well with the flour and slowly incorporate all the ingredients with a fork and your hands. If you prefer, you can use a food processor, fitted with the metal blade. When the dough is formed, press it into a 9-inch pie pan, and chill until ready to use.

Blend all the filling ingredients until they are well combined, but retain some of the "lumpy" texture. Pour the filling into the unbaked crust. Bake for 25 minutes at 250 degrees then raise the temperature to 350 degrees and bake for an additional hour, or until the pie is set but not dry. Serve warm or cold.

Variation: Divide the dough into 2 or 3 pieces and wrap in plastic wrap. Chill the dough for 15 minutes, and then roll the dough out on a floured board to ¼-inch thick. Using a cookie cutter, or the rim of a glass, cut into any shape desired and dip the cookies in sugar. Bake at 350 degrees on a parchment-lined cookie sheet, for 15 minutes or until very light golden brown.

Luna Kaufman

Based on my conversation with Luna

Luna is an activist, humanitarian, educator and recently published author. Her memoir entitled, *Luna's Life, A Journey of Forgiveness and Triumph,* tells the story of her struggles during the Holocaust and how she came to be a champion in the field of Holocaust studies. Luna and Sister Rose Thering, a remarkable Dominican nun, formed a friendship and together they worked tirelessly to erase anti-Semitic references in Catholic textbooks. Luna stresses, "we have to learn to coexist. What we teach our children is that we should accept each other's opinions. Accept everyone for whatever they are." The state of New Jersey considers Luna a regional treasure and has honored her in many ways. The Center for Holocaust Studies at Brookdale Community College hosts an annual Writing & Art contest named for her, and Seton Hall University bestowed on her an honorary doctorate.

When I asked Luna, who was twelve at the time the war started in her home of Cracow, Poland and spent most of the war in various concentration and labor camps, how she defines her life, she answers, "When people ask me what I do or what I did, I ask them when." As she says, "I've worked in everything under the sun." After the war she returned to Poland and then immigrated to Israel where she married her husband, Alex. It was his status as an American resident that helped her secure a visa in 1952. Luna holds a degree in musicology, but her talents run deep, having reinvented herself so many times. From a volunteer at the Lake Placid Olympics, to the head of the New Jersey State Opera, Luna has done it all. Possibly the most intriguing adventure in Luna's reinvented post-war life was on April 8, 1994, when she found herself among a group of 100 survivors who were invited for the first concert of Holocaust music to be performed at the Vatican. Dressed in black, with her head covered, she awaited a meeting with Karol Wojtyla, Pope John Paul II. It just so happens that the Pope was a former classmate of Luna's when she attended the Jagiellonian University in Cracow. Luna remarked, "I had traveled a long way from the concentration camps to the Vatican. I thought, maybe the world will change after all." This trip strengthened Luna's determination to work with the Catholic Church to improve communication between Jews and Christians. It led to her relationship with Sister Thering and the good work they accomplished together. Luna has three children and six grandchildren.

Top left: Luna Kaufman and her mother, Krakow, 1946

Michael Solomonov

Professional contributor

In her moving memoir, Luna describes her arrival in Israel, "We had finally reached the port of Haifa. We had finally come home." She remained in Israel while waiting to immigrate to the United States. Luna closes her chapter by writing, "I wished that my two years in Israel could have lasted forever." To bring a bit of Israel to Luna's story, we have paired it with chef and restaurant owner Michael Solomonov's authentic Israeli beet recipe. And while we are sure Luna ate beets growing up in Poland, we are also sure they never tasted like these!

Beets with *Tehina*

Contributed by Chef Michael Solomonov, Zahav restaurant, Philadelphia

Serves 4

1 pound red beets, all roughly the same size

1 cup kosher salt, plus additional

4 ounces prepared *Tehina* (see recipe)

2 ounces fresh lemon juice

4 ounces extra virgin olive oil

4 tablespoons fresh chopped dill

1 tablespoon freshly chopped mint

4 tablespoons lightly toasted chopped walnuts

Freshly ground black pepper

Preheat oven to 350 degrees.

Scrub the beets under cool running water to remove all dirt and debris. Spread ½ cup of kosher salt on the bottom of a heavy-bottomed sauté pan. Place the beets on top of the salt and cover with the remaining ½ cup of kosher salt. Place sauté pan in the preheated oven and roast for approximately 90 minutes, or until the tip of a paring knife easily pierces the flesh of the beets. Remove the beets from the salt and allow to cool for 20 minutes. Remove skins from the beets while still warm by rubbing with paper towels. Cool beets completely.

Grate the beets using the coarse side of a box grater. Combine the grated beets, prepared *Tehina*, lemon juice, olive oil and herbs in a large mixing bowl and combine thoroughly. Season to taste with black pepper and additional kosher salt, if necessary. Sprinkle the walnuts on top of the beets and serve at room temperature.

Prepared *Tehina*

3 cups warm water

4 cups organic sesame paste (preferably unhulled)

2 garlic cloves, peeled, germ and root-end removed

1 teaspoon ground cumin

½ cup extra virgin olive oil

2 ounces fresh lemon juice

Kosher salt

Combine the garlic cloves and lemon juice in a blender and process until it forms a smooth paste. Let stand for 10 minutes. Add half of the *Tehina* and water and blend until smooth. Add the rest of the ingredients and blend again until smooth. Season to taste with kosher salt. Refrigerate for at least 30 minutes.

Celia Kener

In her own words

I met Celia at the Museum, immediately after she had taken an inner-city elementary school class on a tour. Her energy and willingness to educate young people is consistent with the dedication, strength and resilience she has shown throughout her life.

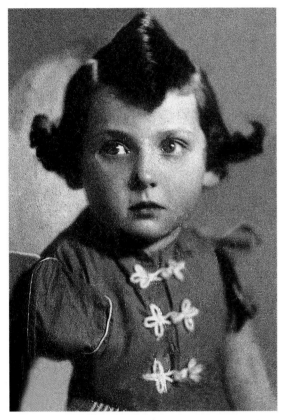

I remember that day in June, 1941, when I was six years old. I was an only child in a middle class traditional home in Lvov, Poland and I posed for a commemorative photo. I was dressed in a blue Shirley Temple-styled costume ready to perform in my dance recital, the one I had been looking forward to for so long. That was the day they forcefully took my father away to serve in the Russian army. Shortly after that, I was playing outside with some children who at one time were my friends. They alerted a guard that I was Jewish, and I was taken away in a truck filled with other Jewish children. I don't know how I got up the nerve, but I approached the guard and asked, why are you doing this to me? I must have touched a chord, because the guard opened the door and tossed me out, essentially saving my life.

I returned home and along with my mother, aunt, uncle and cousins moved into the ghetto. My mother, a beautiful woman, was quickly recruited to work outside of the ghetto. Every several weeks she would come in and check on me. As raids took place, I hid with my extended family, until one day there was no room for me to hide with them. My aunt told me to find a good spot so that the Germans would not find me. I found such a spot, however, the rest of my family was not as lucky. I remember hearing my aunt's voice calling to me in the streets as she was taken away, "Celia, survive and tell our story."

My mother sensed that I would no longer be safe in the ghetto, so one night she came and sneaked me out. She took me to a home in the forest where a devout Christian family had agreed to raise me as their own. They were very kind, and even though I could not go outside, be near windows, or even leave my closeted space, I knew they were doing their best to protect me. I was an obedient child and lived with them for a year and a half. One day, a nearby family who was harboring a Jew was murdered as an example to everyone in the town. My new family panicked and decided to send me to an orphanage. Luckily, the mother could not bear to do this, so without her family's knowledge, she took me to their barn promising to feed me every three days. When I climbed up the rafters to my new hiding spot, I was told there was another person there, and not to be afraid. I had no idea that the person I would now share the barn with was my own mother. She had been hiding there for nearly nine months, having escaped her work camp. My mother was weak and infirm, so I took charge. I would climb down and take the feed intended for the animals. My

Top left: Celia's father carried this photo of his daughter in her recital costume with him throughout the war years

mother eventually gained her strength and by the time we were liberated we were able to walk out of the barn together. When we returned to our home, we were met with letters from my father. He too survived the war in the Russian army and eventually we were all reunited. Amazingly, there was one possession that my father had kept throughout his ordeal: the photo of me dressed in my dance recital costume.

I feel my life started when I came to the United States. The war is a book I put on a high shelf and try never to take down. I do tell my story to schoolchildren who visit the Museum of Jewish Heritage. I would love to sit them all down and cook a traditional Polish meal for them. I think they would enjoy many of the foods I remember as a child. There are several I still make today for my husband of 55 years, and they take me back to a happy time in my home. My three children and seven grandchildren associate many foods with me. They love 'Gigi's' (that's what they call me) inventive food. I hope you enjoy them as well, and remember never to lose hope or faith. Sometimes, it's all we have.

Celia Kener's *Holishkes*–Shortcut Un-Stuffed Cabbage

The distinctive flavors of stuffed cabbage are a fine balance between sweet and sour. Traditionally, the sauce envelopes blanched cabbage leaves that are filled with a meat and rice mixture. The technique can be tricky and the process, time consuming. Celia's short cut is to take these same pungent flavors and create a medley where the meatballs are nestled in shredded cabbage allowing the sauce to gently bubble away and cook all the ingredients as one. Purists might balk, but you'll be the one with a few extra minutes to relax and enjoy the compliments.

Yields: 4 to 6 servings as a main course, 6 to 8 servings as a starter; Start to Finish: Under 2 ½ hours

For the Sauce:

1 large green cabbage (about 2 to 2 ½ pounds), cored and sliced

24 ounces ginger ale

2 tablespoons brown sugar

4 tablespoons honey

For the Meatballs (yields about 30):

1½ pounds ground beef

1½ teaspoons kosher salt

3 tablespoons ketchup

¼ cup seasoned bread crumbs

1 egg

5 tablespoons uncooked long grain rice

To prepare the sauce
In a large Dutch oven, combine the cabbage, ginger ale, brown sugar and honey (to help the honey ease off the spoon, coat the spoon in a dab of oil). Bring to a boil, cover and reduce the heat to low.

To make the meatballs
Mix together all the meatball ingredients (nothing works better than your two hands). Form the mixture into small 1-inch diameter meatballs, adding more bread crumbs if the meat does not hold together. Place the meatballs in the pot of cabbage and gently stir so they incorporate with the sauce. Cover and cook on low heat, for 2 hours, until the cabbage is tender and the meatballs are firm but cooked through.

Feedback
For a stronger tomato flavor, add 1 (14–ounce) can of tomato sauce to the pot while the cabbage cooks. If you like it sour, add lemon juice, white vinegar or a little sour salt to achieve the perfect pucker.

Celia Kener's Citrus Rice Pudding

Somewhere between an old-fashioned rice pudding and a sweet *kugel* (Yiddish for "pudding"), comes one of Celia's inventive specialties, infused with citrus flavors to create a delicately sweet-tart dish.

Yields: 9 pieces; Start to Finish: Under 1½ hours

3 cups cooked white rice

¾ cup sugar

4 tablespoons (½ stick) butter

1 orange peel, zested

1 lemon peel, zested

½ teaspoon ground cinnamon

½ teaspoon vanilla extract

3 eggs

½ cup canned crushed pineapple, with its juice

½ cup golden raisins

Preheat the oven to 350 degrees.

Prepare the rice according to package directions. While the rice cooks, prepare the balance of the ingredients. In a food processor, fitted with the metal blade, combine the sugar, butter, orange zest, lemon zest, cinnamon and vanilla. The mixture will come together and form a ball. With the motor running, begin adding the eggs, one at a time. Blend until smooth, being sure to scrape up any bits of zest that cling to the bottom or sides. The egg mixture will be thin and a golden yellow color, dotted with flecks of brown from the cinnamon.

Pour the egg mixture into a bowl and stir in the pineapple and raisins. When the rice is cooked and cooled a bit, stir it into the egg mixture. Blend thoroughly and pour the rice mixture into an 8x8-inch or 9 x9-inch square baking pan. Bake at 350 degrees for 50 to 60 minutes; the top should be a light golden brown and the pudding should be firm but not dry. The *kugel* can be served hot as a side dish or cold for dessert. If serving cold, try spooning any remaining crushed pineapple over each slice.

Feedback

People who have a zest for life (like Celia) have a spirited enjoyment. The concentrated flavor you get from zesting a lemon or orange has the same effect in your recipe, infusing everything with a zing. While the juice from citrus fruit adds flavor, the concentrated goodness and pure oils are contained in the peel. When you grate or zest the fruit you really capture the true essence. Wash the fruit carefully as the rind is usually coated in wax. Be sure not to grate down to the white portion of the rind, it is bitter, and always zest the fruit before you squeeze it.

Miriam Lesorgen

Karen Banschick's mother, Miriam, came to America having survived the Holocaust with very little except her memories and ambition. She was a practical, pragmatic Polish-born woman who, Karen remembers saying, "For what you spend to eat out one night, you could cook for a week." That prompted her to create meals that were versatile and relatively inexpensive. Through her cooking and her love, Miriam has undoubtedly left an everlasting legacy for her two children and six grandchildren.

Miriam Lesorgen's *Kreplach*

Grandma Mancia, as Miriam was known, was famous for her *kreplach*. Her grandchildren swore that no deli in New York could duplicate their lightness and flavor. The key to good *kreplach* is to roll the dough thin enough so the dough is transparent, but thick enough to hold the filling when boiling. Karen's Mom favored a beef filling, but we've included a chicken with scallion filling as a variation. If you prefer your *kreplach* as a trendy small bite, we've also included an easy dipping sauce to spice things up.

Yields: 24 Kreplach; Start to Finish: Under 1½ hours

For the *kreplach* dough:

1¾ cup all-purpose flour

2 eggs

½ teaspoon salt

3 tablespoons corn oil

1 to 2 tablespoons water

For the beef filling:

½ pound ground beef

1 tablespoon oil

1 small onion, grated

1 teaspoon kosher salt

For the chicken filling:

½ pound ground chicken

1 tablespoon oil

3 tablespoons minced scallions

1 teaspoon garlic powder

1 tablespoon soy sauce

In a medium bowl or the bowl of a food processor, fitted with the metal blade, combine the dough ingredients, dry first then liquid, and process, adding a drop of additional water if necessary, to create a smooth, elastic dough. Turn the dough onto a lightly floured surface and knead for a minute or two. Wrap the dough in a barely damp cloth and let it rest for 1 hour. While the dough sits, prepare the filling.

Heat the oil in a skillet, cook and stir in the ground beef or chicken, over medium heat, until nicely browned, about 10 minutes. Be sure to break up large pieces with the back of a fork or spoon. Remove the meat from the skillet with a slotted spoon and let the meat cool for a few minutes before adding the rest of the filling. Meanwhile, bring a large pot of salted water or broth to boil.

When the beef has cooled a bit, combine it with the grated onion and salt.

For the chicken, combine the scallions, garlic powder and soy sauce with the browned chicken.

On a floured board, roll the dough to ¼-inch thick; it will be very elastic. If you tug at it, it will just snap back, use the rolling pin to stretch. Using a cookie cutter, or rim of a glass, cut the dough into 3-inch rounds. Have a small bowl of water standing by to dip your fingers. Place 1 teaspoon of filling in each round and seal by dipping your fingers in the water, and dabbing the edges. Fold the circle into a half moon and pinch the edges closed. Drop a few filled *kreplach* at a time into the boiling liquid and cook about 20 minutes. Occasionally shake the pot to be sure no shy *kreplachs* cling to the bottom. They are done when they happily float to the top and the dough is soft to the bite. If you cooked the *kreplach* in soup, do nothing more, just enjoy. If you cooked them in water, remove the *kreplach* with a slotted spoon and let them drain on a paper towel.

The *kreplach* can then be dropped into a bowl of soup or lightly fried. To fry the *kreplach*, heat 1 tablespoon of oil for every 8 *kreplach*, and lightly brown, in a skillet, for several minutes. Drain on a paper towel and serve with the dipping sauce below. If adding to soup, simply drop them into a pot of simmering soup and allow them to reheat gently.

Orange Honey Ginger Soy Dipping Sauce

The name of the recipe is also the list of the 4 basic ingredients.

2 tablespoons of orange juice

2 teaspoons of honey

½ teaspoon ground ginger

4 tablespoons of soy sauce

Blend together and serve as a dipping sauce or light dressing.

JFH

Karen Banschick's BBQ Brisket

One of Miriam's favorite dinners was slow roasted brisket with rich brown gravy and sweet onions. As an adult, her daughter Karen wanted to keep that memory alive, but needed a new take. After devouring a famous BBQ brisket, prepared by one of New York's premier butchers, Karen went home and began to work on creating her own version. Here is Karen's fall apart, better the next day, brisket. Don't let the number of ingredients scare you, it's an easy preparation, and the leftover brisket and sauce won't go to waste. You can control the heat by cutting down on the black pepper that is used in the rub.

Yields: 10 to 12 servings; Start to Finish: Step One: Under 30 minutes, then 6 to 8 hours or overnight, Step Two: 5 to 7 hours

For the Rub:

3 teaspoons liquid smoke
(available in most markets)

⅓ cup brown sugar

⅓ cup minced garlic

2 tablespoons Kosher salt

⅓ cup freshly ground coarse pepper

1 tablespoon cayenne pepper

For the Meat:

1 (8 to 9 pound) brisket

For the Sauce:

1 cup tomato sauce

¾ cup honey

¾ cup soy sauce

6 tablespoons distilled white vinegar

¼ cup light or dark corn syrup

3 tablespoons Worcestershire sauce

2 tablespoons hoisin sauce

½ teaspoon cayenne pepper

Kosher salt and pepper

Step One: Combine all the rub ingredients in a blender or food processor. Pulse until thoroughly mixed. Place the brisket in a large roasting pan and rub all sides of the brisket with the mixture. Cover tightly and refrigerate 6 to 8 hours or overnight.

Mix all the BBQ sauce ingredients in a saucepan and stir over medium heat till combined. Lower the heat, cover and cook for 30 minutes. Let the sauce cool and refrigerate till needed (can hold up to 5 days).

Step Two: Preheat the oven to 250 degrees.

Remove the brisket from the refrigerator and let it rest while the oven heats. Cover tightly and bake, 5 to 7 hours, basting every 2 hours, with the juices that collect in the pan. When the brisket is fork tender, but not falling apart, uncover the pan, spoon off about 2 cups of the collected liquid, and pour the BBQ sauce over the brisket, enough to cover but not drown the meat. Cover and continue cooking for 1 hour. When done, cut the brisket against the grain with a non-serrated knife. For pulled brisket, which is great on a sandwich, pull the meat apart with two forks, following the grain.

Next Day Brisket Stuffed Meatloaf

If you manage to squirrel away the tangy sauce and tender brisket, you will not want to waste a bite. Try this recipe where meatloaf, leftover brisket and BBQ sauce make a winning combination.

Yields: 4 to 6 servings; Start to Finish: Under 1½ hours

2 garlic cloves, finely grated

2 eggs, lightly beaten

¼ cup seasoned bread crumbs

½ to 1 cup leftover BBQ sauce (if none remains, use a bottled variety or steak sauce)

2 teaspoons kosher salt

1 teaspoon black pepper

2 pounds ground beef

1 to 2 cups leftover brisket, shredded or cut into small dice

Preheat the oven to 350 degrees.

Mix the garlic, eggs, bread crumbs, ¼ cup sauce, salt and pepper. Add in the ground beef and brisket. Blend with a wooden spoon or your hands to completely incorporate all the ingredients. Do not overwork the mixture. Shape the meat into a loaf. Place the meat loaf in a roasting pan and cook for 30 minutes. Pour ½ cup of sauce on top of the meatloaf and pour ½ cup of water in the roasting pan. Continue to bake until cooked through, an additional 30 to 40 minutes. Serve with any remaining BBQ sauce on the side.

Feedback
When making meatloaf, add the meat as the last ingredient. This will prevent you from overworking the meat, which affects the texture and makes it tough.

JFH

Dina and Jacob Liverant

As told by their daughter Dorothy Liverant Goldberg

In 1997, Dorothy Goldberg went with her family to Lublin, Poland, where her parents had lived both before and during the Holocaust. Her father showed them Majdanek concentration camp, where he was imprisoned and from where he had escaped. He also showed them his former apartment and many places where he hid from the Nazis. He wrote his memoirs so that the family would always know what he endured. Dorothy shares some of that story with us.

Both my parents were from a city, not a small *shtetl*. My parents always felt proud that they had the opportunity for a good education and that my mother graduated from the *Gymnasium* (secondary school). My mother survived the war by passing as a Christian woman. She got false papers and paid a Polish family to hide her. When her money ran out, she had to leave and she hid wherever she could. She bleached her brown hair white using straight peroxide from the bottle to get all the color out. She was the only member of her family to survive. She never forgave herself for not being able to save her 15 year old sister.

My father went to vocational school for bookkeeping before the war and then went into the Polish army. He learned the Christian prayers there, which later helped him survive. After the war started he obtained documents to show he was Christian. The papers, which he acquired through the underground, were authentic, as they were from a deceased gentile man. Even so, he was rounded up as a forced laborer, and sent to Majdanek concentration camp, where he was imprisoned for 14 months. In March of 1944, he escaped from the Majdanek sub camp on Lipowa Street, along with nine others, who dug a tunnel to freedom. He hid in the woods and joined the A.K. (Armia Krajowa) a Polish home army, for a short time. Throughout the entire war, he maintained his false identity as a Christian. Less than six months later, he was liberated and met my mother. They married in the fall of 1944. Many survivors needed to reconnect with people whom they had something in common with; my parents were no different.

When I asked my father how he survived, he would tell me it was more luck than anything. He recalled a night where he said he had a bad feeling about his hiding place, so he didn't return the next night. It turned out that everyone who had hidden there was betrayed and captured. He attributed his survival not to intelligence or strength, but to fate.

I try to keep many of my family's traditions alive. It is important to me to preserve the holidays and the *alte heim* (old home). My mom was a believer in continuing to cook traditional foods. I am always trying different ways to recreate what we ate as children. Her apple cake was delicious, and is a very traditional Polish dessert. Our favorite, was her *kutletela*, her version of a chicken burger, which my family still enjoys today. My parents were married for 53 years had two children and three grandchildren in their lifetime. Since they have passed on, our family has grown to four grandchildren and two great grandchildren (and two more on the way)!

Top left: Dina and Jacob Liverant, with Dorothy

Dina Liverant's *Kutletela*–Small Chicken Burger

Long before the ubiquitous turkey burger was on every menu, ground chicken cutlets were a regular meal in Polish households. A good way to stretch the protein was to grind the chicken and mix it with seasonings, and sometimes vegetables. Some cooks poached the cutlets while others like Dina would fry them as mini burgers. Top them as you wish or sandwich them in a bun and enjoy!

Yields: 4 servings; Start to Finish: Under 15 minutes

1 pound ground white meat chicken

2 eggs, beaten

¼ cup seltzer

Scant ¼ teaspoon baking soda

¼ cup bread crumbs (or matzo meal at Passover)

1 teaspoon garlic powder

1 teaspoon kosher salt

Black pepper, to taste

2 to 4 tablespoons canola oil for frying

Heat 2 tablespoons of oil, in a large skillet, over medium heat. Combine all the remaining ingredients, using a large wooden spoon or your hands. When the oil is hot, drop a generous tablespoon of the chicken into the oil to make small "slider" sized burgers. Do not over crowd the pan. For larger patties, wet your hands lightly and form 4 burgers. Fry the chicken until the bottom side is nicely brown and crisp, about 5 minutes. Flip the burgers and continue frying until the chicken is cooked through and both sides are brown and crisp, adding more oil to the pan if needed. Drain on paper towels before serving.

Feedback

If you prefer a firmer burger, omit the seltzer and baking soda (although Dina maintained the baking soda helped your digestion). You can add minced onion, garlic, or scallions to the chicken mixture before frying, or change up the seasoning blend to your taste. To spice things up, Dorothy suggests a splash of Sriracha (a Thai style hot sauce), sprinkled on the cutlets. The same chicken mixture can be poached for a lighter variation. Bring a large pot of chicken broth to boil. Form the chicken mixture into small ovals (like gefilte fish) or mini meatballs. Cook them for 20 to 30 minutes, until the chicken is completely cooked through.

Lily Mazur Margules
and Edward Margules

In Lily's words

Lily Margules makes several things very clear, the first, "there are other things much more important than hate." Our conversation flowed, and her intellect shows through in everything she says and writes. Her parents were what Lily termed "assimilated intelligentsia" and they imparted to Lily the thirst for knowledge and culture. Her ease at writing has always been Lily's gift. "Ask me about two trains that are traveling at certain speeds in the same direction, which arrives first? I haven't a clue. But ask me to write, that's easy." Her book, *Memories, Memories,* is written in such a way as to help children understand her journey from Vilna to America, with as she writes, "a few stops along the way."

My parents met when they were both students at the University during the Russian Revolution. My mother became a dentist, while my father studied to be a rabbi, but changed his mind and studied to be a pharmacist instead. Although we lived in Vilna, Poland, in my early childhood we spoke only Russian, but later we spoke Polish as

well. The first time I realized I was Jewish was as a student in a private exclusive school with other Jewish children. One day I sat down to eat my non-kosher lunch, which was made fun of. To pacify me, my mother bought a pair of silver candlestick holders and a bag of Shabbos candles and began lighting candles on Friday night. One of my biggest pleasures was to be invited to my friend's house when they celebrated Shabbos, with all the ceremony and traditional food. The best holiday in our house had to be Passover as I was born on the first day of the seder so my mother would shower me with presents.

I learned about anti-Semitism in 1935 when my father, who was a decent guy and employed at a big government pharmacy, was told he did not have enough education to be a pharmacist. This was a ruling directed only at Jewish pharmacists. He went back to school and passed his Master's exam in Warsaw, but was dismissed from his position one year later. The only way he could support his family was to buy his own pharmacy and he could only do so by paying a Polish pharmacist under the table to buy the pharmacy in his name. I still remember his name, it was Wiscniewsty, and the pharmacy was in a small town called Soly. When the Germans came, my father sent first my sister and me, and later came himself, to Vilna to be with my mother's sister, Sonia Lipkowicz Perski. By this time, I was nearly a teenager and I had already suffered the loss of my mother. My father was taken from the pharmacy and deported to Estonia. I managed to

Top left: Lily Mazur, age 6, and her father David, saying goodbye to his nephew, Chacrel, (Herschel) 1930

see him one last time when he was in Kaiserwald concentration camp. One day a girl from our labor camp where I was working together with my sister, Rachel, told us that a man called David Mazur, who came with a transfer of prisoners from Estonia, was asking about his two little girls, Lily and Rachel. The only way I could go and see him was to pretend I had a toothache so they would send me to a dentist in Kaiserwald to have my tooth extracted. I boarded a truck to the camp and I was looking for the barracks where the men were being held. I found my father, who was so relieved to know that my sister Rachel and I were alive and together. I clearly recall his words, "No matter what happens, we will meet at the pharmacy in Soly. You are the oldest sister; take care of Rachel. Keep your head high and conduct yourself in accordance with our good family name." I don't remember everything, but certain things are engraved in my heart, I remember this. After we were liberated we searched for our father, but never saw him again.

It was on September 23, 1943, when Rachel, my Aunt Sonia and I were awakened by screaming guards and ordered out of the ghetto. Rumblings in the crowd told us that the line to the right would live and to the left would not. Knowing my sister Rachel looked very young and small, my aunt removed her high heels and exchanged them with Rachel's shoes. Rachel now looked taller and older and along with me, was spared, but my Aunt Sonia, was not. We were sent to the right, to live and she was sent to the left, to die. Rachel and I moved through numerous work and concentration camps and on March 11, 1945, the Russian army in a small village called Krummau in East Prussia liberated us. It was in Lodz, Poland, that we joined a group of Zionists who planned to go to Israel. We were now part of the Kibbutz, Ihud; we were young, idealistic and full of determination. We traveled from Poland to Prague, Prague to Munich and Munich to Italy. It was difficult for Jewish refugees to get the necessary documents so we posed as Greek peasants who were seeking work in Italy's vineyards. On New Year's Eve, 1946, our caravan of trucks stopped at the foot of the snow-filled majestic Alps. We had to climb to the other side to enter Italy. Much to our surprise, we were not the only refugees doing so. I had no idea that my future husband, Edward Margules, was also crossing the Alps on that same memorable night. He shared a bag of home-baked cookies with his fellow climbers, I ate them with zest, never suspecting that he and I would meet and share a life together.

Upon reaching Italy, Rachel and I stayed in a DP camp in Grugliasco, near the city of Turin. We had heard that in Milan you were able to search for surviving family members so we decided to go there to post notices. While in Milan, we would pass the hours by going to the movies. On one particular day, the movie was being shown in Russian. I helped translate the film for my sister, and this caught the attention of a young man sitting behind me. We were introduced a few days later, and on February 13, 1947 in an ancient synagogue in Turin, Italy, I married Edward Margules. The Rabbi, who had all of three hairs in his beard, had survived Nazi occupation in a Jesuit monastery. This was the happiest day of my life.

Sometime later, we received a telegram from my father's brother, Isaac, who offered to sponsor our trip to join him in Buenos Aries. Although we never made our *Aliyah* to Israel, Rachel, Eddie and I, while still in Italy, listened to the radio on May 14, 1948 when the dream for a Jewish homeland became a reality. I lived in Buenos Aires for nearly a decade, and learned their traditions as well as maintaining my Polish heritage and that of my adopted home of Italy. It has been a long odyssey from Poland to America; I came here in 1956 with a family and a very strange accent. It was a little Russian, a little Polish, some Italian, and some Argentinean. I was shy and quiet and often embarrassed by my unusual accent. I was liberated for a second time when Dr. Henry Kissinger became Secretary of State and I realized that it is what you say, how intelligently you present your ideas that matters, not your accent. It was then that I took a deep breath, opened my mouth and began to express my opinions. I haven't stopped since!

Together Edward and I have two children and one grandchild.

Since completing the book, I sadly learned that Edward passed away. We extend our sincerest condolences to his devoted family. May his memory be a blessing.

Lily Margules' *Tsimmes*–Chicken with Prunes

Lily very clearly remembers cooking with her aunt Fanny Mazur in Buenos Aires. "I didn't know how to boil a cup of tea. My aunt made a delicious *tsimmes*, a dish she ate in Vilna, with chicken parts, large slices of potatoes, sweet prunes, brown sugar and honey. It was cooked on the stove, a long time on a small flame, with my aunt adding water as necessary. The prunes would just melt in your mouth." *Tsimmes*, which in Yiddish means a big fuss, is a good name for this dish inspired by Lily's memories, as everyone who enjoys it will make a big fuss over you.

Yields: 4 servings; Start to Finish: Under 2 ½ hours

1 (3½ to 4 pound) chicken, cut into 8 pieces (skin can be removed)

4 tablespoons vegetable oil

2 cups water

½ cup red wine (or broth)

2 tablespoons brown sugar

2 tablespoons honey

2 cups pitted prunes

Kosher salt and pepper

2 russet (or sweet) potatoes (about ¾ pound), peeled and cut into large chunks

Heat the oil in a large Dutch oven, and brown the chicken parts on all sides, over medium heat, about 15 minutes. Pour off the fat and add 1 cup of the water, the wine (or broth), brown sugar, honey and prunes. Season the dish with salt and pepper and bring to a gentle boil. Reduce the heat to low, cover and cook for 1 hour, and then add 1 more cup of water and the potatoes, being sure to tuck the potatoes into the sauce. Season to taste with salt and pepper. Continue cooking for 45 to 60 minutes or until the potatoes are fork tender. If the sauce is too concentrated, add some boiling water, heat through and serve.

Mark Strausman

Professional contributor

Lily fondly remembers her life in Argentina, where her Italian neighbors taught her to cook many Italian dishes. "I recall eating on Sundays a big Italian dinner, where we served meat slow cooked in tomato sauce. On Sundays it was really enjoyed as a big family lunch." The following recipe contributed by Mark Strausman honors those warm recollections.

Involtini di Manzo–Beef Braciole

Excerpted from two meatballs in the italian kitchen
(Artisan, a division of Workman Publishing, Inc., 2007)

My version of braciole isn't terribly dainty, but it is more moderately proportioned than the old-school dish. I like smaller bundles because then the taste of the flavorful filling doesn't get lost in pounds of meat. Use a cut of beef with a little bit of fat in it–I like top round–and pound the pieces thin to tenderize them and so they'll be easy to roll. Traditionally the dish is served in two courses. First the sauce from the pan is served with some pasta (see recipe for gnocchi below). Then the meat itself is brought out, with a green vegetable on the side. But to make things simpler, I often cut up the braciole and serve them right on top of the sauced pasta, as one dish.

Serves 4

1 tablespoon (15ml) extra-virgin olive oil

1 medium yellow onion, chopped

2 garlic cloves, minced

One 28-ounce (794-gram) can Italian tomato puree, preferably San Marzano

1 cup (240ml) dry red wine

1 teaspoon oregano, preferably Sicilian

½ teaspoon kosher salt

Pinch of crushed red pepper flakes

A small Parmigiano-Reggiano cheese rind (optional) (see note below)

For the filling:

1 tablespoon (15ml) extra-virgin olive oil

1 medium red onion, minced

3 garlic cloves, minced

½ cup (120ml) dry white wine

2 teaspoons chopped fresh oregano

2 teaspoons finely grated lemon zest

½ cup (2 ounces/56 grams) freshly grated Parmigiano-Reggiano cheese (optional) (see note below)

For the Braciole:

Eight 3-ounce (85-gram) pieces of beef, top or bottom round, pounded to a thickness of ⅛ inch (0.3cm)

2 teaspoons kosher salt

1 teaspoon freshly ground black pepper

2 tablespoon (30ml) olive oil

(Continued)

To make the sauce

Place a 10–to 12-inch skillet over medium-low heat, and when it is hot, add the olive oil. Add the onion and garlic and cook until wilted, about 5 minutes. Add the tomato puree, wine, oregano, salt, red pepper flakes, and Parmigiano-Reggiano rind, if using, and bring to a boil. Remove from the heat and set aside.

Preheat the oven to 325 degrees.

To make the filling

Place an 8-inch skillet over medium-low heat, and when it is hot, add the olive oil. Add the onion and garlic and cook until wilted, about 5 to 7 minutes. Add the white wine and simmer until it has evaporated, 5 minutes. Set aside to cool.

When the onion mixture has cooled, stir in the oregano, lemon zest and cheese, if using.

To assemble the braciole

Lay the beef out on a cutting board or work surface and sprinkle both sides with the salt and pepper. Spread some of the onion (and cheese) mixture in the center of each piece of beef, leaving a 1-inch border uncovered. Starting from a short side, roll up the beef and close with a toothpick.

Plae a 10–to 12–inch ovenproof skillet over medium-high heat, and when it is hot, add the olive oil. Add the beef and cook until deeply browned on all sides, about 8 minutes. Cover with the tomato sauce, transfer to the oven, and braise until the beef is tender, 1 to 1½ hours.

Serve immediately.

Editor's Note: The recipe calls for a traditional filling, which includes grated cheese. Obviously, if you are kosher, you will omit that ingredient from your preparation.

Lily recalls "On Thursdays, it was a tradition to have pasta. One of my favorites was a special pasta, gnocchi, with a delicious sauce we made from scratch. The gnocchi would be topped with fresh tomatoes, oregano, olive oil and parsley." Our resident expert on Italian cooking, Mark Strausman shares two earthy mushroom versions to top his homemade gnocchi. The recipes that follow capture the essence of what Lily described.

Gnocchi

Excerpted from two meatballs in the italian kitchen (Artisan, a division of Workman Publishing, Inc., 2007)

The word *gnocco* simply means a single dumpling (or the bump you get after a knock on the head). In northern Italy, potato gnocchi are served every Thursday, although no one quite knows what gave rise to this tradition. Potato gnocchi are so easy to make. Since they don't involved rolling out a dough to super-thin transparency, they take less time than egg pasta...When properly made, gnocchi are soft to the bite, but not mushy or gluey.

When you are boiling potatoes for the gnocchi, pierce them only once or twice to check for doneness. If you poke too many holes in them, they will absorb too much water. Don't overdo mashing the potatoes either, or your gnocchi will become gummy. To make the dough, you will need a large, preferably wooden work surface (although not as large as the one required to make egg pasta), an offset spatula, and a sharp knife. You will also need a strainer for scooping them out of the cooking water. You will know you've added the right amount of flour to the dough when it doesn't stick to your hands anymore. This recipe serves 8 generously, because I believe that if you are going to go to the trouble of making gnocchi, you should make a lot, but you can freeze any extra gnocchi if necessary (see below).

Makes about 120 pieces serving 8 generously

2 pounds (908 grams) Yukon Gold or russet potatoes (6 medium), scrubbed

1½ cups (187 grams) unbleached all-purpose flour, plus additional for dusting

3 tablespoons (21 grams) freshly grated Parmigiano-Reggiano cheese

2 tablespoons plus ½ teaspoon kosher salt

Pinch of freshly grated nutmeg

Pinch of freshly ground black pepper

1 large egg, lightly beaten

Wild Mushroom Sauce or Mushroom Cream Sauce (recipes follow), warm

3 tablespoons (21 grams) freshly grated Parmigiano-Reggiano cheese, if using the Mushroom Cream Sauce

Place the potatoes in a 6-quart stock pot and cover with 3 inches of cold water. Cover the pot and bring to a boil, then reduce to a gentle simmer. Cook until the potatoes are tender and easily pierced with the tip of a paring knife, about 25 minutes. (Do not test too often, or you will waterlog the potatoes.) Drain the potatoes.

Line two baking sheets with parchment paper. Wash and dry your hands (remove any jewelry) and the work surface. A wooden surface is recommended for best results, but stainless steel or marble may also be used.

(Continued)

Lightly flour the work surface. As soon as the potatoes are cool enough to handle—they should still be very warm—peel them. Place the potatoes on the work surface, and slightly mash them. Sprinkle with the flour, Parmigiano-Reggiano cheese, ½ teaspoon of the salt, the nutmeg, and pepper. Place the egg in the center of the mixture. Working quickly, gently knead and squeeze the ingredients together until incorporated, about 1 minute. Avoid overworking the dough.

Dust your hands with 2 tablespoons of flour and rub them together aggressively over the work surface. Dough should fall to the surface, and both hands should now be "working clean." Roll the dough mass gently around the work surface to incorporate any remaining flour and dough particles, then shape it into a large log. The dough should still be warm to the touch. Sprinkle with flour. Unlike fresh egg pasta dough, gnocchi dough should not rest, but should be shaped immediately.

Dust the work surface very lightly with flour. Cut the dough into 8 equal parts. Working with one at a time, roll the pieces into logs ½-inch (1.3-cm) in diameter and 10 to 12 inches (25 to 30 cm) long. As you finish each log, move it away from you and dust it generously with flour.

Lightly flour the work surface and roll 4 of the logs toward you, moving them through the flour to coat them. Line up the 4 logs parallel to one another; then, holding your hand perpendicular to the work surface, separate the logs from each other with the tips of your fingers. Cut the logs on the bias into ½-inch (1.3-cm) pieces. Gently scrape the work surface with an offset spatula, lifting the gnocchi up and tossing them in the flour on the work surface, and then use the spatula to transfer the gnocchi to one of the prepared baking sheets. Arrange them in a single layer.

Repeat with the remaining 4 logs of dough. You should have about 10 dozen gnocchi in all. The gnocchi can be stored in a cool, dry place for up to 2 hours; do not refrigerate. (The gnocchi may also be frozen for up to several weeks. Freeze them on the baking sheets in a single layer. When they are frozen, place them in a strainer in small batches and sift off excess flour, then portion into freezer bags or containers. Do not thaw before cooking, but when cooking frozen gnocchi, boil them in small batches, or they will drop the temperature of the cooking water too rapidly.)

Fill a 10-quart pot with 7 quarts (6.5 liters) of water and bring to a boil over high heat. Add the remaining 2 tablespoons kosher salt. Place the warm sauce in a large shallow ceramic bowl that's been warmed.

Lift one-third of the gnocchi off the pans, shaking them to sift off any excess flour as you do so, and add to the boiling water. At first, the gnocchi will sink to the bottom of the pot. Do not stir them. As the water returns to a boil, after 1 to 2 minutes, the gnocchi will float to the surface. Gnocchi are the rare pasta that is not cooked al dente: the ideal cooked texture is soft and pillowlike, with just enough solidity to hold together without becoming chewy. This is normally achieved after 1 to 2 minutes of cooking time, or as soon as they rise to the surface of the cooking water. Scoop the gnocchi from the boiling water using a strainer, draining them well, and transfer to the bowl containing the sauce.

Before adding the next batch of gnocchi to the pot, stir the boiling water with the strainer; any gnocchi remaining in the water should rise to the surface—scoop them out. Wait for the water to return to a boil, and then cook another one-third of the gnocchi. (Since gnocchi cook quickly, even when cooked in 3 batches, they will still be hot when they are served.)

Season with salt and pepper, as desired. Swirl the bowl to combine. Avoid using a utensil to toss the gnocchi, as cooked gnocchi are very delicate and damage easily. Sprinkle the cheese over the top, if using, and serve immediately.

Sugo al Funghetto di Bosco–Wild Mushroom Sauce

Makes 4 cups (960ml)

2 tablespoons (30ml) extra virgin olive oil

2 garlic cloves, chopped

2 pounds (908grams) mushrooms (Oyster, Shitake, Hen-of-the-woods, Chanterelle, or Porcini, or a combination of two or more), stems removed, caps wiped clean and thinly sliced (about 4 cups)

1½ teaspoons kosher salt

1 teaspoon freshly ground black pepper

1 tablespoon fresh thyme leaves

½ cup (60ml) dry young red wine, such as Chianti

2 cups (480ml) canned Italian plum tomatoes, preferably San Marzano, with their juices, pureed in a food processor or food mill

Place a 12-inch skillet over medium heat, and when it is hot, add the olive oil. Add the garlic and cook until it releases its fragrance, about 1 minute. Add the mushrooms, salt, pepper and thyme, mix gently, and cook until the mushrooms have released all their liquid and are very soft, about 10 minutes.

Add the wine and bring to a simmer, 2 minutes. Add the tomatoes, reduce the heat to low, and cook, stirring occasionally, until most but not all the liquid has evaporated, about 10 minutes.

Sugo di Crema e Funghi–Mushroom Cream Sauce

Makes 4 cups (960ml)

2 tablespoons (30ml) extra virgin olive oil

2 garlic cloves, finely chopped

2 pounds (908 grams) Cremini mushrooms, stems removed, caps wiped clean and finely chopped (the food processor works well; about 4 cups chopped)

½ cup (120ml) dry white wine

1 teaspoon kosher salt, or more to taste

2 teaspoons freshly ground black pepper, or more to taste

½ cup (120ml) heavy cream

Place a 12-inch skillet over medium heat, and when it is hot, add the olive oil. Add the garlic and cook until lightly colored, about 2 to 3 minutes.

Add the mushrooms and cook, stirring constantly, until they have released all their liquid and cooked down, about 10 minutes. Add the wine, salt and pepper and cook until the alcohol from the wine has evaporated, about 2 minutes. Add the cream and cook, stirring frequently, until it has reduced and blended with the mushrooms, 5 minutes. Taste for salt and pepper.

Helen and Henry Ptashnik

As told by their daughter Meira Fleisch

Meira describes the actions both her parents took during their ordeal; each in their own way exhibited heroism and resolve. While she recalls her parents saying "they owe their lives to luck, their siblings and good people here and there," as their story shows, they were active participants in their fate.

Both my parents were from Stopnits (Stopnica), Poland, but because my father was 10 years older than my mother, they didn't really know each other. You could say they were worlds apart. When my Mom was a teenager of about fourteen and my father was in his early twenties, the war changed their lives. My parents were both sent to the same work camp, but both ended up in separate concentration camps. During their internment, my mother was with her two sisters and my father with his two brothers. They were both fortunate that they could be useful to the Germans, as this certainly kept them alive. My father was quite heroic, and was responsible for saving many lives while interned. He and his brother, both carpenters, built a sliding door hideaway in the barracks. They

essentially created a place for sick prisoners to hide. Doing so, they undoubtedly saved those people's lives. Decades later, I remember when my father was in the hospital and dying. A man in a wheelchair came to visit him saying he owed his life to my father who hid him during the war. I felt very proud and my father was very honored.

After the war my father went to a DP camp, while my mother was taken to a rehabilitation camp in Italy. She was actually housed in one of Mussolini's former palaces. From there my mother went to Israel aboard a ship that the British initially turned away. In an active act of defiance, the passengers on board staged a hunger strike, and the British allowed her and eventually all the others to disembark. My father had also immigrated to Israel and one day, while at what I believe was a government building, they bumped into each other. From that time on, my Dad started visiting my mother's home. My mother thought he was courting her sister as they were closer in age, but he was after my mother. My Dad fought in the War for Independence and they remained in Israel for over a decade; that's where I was born.

My mother always cooked fresh foods, never canned or packaged; there were no TV dinners in my house. I use to eat, in my early school days, an Israeli sandwich made from cream cheese and olives; they were the best. I remember loving her chicken soup and her *p'tcha*, with its highly seasoned flavor and lots of garlic. She was a refined cook; even in her noodle pudding, she always used fine noodles. Of her recipes, the one I remember now is a red cabbage dish that she served at holidays. My mother's strength was to make simple food well, and focus on quality. What you put in, is what you get out.

My parents were married 58 years and had two children and four grandchildren.

Top left: Hella and Yeheskel (Helen and Henry), wedding photo, Israel, January 9, 1949

Helen Ptashnik's Braised Red Cabbage and Apples

This could very well be the ultimate sweet and sour recipe. Mild, sweet red onions and tangy cabbage meld together with tart, crisp apples, honey, lemon and brown sugar. The result is a mélange of flavors that roll off your tongue as authentic Polish cuisine. Just like a see-saw, you can tip the balance in whichever direction you please, adding more lemon for a sour flavor or brown sugar to make it sweeter.

Yields: 8 to 9 cups; Start to Finish: Under 2 ½ hours

2 large red onions, thinly sliced

2 tablespoons vegetable or canola oil

1 large red cabbage (about 2 to 2½ pounds), shredded

1 tablespoon kosher salt

4 apples (2 Granny Smith, 2 Cortland or Macintosh), peeled and sliced thin

¼ cup honey

¼ cup ketchup

2 tablespoons brown sugar

¼ cup tomato sauce

1 tomato, pureed or finely diced

Juice of 1 lemon

Heat the oil in a large sauté pan, cook and stir the onions, over medium heat, until just soft, about 10 minutes. While the onions cook, shred the cabbage. Add the shredded cabbage to the pan and sprinkle with the salt. Using a large pair of kitchen tongs, toss the cabbage and onions so the salt works its way into the dish. Continue cooking until the cabbage has cooked down and begun to release its liquid, about 10 minutes.

While the cabbage cooks, peel and slice the apples and prepare the remaining ingredients. Stir the apples into the pan and add the honey, ketchup, brown sugar, tomato sauce, tomato and lemon juice. Cover the pan, reduce the heat to low and cook for 2 hours, stirring the cabbage every 30 minutes. Season to taste with salt and balance the sweet and sour to your liking. Serve hot as a side dish.

Arthur Schwartz

Professional contributor

Who but Arthur Schwartz would we turn to for an authentic, Yiddish, foolproof—recipe, to honor Meira's food memory of her mother's flavorful *p'tcha*?

P'tcha—Jellied Calf's Feet with Garlic

Excerpted from Jewish Home Cooking (Ten Speed Press, 2008)

Most people remember *p'tcha* as jellied calf's feet with chopped raw garlic and, in some versions, slices of hard-cooked egg or chopped hard-cooked egg embedded in the firm gelatin (yoich) just to make it look a little better. In French, *p'tcha* would be called an aspic, which sounds elegant. But even with a name like *p'tcha*, the dish has a cult following. Hardly anyone makes it at home, and it is nearly impossible to find in a restaurant, so it has become legendary.

P'tcha possibly started out as a soup, not a jelly. Refrigeration is required to get the broth to jell. Maybe in the *shtetl*s they chilled their *p'tcha* outside in the frigid air. In the following recipe, chopped fresh parsley is a contemporary touch to improve the looks of the jelly as well as its flavor. If, however, in your memory, *p'tcha* is not *p'tcha* if it doesn't resemble a brownish, suspiciously quivering brick, leave out the herb.

Serves 6 to 8

2 calf's feet or knuckles or both (about 3 pounds), sawed into 2-inch pieces by the butcher

10 cups water, plus additional water for soaking

2 medium onions, quartered

2 cloves garlic, coarsely chopped, plus more for the broth

1 teaspoon salt

¼ teaspoon white pepper

2 tablespoons distilled white vinegar

1 cup finely chopped fresh flat-leaf parsley, for garnish

3 egg yolks, for thickening the hot broth or 2 hard-cooked eggs, peeled and sliced or chopped, for garnish (optional)

Finely minced garlic, for garnish (optional)

1 lemon, cut into wedges, for garnish (optional)

Wash the meat thoroughly. Put the pieces into a large bowl, cover them with water, let soak for a few minutes, then drain. Scrape the skin with a sharp knife until it is smooth. (Sometimes, these days, the calf's feet are already cleaned.) In a 4-quart pot, bring the 10 cups of water to boil over a high heat.

Place the pieces in the boiling water along with the onions, the 2 cloves of coarsely chopped garlic, salt, pepper, and vinegar. Continue to boil until the meat and gristle begin to separate from the bones, about 3 hours. You will probably have to add more water to keep the feet covered, but it is supposed to reduce. Strain the liquid, saving both liquids and solids.

(Continued)

Pull the meat from the bones and cut into small pieces. Taste the broth and adjust the salt, pepper, and vinegar to taste. To serve hot, combine the meat and broth and return to boiling. Remove from the heat and add as much chopped raw garlic as you like. Do not simmer the broth after adding the garlic.

Serve hot in individual soup bowls with meat and garlic, garnished with fresh chopped parsley. Or, beat the 3 egg yolks together in a mixing bowl, then mix in some hot broth. Pour this mixture into the broth; do not allow the broth to boil after adding the raw eggs or the eggs will curdle. Another way to serve the broth is with chopped hard-cooked egg, instead of the raw egg enrichment.

To serve cold, which is more typical, arrange the pieces of meat and gristle in a deep heatproof dish. Add the parsley and chopped garlic. Pour in the broth and refrigerate, covered. Before the gelatin firms completely, place slices of hard-cooked egg over the top. Or, alternately, chop the hard-cooked egg and add it to the broth before you refrigerate it and it starts to jell.

In either case, hot or cold, can be served with wedges of lemon.

Gita Karelitz Roback and Godel Roback

As told by their daughter, Rosy Granoff

Gita's intelligence and chutzpah were two characteristics that served her well. Even as a child, she was a non-conformist who envisioned a strong Palestine. However, her legacy is here in America, as her daughter lovingly remembers her, as a brave, resourceful woman.

My mother was the youngest of three children, born to a well-to-do family in Baranów, Poland. My Mom, who was just a kid before the war broke out, attended parochial school. She benefited from a very good education, and I am proud to say my mother spoke seven languages. She was also somewhat of a free spirit, very dissimilar to her siblings; shunning materialistic things and pursuing Zionist causes. As a young girl, she would sneak out of her house at night and attend meetings and rallies sponsored by Menachem

Top left: Gita and Godel Roback after liberation

Begin's right-wing organization. When the war broke out, she was working as a bookkeeper. Several members of her family were immediately deported to Siberia, and others followed after to find them; they were never heard from again.

When my mother was sent to the ghetto, she worked as an administrative assistant for a German officer. It is hard to imagine, but she witnessed her mother being rounded up and taken away. My mother wanted to go after her, but the officer convinced her to stay, explaining frankly that if she left, she would not survive. While in the ghetto, she and her first cousin plotted their escape, with hopes of joining the partisans. Through ingenious trickery, she made arrangements to sneak over the barbed wire and escape into the woods where they joined a small group of freedom fighters. They spent the next couple of years traveling by night and hiding by day. It was in this group, that she met my father, Godel Roback.

After the war, my mother and father moved to Rome, Italy, where my two brothers were born. Their plan was to realize my mother's lifelong dream and go to Palestine. However, a family member from my father's side offered to sponsor their trip to America and they accepted. My parents surrounded themselves with friends from the war; partisans became the relatives we never had the chance to meet. And while we had a traditional Shabbos dinner every Friday night my mother's cooking traditions were more American and Italian than Eastern European. A family tradition, which stemmed from the time she spent in Italy, was to have pasta every Sunday night. She and my Dad were married over 40 years, and together they had three children, six grandchildren and three great grandchildren.

Gita Roback's Slow Simmered Sunday Sauce

Gita would begin her sauce with the tireless trio of onions, peppers and celery. Slow cooked herbs, crushed tomatoes, and tomato paste simmered the day away till a robust and aromatic sauce emerged. These same ingredients can easily create a quick sauce; you might sacrifice a little in flavor, but if time is crunching, it's still far better than store bought. Gita would bathe waiting pasta in the vibrant sauce and serve it alongside thick, juicy rib steaks, which were simply broiled. For a change of pace, burgers made from freshly ground beef and veal and seasoned with grated onion and garlic would be served bunless alongside the spaghetti.

Yields: 3 cups, Start to Finish: At least 4 hours or up to 6 hours, For quick sauce, under 1 hour

1 medium onion, finely chopped (about ¾ cup)	**2 garlic cloves, minced**
1 medium green pepper, cored, seeded and diced	**2 tablespoons freshly chopped oregano**
2 celery ribs, finely chopped	**2 tablespoons freshly chopped flat leaf parsley plus additional for garnish**
2 tablespoons olive oil	
2 pounds ripe plum tomatoes, peeled, seeded and chopped or 1 (28-ounce) can whole tomatoes with their juice	**2 tablespoons freshly chopped basil plus additional for garnish**
	2 bay leaves
1 heaping tablespoon tomato paste	**Kosher salt and pepper**
1 (8-ounce) can of tomato sauce	

Heat the oil, in a large saucepan, cook and stir the onions, peppers and celery, over medium heat, until lightly browned, about 10 minutes. Stir in the tomatoes, tomato paste, tomato sauce, garlic, oregano, parsley, basil and bay leaves. Season to taste with salt and pepper. Lower the heat to a simmer, cover and cook the sauce, for at least 4 hours or up to 6. For quick sauce, cook for 30-60 minutes. In the last few minutes of cooking add the parsley and basil. Before serving, remove the bay leaves and toss with your choice of pasta.

Feedback
In this slow simmered sauce, parsley and basil are added twice. First they are cooked with the sauce to flavor it and meld with the aromatics. They are also added right at the end to appreciate their full flavor. Usually, the fresh spring taste of soft herbs such as parsley, dill and basil is best preserved if they are chopped right before using and added at the very end. With this recipe, you get the slow cooked flavor from the herbs and their vibrant fresh boost at the end.

Sol and Sally Rosenkranz

In Sol's words

Sol is a born teacher, spending much of his time educating children on the lessons of the Holocaust. His 90+ years do not impede his efforts or his memories. He recalls every name, every incident in such vivid detail that I listened with rapt attention. His is truly a story of perseverance and love.

I remember very clearly my childhood in Krosniewice, Poland. I was the youngest in the family and I recall helping my mother, beginning on Thursday, to prepare for Shabbos. We lived well, and had the money to buy chicken, duck, goose, eggs and butter from the peasants who sold their wares. In 1939, when I was twenty-one, Poland was fully affected by the Nazis. I came from a close-knit family, so much so that when the Nazis came for my older brother, who was married and a father, my middle brother took his place. My younger sister did the same for my older sister. They both did it out of love. When

the town was ghettoized, our building, a corner stone house, became part of the ghetto. We considered ourselves lucky, taking in our aunts and uncles, filling our house with over twenty people. On March 1, 1942 we escaped the ghetto, the night before it was liquidated. The story is one of great luck.

While in the ghetto, I was assigned to shine the boots of the German police who lived in a large building just outside the ghetto. I would go early in the morning and was warned not to wake them up, which was difficult because the floorboards squeaked. If you did wake them, as I did on my first day, you were beaten and told not to come back. One morning, in the first week of February, 1942, I approached the gate and saw a family I did not recognize; it was a mother, father and two boys. I learned from the father, whose name was Harry Greenfield, that his family escaped from their nearby ghetto before it was liquidated. I brought the family home with me and we listened to their warnings and escape plan. The following day, I released the bottom portion of the fence so they could sneak out.

I was asked back to the police station, as I was the last young fellow in the ghetto. Before the war, my family had been in the fur business, and we still had many of our goods. It was freezing cold, and I took a fur collar for the son of the German Chief of Police, Danksom Miller. In exchange, I asked him what was going to happen to the Jews? He told me not to be afraid, until March 1st, which was only two weeks away. On the last day in February, my friend, Aaron Shulman, who took care of their horses, and I were given a very heavy assignment to fill up their stalls with heating supplies of coal and wood. While I was outside the ghetto I used my time to convince five families in town to hide my family for the night. That evening, I sent my

Top left: Sally and Sol Rosenkranz

family out of the same opening in the fence, but I remained behind. In the morning, as I was collecting the boots to shine, I saw three trucks pull up in front of the police station. I camouflaged myself as a worker, waited for the commotion to stop, and I was on their tail. I followed the police as they took up positions on the side of the ghetto. It was probably foolish of me, but I was brazen. I soon reconnected with my family, and we were on the road to escape.

We first went to Lodz, and we bribed a civil servant to direct us to a small cottage where a woman hid my family in her attic. I decided not to go up to the attic but stayed downstairs in the hut about 30 to 45 minutes. Later a German border guard entered with a German shepherd. He sat opposite me and started a conversation since he noticed me wearing a watch. He spoke to me in German, asking to buy the watch. I played dumb that I didn't understand German and responded in Polish, and not about the watch. Instead I spoke about the heavy snow and the severe weather. I must say, he was not a sophisticated border guard. He did not have the slightest clue who was up in the attic or that I was Jewish. He soon went on his way. Soon we did too and finally met with the Greenfields in a city called Piotrkow/Trybunalski. In May, my brother and I were sent to work in separate factories. I worked in Kara, a glass factory beside the railroad. We worked all day, but were allowed to return home at night. Beginning in August, the trains that ran there were taking Jewish people to Treblinka. Every day I would watch the trains, as people on the train would throw notes from the small windows. Kids would run and pick up the notes and we would read them to see if we recognized any names. One evening in September, we went to the gates to leave for home after work, but they were shut and remained shut. We were now detained and cut off from our family. After about a week of being detained, I was opening the notes thrown from the train and sadly read the names of my family. I never saw them again.

I continued working from May, 1942 to November, 1944. The Germans feared the Russians were nearby, so they would scoop us up and move us. We did this over and over, until we arrived in Buchenwald. There I found my first cousin, Phil. We volunteered to be transferred, one time near a gasoline factory, Rheinsdorf Leipzig, where we were almost killed by Allied bombs. We were not fed, and every day we each collected two cigarette rations in Buchenwald, which we later used to bribe a guard to transfer us to field work. We were again loaded on to trains and by now we learned never to be the first and never to be the last. We stayed in the middle of the train that was nearly 60 cars long. We were lucky, because Allied planes dropped bombs that blew up the front of the train. We were in a large forest in Austria before approaching Strasbourg. We used that timing to run as fast and as far as we could, heading into the forest. Once again, we were scooped up, and marched from town to town, through Strasbourg and into Czechoslovakia and ending up in Terezin. A few weeks later, the Russians liberated us. I survived because I always had an eye open, and I was very lucky.

My wife, Sally, came from a large family. She was second to the youngest, and was thirteen when taken to the camps. Sally went through many camps in Poland and Germany. She ended up in Bergen-Belsen where the British liberated her. I also came to Bergen-Belsen after the war and that's where we met. Sally learned she had family who had survived the war and were living in Stuttgart. She wanted to go there to find them. We had just gotten acquainted, but I took her to the train station. The train was packed. Luckily one window on the train was open and I pushed Sally through the window onto the train on top of everyone's shoulders. This was the only way to go from place to place. She told her family all about me, and they invited me for Pesach. I went to Stuttgart and I was given an interview by the family. A Jewish military chaplain married us April 27th. My future brother-in-law worked for an American military office, and he was given all the affidavits needed for all of us to come to America in July, 1946.

Sally learned all the cooking and baking from her Aunt Toby, also a survivor. She became an excellent cook and baker under Aunt Toby's guidance and then by figuring things out on her own. We had a truly wonderful life together, and I knew she was my *bashert*. After 50 years of marriage, Sally suffered a heart attack and as fitting with our life story, died in my arms. We have three children and one grandchild.

Jeff Nathan

Professional contributor

Sol remembers as a young boy, preparation for Shabbos dinner beginning Thursday and he recalls a home where chicken, goose and duck were enjoyed for Friday night dinner. Jeff Nathan adds, "There was a time in early Jewish American history when the duck for a Shabbos dinner was as commonplace as today's chicken. This recipe is classy, yet relatively easy to prepare with pantry ingredients."

Duck with Apple and White Raisin Sauce

Presented by Chef Jeff Nathan, host of Jewish Television Network's New Jewish Cuisine.

Yields: 4 servings

1 apple, quartered

1 orange, quartered

(2) 5 pound ducklings

Butcher cracked black pepper (also known as quarter cracked)

Preheat the oven to 450 degrees.

Place the quartered apple and orange in the cavity of each bird. Prick ducks with a fork all over.

Roast, breast side up on a foil rack in baking pan. Bake at 450 degrees for 1 hour.

Lower the temperature to 400 degrees for one half hour more.

Remove ducks from oven. Let them rest approximately 20 minutes. Carve or refrigerate overnight.

Apple with White Raisin Sauce

4 tablespoons sugar

1 piece star anise

¼ cup apple cider vinegar

2 Granny Smith apples, peeled and cored; tossed with lemon juice

¼ cup golden raisins

½ cup apple cider or juice

⅛ teaspoon ground cinnamon

Fruit liquor

Cornstarch

In a small saucepot place the sugar, star anise and cider vinegar. Cook until caramel colored.

Carefully add the apples, raisins, cider and cinnamon. Slowly simmer until rich and flavorful. Thicken with a slurry of fruit liquor and cornstarch as needed.

Sally Rosenkranz's Honey Cake

Sally's daughter Rita writes, "My late mother, Sally Rosenkranz, who was from Radom, Poland, lost her mother in the Holocaust. Mom learned to cook and bake from her aunt, refining recipes over the years. I bake this crowd-pleasing honey cake for the holidays, and also freeze individual slices for drop-in guests."

Yields: Two 9-inch loaves, 12 to 16 slices each; Start to Finish: Under 1½ hours

½ cup brewed coffee, cooled

3½ cups sifted all-purpose flour

¼ teaspoon salt

2 teaspoons baking powder

1 teaspoon baking soda

1½ teaspoons ground cinnamon

¼ teaspoon ground nutmeg

⅛ teaspoon powdered cloves (optional)

1½ teaspoons powdered ginger (optional)

4 eggs

1 cup sugar

1 cup vegetable oil

2 cups dark honey

1½ cups coarsely chopped walnuts or almonds

1 cup raisins (optional)

Preheat the oven to 325 degrees and grease two 9-inch loaf pans or a 16 x 11 x 4-inch baking pan.

Brew the coffee and set it aside to cool.

In a medium bowl sift the flour, salt, baking powder, baking soda, cinnamon, nutmeg, cloves and ginger. In a separate large bowl, beat the eggs on medium speed, gradually adding the sugar and beating for several minutes, until the mixture turns a pale yellow. Beat in the oil, honey and cooled coffee. Gradually add the flour mixture to the egg mixture, beating on low speed to prevent the flour from flying out of the bowl. Turn the speed up to medium and beat for several minutes, until a smooth thick batter is formed. Stir the chopped nuts into the batter. If adding raisins, stir them in at this time.

Fill the prepared pans halfway with batter. The cake rises considerably when baking. (Any extra batter can be used to make delicious muffins). Bake at 325 degrees for 1 to 1¼ hours until the top of the cake is a cinnamon brown, but not burnt, and a bamboo skewer inserted in the center comes out clean.

Cool completely before slicing.

Feedback
Honey is a great way to sweeten just about anything. Your taste buds interpret it as being sweeter than sugar, so start slowly when adding it to your dish. Honey is one of the only foods that does not spoil. Some say honey was actually found fresh, in the unearthed tombs of the Pharaohs, so when adding honey to your cakes and recipes you prolong their freshness. If the honey crystallizes, place the jar or container in a warm water bath and let it liquefy. You can do this over and over. Important to note, honey should never be given to an infant, their bodies cannot always process it safely.

Maks and Gita Rothman

As told by their daughter Sylvia Rothman Nirenberg

Maks and Gita were a mixed marriage, he from Poland and she from Romania. We placed their story in the Polish section, as Sylvia's home traditions leaned more toward the Polish style. But we honor her mother's Romanian heritage with an interesting twist on a classic dessert.

My parents began their new lives in Canada, but they started them in very different places. My father, Maks, was born and raised in Poland, and like so many others during the war, came home one day to find his house burned to the ground and his family gone. My Dad was a resourceful teenager and spent the war years surviving on his own, hiding by day, scavenging for food at night. He drifted from border to border, always evading capture. Eventually he immigrated to Israel and fought in the Israeli army. My father learned that most of his family had survived. He traveled to Canada to be reunited with his parents, two sisters and two brothers. Amazingly, another sister whom the family did not believe had survived resurfaced recently and was reunited with the rest of the family more than 50 years after she was presumed dead.

I know little about my mother's story during the war, as she was reluctant to talk about her experiences. I know that her family fled Romania to Siberia and that she eventually came to Canada where she met my Dad. When they moved to America, I remember my mother cooking the traditional Shabbos meal, and then we would eat the leftovers for days. My parents have two children, four grandchildren and one great grandchild.

Top left: Maks and Gita Rothman on their wedding day

Sour Cream Strudel with *Loukoum* Filling

Sylvia described in vivid detail a very unusual yeast and sour cream pastry that her mother, Gita, would stuff with *Loukoum*, Turkish delight candy. Because of Romania's close proximity to Turkey, their cooking style often reflected an influence from Turkish cuisine. Sylvia described her Mom pulling and stretching the candy of varying colors and flavors. I searched everywhere to find a recipe that would honor this memory. One day, I wandered into a Middle Eastern market where a lovely woman of Armenian descent helped me recreate the recipe Sylvia recalled. The basic dough is a sour cream rugelach, provided by Nancy Apfel, a wonderful baker. The tricky part was finding a way to blend the candy into the cookie so it retained its soft chewy texture while not overpowering the pastry. The recipe that follows does just that. You can, of course, fill the strudel traditionally with nuts and raisins, but if you want to try this Romanian version you might just find it hides a pleasant surprise in every bite.

Yields: 64 pieces; Start to Finish: Step One: Under 30 minutes, then refrigerate 6 to 8 hours or overnight, Step Two: Under 1 hour

For the dough:

3 cups all-purpose flour

1 package dry yeast

½ teaspoon salt

1 tablespoon sugar

½ pound (2 sticks) butter, room temperature

3 egg yolks

1 cup sour cream

Filling:

1 pound *Loukoum* (Turkish Delight candy), assorted flavors (avoid rose water), cut into 1-inch pieces (you will need 64 pieces)

1 cup sugar combined with 4 teaspoons of ground cinnamon

1 cup apricot preserves, room temperature

Egg wash glaze:

1 egg beaten plus a tablespoon of water

Topping:

Sanding sugar

Step One: In a large bowl or the bowl of a food processor fitted with the metal blade, combine the flour, yeast, salt and sugar. Using a pastry blender, or the pulse action of the food processor, blend in the butter until the ingredients are thoroughly mixed and crumbly. In a separate bowl beat the egg yolks and sour cream. Stir the egg mixture into the flour mixture. Blend till completely combined and a dough forms; it will be a little sticky. Separate the dough into 4 equal parts, flatten each into a disc and wrap in plastic wrap. Refrigerate for 6 to 8 hours or overnight.

Step Two: Preheat the oven to 350 degrees.

Remove one section of dough from the fridge and let it come to room temperature.

Take the *Loukoum* and warm it in the microwave for about 30 to 60 seconds, you want the candy soft and pliable enough to stretch and flatten with your hands, but not melted.

Generously flour a work surface and roll the dough out into a 12-inch circle, about ¼–inch thick. With a spatula, spread a thin layer of the preserves over the entire circle, and then sprinkle with ¼ cup of the sugar and cinnamon. Using a pizza cutter, cut the circle into fourths, then cut each fourth into fourths again. You should have 16 pieces.

Take a piece of the softened candy and press it between your fingers to stretch and flatten it. Place 1 piece of candy at the wide end of each wedge, and then roll the wedges. When rolled you should have a nice crescent shape. Place each piece on an un-greased cookie sheet. Brush lightly with the egg wash and sprinkle with a touch of sanding sugar. Bake at 350 degrees for 20 minutes or until golden brown. While that batch bakes, take the next disc of dough out to warm up, and repeat.

JFH

Judy Bart Kancigor

Professional contributor

Maks Rothman was famous for his pickled herring. Sylvia recalls, "When my father made it, I would run the other way. This was a dish he would make for breakfast gatherings at his synagogue." Not only did Polish Jews consume a lot of herring, they were herring traders and importers as well. Because the fish was pre-salted, and inexpensive, it became a staple in the diet of Eastern European Jews. The great debate is wine sauce or cream sauce? You decide. To turn this recipe, contributed by Judy Bart Kancigor, into herring in cream sauce, simply cut the herring into bite-size pieces, stir in some sour cream, and correct the taste with sugar.

Louis Selmanowitz's Chopped Herring

*Excerpted from Cooking Jewish; 532 Great Recipes from the Rabbinowitz Family
(Workman Publishing Company, Inc. 2007)*

Serves 6

2 salted herrings, filleted

1 small white onion, chopped

1 large tart apple, peeled and finely chopped

2 tablespoons distilled white vinegar

1 large egg, hard-cooked and mashed

⅛ teaspoon freshly ground black pepper

Romaine lettuce, for serving

Grated hard-cooked egg and finely chopped onion, for garnish

Plain crackers, for serving

Soak the herrings in cold water to cover for 24 hours. Then rinse them well and grind them by hand.

Combine the ground herring, onion, apple, vinegar, egg and pepper in a bowl, and mix thoroughly.

Spoon the mixture onto a platter lined with romaine lettuce leaves and garnish with grated egg and chopped onion.

To serve, *shmeer* on plain crackers.

Feedback

Many of the recipes in the book call for hard-boiled (hard-cooked) eggs. If you can boil water, you can hard-boil an egg. Use eggs that are several days old, farm fresh just plucked eggs are harder to peel after being cooked. Place the eggs in a saucepan filled with enough cold water to completely cover the eggs by at least an inch or two. (Some people add vinegar to the water to stop the whites from leaching out if the shells crack. I think the eggs pick up a vinegary taste and would not recommend that method.) Bring the water and eggs to a boil. Once the water boils, lower the heat, but maintain a slow boil for 10 minutes. Plunge the cooked eggs in ice-cold water until cool enough to peel. This helps keep the yolks bright yellow, prevents the greenish ring that sometimes collects on the sunny yolk and makes peeling easier.

Helena Pradelski Sabat and Benjamin Sabat

As told by their daughter Anna Sabat

Many of Anna's childhood memories are built around food and family gatherings. With lots of humor and great respect for those traditions, she shares her memories with us.

My mother, whose maiden name was Helena Pradelski, was born on February 22, 1921 in Sosnowiec, Poland, the fourth of six children. Her brother, Henry, the eldest, was the only son. During the war, he was shuttled through various concentration camps, while my mother spent five years in one work camp, where she and other young women made machinery parts to be used in the war. Unlike my father, Benjamin Sabat, who was in Auschwitz, my mother had no number tattooed on her arm. When the war ended, my mother was deliriously happy to be finally reunited with her brother Henry, but as they continued their search for the rest of their immediate family, they eventually learned that their parents and four sisters perished in the camps. As did many survivors, after the war, my

Top left: Anna Sabat with her parents, Helena and Benjamin, Regensburg, Germany

mother quickly married and became pregnant (with me). We came to America in the summer of 1949 and settled in Brooklyn, New York, where my sister Mary (!) was born in 1951. Of course, food took on a significant role in our household, almost becoming another member of the family. The centerpiece of many family stories focused on how I, at two-years old, barely ate for the weeklong ship voyage to America. I remained quite thin throughout my girlhood and adolescence, despite my parents' never-ending quest to fatten me up. For Holocaust survivors, it was almost shameful to have a thin child. The following are some recollections, mostly brief sketches, related to food in the home where I grew up:

My mother shopped for food daily, buying just enough for that day's meals, as she had in Europe. Everything had to be fresh. Our freezer stored nothing but ice cubes. She was not much of a baker, but she visited Jeffrey's Bakery on Church Avenue daily for bread and cakes. At night, after dinner, my sister and I were served absurdly large pieces of cake, along with glasses of milk or sometimes malteds that my father picked up on his way home from work at the local candy store with a soda fountain. My favorites were Jeffrey's chocolate eggs, which were individual-sized oval-shaped yellow cakes covered with chocolate. The centers were filled with a butter cream that even now makes my mouth water as I think of them. While my sister and I ate those or strawberry shortcake or seven-layer cake, my parents usually had sponge cake and tea in glasses.

My father insisted on fresh rye bread with his meals. Sometimes on Saturday mornings I was sent out to fetch the bread, one-quarter to one-half loaf at a time, sliced without seeds, as my father liked it. I recall the bakery clerk selecting the bread, which had a sticker on the end (I guess to distinguish the seeded from non-seeded ryes), and then putting it through the slicer. Sometimes I nibbled on the end piece as I carried the wax bag home. However, the morning's bread would not do for dinner that same day. Once again, I or my sister or my mother (never my father) would go to the bakery to get another quarter loaf. Sometimes as I stood at the counter waiting my turn, I looked at the breads and rolls piled high on the shelves and thought of the stories my mother told of the days just before she and her sisters were sent away, when there was little food, and they traded their beautiful embroidered nightgowns to townspeople, only to be given pieces of stale bread in return.

My mother made gefilte fish from scratch for all the holidays. She would cover her ironing board with a cloth and clamp on a metal hand grinder into which she fed the fresh fish that she then mixed with other ingredients, shaped into oval patties, and cooked. My mother made the best potato *latkes* I've ever had. They were completely different from the dense ones I've been served throughout my adult life on many occasions and in various settings. My mother's were light, airy, golden, and crisp, never greasy. We usually ate them with only a light sprinkling of sugar – no sour cream or applesauce. One of my biggest regrets is that I didn't get the recipe when she was alive. My mother regularly made chopped liver. I can still hear the rhythmic sound of her wielding a hand chopper to mince chicken livers, hard-cooked eggs, and onions in a round wooden bowl that was covered with tiny nicks from years of use.

Attempts at American fare resulted in hamburgers round and dense as baseballs. Chopped meat was mixed with eggs and garlic and served not on buns, but on white bread. She sometimes packed them for me to take to school for lunch. I was embarrassed about how un-American they looked, but my friends loved them and gladly traded their "American" peanut butter and jelly sandwiches for my "refugee" hamburgers.

When I'd balk at a family dinner as my mother filled my plate to the brim and cut those absurdly large pieces of cake, my Uncle Henry would advise me to humor her. "You have to remember," he said, "the war made us all a little crazy about food." My parents were married 31 years, as we lost my Mom at a relatively young age. She knew my son, Matthew, but not my daughter, Helena, who was born in 1979 and is named for the grandmother she never knew.

Ina Garten

Professional contributor

While we can't bring back the sound of the *hak messer* chopping liver, we can ignite Anna's memories with a new version. We are sure the fabulous Ina Garten's recipe will bring back great memories for Anna, and will provide us all with a new way to make this timeless classic.

Chopped Liver

Excerpted from Barefoot Contessa Parties! by Ina Garten (Clarkson/Potter Publishers), Copyright 2001. All Rights Reserved

Around the Jewish holidays, all our (Barefoot Contessa) customers wait for us to make chopped liver. It's like your grandmother's, if you have a Jewish grandmother, but better. The Madeira adds a bit of sweetness without your knowing what it is. Be sure not to overprocess this spread; you want it chunky. I serve it with pieces of matzo.

Makes about 5 cups

2 pounds chicken livers

1 cup rendered chicken fat

2 cups medium-diced yellow onion (2 onions)

⅓ cup Madeira wine

4 extra-large eggs, hard-cooked, peeled, and chunked

¼ cup minced fresh parsley

2 teaspoons fresh thyme leaves

2 teaspoons kosher salt

1 teaspoon freshly ground black pepper

Pinch cayenne pepper

Drain the livers and sauté them in 2 batches in 2 tablespoons of the chicken fat over medium-high heat, turning once, for about 5 minutes, or until just barely pink inside. Don't overcook the livers or they will be dry. Transfer them to a large bowl.

In the same pan, sauté the onions in 3 tablespoons of the chicken fat over medium-high heat for about 10 minutes, or until browned. Add the Madeira and deglaze the pan, scraping the sides, for about 15 seconds. Pour into the bowl with the livers.

Add the eggs, parsley, thyme, salt, black pepper, cayenne, and the remaining chicken fat to the bowl. Toss quickly to combine. Transfer half the mixture to the bowl of a food processor fitted with a steel blade. Pulse 6 to 8 times, until coarsely chopped. Repeat with the remaining mixture. Season to taste and chill. Serve on crackers or matzo.

Feedback

Ina Garten's chopped liver has a delicious gourmet twist and a perfect texture. The chicken fat added to the mixture makes it rich and smooth. If you are kosher, then you know you must broil the liver first.

Ruth Baumwald Stromer and Moty Stromer

As told by their daughters Nina Gaspar and Sue Talansky

Nina and Sue speak in tandem, as many sisters do; one begins a sentence and the other finishes. When they exuberantly spoke of their parents, you could hear the joy in their shared memories. They described their father as a character, their mother as a lady. They also shared their Dad's diary with me, published by Yad Vashem. *Memoirs of an Unfortunate Person* is Moty's accounting of his time in hiding. The first person narrative is revealing and chilling, and provides great insight into their father. What is written here comes from his diary and from the eloquent introduction written by Sue.

Our father, Moty, was born in 1910, in Kamionka-Strumilowa (Kaminke), in southeastern Poland. According to his diary, he enjoyed the period of time between August, 1939 and June, 1941, when this part of Galicia was under Soviet rule. Everything was forever destroyed on Sunday, June 22, 1941, when German tanks and troops entered Kaminke. Ten days later, his grandfather and great uncle were murdered. Moty fled to the Lemberg ghetto where he remained till it was liquidated in June of 1943. By then he had lost much of his family. Soon after, Moty escaped from a transport train and fled into the woods. He tried to find shelter with people he knew before the war: Jozef and Rozalie Streker, an ethnic German couple who had a farm in an area called Jagonia. The Strekers, at great risk, hid him in their attic for ten months, until the

approaching Soviet armies and the implicit threat they posed to ethnic Germans, forced them to abandon their home and its terrified hidden tenant. Decades later, the Strekers were honored at Yad Vashem as "Righteous Among the Nations."

It is in the last two months of hiding, from April 6 to June 2, 1944 that our father wrote his memoir. He asked for paper and pencil in order to write down his thoughts and memories. Writing in Yiddish, in painfully neat and tiny script, he recounted as best he could the fate of those he knew and loved. There is a sense of urgency in these lines and the script becomes larger and larger, as if he were shouting these directions on paper with his last ounce of mental and physical strength. He needed to do everything in his power to insure this manuscript's survival, if not his own. He wrote:

With the help of God
I am writing these words on the night before I have to leave my place, this attic, where I have been more than–or exactly–300 days and nights. The days in this place were no brighter than the nights; but what do I want? To be able to spend more time in this place–or find one like it. May God help me! Please convey this to my brother Meyer Stromer, or my sister in America Henia Edelstein, to let them know

Today is Thursday, April 6, 1944
I had a difficult time trying to decide whether to write this or not, because I had always hoped I

Top left: Ruth and Moty Stromer

would live through the greatest disaster...Once everything is on paper, [will I find] the right person to hide the manuscript? God has helped me. The fact is that my personal tragedy is the tragedy of hundreds of thousands of Jews. But be it as it may, I hope that I survive long enough to see my remaining family. Then I will laugh at life, because on more than one occasion I have looked death in the eye.

Soon after the last page was written, the war came to an end and Moty returned to Kaminke. There he met our mother, Ruth Baumwald. She was a beautiful woman, twelve years our father's junior, and like his sister, Henia, a graduate of a Polish *Gymnasium* (secondary school). Our mother was far more reticent about her war experiences than our Dad. We know that a Christian woman in Lemberg proper hid her. We know she spent much of the war terrified beyond description and we know she survived with her nuclear family intact—a miracle indeed. My parents-to-be fell in love and were married in 1947 by the Chief Rabbi of Cracow, who years later, in New York, officiated at my wedding, as well as my sister's.

After a brief sojourn in Belgium the family moved to the Upper West Side of New York City. Once transplanted to America our mother learned English quickly and her kitchen was the center of our household. She served up standard American fare, burgers and fries, spaghetti and meatballs, steak and mashed potatoes. Thursday night was always "dairy" with creamy potato soup, fried fish, *lokshen* (noodles) and Schrafft's ice cream for dessert. Eastern European foods found their place on our Shabbos and holiday tables; gefilte fish, chicken soup, *tsimmes* and her wonderful chopped liver. Our mother's delicious stuffed cabbage took almost a full day to prepare. When I was first married and living on the north shore of Long Island, I taught classes till late on Friday afternoons in Manhattan. In the winter I did not have a chance to prepare a Shabbos meal, so my mother would cook and pack up a five course dinner and then meet me at the 103rd Street IRT subway stop and simply hand it to me when the train doors opened. All of a sudden as we pulled out of the station, this subway car packed with harried New Yorkers, filled with the aroma of a *shtetl* Shabbos.

My father loved to cook chicken soup. He would put on a huge chef's apron and prepare gallons at a time. More than cooking, our Dad loved food shopping. Every Sunday he went to Zabar's to buy appetizing lox and all the trimmings for our lavish brunches. He especially enjoyed chatting with a *landsman* behind the counter. Moty later learned that this same man who sliced nova for him every Sunday, was also a survivor. But, Moty hated the lines. Not to worry. He simply searched the floor for discarded numbers and then skipped to the head of the line. It's things like this that helped him survive; he was always resourceful and knew how to bend the rules. We had the typical upbringing of survivor's children. We rarely ate out, never had babysitters, avoided pets, paid in cash and stuck together. We were the center of our parents' universe and as often as not, much of their attentiveness expressed itself in the foods they so lovingly prepared and served to us. Their true legacy is their seven grandchildren and seven great grandchildren.

Ruth Stromer's Honey and Lemon Stuffed Cabbage

Pure genius! That's the only way to describe Ruth's technique for preparing the uncooperative cabbage leaves necessary for stuffed cabbage. Instead of battling with boiling water, Ruth would freeze the cabbage for about a week. The night before she was going to prepare the stuffed cabbage, she would thaw the frozen head (overnight in the fridge will do it). The next morning, as if to say, "stuff me," the leaves would fall away, limp, pliable and ready to go. Granted you have to think ahead, but give this method a whirl when you have a premonition of craving stuffed cabbage.

Yields: 14 to 16 rolls; Start to Finish: Under 2 ½ hours (plus the time to freeze and thaw the cabbage)

1 medium head of cabbage, frozen for one week, and then thawed overnight in the fridge

For the sauce:

1 large onion, coarsely chopped

2 tablespoons olive oil

24 ounces canned tomato juice

2 beef bones (shin bones work well)

2 teaspoons kosher salt

½ teaspoon black pepper

For the filling:

1 cup cooked rice

1 pound ground beef

2 teaspoons kosher salt

½ teaspoon black pepper

1 teaspoon onion powder or minced dried onion

1 egg

To finish the sauce:

½ cup honey

2 to 3 tablespoons lemon juice, or ½ teaspoon sour salt

After the cabbage has been thawed, separate the leaves. You will need to cut the hard end (tip of the core) so that the leaves release from the head, and cut out the thick white rib on each leaf. You should have at least 14 to 16 leaves, large enough to stuff. Let the leaves drain and rest on a paper towel while you prepare the sauce and filling.

Heat the oil in a large Dutch oven, cook and stir the onions, over medium heat, until lightly browned, about 10 minutes. Pour in the tomato juice, add the bones and season with salt and pepper. Let the sauce simmer, uncovered, while you prepare the filling.

Cook the rice, according to package directions. Let the rice cool for a few minutes then combine it with the rest of the filling ingredients. Fill each leaf with about ¼ cup of filling; don't over fill (the amount depends on the size of the leaf). Roll the end toward the middle, tuck in the soft sides and roll into a tight package. Place the rolls in the sauce close together, this will help prevent them from unrolling while they simmer. Cook, covered, on a low heat, for about 1½ hours, and then push the cabbage rolls to the side so you can stir in ½ cup honey and fresh lemon juice or sour salt to the sauce. Gently stir, and season to taste with salt and pepper. Cook, covered, for 30 minutes longer.

Feedback

There is no question that the texture of the cabbage leaves using this method is different than when boiled. This same recipe can be prepared using the more traditional method of boiling the cabbage to obtain the wilted leaves (see Freda Lederer's recipe on page 270 for that technique).

Capsuto Freres Restaurant

Professional contributor

Shopping for nova on Sundays was a ritual for Moty, but he would not have had to jump the line if he had home cured *gravlax*. How do you take a piece of fresh salmon and create silky, smooth, *gravlax*—right in your own fridge? Simple. Just a few ingredients and a few days is all it takes. Samuel Capsuto, owner of the wonderful restaurant, Capsuto Freres, serves this classic dish with garnishes such as capers, chopped egg, minced red onion and cornichons. Here they are presenting it with a sweet mustard sauce. Dress it up or serve it simply, but for goodness sake, don't call it lox!

Basil Cured *Gravlax*

Contributed by Capsuto Freres restaurant, New York City

2 (1 pound) salmon filets with skin

¼ cup kosher salt

¼ cup sugar

2 tablespoons crushed peppercorns

1 bunch basil, washed and chopped (reserve 1 tablespoon for the sauce)

Cheesecloth

Spread filets side-by-side, skin side down, on cheesecloth. Sprinkle salt, sugar and peppercorns evenly over both filets. Pat the basil on both sides. Using the cheesecloth, fold one filet on top of the other. Skin should be facing outward, basil sides together. Wrap in the cheesecloth. Place on plate with heavy weight on top.

Refrigerate for 3 days. Slice thin with a long sharp knife.

Honey Mustard Sauce

½ cup Dijon mustard

¼ cup honey

1 tablespoon reserved chopped basil

Blend all three ingredients together. Adjust honey and mustard to taste. Serve on the side with the *gravlax*.

Florence Tabrys

In her own words

Florence imbued in her daughters the responsibility to continue the traditions rooted in her Eastern European home. She doesn't talk often about her experiences during the war, but she was more than willing to share her cherished recipes.

I was born in a small town called Szydlowiec, near Radom, in Poland. My family consisted of my parents and six other siblings. In September, 1939, when I was 14 years old, the Nazis occupied our town. For three years we continued to live in our house along with the other people in the town. It was not a formal ghetto, but the Polish people and the Nazi SS surrounded us. We were forced to do various jobs, and survived as my father, a cobbler, bartered for food and supplies. In 1942, my younger sister and I were separated from the rest of our family and we never saw them again. My sister and I were sent to a munitions factory where we worked 12-hour shifts and managed to stay alive. As the Russian army grew closer, the SS moved us from camp to camp and while confined in Bergen-Belsen, the British army liberated us. Miraculously, I stayed with my sister the entire time. After liberation, like many other displaced persons, I went to a DP camp. There I met and married my husband, Harry. Together we immigrated to the United States and raised two beautiful daughters, who gave us four wonderful grandchildren.

Despite the hardships I endured and the losses I sustained, I feel very lucky to have been able to re-build my life. One of the things that kept me going during the war were memories of my family, and so many of those revolved around family gatherings and food. We would remind ourselves of the simplest things that we ate at home, especially during the holidays. I would think about how I helped my mother prepare the necessary dishes such as gefilte fish, chicken with matzo ball soup, *kreplach*, stuffed cabbage and apple cake for Shabbos. I can still taste the sweet blintzes that my mother would make. Those memories came with me to America and those are the recipes I still lovingly prepare today.

Since completing the book, I sadly learned that Florence's husband, Harry, also a survivor, passed away. We extend our sincerest condolences to his devoted family. May his memory be a blessing.

Top left: Florence and Harry Tabrys in the U.S., circa 1949-early 1950s

Florence Tabrys' Sweet and Creamy Cheese Blintzes

These cheese blintzes have always been a favorite with everyone in Florence's family. Serve them for a casual brunch or light lunch. The filling is a combination of soft cheeses that melt into the blintz for a sweet and creamy burst of flavor with every bite. They make a great late night snack and ready to heat treat, as they freeze perfectly.

Yields: 10 blintzes; Start to Finish: Under 30 minutes

For the batter:

6 large eggs

½ cup warm water

½ cup whole milk

1 cup all-purpose flour

For the filling:

1 (4-ounce) package cream cheese, softened at room temperature

1 cup (7.5-ounce package) farmer's cheese

1 teaspoon melted butter

¾ teaspoon ground cinnamon

½ cup sugar

1 egg, beaten

Butter for frying

Toppings:

Sweetened sour cream, cinnamon sugar, confectioner's sugar, orange zest (optional)

Prepare the batter by whisking together all the ingredients. The batter should be thinner than a pancake batter, and a golden yellow color. Refrigerate the batter while you prepare the filling. For the filling, combine all the filling ingredients and gently blend until smooth.

Heat a pat of butter in an 8-inch non-stick skillet. Ladle about ¼ cup of batter into the center of the pan and quickly swirl the pan in a circular motion to evenly distribute the batter. Fry for 1 minute and then flip the blintz over. Cook for just a few seconds on the flip side and remove to a waiting paper towel. Cover with a second paper towel to prevent the blintzes from drying out. Wipe the pan clean of the residual butter, add a fresh pat and follow the same process until you have used all the batter.

When cool to the touch, begin filling the blintzes. A large tablespoonful plopped right in the middle of the blintz should do it. Fold the blintz, by bringing the two ends to the middle, and then fold the two sides into the middle, creating an oblong little package. Their irregular shape lets people know they are homemade, so don't fret if they don't look perfect. The blintzes are ready to fry. Heat several pats of butter in the same skillet you used to cook the batter, and fry them for several minutes or until golden brown. You can freeze the prepared blintzes, and fry them at a later time.

Enjoy the blintzes as is, or top with any of the suggested toppings. A classic fruit sauce makes an elegant choice, (see our recipe on page 151). Don't be surprised if people begin calling your blintzes crepes—they mean it as a compliment.

David Waltuck

Professional contributor

So now that you have mastered sweet cheese blintzes, are you ready to tackle a gourmet interpretation of this classic dish? There is no one better to guide you than masterful chef, David Waltuck. David discovered that his Jewish roots could be elevated to fine cuisine as evident in the following recipe.

David Waltuck's Blintzes of Fresh and Smoked Salmon with Caviar Cream

Excerpted from Chanterelle (Taunton Press, 2008)

Years ago, while dining at one of New York's finest restaurants—an upscale, American-owned establishment with French-leaning food—I was served a miniature bagel topped with a drizzle of truffle sauce. I was startled to see a Jewish-American staple in that setting. I was instantly liberated. It had never occurred to me to bring foods from my own ethnic heritage into Chanterelle, but as I sat there eating this gussied-up bagel, I thought, "Why Not?"

It wasn't long before little nods to knishes, blintzes, and other Middle European favorites began to find their way onto my menu. This is one such dish, which combines the form of a blintz with another cornerstone of my culinary heritage, smoked salmon. To balance the flavor and make the dish suitable to the elegant surroundings of Chanterelle, I add fresh salmon and finish the blintzes with a simple caviar cream. Try to find a nice, smoky salmon, such as a Norwegian-style one.

Rather than make blintz dough, I use *feuille de brik*, the crepe-like wrappers found in North African cooking. They can be purchased from specialty suppliers and are usually sold frozen and are very much my first choice for this dish, as they are much thinner and more delicate than spring roll wrappers. That said, you may use spring roll wrappers as an alternative.

Makes 24 pieces, enough to serve 6

½ cup heavy cream, plus more for serving

3 tablespoons crème fraîche or sour cream

1 teaspoon sherry vinegar

1 cup diced (¼–inch) sushi-grade salmon with skin removed (from about an 8-ounce fillet)

¼ cup diced (½–inch) smoked salmon (about 4 ounces)

½ teaspoon freshly squeezed lemon juice, plus more to taste

Pinch of kosher salt

1 large egg

2 tablespoons cold water

Six 12-inch *feuille de brik* sheets or large spring roll wrappers

Canola or other neutral oil, for frying

2 tablespoons American black caviar, such as paddlefish

To make the caviar cream, put the cream, crème fraîche, and vinegar in a medium bowl and stir together. Cover with plastic wrap and set aside to thicken at room temperature for 10-30 minutes, then transfer to the refrigerator to chill for at least 1 hour and up to 2 hours. If it becomes too thick, stir in a teaspoon or two more cream to make it pourable.

Put the fresh and smoked salmon in a medium bowl. Add the lemon juice and salt, toss gently, and set aside.

Prepare an egg wash by whisking together the egg and water together in a small bowl.

Arrange the *feuille de brik* sheets on a clean, dry surface, with one corner pointed at you. Using a pastry brush, brush each one with a thin coat of egg wash. Place 3 tablespoons of the salmon filling in the center of each wrapper. Then, if you think of each corner as a compass point, fold the south corner upward and hold it down with a thumb as your pointer fingers fold in the east and west corners, encasing the filling. Roll the *feuille de brik* carefully and tightly away from you, sealing the blintz with a bit more egg wash if necessary.

Line a plate with paper towels. Heat a wide heavy-bottomed sauté pan over medium heat for 3 to 4 minutes. Pour in the oil and heat until a scant drop of water sizzles when flicked into the pan, about 2 minutes. Carefully place the blintzes in the hot oil and fry until crispy (the filling will be slightly undercooked in the center), 2 to 3 minutes per side. Use tongs to remove them from the oil to drain on the paper towels.

Use a serrated knife to cut each blintz into quarters. Stir the caviar into the cream. Arrange the blintz pieces on a platter. Serve hot with the caviar cream alongside as a dip.

Florence Tabrys' Polish Apple Cake

If Polish women are tired and cranky, I understand why! This cake is a lot of work, but the final result is worth it. A delectable compote of apples and raisins is baked between layers of crunchy dough to create the national treasure that is *Jablecznik*, Polish for apple pie. Dina Liverant (see page 106) and Florence must have swapped recipes, as their versions were very similar. Florence's twist is an added layer of grape jelly that introduces another flavorful note to every bite.

Yields: 24 pieces; Start to Finish: Under 1½ hours

For the Dough:

4 eggs

4 tablespoons orange juice

1 teaspoon orange peel, zested

4 tablespoons vanilla extract

1⅓ cups sugar

2 rounded teaspoons baking powder

1 cup vegetable oil

5 cups all-purpose flour

For the Filling:

2½ pounds (8 to 10) Macintosh apples, peeled, cored and grated

½ cup raisins, or more to taste

½ cup sugar mixed with 2 teaspoons ground cinnamon

Topping:

¼ cup sugar mixed with 1 teaspoon ground cinnamon

For the Layering:

1 cup grape jelly, room temperature

Preheat the oven to 375 degrees and grease a 13x9x2-inch Pyrex baking dish.

To make the dough, in a large bowl, beat the eggs, orange juice, orange zest, vanilla, sugar and baking powder on medium speed until well blended and frothy. Pour in the oil and continue to mix on medium speed. Turn the speed to low, begin adding the flour. When you have added 5 cups, remove the dough from the bowl and begin kneading on a floured surface, by hand. It is the best way to determine if you need additional flour (up to ½ cup) to form a smooth, elastic dough. Let the dough rest, covered, while you prepare the filling.

For the filling, peel, core and grate the apples on a box grater or with a food processor shredding disc.

Spoon the apples into a bowl and stir in the raisins, sugar and cinnamon. Toss to completely coat the apples. On a floured board, roll out a little more than half the dough, to fit the bottom of the baking dish. (Keeping the dish beside you as a reference will help you judge the size of the rolled dough more accurately.) Use the rolling pin to roll up the dough and carefully lay it in the bottom of the dish. Use your hands to evenly spread the dough, bringing it halfway up the sides of the dish and patching empty spots as needed with the excess dough you trim from the sides. Think of this as an edible arts and crafts project.

With an offset spatula, spread a thin layer of grape jelly on top of the dough. Sprinkle a light dusting of flour over the jelly and then spread the apple mixture, as you would pie filling. Roll out the remaining half of the dough and lay it on top of the apples. Smooth it out and cut off any excess. Press down lightly on the sides to form a seal around the edges. Sprinkle with the sugar & cinnamon topping. Lightly score the cake into 24 pieces and bake at 375 degrees for 1 hour, or until the top of the cake is golden brown. Allow the cake to cool completely allowing the juices to settle, before cutting all the way through.

Be sure you get the largest slice and a back rub. You've earned it!

Ruth Goldman Tobias

In her own words

Ruth Tobias is all about family and community. The day I met her, she was cooking for an Orthodox Jewish tradition called *Sheva Brochos*—Seven Blessings, when the bride and groom celebrate their nuptials for one week. Ruth is a creative cook and as a result of her internment in Italy during the war, has studied Italian cooking. I devoured her delicious *mandelbrot*, a recipe that will remain Ruth's secret. She did, however, share her story and several other wonderful recipes with me.

My parents both came from the same small city in Poland. My father, Avram, left pre-war Poland and headed to Germany to study. Sabina, my mother, came from an Orthodox family and also went to Germany. There they met and married. The mood in Germany was changing, and my father knew they had to relocate. He traveled to Italy to secure passage on an illegal ship to Palestine. In a twist of fate he met a man on the train who convinced him to go to Milan. My father took that man's advice and together my parents left Germany to settle in Italy. On June 10, 1940, Hitler and Mussolini made a pact and the following day the Allies bombed Milan. Shortly after the bombing, Sabina went into labor and I was born on the holiday of Shavuos, the 12th of June. A year later, my mother and I were sent to an internment camp in Potenza. My father was not home at the time and therefore continued to live in a "safe" house in Milan. Eventually he was arrested and sent to Italy's largest concentration camp, Ferramonti. After some time, my father was able to transfer to Potenza where we were reunited. Growing up in an internment camp seemed normal to me. There, I played with friends, lived simply but comfortably and remember cooking with my mother. Although we were under the protection of the Italian people, we held on to our Jewish traditions. We baked matzo on a big open fire and observed Passover and the other Jewish holidays.

Shortly after the Germans took control of Italy in September, 1943, our camp was dispersed and we were sent to a small town called Tito where several Jewish families were harbored. I remember the Italians being compassionate, and I am grateful to them for keeping us safe. We could have easily been transported to a death camp, but because of their protective nature, we were spared. The Canadians liberated us and the two things I remember were tasting chocolate and gum for the first time.

I know my upbringing was far from conventional, yet through the disruption and movement, I learned many things. I am very family-oriented because I felt so isolated growing up. I enjoy family gatherings and I cherish the traditions my parents imbued in me. Because of my love for Italy and the Italian people who saved me, I have spent time in Tuscany and Bologna learning to prepare the traditional Italian foods that I did not explore as a child. I prepare both the traditional Jewish specialties as well as my Italian dishes. But mostly, I learned how to look at life. My father always said, "cope with the problems that life brings and be thankful for what you have." I remember my Dad singing all the time and my Mom maintaining an amazingly positive outlook.

No one goes through life without disappointment; it is how you handle it that makes you who you are. I have tried to pass that philosophy on to my three children and three grandchildren.

Ruth Tobias' *Peperonata*–Bell Peppers

Certainly this flavorful and colorful recipe was influenced by Ruth's adopted home, Italy. It makes a lively side dish or delivers a wake-up call for your taste buds as a savory starter. Try tossing the vibrant peppers with rigatoni or ziti, for a sizzling hot dish, or chilling the peppers and pasta for a fiery summer salad.

Yields: 4 servings; Start to Finish: Under 1 hour

1 medium red onion, sliced

4 tablespoons olive oil

1 garlic clove, crushed

2 medium red bell peppers (about 1 pound), cored, seeded and cut into chunks

2 medium yellow peppers (about 1 pound), cored, seeded and cut into chunks

½ cup tomato sauce or 2 ripe plum tomatoes, peeled, seeded and diced

Kosher salt

Freshly ground black pepper

Basil, for garnish

Heat the oil, in a large skillet, cook and stir the onions, over medium heat, until lightly browned, about 10 minutes. Add the crushed garlic and cook for 5 minutes longer. Stir in the peppers, tomato sauce, salt and pepper, reduce the heat to low, cover and cook for 15 minutes. Uncover the skillet and cook 30 minutes longer. Garnish with fresh basil leaves.

Sabina Goldman's Bursting with Blueberries Tart

There are two kinds of blueberries, those that are shy and drawn and not really worth eating, and those that are so ripe with blueberry flavor that they are ready to burst out of their skin—those are the blueberries you want for this simply divine tart. Ruth's Mom, Sabina, added vinegar to the crust, which acts as a stabilizer and adds a subtle bite to balance the buttery flavor. The blueberries bubble and create their own sweet syrup.

Yields: About 8 servings; Start to Finish: Under 1½ hours

For the crust:

2 cups all-purpose flour

Pinch of salt

3 tablespoons sugar

1 cup (2 sticks) cold butter or margarine

2 tablespoons white vinegar

For the filling:

4 cups fresh blueberries

½ cup sugar

⅛ teaspoon ground cinnamon

2 tablespoons all-purpose flour

Garnish:

2 cups fresh blueberries

Confectioner's sugar

Preheat the oven to 400 degrees.

In a medium bowl, or in the bowl of a food processor fitted with the metal blade, combine the flour, salt and sugar. Using a pastry blender or in the processor, cut in the chilled butter and pulse or blend to form a crumb-like consistency. Allow bits of butter to remain visible, they melt and create steam during the baking process for a very tender and flaky crust. Sprinkle with vinegar and blend until you have created a soft dough.

With lightly floured hands, press the dough into a 9 x 2-inch spring form pan, or a 9 x 1-inch pie pan with a removable bottom. The crust should be about ¼-inch thick on the bottom; the sides should be a little thinner and come up about 1-inch (you might have some dough remaining). You can refrigerate the crust until ready to fill.

In a separate bowl, gently toss the filling ingredients. Spoon the filling into the pan and bake, on the lower rack, at 400 degrees for 1 hour. When the tart cools, garnish with blueberries and a sprinkling of confectioner's sugar.

Ruth Tobias' Orange Flavored Sponge Cake

Ruth's pure recipe will change your impression of sponge cake. Long considered the wallflower in the bakery, which you are obligated to buy for the holiday, this version is moist, citrusy and sweet. For a nice variation, the cake can be made with lemon juice and zest instead of orange.

Yields: 10 to 12 servings; Start to Finish: Under 1½ hours

6 eggs, separated

1 cup sugar

1 orange peel, zested

Juice of half an orange

1 cup all-purpose flour

1 teaspoon baking powder

Pinch of salt

Preheat the oven to 325 degrees.

Beat the yolks and sugar, in a large bowl, on medium speed, until light and fluffy. First zest (grate) the orange peel, and then squeeze it for the juice. Stir in the orange juice and grated peel. In a separate bowl, sift the flour and baking powder three times. Add the flour to the egg mixture, on low speed, and then beat for a minute or two on medium speed.

In a separate bowl, beat the egg whites with a pinch of salt until they are stiff but not dry. Gently fold the whites into the batter. Spoon the batter into an ungreased 9 x 3-inch tube spring form pan and bake at 325 degrees for 50 to 60 minutes. When done the top will be golden brown and a bamboo skewer inserted in the center should come out clean. To cool, invert the cake on a wire rack, and then remove from the pan. Sprinkle with a dusting of confectioner's sugar or garnish with candied orange peel.

Candied Orange Peel

Candied citrus peels make a beautiful and delicious garnish or dipped into melted chocolate become a sweet treat. Six lemon peels can be substituted for the three orange peels, if making the lemony version of Ruth's sponge cake.

Yields: 2 cups; Start to Finish: Under 2 hours, then several hours to overnight

3 large navel orange peels, cut into strips about ¼ to ½-inch thick (avoiding the bitter white pith)

1 cup granulated sugar (or ½ cup sugar plus ¼ cup honey)

3 tablespoons light corn syrup

Pinch of salt

¾ cup water

Garnish:

Superfine sugar or melted chocolate, (optional)

In a medium saucepan, cook the orange peels in enough water to cover. Bring to a boil and then cook over low heat for 20 to 30 minutes. Drain and repeat. You might need to do this several times until the peel is soft to the bite. Remove the peel. Heat the sugar (or honey and sugar), corn syrup, salt and water, in a medium saucepan, stirring to help dissolve the sugar. When the sugar is completely dissolved, add the peel. Lower the heat and cook the peels until the syrup has been reduced by at least half. Take the pot off the stove, cover and let the peels sit in the syrup for several hours or overnight so they can soak up the sweet flavor. Lay the peels on a piece of wax paper. Use as a garnish or roll them in super fine sugar or melted chocolate for an added layer of sweetness.

JFH

Hanna Kleiner Wechsler

In her own words

Hanna was one of my last interviews, and confirmed what I learned from my very first. Those willing to share their stories have an amazing spirit, an outlook on life that inspires and a perspective that we can all benefit from. Hanna began our conversation by saying, "If you overcome this, you can do anything. There are seven wonders in the world, I consider my survival the eighth." After speaking with her, and getting to know her well, I would have to agree!

I was born in my grandfather's house in Nowy Korczyn, a little town in Poland. I had a few nice years before the war, but my memory of those years is almost zilch. I was the first grandchild on either side and within a few years of my birth, it was unquiet in Poland. At first Polish people, for a very short time, hid us. We lived in their barn, underneath the floor. There were 11 people in a very small space. One night the lady of the house came down and told us that she felt her neighbors were suspicious, and that she could not keep us anymore. We left at night in order

Top left: Hanna, Mordechai, Rozalie Kleiner, 1945

not to give her away. We went to a place where the Jews were picked up in the morning to go to the Cracow ghetto. My whole family stayed there, with my parents going to work every morning. By some miracle one of my uncles got a connection to the outside; with money, you really could still be a little bit innovative and help yourself. My mother, Rozalia, looked like a 100% gentile woman; blonde hair, blue eyes, fair skin and very gutsy. There was a family meeting and my mother volunteered to go to our connection on the outside and obtain papers, so we could sneak out of the ghetto. Now we retell these things in a quiet way but at the time, this was all a matter of life and death. It was a hair-raising moment.

She boarded a tram where a German soldier said to her in German, "Please sit down young lady." She never stopped telling us where her heart was at that time, you can only imagine. She went to the address she had for the papers. At that time there were rumors that in Romania and Hungary the situation was not so bad and even Polish Jews were fleeing to those countries. Our new name was Koslovska. She came back with the papers and I remember all the time she was gone, praying, "Please let my Mommy come back." When I saw her you can imagine how happy I was, it was a happy, terrible feeling.

We got out, the whole group, sneaking out at night. One uncle who was extremely shrewd, smart and capable arranged for two men to act as guides who would help us cross into Czechoslovakia then to Romania and on into Hungary. Like when Moses took us out of Egypt, it worked. On the way, we lived on berries and water from the morning dew that collected on the leaves. The roads were extremely dangerous and hard to walk. I remember being carried on the shoulders of one my family members. We went out and crossed most of the borders, except when we came to Romania. The guides suddenly left us in no-man's land. We realized we didn't know where to go, we didn't know what to do. From out of nowhere, two shepherds showed up—they spoke Hungarian and Romanian, we spoke only Yiddish and Polish, but money was a common language. Guess what? They took us directly into a German police station. We were thrown into a prison, even though we claimed we were not Jewish.

Somehow, we got out, I don't remember how, and we lived for a short time in Hungary. We lived freely until they began collecting the Jews there. My mother and I were lucky. The guard at the prison where we were housed had a little more heart; I looked like his daughter, my mother looked like his wife. He never took advantage of my mother, which we feared he might. What did he do for us? Each time someone came in to transfer inmates, he would shuffle our papers underneath, so we were among the last to be shipped to Auschwitz. One day he disappeared, we suspected he had been sent to the Russian front as a punishment because he was too good to the Jews.

We were separated from my father; my mother and I were sent to a camp that had housed gypsies. It was liquidated in anticipation of the arrival of Hungarian Jews. We were also interned in Auschwitz where we spent about six to seven months. Every night my mother would sneak out of the barracks and go to a friend who

had stolen food from the kitchen. I always say that my mother gave birth to me every day we lived in Auschwitz, because without her I would not have survived. I also know that I gave her a reason to survive. She was my God and my angel that protected me always. Mother kept telling me all the time, not to be seen, not to be heard and to try and survive.

My father, Mordechai, was shipped to Dachau while the Russians freed my mother and me. We returned to Cracow after the war hoping to be reunited with my father and the rest of the family. We registered with an organization that tried to reunite families. While my father was sitting at a train station in Germany, an acquaintance from his hometown noticed him, looking so despondent and told him that my mother and I had survived. My father came to Poland to look for us. Meanwhile, we had notified the organization that we were living with a friend on Long Street, and a long street is what it was. Very much like Fifth Avenue, it went on forever. My father knew the name of the street, but not the number. He was determined to find us, but reluctant to give out our real name, as Poland was still so anti-Semitic. He asked everyone if they saw a blonde woman with heavy legs and a nine year-old daughter. For four days and nights, my father walked up that street going door to door and floor to floor. On the fourth day, at 5 a.m. he rang our bell; we thought it was the milkman. When my mother's friend opened the door, my mother heard my father's voice and fainted.

We returned to Germany, and then immigrated to Israel, where we had a very nice life. We always talked about Auschwitz; my mother never got over it. I married an American and I reluctantly left Israel and moved here in 1968. But, God was good to me—I have two daughters, two grandchildren and I am still married to my wonderful husband of 47 years. We moved to Paramus, New Jersey, which I have to admit, I thought was the sticks. I cooked very few things like my mother. I became a Hebrew teacher and a real estate agent and I enjoyed them both tremendously. I have had much *naches* in my life.

Since our last printing, I sadly learned that Hanna's husband, Harry, passed away. We extend our sincerest condolences to his devoted family. May his memory be a blessing.

Left: Hanna Kleiner, Chanukah, 1945

Hanna Wechsler's Strawberry Filled *Naleshniki*–Blintzes

Hanna Wechsler spoke lovingly of her mother's blintzes, a cross between a thin crepe and a traditional blintz. She recalled her mom filling them quite simply with strawberry preserves, chopped nuts and a touch of sugar. Hanna proudly says, "this recipe has continuity, it has endured for four generations." Pair it with Florence Tabrys' blintz recipe (see page 139), for a sweet variation and top with the strawberry sauce (recipe follows).

Yields: About 1 cup of filling; Start to Finish: Under 15 minutes

1 cup strawberry preserves

¼ to ½ cup chopped almonds or walnuts; your choice

1 teaspoon sugar, more or less to taste

Combine all three ingredients in a bowl and use as filling.

Strawberry Sauce

While Hanna's mother served her blintzes with fresh fruit, a pureed strawberry sauce is a colorful topping and helps bring out the strawberry goodness packed inside the blintz.

Yields: 2 cups; Start to Finish: Under 30 minutes

1 (16-ounce) bag frozen strawberries

3 tablespoons sugar

¼ cup water

1 teaspoon cornstarch

Juice and grated peel of half a lemon

In a medium saucepan, cook the strawberries, sugar, water and cornstarch, over medium-low heat, until the berries are very soft, about 15 minutes. Puree the berries and stir in the lemon juice and grated peel. Serve hot or cold over blintzes, cake or ice cream. The sauce will hold for 1 to 2 weeks in the fridge. You can also follow the same preparation if using frozen blueberries or raspberries.

JFH

Michael Solomonov

Professional contributor

There is nothing quite like fresh homemade Israeli hummus, just ask anyone, like Hanna, who has spent time in Israel. Before opening his popular Philadelphia restaurant, Chef Solomonov took his staff to Israel for inspiration. One day, they visited five hummus parlors. He spent months perfecting his signature dish, and he points out that "Americans have this misconception that hummus is strongly lemony and garlicky or worse that it comes in lots of flavors. Israelis don't do flavors." Here is his straightforward, smooth and creamy, perfectly flavored hummus that you can easily replicate at home, even if your home is in Paramus, New Jersey!

Tehina-Hummus

Contributed by Chef Michael Solomonov of Zahav restaurant, Philadelphia

Serves 6

1 pound dry chickpeas

1 tablespoon baking soda

1 whole head of garlic with the skin on, plus one clove with the germ removed

2 ounces of fresh-squeezed lemon juice

12 ounces un-hulled sesame paste

4 ounces extra virgin olive oil (preferably from Lebanon or Israel)

Kosher salt

Ground cumin, to taste

¼ cup Italian parsley, chopped

Paprika (preferably sweet, smoked Spanish paprika)

Cover the chickpeas and baking soda with at least double their volume of water and soak, refrigerated, for 18 hours. Drain the chickpeas and rinse thoroughly in cold water. Place the chickpeas in a large pot with the whole head of garlic and cover with water. Bring the water to a boil and reduce the heat to low. Simmer the chickpeas over low heat for approximately three hours, or until very tender. Drain the chickpeas, reserving one cup of the cooking liquid. Discard the garlic bulb.

In the bowl of a food processor, add the sesame paste and the cooked chickpeas. Puree the mixture with the olive oil and lemon juice, adding enough reserved cooking liquid to achieve a smooth, creamy consistency. Season to taste with kosher salt and ground cumin. Garnish with extra virgin olive oil, chopped parsley and paprika.

Feedback
Tehina (also called *tahini* or sesame paste) has a taste similar to peanut butter, and a consistency to match. In Middle Eastern homes, *tahini* is used like peanut butter as a spread, a dip or to enhance other dishes. It is available in most supermarkets; look in the aisle with Asian/Middle Eastern foods or where the condiments are found. If your market does not stock it, you can find it in a Middle Eastern specialty market. While the chef feels this recipe serves 6, as a dip it can feed an army.

Jennifer Abadi

Professional contributor

What better way to enjoy homemade hummus than with homemade pita. Jennifer Abadi, an expert in Syrian and Middle Eastern cooking, guides us through the steps to making homemade pocket pita. I am not saying it is as easy as a trip to the store, but it certainly tastes more authentic.

Chibiz–Syrian Pita or Pocket Bread

Excerpted from A Fistful of Lentils: Syrian-Jewish Recipes from Grandma Fritzie's Kitchen, by Jennifer Abadi (© 2002, used by permission from The Harvard Common Press)

The pocket this bread forms when baking makes it perfect for sandwiches or scooping up all kinds of meats and dips. Fresh or toasted, you'll enjoy this low-calorie bread found everywhere in the Middle East.

3 teaspoons active dry yeast

2 ½ cups warm water

1 tablespoon honey or sugar

1 tablespoon vegetable oil

6 cups enriched white bread flour

2 teaspoons salt

In a small bowl, combine the yeast, ½ cup of the warm water, and the honey. Let stand until slightly frothy, about 5 minutes. Add the oil and mix.

In a large bowl, combine the flour and salt. Make a well in the center of the flour and pour the yeast mixture into it, mixing it into the flour with a wooden spoon. Add the remaining 2 cups warm water, ½ cup at a time. Shape the dough into a sticky ball and knead on a clean, well-floured work surface until very smooth and elastic, a good 10 minutes (add more flour as needed, a little at a time, if your dough is too sticky to knead).

Place the dough in a greased glass or plastic bowl and cover with a towel. Let rest in a warm place for 1½ hours to rise and double in size.

Knead the dough on a floured surface for another 10 minutes (again, adding flour as needed) and roll it into a tube about 1 foot long and about 3 ½ to 4 inches in diameter. Using a sharp knife, mark 16 equal lines on the roll of dough, then break the dough into 16 pieces of equal size and roll each into a ball.

On the same floured surface, roll out each ball with a rolling pin or tall glass until the dough is ¼ inch thick and 6 inches in diameter, resembling a small pizza. Place each rolled-out piece of dough on a floured piece of foil cut to the same size as a baking sheet, 4 to 5 at a time, until all 16 have been made.

Cover the flattened dough pieces with a kitchen towel and let them rise in a warm spot for another 2 hours. (At this point, preheat the oven to 550 degrees for 2 hours. It is important to get the oven temperature as high as possible so that each pita bakes quickly and forms a pocket.)

(Continued)

Carefully lift up one sheet of foil with the risen dough pieces and place on a baking sheet. Bake on the middle rack in the oven for 4 to 5 minutes. *Do not open the oven more than a crack until you see the bread puff up.* Take the sheet out and remove the baked pita breads, placing them in a basket and covering them with a clean cloth to keep warm. Discard the used foil and transfer another sheet of unbaked pieces to the baking sheet. Continue to bake in this manner, one sheet at a time, until all the pitas are baked.

Serve immediately alongside any *maazeh* salad or spread or as a sandwich with *ijeh* (spiced patties or omelets) in its pocket. These really don't stay soft and fresh past a day, but if you have a lot leftover, store them in a Ziploc plastic bag for up to 2 days on the counter or 1 week in the freezer, toasting them in the oven when needed.

Rachela Introligator Weisstuch and Victor Weisstuch

As told by their son Mark Weisstuch

Mark, a Jewish scholar, retells his parent's story with great precision and love.

My parents were married in 1935 and living in Dabrowa, southwestern Poland, with their two daughters, Sarah and Hannah, when World War II began. Within a week of the Nazi invasion, their area was over-run. My father was taken to numerous forced labor camps. In one, which served as a construction site, he befriended a German worker. They developed a relationship and my father asked him if he would be willing to find my mother, to give her a message and retrieve supplies from her. For several months, this German laborer was a go-between for my parents. My mother remained at home with her two children until mid-1943 when she, her two

children, her sister and her daughter were taken to the Srodula ghetto. There they hid in a cellar for several months. On January 13, 1944, they were all put on the last transport out of the ghetto and were sent to Birkenau; it was the last time she saw her daughters. In winter of 1944-1945, the Germans evacuated Birkenau, and my mother and aunt were force marched into the German heartland and eventually ended up in Bergen-Belsen. They were liberated from that camp by the British army in April, 1945.

Bergen-Belsen became a DP camp and my mother and aunt stayed there to recuperate. My father, learning they had survived, journeyed to Bergen-Belsen to find them. He continued his journey and eventually found my mother. After she recovered, they stopped in one town and were walking in the street and chatting in Yiddish. They used the Yiddish word for spoon, loffel. Three guys who were following behind them inquired who they were and where they were from. They said, "I knew a guy in the camp who used the word spoon in the same dialect as you." They discovered that these strangers were talking about my father's brother, Karl. That's how they learned that my uncle was alive. They settled in Münchberg, Germany, where I was born. It was a Yiddish household, like a little shtetl. My mother cooked Jewish, which is, of course, Polish. There is no such thing as Jewish food, matzo is the only real Jewish food, and the rest is all borrowed, adapted and adopted from other countries. My parents and I came to New York in 1949. One distinct memory I have is that whenever my parents got together with their friends, all of whom were survivors, they always ended up meandering into and focusing on their war experiences. I would remember often hearing it, like music playing in the background. My parents were married 58 years, had one more child and two grandchildren.

Top left: Victor and Rachela Weisstuch, Münchberg, 1946

Chilled Cherry Soup

Mark remembers a time his family visited Poland. They were in Galicia and stopped at a roadside restaurant for lunch. They served cold cherry soup. "I ate this soup and said, 'oh my, this is what my mother used to make'. This extraordinary cold cherry soup is what my mother made as a dessert or entree. This is exactly the same thing." This recipe replicates that memory and captures the tart and sweet flavor of the black cherries in a cold soup balanced by sour cream and lemon.

Yields: 4 to 6 servings; Start to Finish: Under 30 minutes, then time to chill

2 packages frozen black cherries, thawed with their juice

1 cup bottled cherry juice (red wine can be substituted)

Juice of 1 lemon

1 cinnamon stick

¼ cup of sugar

1 cup sour cream

¼ cup heavy cream

In a medium saucepan, simmer the cherries with their juice, 1 cup of water, bottled cherry juice, lemon juice (throw in the lemon), cinnamon stick and sugar. (If using red wine, simmer separately in a small saucepan to allow the alcohol to evaporate, then add to the soup in place of the cherry juice.) Cover and cook over medium heat until the cherries are soft, about 15 minutes. If the soup is too tart, add additional sugar and continue to simmer. If too sweet, add more water or lemon juice. When the cherries are soft, remove the lemon and cinnamon stick. Ladle two-thirds of the soup into a blender and process until smooth. Combine the pureed and un-pureed soup and chill in a large sealed container for several hours or overnight until very cold. Remove from the fridge, and stir in the sour cream. Ladle the soup into individual bowls. Gently swirl a spoonful of heavy cream into the bowl to create a white ribbon in the pink soup; the presentation is beautiful.

JFH

Eva Young

In her own words

I met with Eva and her husband Julius in their New York apartment. I juggled my notebook while sipping delicious peppery cabbage soup. I peered into Eva's fridge and saw the wonderful array of foods she had prepared. Her New York City kitchen is stocked with all the best ingredients and a recipe file filled with traditional Polish and Hungarian dishes that all have the Eva touch. Her life has been filled with remarkable moments, all contributing to the independent and accomplished woman she is today.

I was born to an affluent family in Wisla, Poland. I remember a childhood filled with holiday meals, stuffed Cornish hens and home-baked challah. I also remember the day my father hollowed out a tooth and hid a diamond inside it. He told me it was for me to use one day to save my life. In 1942, when I was 15, I was a prisoner working in a Polish labor camp manufacturing weapons. I knew I could not survive much longer, so I used the diamond to bribe a guard. I shared the proceeds with another prisoner and I feel that saved his life as well. Three years later, as we were marched through the woods of Germany, I escaped and found safety in a farmhouse where I met other girls who were in hiding. I only had my uniform to wear, so one of the girls gave me a sheet, from which I made a skirt. That skirt survived with me and is now part of the Museum's collection.

After the war, I went to Holland, arriving in May of 1945. We were transported along with returning Dutch soldiers, and Queen Wilhemena was there to greet them. Our picture was taken for public relations posters, as we were the first survivors to arrive in Holland. I also helped rescue and transfer children to Israel, where I eventually immigrated. Because I was multi-lingual and had weaponry experience during the war, I was recruited to work with the Israeli brigade in developing among other things, the Molotov cocktail. Even my husband did not know the secretive and sensitive nature of my work. On a family trip to America, my husband became ill and died, leaving me with two children in a new and unfamiliar country. I chose to stay here and began taking classes and eventually received a degree in business. I accepted a job as a jewelry buyer for all of the Klein's department stores. I had a good business sense, and developed a strategy to increase sales. I would collect small deposits on merchandise and hold the jewelry until it was paid in full. When my boss came to my counter to see what I was doing, I showed him how I put-away jewelry and collected small weekly payments. I suppose you can say that I invented the layaway!

I was promoted and given tremendous responsibility, which weighed heavily on me. I couldn't sleep at night. What was I going to do? So, I would head into the kitchen and come up with all sorts of ideas about cooking. I developed my own taste, which brought back memories from my mother. If I'm going to relax, I'm going into the kitchen, because cooking is a huge part of my life. I met my husband, Julius, when I was a jewelry buyer and he was a jewelry manufacturer. During the war, as a Hungarian citizen, Julius served in the army and was captured, along with German soldiers, and become a Russian prisoner of war. After three years as a POW, Julius made his way to America.

I love to be inventive with my cooking. Whatever I cook is in one pot or one dish. Everyone is unique; cooking helps me share with people. I have been married to Julius for 37 years and we have two children, six grandchildren and seven great grandchildren.

Since completing the book, I sadly learned that Julius passed away. We extend our sincerest condolences to his devoted family. May his memory be a blessing.

Eva Young's Creamy Cheese Noodle *Kugel*

"She makes the best noodle *kugel*," exclaims Eva's husband, Julius. Eva adds several secret ingredients, like sour cream, and whipped egg whites, but the crowning glory is the buttery baked graham cracker topping. Warm or cold, it makes a sweet ending, a luscious starter or a terrific mid-day nosh.

Yields: Servings vary depending on how you cut the kugel, but Eva wants you to know, it feeds a big family; Start to Finish: Under 1½ hours

For the noodles:

1 (12-ounce) package uncooked broad noodles

6 tablespoons (¾ stick) butter

6 eggs, separated

1 (8-ounce) package cream cheese, softened

1 (16-ounce) container small-curd cottage cheese

1 pint (8 ounces) sour cream

1 teaspoon vanilla extract

½ cup sugar

For the topping:

⅔ cups crushed graham crackers (about 8 crackers)

½ cup sugar

1 stick (½ cup) butter, melted

Preheat the oven to 350 degrees and lightly grease 13x9x2-inch baking dish.

Put a large pot of lightly salted water to boil, and cook the noodles according to package directions, drain. Return the drained noodles to the pot and stir in the butter. In a separate bowl, beat the egg yolks, cream cheese, cottage cheese, sour cream, vanilla and sugar, on medium speed, until light and fluffy. Stir the egg mixture into the noodles.

In a separate bowl, beat the 6 egg whites until stiff but not dry. Gently fold the egg whites into the noodles. Pour the noodles into the prepared baking dish.

Prepare the topping by mixing together the three ingredients. Sprinkle the topping over the noodles and bake at 350 degrees for 1 hour, or until the top is lightly browned.

Abraham and Millie Zuckerman

Based on Abe's memoir

Drive through numerous New Jersey housing developments and you might notice an interesting trend with regard to the names of many of the streets. They all honor Oskar Schindler, who was responsible for saving the lives of 1200 Jewish men, women and children. These street names would seem curious unless you knew the story behind the men who developed those communities. In his moving memoir, *A Voice in the Chorus; Memories of a Teenager Saved By Schindler,* Abraham Zuckerman recounts his good fortune of being a "Schindler Jew" and how he survived the Holocaust. The following is based on details described in his memoir and conversations with his son-in-law.

Abe was born in Cracow, Poland in 1924. He was fourteen years old when the war came to his beloved homeland. Abe recounts watching in horror as his parents and two sisters were taken by the Nazis. Abe managed to flee and stayed with a farmer in Wieliczka. He was chased by the Nazis on numerous occasions and was sent to several work camps. Eventually, he was sent to Plaszow work camp where he was reunited with

his childhood friend, Murray Pantirer. Together they were selected to work in Oskar Schindler's enamelware factory. Abe describes Schindler as "a living saint." He recalls how Schindler greeted Abe when he saw him and how he was immaculately dressed and had a protective, fatherly feeling. "He was very handsome, like a statesman; with him I felt I might survive." In August, 1944, Abe was moved from Plaszow to Mauthausen, where two American soldiers liberated him in May, 1945.

Following his liberation, Abe spent four years in a displaced persons camp in Bindermichel, Austria. It was there that he met and married Millie, his life partner for more than 60 years. Millie, also, had a protector—a Polish woman, Michalina Kedra. Before the war, Michalina had been a patron of the grocery store owned by Millie's Dad. The Nazis liquidated the entire town of Humniska, where Millie was born and raised. For two years, Millie, her sister and their parents hid above a trap door in Michalina's barn, never seeing the light of day. It was in Bindermichel that Abe and Millie began a new life. After their liberation and immigration to the United States, the Zuckermans stayed in touch with Schindler and hosted him many times. Abe and Murray, who became business partners, were especially proud to drive him through their developments and show him the more than twenty-five streets named in his honor.

There was never a festive meal that ended without her handmade sugar cookies. To this day, her three children, ten grandchildren and three great grandchildren enjoy them.

Top left: Millie and Abe Zuckerman in DP camp, Bindermichel, Austria

Millie Zuckerman's Sugar Cookies

While Millie's cookies are a nice blend of ingredients, her family feels "The most important ingredients included in Millie's cookies are her love, sweetness and kindness." A nice sprinkling of sugar gives the cookies a sweet crunch, but we are sure Millie wouldn't mind if you indulged in sprinkles, shredded coconut or ground nuts. For an extra kick, grate 2 tablespoons of orange peel into the dough. This is a very soft dough, which is why this cookie doesn't crumble, so work quickly and do not over roll it or it will become too hard to handle.

Yields: About 5 dozen 2-inch cookies; Start to Finish: Step One: Under 30 minutes, then refrigerate at least 6 hours or up to 24, Step Two: Under 30 minutes

½ pound (2 sticks) margarine, room temperature

2 egg yolks

¾ cup sugar

½ cup orange juice

1 teaspoon vanilla

3 cups all-purpose flour

1 tablespoon baking powder

Granulated or sanding sugar for topping

Step One: Beat the margarine, egg yolks and sugar, in a large bowl, on medium speed, until smooth and creamy, about 3 minutes. Slowly pour in the orange juice and vanilla. The liquids will cause the mixture to separate, so continue beating and scraping down the sides until they are well incorporated. In a separate bowl, sift together the flour and baking powder. With the mixer on low speed, add the flour to the butter mixture and beat on medium speed, until all the ingredients are well combined. Divide the dough in half, flatten each into a disc and wrap tightly in wax paper. Refrigerate 6 hours or overnight.

Step Two: Preheat the oven to 350 degrees, lightly grease a large baking sheet, and have sugar ready to sprinkle on top of the cut cookies.

Remove one piece of dough from the fridge and cut it in half (it's easier to roll). Place the remaining dough back in the fridge. Lightly flour a work surface, and roll the dough to ¼-inch thick. Using a cookie cutter, or the rim of a glass, cut the dough into the desired size and shape. Gather and re-roll the scraps. If the dough is too soft, place it back in the fridge. Place the cookies on the prepared baking sheet and sprinkle with sugar (or your choice of topping), and then gently pat down to help the topping adhere. Bake at 350 degrees for about 10 to 12 minutes, or until the cookies are a light golden color with lightly brown tinged sides. Repeat with the remaining dough, or freeze the dough (wrapped tightly, thaw before baking) for later use.

Feedback

This same dough makes a terrific foundation for *hamantashen*. Following the same procedure as above, have preserves (see Katherine's recipe on page 282) or your choice of filling ready to dollop in the center. Cut the dough into 3-inch rounds. Place a teaspoon of filling in the center, then pinch the dough to form the 3-points (the corners of Haman's hat). Bake as directed above. Yields about 3 dozen cookies.

Artifacts

Artifacts tell the stories that words sometimes cannot. They are pieces of history with a time and place, which have been lovingly preserved and protected by the generations that followed. The Museum of Jewish Heritage hopes to insure their legacy and give voice to what came before. Unless otherwise noted, all artifacts in this section are from the collection of the Museum of Jewish Heritage—A Living Memorial to the Holocaust. For a more extensive view of the Museum's collection we invite you to explore their database at: www.mjhnyc.org and click on Exhibitions and Collections.

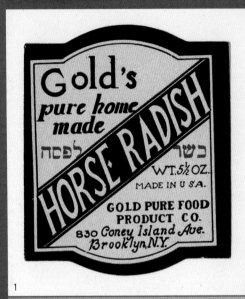

1. Label designed for Gold's first bottle of horseradish; Gift of Pure Food Products Company, Inc. 2. Bowl from Germany, used to hold salt water at the Passover seder; Gift of Edith Riemer 3. Fleishmann's yeast tin.

4. Copper, wood and steel meat cleaver from Poland; Gift of Harry Benet 5. DP camp photo 6. Silver kiddush cup brought to the Chechelnik Ghetto in the Ukraine by Berl and Lota Landau who were deported from Bukovina; Gift of Iser Volkhovitser in memory of Perl Volkhovitser. 7. Wooden spoon from Bergen-Belsen; Gift of Erna Rock, Yaffa Eliach Collection donated by the Center for Holocaust Studies.

8. Silver kiddush cups kept by Leah Kats in the Shargorod Ghetto; Gift of Arkady Aleksandrovsky in memory of Basya Basenkis. 9. Round cutter used to cut rolled dough; Gift of Rabbi W. Gunther and Elizabeth S. Plaut. 10. This metal cooking pot made its journey from Germany to America; Gift of Rabbi W. Gunther and Elizabeth S. Plaut. 11. Rosh Hashanah menu for Jews interned as enemy aliens on the Isle of Man. Gift of Robert R. Frankel.

12. Large spoon from Auschwitz; Gift of Sugar siblings in memory of Rosenfeld & Schwartz families. 13. Black and white print advertisement devised by Morris Gold for Gold's Borscht. Gift of Gold Pure Food Products Company, Inc. 14. Silver Kiddush cup of Richard Oppenheimer, Hanover, Germany, 1863 Gift of Lili Fischer.

15

16

17

18

15. Cookbook designed for new immigrants to Palestine, c, 1930. 16. Engraved pewter seder plate; Gift of Lilly Teitelbaum. 17. A typical funnel cake pan; Gift of Rabbi W. Gunther and Elizabeth S. Plaut. 18. Salted herring recipe book; Gift of Rabbi W. Gunther and Elizabeth S. Plaut.

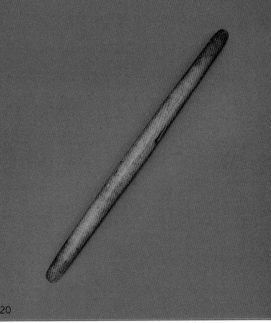

19. A simple noodle maker; Collection of the Museum of Jewish Heritage-A Living Memorial to the Holocaust, NYC. 20. Simple wooden tapered rolling pin; Gift of Stephen S. Bressler. 21. Workers in the kitchen at the Foehrenwald displaced persons camp, 1946; Gift of Evelyn Cohen.

22

23

24

22. "Krigel," a pot used to buy fresh milk from farmers, Poland, 1920s; Gift of Ruth Metzger Bader. 23. Joke Hanukkah menu, Isle of Man. Dishes marked with x cannot be served because the kitchen ran out of them. Gift of Robert R. Frankel. 24. Silver challah knife with Hebrew inscription "to honor the Sabbath;" Gift of Rabbi W. Gunther and Elizabeth S. Plaut.

Germany and Austria

The food of Germany and Austria has always been influenced by its geographic location. The result is a flavorful blending of both Western and Eastern European cuisine. French influences are especially felt in southwestern Germany, where several of our survivors were born. Their recipes reflect a sophisticated style of cooking and ingredients that have a French flare. Rich chocolate, slow marinades and the restrained use of sweet, balanced by sour, are elements borrowed from their Polish and Czech neighbors, and can be seen in many preparations from the contributors of this region.

German and Austrian cooks brought many of their cooking traditions with them to America, but none have left as firm an imprint on the culinary landscape as their cakes and pastries. Buttery streusel, mürbeteig dough and twice-baked *Mandelbrot* were all popularized in this region and can still be found in every local bakery today.

Because Germany and Austria experienced a wave of emigration as unrest began to build, we have a number of contributors who found themselves as refugees, with one foot firmly planted on safe soil and another tenaciously grounded in the rich culture they left behind. The result was a curious melding of culinary customs that you will find interesting and unexpected.

We invite you to prepare and enjoy the varied and creative recipes remembered by our stouthearted contributors from Germany and Austria.

RECIPES

Inge Auerbacher: *Weincreme*–Whipped Topping

Edith Hamburger Blumenthal: Chocolate Macaroons

Edith Hamburger Blumenthal: *Streuselkuchen*–Crumb Cake

Ruth Eggener: Braised Sauerbraten–Marinated Roast with Chunky Applesauce, Mushroom and Onion Stuffing

Reni Hanau: *Waffeln*–Waffles

Reni Hanau: Winter Celeriac (Celery Root) Salad

Ellen Katz: Veal Marengo

Ellen Katz: Apricot Squares

Ruth Kohn: *Arroz con Pollo*–Chicken with Rice

Ruth Kohn: Fried *Platanos*–Fried Plantains

Miriam Margulies: *Palatschinken*–Thin Pancakes

Miriam Margulies: Sweet and Sour Red Cabbage

Marsha Meyer: Fruit-Filled *Knodels*–Dumplings

Marsha Meyer: German Potato Salad

Gisela Obernbreit: *Wiener Schnitzel*–Breaded Veal Cutlets

Gisela Obernbreit: *Gluwein* - Mulled Wine

Ruth Obernbreit: *Tres Leches*–Three Milk Cake

Ruth Obernbreit: *Café con Leche*–Coffee with Warmed Milk

Ruth Orvieto: Risotto

Ruth Orvieto: *Gnocchi Alla Romana*–Semolina Gnocchi with Cheese

Judy Prussin: Spiked *Mandel* Bread

Wolfie Rauner: *Matzo Kloesse*–Matzo Dumplings

Henny Bachrach: Almond and Apple Cake

Melly Resnicow: Chocolate Roll

Evelyn Pike Rubin: Sweet Summer Peach Cake

Doris Schechter: Blackout Cake

Ruth Schloss: *Spaetzle* with Cooked Dried Fruit

Helen Wallerstein: Potato *Latkes*

Helen Wallerstein: *Gesundheit Kuchen*–Chocolate Cake

Dr. Ruth Westheimer: Celebration Cake

PROFESSIONAL CONTRIBUTORS

Daniel Boulud: Tender Beef with Horseradish, Parsnips, and Celery Root

JFH: *Schlagzahne*–Whipped Cream

JFH: Celery Root and Apple Salad

JFH: Gruenkern Soup with Mini Turkey Meatballs

JFH: Parsley Red Bliss Potatoes

JFH: Chocolate Ganache

Mark Schachner: Tongue Polonaise

Jonathan Waxman: Sweet Onion Tart

Inge Auerbacher

In her own words

Inge is an author, a lecturer and an activist for human rights. She has been awarded numerous honors for her work. She is the recipient of the Ellis Island Medal of Honor, Woman of Distinction Award, given by the New York State Senate, the Louis E. Yavner Citizen Award, and an honorary Doctor of Humane Letters from Long Island University. She is the author of six books. In her first book, *I am a Star,* Inge writes, "We must speak out against evil and injustice. Let us build bridges of understanding and love to join mankind in every land. My hope, my wish, and prayer is for every child to grow up in peace without hunger and prejudice."

I was the last Jewish child born in Kippenheim, a small village located in the southwestern portion of Germany. My father's family had lived there for over 200 years, and our house still stands today. Although I was only three years old during Kristallnacht, I remember it very clearly. After being detained in Dachau for several weeks, my grandfather and father were released, and we chose to go to Jebenhausen, an even tinier village of only one thousand people, to live with my grandparents, who were the only remaining Jewish family in that town. My grandmother was a wonderful cook and I remember eating many dishes that you would associate with Swabian (southern German) cooking. Albert Einstein's family once owned the bakery in the village where we brought our challahs and cakes to be baked in their ovens. Because my hometown, Kippenheim, was near Alsace, our food was influenced by French cuisine. My grandmother was deported to Riga in 1941, and we were moved to a designated Jewish house, where we stayed until August, 1942, when my parents and I were deported to Terezin.

Above: Inge, holding her favorite doll, with her family .

While we were imprisoned in Terezin, the International Red Cross requested permission to inspect a camp. The Nazis chose Terezin for that purpose. Certain parts of the camp were cleaned up. Some people were given new clothing and good food to eat. A few children received chocolates and sardine sandwiches just as the commission walked past them. I was not one of the lucky ones. The International Red Cross inspection team left the camp believing the immense deception that Terezin was a "model" place for Jews to live. The truth was, conditions in Terezin were very harsh and of the 15,000 children imprisoned there between 1941 and 1945, a very small number survived. I was one of them. I spent three birthdays there. One year I received a potato cake the size of my palm, prepared from a mashed boiled potato with just a hint of sugar in it. Another year my doll Marlene, that survived Terezin with me, was given a new outfit sewn from rags. On my tenth birthday my gift was a poem my mother had written especially for me.

Miraculously, on May 8, 1945, the Soviet army liberated us. The first thing we did was rip off the yellow star from our clothes. All of us felt joy, pain and relief. We first went to a DP camp, then back to Jebenhausen to look for surviving family members. When we arrived in Jebenhausen, we faced the awful truth. Grandma and twelve other family members had not survived. The new owners of grandma's house prepared a room for us. Our return after so many years was greeted by a vase filled with field flowers, which stood on the table.

We soon found more permanent living quarters in the neighboring town of Göppingen. The mayor invited us to visit him at City Hall. As soon as we stepped into the mayor's office Mama noticed the oriental carpet—it was ours. The mantel clock had a familiar chime, it too, had once been our property. Our new home became a familiar place for the American soldiers to stop by. They showered us with personal goods and candy. Some ran with their melting ice cream rations to our home so that I could have a special treat. To my knowledge, there were only two Jewish child survivors who had been in concentration camps who were now in the state of Württemberg. I spent my eleventh birthday there; it was a sensation.

Life slowly returned to normal again, but it was still lonely. We took the first opportunity we could to immigrate to America, in May, 1946. We arrived in New York harbor at night. I stood in awe of the blinking lights of Manhattan, which seemed like a wonderland to me. Lady Liberty was especially bright as her lamp's light welcomed and guided us to a new life. The next morning we disembarked just as the sun rose on a new day. In America, after I spent a few years fighting a serious sickness that I contracted in the camp, I was able to continue my education and not only graduated high school and college, but did post graduate work in biochemistry. Since 1981, my mission has been to educate children about the Holocaust, which I have tried to do in all my books and in several documentaries that tell my story.

Inge Auerbacher's *Weincreme*–Whipped Topping

This custard-style preparation that Inge enjoyed every year as a Passover topping for nut torte (see Henny Bachrach's and Dr. Ruth Westheimer's recipes on pages 219, 235), combines wine, sugar and a subtle lemon kick. Substitute apple juice or grape juice for the wine to create a child-friendly holiday treat.

Yields: 2 to 3 cups; Start to Finish: Under 30 minutes

1 cup dry white wine

3 tablespoons sugar

2 eggs, separated

Juice of 1 lemon

½ teaspoon grated lemon zest

1 teaspoon vanilla extract

2 tablespoons potato starch (1 tablespoon corn starch can be used for non-Passover preparation)

In the top of a double boiler, over gently simmering water, combine the wine, sugar, egg yolks, lemon juice, zest and 1 cup of water. Whisk until the mixture begins to thicken and develops a custard-like consistency, about 15 minutes.

Combine the potato starch with ½ cup of water and stir until you create smooth slurry. Slowly pour the slurry into the wine mixture, continuing to whisk so they custard thickens but does not clump. When the custard is thick like pudding, remove from the heat and cool.

When the mixture is cool and you are ready to serve, whip the egg whites, in a medium bowl, until stiff but not dry. Gently but thoroughly fold the egg whites into the mixture. Always stir up from the bottom to incorporate all the ingredients. Serve at once to prevent the whites from loosening and settling.

Feedback
To test when a custard or pudding preparation is thick enough try a technique called "coating the back of a spoon." Take a large spoon, wooden works best, and dip the flat side into the mixture. Run your finger down the middle of the back of the spoon. If your finger leaves a trail, like the parting of the Red Sea, and the coating does not fill in the line, the custard is ready.

Jonathan Waxman

Professional contributor

While talking to Inge about her food memories, she described several dishes that have stayed with her over the years. One favorite is a sweet but salty onion tart that her grandmother would make, and for which Inge no longer had a recipe. Jonathan Waxman, one of America's best chefs, guides us in preparing his version of this established dish rooted in Alsace Lorraine, Inge's childhood backyard.

Sweet Onion Tart

Excerpted from A Great American Cook: Recipes from the Home Kitchen of one of our most Influential Chefs (Houghton Mifflin, September 2007)

The onion tarts I encountered in Europe were light, tasty, and delicious. The versions I had eaten in America were leaden, coarse, and often the pastry wasn't cooked through. The best of the versions in Europe were the ones made with puff pastry or semi-puff pastry. I decided to create a version as light as the European tarts. Not wanting to reinvent the wheel, I played around with an even lighter and fluffier tart that used fewer eggs and little cream. The trick was to extract as much liquid and flavor from the onions as possible without losing the texture components. This light but tasty tart tastes complex—with just six ingredients.

Yields: 6 servings

3 Maui onions, or other sweet onions, such as Vidalia or Walla Walla

2 tablespoons butter

½ cup balsamic vinegar

Salt and freshly ground black pepper

½ pound puff pastry

2 large eggs

½ cup heavy cream

Thyme blossoms, or 1 teaspoon fresh thyme leaves

Slice the onions crosswise as thinly as possible. Place a large skillet over very low heat. Add the butter, and when it melts, stir in the onions. Cook, stirring, for 30 minutes. Add the vinegar and cook until it's reduced, about 5 minutes. Let the mixture cool, and then season with salt and pepper.

Heat the oven to 400 degrees. Roll out the puff pastry as thinly as possible. Fit the pastry into an 8-inch tart pan. Dock the pastry by poking it all over with the tines of a fork. Bake the bare pastry for 25 minutes or until dark golden brown, especially the bottom crust. Don't be afraid that the tart will burn later when it is filled—the filling will prevent that from happening.

Whisk the eggs lightly in a bowl, and add salt and pepper. When the pastry has browned properly, take it out of the oven and let it cool for 10 minutes. Spread the onion mixture evenly into the tart shell. Add the cream and the thyme blossoms or thyme leaves to the whisked eggs, blend well, and then pour the mixture over the onions. Stir gently with a fork. Don't worry about mixing it perfectly. Bake the tart for 25 minutes or until just set. Remove and let the tart cool. Serve warm or at room temperature.

Edith Hamburger Blumenthal and Siggi Blumenthal

In her own words

Despite upheaval as a child and medical setbacks as an adult, Edith demonstrates a quiet inner strength and a gentle resolve. But the true measure of this woman was the love, respect and devotion shown to her by her youngest son, David, who joined in the interview, and her older son, Michael who participated via speakerphone. Humor permeated every aspect of our conversation, and together we marveled at Edith's organizational skills and keen memory.

My great-uncle Felix Levy was the second youngest of eight children born to my grandmother. Years before the war, a relative visiting from America suggested to my grandparents that they send Felix back with him to the United States. Felix was unmarried and it seemed like a good idea. It wasn't until the 1930s that we realized what a good idea it really was. In 1938, on the night of Kristallnacht, in our town of Hanau, Germany, many of the men were taken to a work camp. My father, Julius Hamburger, was one of those men taken. Oddly enough, among the things he took with him was a document that said he had served in the First World War on the German side. It was just a coincidence that he had that with him. After three weeks, all the men with military papers indicating service in the German military were released from that camp, and my father returned home in January, 1939.

It was very difficult to survive in Germany at a time when Jews were being persecuted for simply being Jews. It was hard for my father to find work, and it was difficult for me, who was

almost eleven, and my brother, Theodore, who was nine, to deal with the persecution and harassment in school. At that point, we were anxious to leave Germany. My family could have actually left Germany more than eighteen months earlier, but my father gave our papers to his pregnant sister, Ida, so she could travel safely to the United States and have her child. Uncle Felix arranged for our affidavits to be filed and sent for the entire family to join him in the United States. In March, 1940, my parents, brother and I boarded the "Washington," which I believe was the last ship to leave Italy for America. We finally arrived in New York in April, 1940, after spending Passover on the ship. My late brother Theodore was the youngest boy on the ship and recited the *Ma-Nishtana* (four questions) for everyone at the ship's seder. One of the treasured items that we brought on our voyage was a cookbook my mother had received from her mother. The book was called *Kochbuch für einfache und feine jüdischen Köche*, which roughly translates to mean, "Cookbook, for Simple and Fine Jewish Cooks." We arrived in New York on the last day of Passover, April 12, 1940. My father, a religious man, insisted on walking to our next destination, but was told at Ellis Island that walking to Manhattan was not possible. So, for the first and only time in his life, he rode in a car on a Jewish holiday.

My job was to learn and study. At first it was very hard since I spoke no English, and was shy. I tried very hard to be a good student and I still have my very first report card where my teacher

Top left: Edith with her parents and brother, Theodore.

wrote when commenting on my first semester, "a courageous beginning." The following December, in seventh grade, I wrote an article for our school newspaper, entitled "The Best Time I Ever Had." In it I wrote:

When I consider the best time I ever had I have to look back on my past life. I find that I had the best time right after the worst time. This was about six months ago when I arrived in this country. I realized then the difference between a free country and a land ruled by a dictator. In Germany, as a Jew, I was considered an outcast. My family was persecuted and my father was taken to a concentration camp. But in this country I have found friendship and understanding. I can associate with other girls of all creeds in the school I attend. I didn't understand the language but teachers as well as pupils realized my position and they helped me as much as they could. I will always consider the time when I came to the " Land of the free" as the best time of my life and will be grateful to this country, which gave me refuge. By being loyal and a law-abiding citizen, I can repay my new country for its kindness.

Edith Hamburger, 7B1

I attended Washington Irving High School, where I was valedictorian, and then matriculated at Hunter College where I majored in Spanish and was voted the girl most likely to succeed. I married Siegmund Blumenthal in May, 1953.

My husband Siggi's life was challenging as well. When the Nazis came to power, his father, David Blumenthal, realized things could only get worse. He sold his farm, and the week after Siegmund's Bar Mitzvah, my husband, his brother, Alfred, and his parents, David and Johanna, left Germany for Catskill, New York. Siggi had very little schooling in New York, as he needed to work. Between 1934 and 1939, David, Johanna and their sons sacrificed and worked tirelessly, and during that five year period sponsored more than 50 family members and friends to come to America. Shortly after Pearl Harbor, Siggi enlisted in the U.S. military and spent three years serving his country in active combat in the Pacific Theater. When he returned to the United States, he held a number of jobs in the food industry, and eventually he and his brother Alfred, along with their father David, opened a small supermarket in New York City on Columbus Avenue, between 86th and 87th Street, where the two brothers worked side by side until 1981. Siggi then took a job at the local kosher market in Teaneck, New Jersey, where he befriended almost every child in Teaneck, until his death in 1990.

Siggi and I had two sons, who married two wonderful women. I have nine grandchildren, two girls and seven boys ranging in age from seven to twenty-two. I am truly grateful to everyone who helped me arrive at this point in my life.

Top right: Edith's mother pitting plums.

Edith Blumenthal's Chocolate Macaroons

No need to wait until Passover to enjoy these light, little flourless chocolaty treats.

Yields: 60 to 65 cookies; Start to Finish: Under 30 minutes

5 whole eggs

1 cup sugar

½ teaspoon ground cinnamon

1 tablespoon cocoa powder

½ pound ground semi sweet chocolate

1 pound ground almonds (about 4 cups)

Sugar for dipping

Preheat the oven to 350 degrees and line a cookie sheet with parchment paper or a non-stick silicone mat. Beat the eggs with the sugar, ground cinnamon and cocoa powder, in a large bowl, on medium speed, for several minutes, until the mixture is light and fluffy. Grind the chocolate with a coffee or nut grinder or serrated knife. Stir in the ground chocolate and almonds to form a stiff dough.

Pour about ½ cup sugar into a small bowl and have a second bowl of warm water nearby. Dip your hands into the water, shake off the excess and roll 1 teaspoon of dough in your hands to form a small ball about 1-inch in diameter, and then roll the ball in the sugar. Place on the prepared cookie sheet and bake at 350 degrees for 10 minutes. Let the macaroons cool slightly before removing them to a plate.

Edith Blumenthal's *Streuselkuchen*–Crumb Cake

From the German, *streusel*, meaning strewn together and *kuchen* meaning cake, we have the definitive German dessert. Edith's no fuss version is delicious as is but we thought a lovely addition would be to incorporate blueberries into the batter. While the cake is a wonderful way to end an evening, it is also an awesome way to start the day. Preparing the cake in a deeper dish, creates a moister finish, however, the jellyroll pan is what a true German baker would use.

Yields: 12 servings; Start to Finish: Under 1 ½ hours

For the batter:

1 stick (½ cup) butter, room temperature

1 cup sugar

3 eggs

1 teaspoon vanilla extract

¾ cup whole milk

2 ½ cups all-purpose flour

2 ½ teaspoons baking powder

1 teaspoon salt

1 cup fresh or frozen blueberries (if frozen, thaw and drain) (optional)

For the crumb topping:

½ cup granulated sugar

¼ cup brown sugar

2 ½ cups all-purpose flour

1 teaspoon salt

1 teaspoon ground cinnamon

2 sticks (1 cup) cold butter, cut into small pieces

Preheat the oven to 350 degrees and grease a 13x9x2-inch baking dish or 15 ½ x10 ½-inch jellyroll pan. While the butter comes to room temperature, create the topping by combining the two sugars, flour, salt and cinnamon. Stir the ingredients until completely blended. Cut in the cold butter, using a pastry blender, a fork or your hands. Work the butter into the flour mixture until soft crumbles form. Resist the urge to break up all the large clumps; it's nice for the *streusel* to have different sizes and textures. Refrigerate the topping until ready to use.

Prepare the batter in a large bowl. Beat the butter and sugar, on medium speed, until light and creamy, about 3 minutes. Beat in the eggs, one at a time, mixing after each addition. In a small bowl add the vanilla to the milk. In another bowl, combine the flour, baking powder and salt. While beating on low speed, begin adding the milk and flour to the butter mixture, alternating between the two, until all the ingredients are incorporated. The batter will be thick and gooey. Toss the blueberries, if adding, with a tablespoon of flour; to help prevent them from sinking to the bottom of the batter. Gently stir in the blueberries, and then evenly spread the batter into the prepared dish or pan. Scatter the *streusel* topping over the entire cake and bake for 35 to 40 minutes, or until the top is lightly browned and a toothpick inserted in the center of the cake comes out clean. When cool, slice and serve just as is or sprinkled with confectioner's sugar.

Feedback
To make a terrific blueberry *streusel* muffin, follow the directions above. Spoon the batter three-quarters of the way full, into a muffin pan that has been lined with 2½ -inch muffin cups. Spoon 1 to 2 teaspoons of *streusel* on top of each and bake at 350 degrees for 20 minutes. You will have *streusel* topping leftover. You can cut the recipe in half or refrigerate any remaining topping in an airtight container for up to 2 weeks.

Ruth and Julius Eggener

As told by their daughter Evelyn Seroy

Evelyn's parents were among the fortunate group of German Jews who were able to obtain affidavits and immigrate to America before the full extent of Nazi oppression was felt. She has become a tireless teacher on the subject of the Holocaust as part of the Museum of Jewish Heritage's Gallery Educator family.

My mother was the only child of Sol Stern and Henny Gerson. She was born in Fritzlar, Germany in 1911 and attended a private girl's school taught by nuns. In 1933, her parents realized that there probably wouldn't be much of a future for her in Germany. Her paternal aunt signed the affidavit, and in February, 1934, my mother set sail from Copenhagen for New York City. Upon arriving at her aunt's apartment, she was told that "tonight you'll sleep in the bathtub and tomorrow you'll get a job." My mother first worked as a governess, then as a housekeeper at The Essex House. She taught herself how to speak English by going to the movies.

My father, Julius, was born in Mayen, Germany to Max and Caroline (Klein) Eggener. In 1938, my father came to America. How my parents met is a lovely story. From time to time, my mother would see my father on the subway. When she and a girlfriend went one evening to a dance, my Mom told her chum, "that's the man I see on the train, I'm going to marry him." Her friend knew my father and introduced them. One month later, on the day that would have been her mother's birthday, my parents were married. The big splurge for them on their wedding night was to share a bottle of Coca-Cola.

My parents settled on Laurel Hill Terrace, in Washington Heights. When they first married, my mother didn't know how to cook. She asked someone at The Essex House to give her seven recipes, one for each night of the week. After about a month, my father suggested that she should get seven more recipes, because he was tired of riding the subway up to Washington Heights, knowing what's for dinner. My mother prepared mostly German dishes. Everything she cooked and baked was always made from scratch with fresh ingredients. No short cuts for her! My mother was still shopping and cooking and baking up until she died at the age of 94 years. As her only child, I enjoy continuing her deeply rooted traditions. I know that all children are proud of their parents. As a result of the training, which I received prior to becoming a gallery educator at the Museum of Jewish Heritage, I learned more of what my parents went through, and am even prouder. I want to leave something so others will know my mother and father were here.

Top left: Ruth and Julius Eggener with their daughter, Evelyn. Fort Tryon Park, NYC

Ruth Eggener's Braised *Sauerbraten*–Marinated Roast

Sauerbraten translates to mean sour roast, but that doesn't begin to convey the pungent and delicious result from marinating a simple cut of beef for several days in a mixture of wine, vinegar and spices. The chunky applesauce has just enough sweetness to balance the dish, and the mushroom stuffing soaks up the robust gravy.

Yields: 6 servings; Start to Finish: Step One: marinate 3 to 4 days, Step Two: under 3 hours

Marinade:

½ cup apple cider vinegar

½ cup red wine

2 bay leaves

8 whole black peppercorns

¼ cup sugar

2 medium onions, sliced

1 (3 to 4 pound) chuck, rib, silver tip, or French roast

Flour for dredging

2 tablespoons oil

Kosher salt and pepper

Step One: Bring all the marinade ingredients to boil in a medium saucepan. Reduce the heat, cover and simmer for at least 10 to 15 minutes. Allow the liquid to cool. Place the roast in a large resealable bag and pour the cooled marinade into the bag. Seal, then lay the bag in a shallow pan and refrigerate for 3 to 4 days. Turn the bag twice a day to evenly distribute the marinade.

Step Two: Preheat the oven to 350 degrees and remove the roast from the marinade. Dry the meat with a paper towel and dredge in flour. Heat the oil in a Dutch oven or covered roasting pan, brown the meat on all sides. Strain the marinade, discarding the solids, and add half the marinade to the pot, reserving the rest of the marinade for later. Place the pot in the oven, cover and roast at 350 degrees for 2 ½ hours or until the meat is tender, but not falling apart. Check the pot several times while roasting to add water as necessary to loosen the gravy. When the meat is nearly done, heat the remaining marinade in a small saucepan, bring to a boil and cook for 10 minutes, and then simmer uncovered, allowing it to reduce. Reserve the marinade for the final step.

Remove the roast and slice thin. Add the sliced meat back into the pot. Pour the reserved marinade over the meat and season to taste with salt and pepper. Serve with Ruth's chunky applesauce (recipe below) and mushroom stuffing (recipe follows).

Feedback

Anytime you have a marinade that has come in direct contact with raw meat, you MUST boil it to reduce the risk of contamination from bacteria that can develop. The reduction also intensifies the flavor. Boil the marinade for 10 minutes, then lower the heat and let it simmer uncovered until it is reduced. The more it reduces the more concentrated the flavor becomes. If you prefer, you can make a new batch of marinade, allow it cook down and reduce by half before adding to the roast.

Ruth Eggener's Chunky Applesauce

No excuse for ever buying jarred applesauce again. Crisp fresh apples and pure ingredients make homemade applesauce a no-brainer.

Yields: 3 cups; Start to Finish: Under 30 minutes

4 crisp apples (about 1 ½ to 2 pounds). Use at least 2 different varieties (Macintosh, Golden Delicious, Cortland) peeled, cored and cut into bite-size pieces

½ cup water

¼ cup sugar

½ teaspoon ground cinnamon or 1 to 2 cinnamon sticks

2 teaspoons vanilla extract

Place all the ingredients in a medium saucepan and bring to a boil. Reduce the heat and simmer for 20 minutes, stirring occasionally. There should be a nice blend of chunky, firm and soft apples. Cool and serve.

Ruth Eggener's Mushroom and Onion Stuffing

So simple, you won't believe you ever bought stuffing in a box.

Yields: 4 cups; Start to Finish: Under 30 minutes

2 medium onions, chopped (about 1½ cups)

2 tablespoons oil or margarine

3 celery ribs, chopped (about 1½ cups)

¾ pound mushrooms, chopped

1 pound (about 12 to 16 thin slices) white bread

1 egg, beaten

Kosher salt and pepper

Freshly ground nutmeg (a pinch of bottled ground nutmeg can be substituted)

Heat the oil or margarine, in a large skillet, cook and stir the onions, over medium heat, until lightly browned, about 10 minutes. Stir in the celery and mushrooms, cover and simmer for 15 minutes. Allow the vegetables to cool for a few minutes while you prepare the bread.

Tear the white bread into small pieces, crust and all, and place in a medium bowl. Stir in the beaten egg and combine so all the bread is thoroughly coated. Spoon in the cooled vegetables and stir. Season to taste with salt, pepper and if you like, a touch of nutmeg. Spoon the stuffing into a saucepan and cook, over low heat for several minutes so the egg cooks through. If stuffing a bird, no need to cook the stuffing separately.

Reni Hanau

In her own words

Talking to Reni is like having a conversation with an old friend. She has a warmth, humor and vibrancy that pervade the stories and memories which she shares with Museum visitors in her role as a gallery educator. On a cold December day, she shared her remembrances with me.

I grew up in a small town in Germany where my father was a teacher of both religious and secular studies, and director of rituals; he was the *Shoichet* (butcher), or, as I like to say, a one-man *Kli Kodesh* (clergy). He worked for the German government, which as you might know, has no political atheists. Despite his connection to the government, he was taken to Buchenwald, from which he was released after presenting his papers. Our family knew that now was the time to leave. We moved to Frankfurt, Germany, from our comfortable home, which was situated next door to the synagogue. In Frankfurt my father applied for a visa to England where they were proficient in de-veining, among other meats, ox tails, which is very difficult. My father wanted to learn that skill. The visa was granted and we made our way to London.

Our family was relieved to be leaving a hostile country for safe harbor in England. After all, England was an ally nation and we felt we would be safe there. However, upon arrival, our German passports were scrutinized and the British government deemed us "enemy aliens." We were banished to the Isle of Man, where, although we were safe, we were not free. My mother and I lived apart from my father as the men and women were separated. We were given chores to do including cleaning the hotel where we resided. My mother, who had never done such housework, would pay a certain Christian "enemy alien" to do her work. She would say, "don't spend my money on non-kosher lobster and shrimp!" We remained there until the end of the war when we departed for America. When we arrived in the United States, a photographer on the dock wanted to snap my photo because I was declared the youngest prisoner of war. My mother would not allow the photo, and to this day I feel I was deprived this celebrity status.

After my mother's passing, I found comfort in making the foods my mother used to make. If you make the same things your mother made, you feel a little less alone. That includes making Shabbos dinner the way I remember it. There is a bakery in Washington Heights that makes a particular water challah that was so reminiscent of what I ate as a child. No wonder. It turns out that the baker is the son of the baker from my home village! The bread, which we called *berches* is shaped like a rye bread, it has something like a braid on top and it is sprinkled with lots and lots of poppy seeds. Maybe people got a little high on that, who knows?

There are survivors who had the opportunity to save and bring to America, not only their traditions, but the actual utensils they used. It's like bringing a part of their old life into their new life. My husband, Walter, of 55 years, and our two sons and our seven beautiful grandchildren make my life richer.

Top left: Reni Hanau, age 10, in America

Reni Hanau's *Waffeln*–Waffles

Reni left Germany as a child, but her memory of her mom's cooking traveled with her from Germany to England and on to America. Her snowy Sundays were warmed by these light waffles that scream with delight when covered in confectioner's sugar and fresh *schlagzahne*–whipped cream. In the time it takes to brew a good cup of coffee or squeeze fresh orange juice, you can have homemade waffles.

Yields: 4 to 6 servings; Start to Finish: 15 minutes

4 tablespoons butter, melted

½ cup sugar

1 cup whole milk

¼ cup sour cream

3 eggs, separated

1 ½ cups all-purpose flour

2 scant teaspoons baking powder

To create the batter, whisk together the butter, sugar, milk, sour cream and egg yolks, in a large bowl. An old-fashioned eggbeater or wire whisk works great. In a separate bowl, combine the flour and baking powder. Stir the flour into the egg mixture, until the flour is incorporated and the batter is smooth.

In a separate bowl, beat the whites until stiff but not dry, and gently but thoroughly fold them into the batter. The batter will be very light and airy. Let the batter rest while you heat the waffle iron. Ladle the batter onto the waffle iron, following the manufacturer's directions for how much batter the pan can hold, do not overfill. Cook until light brown, or the indicator on the waffle iron says they are done. Serve with a light dusting of confectioner's sugar or lightly sweetened whipped cream (recipe below).

Feedback

If you do not have a waffle iron, you can turn these into delicious pancakes. Heat a large skillet or griddle with butter, over medium heat. Drop the batter by small ladlefuls and cook on the stove until lightly brown on both sides.

Schlagzahne–Whipped Cream

1 cup, cold heavy cream

2 teaspoons vanilla extract

2 tablespoons, confectioner's sugar (you can use regular sugar or even sugar substitute)

Make sure the cream, mixing bowl and utensil you are using are cold. Whip all the ingredients together, with a whisk, electric mixer or standing mixer fitted with the whisk attachment, until the cream forms firm but not hard peaks. Do not over-whip or you'll end up with butter. You can add additional flavorings to taste such as almond extract or flavored liquor.

JFH

Reni Hanau's Winter Celeriac (Celery Root) Salad

Reni enjoys this classic German provincial dish built around celery root (aka *celeriac*) that her mother would prepare. This alien-looking vegetable is not only homely, but suffers from an identity crisis. It has a taste similar to celery, with the texture more like a carrot. It stands up to pickling very well, stays in the fridge for days and makes a very healthful salad that Reni invites you to enjoy all winter long.

Yields: 6 to 8 servings (about 6 cups); Start to Finish: Under 1 hour, then overnight

1 celery root (about 1 ½ pounds), peeled and cut into 1-inch chunks

3 carrots, peeled and cut into 1-inch chunks

½ cup diced kosher pickles

½ red onion or 2 to 3 shallots, finely diced

¼ cup olive or canola oil

½ cup white vinegar

Pinch of sugar

Kosher salt and pepper

Bring a medium size pot of salted water to boil, and cook the celery root and carrots until tender, but not too soft, about 20 minutes. Drain and add them to a bowl along with the pickles, onion or shallot, oil, vinegar and sugar. Season to taste with salt and pepper. Cover tightly and refrigerate. The salad will marinate in the fridge, stir it occasionally so each ingredient has the chance to pick up all the flavors.

Celery Root and Apple Salad

This celery root slaw is a 21st century interpretation of Reni's original celery root salad. The crunch of the Granny Smith apples lends a tart contrast to the subtly sweet celery root.

Yields: About 6 to 8 servings (about 6 cups); Start to Finish: Under 15 minutes

1 celery root (about 1½ pounds), peeled and cut into matchstick pieces

½ cup mayonnaise

4 teaspoons Dijon mustard

1 tablespoon apple cider vinegar

2 tablespoons freshly squeezed lemon juice

2 tablespoons shallot, minced

½ cup finely chopped cornichons or sour pickles

1 tablespoon Herbs de Provence, or a combination of dried herbs such as chervil, tarragon, thyme

1 Granny Smith apple, peeled, cored and cut into matchstick pieces

Kosher salt and pepper

⅓ cup pecans, toasted for garnish (optional)

Bring a medium pot of water to boil and blanch (quickly cook in boiling water) the celery root, for 2 to 3 minutes. Drain and place in a bowl filled with very cold water to stop the celery root from continuing to cook. While the celery cools down, prepare the dressing by whisking together the mayonnaise, mustard, vinegar, lemon juice, shallots and cornichons or pickles, and herbs. Spoon the celery root into the bowl and blend until all pieces are coated with the dressing. Stir in the apples. Season to taste with salt and pepper. Cover and chill in the fridge until nice and cold. Before serving, heat the pecans in a skillet for several minutes to help develop their full flavor. Toss them on top of the salad as a garnish.

JFH

Feedback
You can forego blanching the celery root if you prefer a crisper slaw. Alternatively you can shred it using a box grater. The root has a tough texture similar to jicama when eaten raw.

Daniel Boulud

Professional contributor

Now that we've gotten you to acknowledge the celery root, let's take it to another level where the great Daniel Boulud introduces it to fresh horseradish in a deliciously rich beef dish.

Tender Beef with Horseradish, Parsnips and Celery Root
Excerpted from Braise (Ecco 2006)

There's nothing that has quite the same extreme pungency as fresh horseradish. If you can't recall if you've ever eaten it, then you definitely have not. It's a forceful sensation you would remember, much more concentrated than the stuff in the jars. It's a classic accompaniment with braised fatty meat dishes, and for good reason. The sharpness is an excellent contrast to the richness of the meat.

You do need to take care when grating the horseradish, especially if your eyes are sensitive (though you will also feel it in your nose). If you use a food processor (and that's a good idea), whatever you do, don't lean over the machine when you take off the cover. Stand back!

Yields: 6 servings

1 (3-pound) beef bottom round

Coarse sea salt or kosher salt and freshly ground black pepper

1 tablespoon all-purpose flour

½ cup extra-virgin olive oil

1 large onion, peeled and cut into large dice

20 juniper berries (see note)

¼ cup red wine vinegar

1 tablespoon tomato paste

¾ cup vodka

2 medium parsnips, peeled and trimmed, and cut into large dice

1 large turnip, peeled, trimmed, and cut into large dice

¼ celery root, peeled, trimmed, and cut into large dice (about 1 cup)

3 bay leaves

2 tablespoons chopped fresh dill

5 ounces peeled, finely grated fresh horseradish (about ¾ cup; see note)

½ cup heavy cream (optional) (see Editor's Note)

Center a rack in the oven and preheat the oven to 300 degrees.

Pat the beef dry and season with salt and pepper. Dust the beef with flour. In a medium cast-iron pot or Dutch oven over high heat, warm the olive oil. Add the beef and sear until golden brown on all sides, 12 to 15 minutes. Transfer the beef to a plate.

(Continued)

Lower the heat to medium. Add the onion, juniper berries, and 1 teaspoon black pepper to the pot and cook stirring 6 to 8 minutes, until the onions are translucent. Stir in the red wine vinegar and tomato paste and cook until almost all the liquid has evaporated. Pour in the vodka and red wine and bring to a boil. Add the parsnips, turnip, celery root, bay leaves, dill, ½ cup of the horseradish, and 2 cups water. Return the beef to the pot and bring to a simmer.

Cover the pot and transfer it to the oven to braise for 2 ½ hours, turning the meat two or three times.

Editors Note: *Mr. Boulud prepares a horseradish whipped cream to serve on the side. For those choosing to follow that preparation, we are including the final step. For those who would not, we suggest you serve the beef with the vegetables spooned on top of the meat, and spoon a bit of the fresh horseradish on the side. You can also adjust the cut of meat.*

Meanwhile, whip the heavy cream to medium peaks and stir in the remaining horseradish. Season to taste with salt and pepper. Serve the beef and vegetables with the horseradish whipped cream on the side.

Juniper Berries

These small purple fruits of a high-altitude evergreen tree have a clean, resinous taste and are used to flavor meats, pates, and marinades.

Horseradish

In the same family as cabbage and mustard, and a friend of both, the bitingly pungent horseradish root looks like a dirty-encrusted white carrot. It has to be peeled before cooking, and if it is tough, the root should be quartered lengthwise and the core cut away, jobs that will sting the eyes. The sharpness of raw horseradish, often mixed with vinegar or cream to be used as a relish, is lost when the root is cooked, as heat renders it a mild root vegetable with a pleasantly soft texture. Look for horseradish in well-stocked produce aisles, particularly around the spring Jewish holiday of Passover, during which it is used to represent the bitterness of affliction.

Gruenkern Soup with Mini Turkey Meatballs

Together, Reni and I developed this recipe, which features *gruenkern*, rich chicken broth and mini turkey meatballs. *Gruenkern* has an interesting nutty flavor and is a nutritious substitute for rice, pasta or noodles in a soup, salad or as a side dish. It has similar properties to farro, spelt or wheat berries. While this forgotten grain is not easy to find, most German specialty stores, or kosher suppliers can usually order it for you.

Yields: 6 servings; Start to Finish: Step One: 6 to 8 hours or overnight, to soak the gruenkern, Step Two: Under 2 hours

For the soup:

1 cup *gruenkern*, soaked

1 large onion, finely chopped (about 1 cup)

2 carrots, peeled and finely chopped (about 1 cup)

2 celery ribs, finely chopped (about 1 cup)

3 tablespoons olive oil

2 quarts water or chicken broth (if using water, you will need to add a bouillon cube or chicken flavor seasoning packet)

Soup bones (optional)

Kosher salt and pepper

For the meatballs (makes about 30):

⅓ cup plain bread crumbs

2 teaspoons garlic, minced

3 tablespoons chopped fresh flat-leaf parsley

1 large egg

Kosher salt and pepper

1-pound ground turkey

Chopped fresh parsley for garnish (optional)

Step One: Soak the *gruenkern* for 6 to 8 hours or overnight, in cold water, enough to completely cover the kernels.

Step Two: Heat the olive oil in a large soup pot, cook and stir the onion, carrots and celery, over medium heat, until they have softened a bit, about 15 minutes (you'll begin to smell their sweet aroma). Pour the broth (or water) into the pot, add the drained *gruenkern*. Season with salt and pepper. If you have any soup bones, feel free to add them to the pot for extra flavor. Cover and cook over low heat for 1½ hours.

While the soup cooks, prepare the turkey meatballs. Preheat the oven to 350 degrees and lightly grease a baking sheet.

In a bowl, combine all the meatball ingredients, adding the turkey meat last. Form mini meatballs, about the size of a marble. Place them on the baking sheet and bake at 350 degrees for 15 minutes. Turn them over and continue baking until they are lightly browned and cooked through, about 15 minutes longer.

Remove them from the oven and gently drop them into the soup. Add the bouillon cube or flavoring packet (if you used water). After 1½ hours, check to see that the *gruenkern* is done, it will retain a soft, slightly grainy bite. Serve piping hot with a sprinkle of chopped fresh parsley and a drizzle of olive oil.

JFH

Ellen and Ernest Katz

In their own words

Ellen and Ernest Katz are a wonderful couple, who smile broadly as they listen to each other tell their respective stories. They both have a very positive attitude and have built a beautiful life together. We spoke shortly after President Obama was inaugurated and Ellen referred to his outlook on life, an attitude, which she shares, "you pick yourself up and dust yourself off." Ellen adds, "It is what we do. We always land on our feet."

Ellen

I remember a very pleasant life as a little girl in Offenbach, Germany. I remember cooking with my mother, when she baked I would be licking the spoons like any child would. It wasn't until 1939 that we started to feel ostracized. I didn't look Jewish at all, because I was blonde with blue eyes, but when it came my turn to be waited on in a local store I was told, "you can't have this." All of a sudden I realized it was because I was Jewish. I was young, only twelve, so I was eligible to leave on a *Kindertransport*, for America. My father arrived in America one month before me, while my mother stayed behind with my sister. My sister was over sixteen and too old to leave with me. She and my mother never made it out of Germany. I first went to Italy by train and met up with five or

six other children and a woman who was in charge. We boarded a ship and came to America. I arrived in May of 1940, and by the time I started school in September I had no problem speaking English, as I had learned a little when I was in Germany. We were determined not to speak German, we didn't want the culture, we wanted to forget. At first we lived with my aunt and uncle who had immigrated here a year earlier, then my father and I moved out and made it on our own.

Ernest

Although I was born in Düsseldorf, I lived in the same town that Ellen did, as Offenbach was the center for handbag manufacturing, and that was my trade. I left Germany in 1938 and went to England, by way of Italy. When I arrived in England with my German papers, I was deemed an enemy alien, prisoner of war and sent to Australia. I was interned on a prisoner of war ship named the "Dunera," which was actually hit by a torpedo in transit. We arrived in Sydney after two months and were put on a train for as far as it would go. I spent four years in a POW camp where we were treated fine and there was little anti-Semitism. The Australians eventually realized they had made a mistake and told us we could join the British army. I joined the Australian army instead and served for four years in the labor corps. My sister lived in America, so I came on a visit and decided to stay.

(*Ellen joins in the conversation:* "Ernie had a girlfriend then, and it wasn't me! Eventually it was.")

Ellen and Ernie are married 60 years, they have two children and five grandchildren.

Top left: Ellen's travel document for Kindertransport to America

Ellen Katz's Veal Marengo

Although Ellen easily assimilated when she came to America, her cooking traditions are European. One of her favorite recipes is this hearty Italian veal stew flavored with crisp white wine, plump tomatoes and sautéed mushrooms. Although Ellen never lived in Italy, both she and Ernest made their way to America via Italy. This preparation is Ellen's homage to their gateway country.

Yields: 4 to 6 servings; Start to Finish: Under 1½ hours

4 large ripe tomatoes, peeled and cut into chunks

1½ pounds veal, cut into 1-inch cubes and patted dry

3 tablespoons vegetable or olive oil

1 large onion, coarsely chopped (about 1 cup)

2 tablespoons all-purpose flour

½ cup semi dry white wine (Sauterne)

1 cup chicken broth

1 clove garlic, finely chopped

Kosher salt and pepper

½ pound white button mushrooms, sliced

1 tablespoon margarine

To peel the tomatoes remove the small stem and then with a sharp paring knife, carefully remove the skin. If you do not have great knife skills, instead bring a medium pot of water to boil. Prepare a bowl with ice water. Make a small "X" in the bottom of each tomato. Drop the tomatoes, one at a time, into the boiling water. After 30 seconds, remove with a slotted spoon. Plunge the tomato into the ice bath; the skin should begin to fall away. Chop and reserve.

Heat the oil in a Dutch oven or deep covered pan, brown the veal on all sides, over medium heat, about 5 minutes. Stir in the onions and tomatoes and continue to cook for 2 minutes longer. Stir in the flour until evenly blended and no longer visible. Gradually add the wine, broth and garlic. Season with salt and pepper. Cover tightly and simmer over low heat for 1 hour, or until the meat is fork tender.

While the veal cooks, heat the margarine, in a separate skillet, and cook and stir the sliced mushrooms, over medium heat, until lightly browned. Add the mushrooms to the veal just before serving. The sauce can be thickened by creating a slurry (see feedback). Heat for an additional 10 minutes.

Feedback

A slurry is created by mixing flour, and corn or potato starch (thickener) with water. Never add the thickener directly into the sauce, it will cause lumps. Cornstarch is the best thickening agent: 1 tablespoon mixed with about 2 tablespoons of water will thicken 1 ½ to 2 cups of sauce. Whisk the two together (it should resemble the consistency of thin Elmer's Glue), and then whisk it back into the pot. Cornstarch thickens and glosses the sauce almost instantly. Repeat if necessary for further thickening. You will need twice as much flour, or potato starch to thicken a sauce, but the ratio is the same: 1 tablespoon of flour or potato starch mixed with 2 tablespoons of water will thicken about 1 cup of sauce. Allow the dish to cook for several minutes to lose the pasty flour taste. Repeat the process until you achieve the desired thickness.

Ellen Katz's Apricot Squares

These sublime bites are Ellen's entrance fee when visiting her grandchildren. The dough is a classic *mürbeteig*: lightly sweet short crust pastry, covered with flavorful apricot preserves, buttery *streusel*, crunchy walnuts and flaky coconut.

Yields: 40 mini squares; Start to Finish: Step One: 15 minutes, then refrigerate at least 2 hours or up to 24 hours, Step Two: Under 1 hour

For the dough:

1 cup all-purpose flour

1 tablespoon sugar (more or less to taste)

Pinch salt

1 stick (½ cup) cold butter, cut into small pieces

1 egg yolk

1 tablespoon orange juice

For the crumble:

1 stick (½ cup) butter, melted

⅔ cup all-purpose flour

1 cup sugar

For the topping:

½ cup finely chopped walnuts (about 2 to 3 ounces)

½ cup coconut flakes

For the filling:

1 cup apricot (or your favorite flavor) preserves

Step One: Mix the flour, sugar and salt in a food processor, fitted with the metal blade, or in a bowl using a pastry blender. Cut in the cold butter, egg yolk and orange juice. Pulse or blend the mixture. The dough will start out very crumbly, but comes together as you pulse or blend it. Do not over-process. The finished dough will be very soft but not sticky (add a drizzle more juice if the dough is dry). Press the dough into a 12 x 9-inch jellyroll pan. Spread the preserves over the dough, cover and refrigerate for 2 hours, or up to one day.

Step Two: Preheat the oven to 350 degrees.

Create the crumble by melting the butter in a saucepan or in the microwave. Pour the butter into a small bowl and let it to cool for a few minutes. Stir in the flour then sugar and mix with a fork to create crumbly, moist bits. Remove the dough pan from the fridge and sprinkle the crumbs all over the preserves. Sprinkle the nuts and coconut over the crumbs.

Bake at 350 degrees for 30 to 40 minutes, or until the crumble is lightly browned. When slightly cool, cut into bite-size squares. Allow the cookies to completely cool before removing from the pan. They store well in a closed container for several days.

Feedback

Mürbeteig is a mainstay in German regional baking. Ellen's recipe is similar to the one many of our German bakers – Ruth Eggener, Reni Hanau, Melly Resnicow and Helen Wallerstein – described and all prepare. The key is to use chilled butter, work quickly, and be sure not to over-process the ingredients. The reward is a flaky go-to crust that can be used for pies and tarts, with a variety of fruit or custard fillings. *Mürbeteig* can be prepared in advance and kept frozen for up to one month, till ready to use. Thaw the frozen crust overnight in the fridge before baking. Ellen's recipe makes enough pastry for one 8 or 9-inch pie or tart.

Blind Baking

If you will be filling the crust with a filling that does not need to bake (such as prepared lemon curd, cream pies or meringues) you will need to bake the crust first. Prepare the dough as Ellen describes. For a more neutral flavor, substitute ice water for the juice. Wrap the dough tightly in plastic, flatten into a disc and chill for at least 1 hour. Alternatively, you can press the dough into your pan and chill. After the dough has chilled for 30 minutes, preheat the oven to 375 degrees.

Roll the dough out into a circle, on a lightly floured surface, to about ¼-inch thick, turning the dough a quarter turn with each roll to help retain its shape and to prevent it from sticking to the surface. Flour as needed. Drape the dough over your rolling pin, and firmly press the dough into your pan. Take the rolling pin and run it across the top to trim the edges flush to the pan. Use any scraps to help mend tears or fill in gaps. Prick the dough with a fork (this is called "docking" and is done to prevent air bubbles from forming in the dough as it bakes, which causes lumps and bumps) and brush with cool melted butter. Line the dough with wax or parchment paper and cover with ceramic baking weights or dried beans, this will help the pastry lie flat and retain its shape while baking. Bake at 375 degrees for 30 minutes, carefully remove the weights (they will be very hot) and paper and bake an additional 10 minutes or until the crust is nicely browned. If the edges of the crust brown before the crust is done, create a ring of aluminum foil and drape it around the edges. Take the finished crust out of the oven and allow it to cool before filling.

If the filling needs to bake, you do not need to blind bake the crust, but the dough does need to be chilled before filling. Either roll the chilled dough out or press the dough into your pan and put back in the fridge while you prepare the filling.

Zwetschge (prunes) or *pflaume*, a sugary plum presentation, is a very popular filling. Be sure you use sweet plums, pitted and sliced (or any combination of stone fruit or berries). Toss the fruit with 2 tablespoons of cornstarch to help absorb its juice, and mix with either ½ cup of brown sugar, cinnamon sugar, granulated sugar, or ½ cup of sweet preserves. A squeeze of lemon and a pinch of salt bring out the fresh fruit flavor. Arrange the fruit in a pattern, by overlapping and nestling the sliced pieces. If using several types of fruit, alternate the colors, or lay one fruit in the center and another around the rim for an eye-catching design. If all else fails, simply dump the fruit in the shell- it will taste just as good! For added texture and flavor, you can top the fruit with Ellen's streusel, or another layer of dough to form a top crust. Bake at 375 degrees for 40 to 50 minutes or until the fruit is soft and bubbly and the crust is nicely browned around the edges. Dust with confectioner's sugar when cool.

Ruth Kohn

In her own words

Ruth Kohn proudly wears both an American flag pin and a Dominican Republic flag pin on her lapel, something you might not expect from a nice Jewish girl born in Germany. She happily shares her story and why her granddaughter says, "The sweet Dominican souls saved my grandma and grandpa."

I was six years old when Hitler came to power. Before then I remember a house where everyone was happy. We lived in Berlin from the time I was four until I was fourteen. My father had a cousin in America who wanted us to come, but my father, an Orthodox Jew, and decorated German soldier, felt nothing would happen to us if we stayed. He once said, "If I ever leave Germany, it will be on the last train." That's exactly what happened. I had an uncle who was arrested on Kristallnacht. He paid the Nazis for his release. He traveled to Belgium where he was arrested again. This time, he was sent to Portugal, and was detained in a camp. He managed to escape by walking over the Pyrenees to Lisbon. Once in Lisbon, he met with the American Joint Distribution Committee, who told him of Sosua, a settlement in the Dominican Republic. Trujillo, the dictator there, was offering safe haven to Jews who would commit to agricultural work. My uncle accepted the offer and sent visas for us to join him.

I was told we boarded the last train out of Germany. The age restrictions were changed the day after we left, and my parents would not have been able to leave if we had stayed one day longer. We arrived in the Dominican Republic the day Pearl Harbor was bombed. "OK, now what" we thought? It was very bittersweet. We felt we were out of this world somewhere; the climate and the language in Sosua were so different. We went to a German school, but had to learn Spanish, which was a very good thing. There were certain foods we could not get there, like white potatoes, so we adapted and ate sweet potatoes, fruits like plantains and papayas, all new foods to us.

The Dominicans were very kind, there was no anti-Semitism. It was a very strange feeling being able to walk down a street without harassment. When we first arrived, a young doctor from the hospital in town came and took our photos. The pictures were used for our Dominican documents. Years later, I worked as a nurse at that same hospital, and dated that same doctor. I was later told that after he took my picture, he returned to the hospital and told everyone, "I am going to marry that girl someday." Six years later he did. He waited for me! We were the first couple married at the Temple in Sosua.

My parents brought me up to be a happy person. I haven't forgotten anything, but I am happy. I really admire the Dominican people. It was a horrible time, but they brought us through. We went from one dictator in Germany to another in the Dominican Republic, but the Dominican dictator saved our lives. Many Jews were saved by the Dominicans, 700 in Sosua alone. After the war I said, "what now?" It was like we were on hold, like you put clothes over the summer in mothballs. But my life now is really a happy ending. I was married 45 years and have three children and two grandchildren.

Top left: Ruth Kohn, in Sosua, Dominican Republic.

Ruth Kohn's *Arroz con Pollo*—Chicken and Rice

This classic Latin American dish is a one-pot-wonder. Juicy chicken, tender rice and a splash of green from the peas and olives make this a hearty and visually satisfying dinner.

Yields: 4 to 6 servings; Start to Finish: Under 2 hours

1 (3 to 4 pound) chicken, cut into 8 pieces

½ cup olive oil

2 large onions, chopped (about 2 cups)

1 clove garlic, crushed

½ teaspoon crushed red pepper

1½ teaspoons kosher salt

½ teaspoon black pepper

2 cups, uncooked converted white rice

1 (28-ounce) can tomatoes, with their juice

1 (10 ½-ounce) can chicken broth

1 can green chili peppers, chopped (optional)

1 cup frozen peas

½ cup pimento stuffed green olives, sliced

1 (4-ounce) can pimentos, drained and sliced

Preheat the oven to 325 degrees.

Wipe the chicken pieces with a damp paper towel. Heat the olive oil in a heavy, 6 quart Dutch oven, and brown the chicken, in batches, over medium heat, until golden brown on all sides. With a slotted spoon, remove the cooked chicken to a plate.

In the same pot, cook and stir the onions, garlic and red pepper, over medium, heat until golden, about 10 minutes. Stir in the salt, pepper and rice and cook for 10 minutes longer, stirring occasionally, until everything is lightly browned. Stir in the tomatoes and their liquid, chicken broth and chili peppers, if using. Place the chicken back into the pot (do not add the liquid that collected on the plate) and bring to a low boil. Place the covered pot in the oven and bake at 325 degrees for 1 hour.

After one hour, add ½ cup of water, sprinkle in the peas, olives and pimento strips—do not stir. Cover and continue to bake for an additional 20 minutes. The chicken should be tender and moist and cooked through. Serve family style right from the Dutch oven.

Ruth Kohn's Fried *Platanos*–Fried Plantains

There is possibly no dish more iconic to Caribbean cuisine than fried plantains. Starchy foods normally eaten by Eastern European Jews were not readily available on the island, so indigenous ingredients such as plantains and yucca were obvious substitutes. Don't confuse plantains with bananas: although from the same family, plantains are firmer, starchier and less sweet. Ruth enjoyed this preparation as a light dessert, with a preference for plantains that are dark yellow, black spots and all, but they can also be eaten as a side dish.

Yields: About 6 servings; Start to Finish: Under 15 minutes

3 very ripe plantains, peeled and sliced lengthwise ¼-inch thick

Vegetable oil for frying

Sugar for dusting

Heat several inches of oil, in a large skillet, until sizzling hot, about 350 to 375 degrees. Fry the plantains until golden, about 3 to 5 minutes per side. Drain on paper towels then serve with a sprinkling of sugar on top. Omit the sugar if serving as a side dish.

Feedback

To prepare a similar and popular Latin dish called *tostones*, use green plantains and cut them in 1-inch pieces. Fry them in plenty of vegetable oil. Remove them from the pan and flatten them with the heel of your hand. Let the plantains drain on a paper towel. Season them with salt and let them sit for several minutes. Place them back in the skillet and fry for several minutes more. Drain and serve with additional salt and a squeeze of lemon or lime.

Miriam Margulies

In her own words

Miriam spent most of the war years living in America as a new immigrant. Even as a child, she assumed many of the roles of a traditional homemaker while her mother worked to support them both. As a result, she is an accomplished and eclectic cook with German, Austrian, Hungarian and Czech specialties.

I was born in Vienna, Austria. My family enjoyed a very normal existence, until I turned eight, when the Nazi regime took control. After two years living under Nazi rule, an uncle in America secured papers for my mother and me. We arrived in America in 1940 and took refuge in the German Jewish community of Washington Heights, New York. Although I was only ten, I assumed many traditional roles, such as preparing meals. When you are a refugee coming to a strange country where you don't know the language or culture, you just do it! After the war ended, we reunited with my father. I feel you should always be optimistic. It is wonderful living in this marvelous country that saved our lives, and we keep hoping for a good future. I have two children, seven grandchildren and one great grandchild.

Top left: Miriam Margulies, 1950

Miriam Margulies' *Palatschinken*–Thin Pancakes

This Hungarian-Viennese specialty is a very light and thin pancake, the Viennese version of a blintz on a diet. The filling is almost always preserves, Miriam favors apricot. Dust with confectioner's sugar for a light dessert or elegant breakfast. The pancakes freeze well, unfilled. To freeze, layer parchment or wax paper in between each pancake and seal tightly.

Yields: 10 pancakes; Start to Finish: Under 30 minutes

1 cup sifted all-purpose flour

1 tablespoon sugar

⅛ teaspoon salt

½ teaspoon vanilla extract

2 eggs

½ cup water and ½ cup milk or 1 cup water

1 tablespoon butter, melted (you can substitute oil)

Confectioner's sugar, for sprinkling

Combine all of the ingredients in a blender and process until smooth. The batter should be thin, but not watery, so add more flour if needed to create a smooth, flowing batter.

Heat a touch of butter (or oil) in an 8-inch skillet, over medium heat. When a drop of water dances in the pan, you are ready to add a small amount of batter, about ¼ cup. Swirl the pan so the batter coats the entire bottom of the pan. When the pancake bubbles then begins to look dry, turn the pancake over and cook an additional 30 seconds. Remove to a waiting plate and cover to prevent the pancakes from drying out. Continue this process until you have used all the batter.

Fill then roll the pancakes with any type of jam or preserves; apricot is most traditional. (See Katherine Noir's apricot preserves on page 282). Sprinkle with confectioner's sugar just before serving.

Miriam Margulies' Sweet and Sour Red Cabbage

This dish is totally iconic German cuisine: red cabbage shredded and lightly sautéed, combined with its best friends, sugar and apple cider vinegar. The result is a tangy, tart, satisfying slaw that complements braised meat dishes. The recipe easily doubles and triples, so feel free to make a batch —it keeps for days in the fridge.

Yields: 4 to 5 cups; Start to Finish: Under 45 minutes

1 large onion, peeled and sliced

2 tablespoons vegetable oil

1 small head (about 1 pound) red cabbage, cored and shredded (about 4 cups)

1 teaspoon all-purpose flour

¼ cup apple cider vinegar

¼ cup sugar

In a large skillet, heat the oil, cook and stir the onions, over low heat, until soft, about 15 minutes. While the onions cook, shred the cabbage. When the onions are ready, stir in the cabbage and ¼ cup water. Cover the pan and cook over low heat for about 15 minutes, until the cabbage is nicely wilted and soft. Stir in the flour, vinegar and sugar. Cook for an additional minute or two. Season to taste with salt and pepper, and additional vinegar or sugar to achieve your desired sweet and sour flavor. Serve hot or cold.

Marsha Meyer

In her own words

I was born in a small town called Burghaun, Germany, that had about 30 Jewish families. In 1939, I was able to leave Germany and went to London where I worked and lived with a Jewish family. I stayed only six months, before coming to America. I enjoy cooking, and there are certain specialties I make that my two children and four grandchildren think are wonderful. My favorite recipe is for an unusual dumpling that you cannot buy in any store. It is a traditional German treat, called *knodels*. I serve it for dessert and stuff it with fresh or dried fruit. The late spring and early summer is the perfect time to prepare them, when the plums and apricots are their ripest. It's quite a job to make, but my family is crazy about them. I like to set myself up at the kitchen table, turn on the TV and make these leisurely.

Marsha Meyer's Fruit-Filled *Knodels*–Dumplings

Yields: About 18 knodels; Start to Finish: Under 45 minutes

For the dough:

½ **pound red potatoes, peeled, boiled and mashed**

½ **pound (1 cup) ricotta cheese**

2 **cups all-purpose flour**

2 **egg yolks**

Pinch of salt

For the filling:

18 **dried pitted prunes or 36 dried apricots or 18 fresh small plums or 18 fresh apricots**

Sugar to sweeten the fruit

For the topping:

½ **stick (4 tablespoons) butter**

½ **cup un-seasoned bread crumbs**

3 **tablespoons sugar**

½ **teaspoon ground cinnamon**

To make the dough, bring a medium pot of water to boil and cook the potatoes until soft, about 15 minutes. Drain, then mash the potatoes by hand or use a ricer (creates a smoother texture.) In a large bowl combine the mashed potatoes with the ricotta cheese, flour, egg yolks and salt. Mix thoroughly and then knead, on a lightly floured surface, until a dough forms. If the dough is too sticky, you can add a little more flour.

Bring a fresh pot of salted water to boil.

Prepare the fruit by softening the dried apricots or prunes. Heat them for a few minutes with a little water in a small saucepan. Drain and dry them thoroughly. For the fresh fruit, simply wash the fruit, Marsha does not even remove the stone pit, but you can if you want to.

Separate the dough into manageable pieces for you to roll out on a floured board. Using a cookie cutter, cut the pieces large enough to wrap around the fruit that you will be using. For the fresh plums and apricots the dough will need to be cut larger than for the dried fruits. For extra sweetness, dab a little sugar between the pieces of dried fruit before placing in the center of the dough. Wrap the dough around the fruit, sealing all edges tightly. You should not be able to see the filling through the dough. If you can, you have stretched the dough too thin. Roll the filled dough in your hands to form the *knodel*. It is a very forgiving dough and easy to work with.

Drop the *knodels* in the boiling water and cook about 10 minutes. Gently move them around the pot so they don't stick to the bottom or to each other. Remove with a slotted spoon and allow them to drain on a paper towel.

While they drain, prepare the topping, by melting the butter in a small skillet and lightly browning the bread crumbs with the sugar and cinnamon. After a few minutes, the topping should be light brown and you are ready to roll. Pour the topping into a small bowl and roll the *knodel* in the browned crumbs. If you like, you can sprinkle the *knodels* with vanilla sugar, confectioners sugar or poppy seeds. Eat at once.

Feedback

Vanilla sugar is a favorite sweetener for many German cooks. Take one or two vanilla beans and split down the center. Place them in a tight container filled with confectioners or granulated sugar. Let the flavor permeate the sugar for several days before using. Vanilla sugar is also sold in specialty food stores and on-line.

Marsha Meyer's German Potato Salad

Don't you dare open that jar of mayonnaise! Marsha's German potato salad is all about the apple cider vinegar, scallions and shallots and her secret ingredient, chicken broth. Together they provide all the flavor you need for this home-style favorite.

Yields: 4 to 6 servings; Start to Finish: Under 30 minutes

1½ pounds Red Bliss or Yukon Gold potatoes, peeled

⅓ cup chicken broth

⅓ cup apple cider vinegar (more or less to taste)

Pinch of sugar, to taste

½ small red onion, finely chopped (about ½ cup)

4 scallions, white and light green part only, thinly sliced

1 large shallot, finely minced

6 small gherkins, finely chopped

Kosher salt and pepper

Garnish:

Chopped fresh flat-leaf parsley, chives, or chervil

Bring a large pot of salted water to boil and cook the potatoes until they are fork tender, about 20 minutes. You want them soft but not mushy, drain and reserve. While the potatoes cook, prepare the dressing. In a large bowl, whisk together the chicken broth, vinegar and sugar. Stir in the onion, scallions, shallot and gherkins. When the potatoes are cool enough to handle, slice them into thin rounds. Gently toss the potatoes with the dressing. Season to taste with salt and pepper. Cool and serve topped with freshly chopped herbs. The salad is even better after a day or two, so feel free to make it in advance of serving.

Kurt and Gisela Obernbreit

As told by Kurt's daughter, Ruth Obernbreit

Ruth is an accomplished writer with a colorful family history. Her father, an Austrian refugee fled Nazi oppression for safe haven in the Dominican Republic. Ruth, Kurt's only child, wrote his story in a piece she entitled "Paradise 1943." The following is an excerpt from that essay originally published in *The Westchester Review.*

After the Anschluss, as Hitler marched into Austria in 1938, my father's family began to feverishly figure out how to leave Vienna. The small family included my grandfather, the fastidious Edmund; my grandmother, Gisela, a middle-class hausfrau; and my father, Kurt, an only child who at eighteen was a *Gymnasium* (secondary school) graduate with an academic diploma. They were desperate. One afternoon, my grandmother was in the butcher store on the Wenggasse. She overheard a woman describe how her son was able to get out of

the country. He had mailed the instructions written in invisible ink on the wrapping of a package. The directions were shared with my grandmother... In a certain village you bribed the local Nazi officer. You then found a certain spot at the end of the village and walked several hours in the woods where you were met by representatives of the "naturefriends" a group in Switzerland that housed refugees... This is exactly what my eighteen year-old father did.

He lived with the Swiss for two years while he looked for a place in the world that would take him. While my father and the other refugees were requesting visas, President Roosevelt was organizing an international conference in Evian, the one where the only head of state to offer refuge was a malevolent dictator (Trujillo) who said he would take 100,000 Jews. My father found out about this possibility and somehow in the first winter of the war, in 1940, he arrived in Portugal awaiting a ship to what was then called Santo Domingo.

"It was like a kibbutz," my father would tell me of the living and working arrangements of Sosua. Every Jewish immigrant was given the equivalent of 80 acres, 10 cows, a mule and a horse. My father milked cows; he learned to love the smell of hay and manure. Whatever Trujillo's motivation, my father and his new friends were riding horses, planting tomatoes and were spared the ravages of the ghettos and concentration camps where others met their fate.

In 1943, my father was able to secure a visa for his father, Edmund, to come to Sosua. He was on the last shipload of settlers to arrive. Once there, he suffered a heart attack and it was my father's obligation to write his mother and inform her of his death. At the time, his mother was working in England as a domestic. She was now able to secure a visa to Ecuador and persuaded my father to leave the Dominican Republic and meet her there. My father loved the Dominican people, knowing them to be warm and accepting of him and his people. They did not just save him physically, but more importantly, I think they saved his soul.

Ruth has two daughters who proudly carry on the family traditions.

Top left: Kurt Obernbreit (center), Sosua, Dominican Republic

Gisela Obernbreit's Thin and Crispy *Wiener Schnitzel*– Breaded Veal Cutlets

Ruth relates memories of her grandmother Gisela's cooking. "My Viennese grandmother was a very fine cook. When I was a little girl, I would sleep over at her apartment on West 78th Street and she would make my favorite meal, *Wiener schnitzel* and creamed spinach! Then we would watch Lawrence Welk together. The next day, in the afternoon, her lady friends would come over and visit. They knew each other from Vienna since they were children, even before World War I, yet they still referred to each other using last names only. She made all these things in a windowless kitchen, which clearly had been transformed from a closet, [with] a tiny stove, small fridge and little table on which she would pound, roll and mix by hand."

Yields: 4 servings; Start to Finish: Under 15 minutes

1 pound veal cutlets, pounded very thin

½ cup solid vegetable shortening (such as Crisco)

½ cup all-purpose flour, seasoned with kosher salt

2 eggs, beaten

¾ cup plain bread crumbs

Garnish:

Freshly chopped flat-leaf parsley and lemon wedges

Have your butcher pound the cutlets very thin, or place them in an un-sealed resealable bag, pound the veal until paper thin, using a meat mallet or the bottom of a heavy pan, to about ⅛-inch thick. The pounding not only thins the cutlets, but also breaks down the sinewy tissue that makes the meat tough.

Heat the shortening in a skillet until it is very hot. You can use vegetable oil, but a solid vegetable shortening is preferred. The oil is ready when a few bread crumbs dropped in the pan, sizzle and brown up quickly. True crispy *schnitzel* should soak up very little oil. Maintaining the proper temperature reduces the amount of oil absorbed.

Dip the veal first in the seasoned flour, then beaten eggs and then in the bread crumbs. Do not press the crumbs into the meat. Lightly shake off excess. Fry the veal, over medium heat, until crispy and golden brown, about 4 minutes on each side. Swirling the pan helps create those waves and ripples in the crust that *schnitzel* is known for. Serve immediately, sprinkled with freshly chopped parsley and a wedge of lemon. Parsley Red Bliss potatoes (recipe follows) make a great accompaniment.

Parsley Red Bliss Potatoes

The perfect accompaniment to authentic schnitzel.

Yields: 4 servings; Start to Finish: Under 30 minutes

10 to 12 small Red Bliss potatoes (about 1½ pounds), quartered

½ cup finely chopped fresh flat-leaf parsley

2 to 3 tablespoons margarine

Bring a medium pot of salted water to boil, and cook the potatoes until fork tender, about 15 minutes. Drain the potatoes and toss them with the parsley and margarine. Serve alongside the schnitzel.

JFH

Gisela Obernbreit's *Gluwein*–Mulled Wine

While Ruth's father craved a good cup of Dominican *café con leche* with his *Tres Leches* cake (recipes to follow) on a cold winter night, nothing was more appealing than a mug of steamy Austrian *Gluwein*, which translates to mean "glow wine," a heady combination of red and white wine, with spices and a hint of lemon.

Serves: 10 to 12; Start to Finish: Under 15 minutes

2 cups water

1 cup sugar

¼ cup brown sugar

3 sticks cinnamon

6 cloves

½ lemon, zested

1 quart red wine, a mild merlot works well

1 quart white wine

In a saucepan bring the first 6 ingredients to boil, stir to completely dissolve the sugar. Add the red and white wine and bring to a slow, low boil. Serve hot in glass mugs.

Ruth Obernbreit's *Tres Leches*–Three Milk Cake

Ruth recalls, "When my father was missing the Dominican Republic he would have a yen for a really good cup of *café con leche* and a piece of this cake, which is totally out of this world. Don't be concerned that the cake seems soggy when first prepared. It absorbs the three varieties of milk as it sits overnight in the fridge."

Yields: 12 to 16 pieces; Start to Finish: Under 1 hour, then refrigerate for 6 to 8 hours or overnight

1½ cups all-purpose flour

1 teaspoon baking powder

1 stick (½ cup) butter, room temperature

1 cup sugar

5 eggs

½ teaspoon vanilla extract

1 cup whole milk

1 (14-ounce) can sweet condensed milk

1 (12-ounce) can evaporated regular or skim milk

Preheat the oven to 325 degrees and grease and flour a 13x9x2-inch Pyrex baking dish.

Sift together the flour and baking powder. In a separate bowl, beat the butter and sugar on medium speed, for several minutes, until light and creamy. When the butter is a pale yellow, beat in the eggs, one at a time. Stir in the vanilla. With the mixer on low, begin adding the flour until all the ingredients are well combined. Pour the batter into the prepared baking dish and bake at 325 degrees for 30 minutes, or until the top of the cake is a golden yellow color, firm to the touch, with brown tinged edges.

Let the cake cool for at least 10 minutes.

Combine the three milks and pour them over the cooled cake. Cover tightly with plastic wrap and refrigerate for 6 to 8 hours or overnight. Top with fresh whipped cream, smother with berries or a drizzle of melted chocolate—or all three!

Ruth Obernbreit's *Café con Leche*–Coffee with Warmed Milk

This should really be called "*leche con café*" as it is really milk with coffee! This is what Dominicans have each morning for breakfast with their large slice of toasted bread or in the evening to accompany their *Tres Leches* cake.

Yields: 1 cup of café con leche; Start to Finish: Under 15 minutes

Whole, evaporated or soy milk

Pinch of salt

1 to 2 shots of espresso or strong brewed coffee

Sugar to taste

Heat the milk in a small saucepan with a pinch of salt. When the milk begins to scald (right before it boils), take it off the stove. Pour the hot milk into a mug, filling it one half to two-thirds full, depending on how milky you like it. Add a shot (or 2) of espresso or very strong coffee. Sweeten to taste.

Ruth and Vittorio Orvieto

In Ruth's words

Ruth's story is very international. From a childhood in Germany, coming of age in Ecuador and a 57-year marriage to Vittorio, an Italian survivor, Ruth's life experiences have truly covered the globe.

I was born in Breslau, Germany and had one older brother. On Kristallnacht, my sixteen-year-old brother was almost taken to a labor camp, so shortly after that my family shipped him off to Palestine. My father was sent to Buchenwald, and my mother went everyday to the Gestapo to negotiate for his release. At that time they would still let him go if she could secure a visa for him to another country. She secured visas for him alone to Shanghai, but he would not go without us. We scrambled and quickly got visas for the entire family to Ecuador instead. We arrived in Ecuador in 1939; I was twelve at the time. Life was very different for us. In Germany, my father was a successful manufacturer, in Ecuador, he sold butter. Before leaving we had packed our suitcases with items to use for bartering. When we arrived at the docks to leave Germany, the Gestapo confiscated our bags. We arrived in Guayaquil, Ecuador literally with nothing but the clothes on our backs. When I was thirteen, I had to stop school and go to work to help support our family.

In Ecuador, I didn't consider myself to be German. I had only one dream and that was to get out of there and go to America. I had an affidavit, and I could have gone, but I met and married my husband and we began raising a family. My husband, Vittorio, was born in Genoa, Italy, and left there at nineteen to escape the Holocaust. He often recalled the enormous kindness of the Italian people who helped him board a ship to Ecuador. I always say that was the only good thing Hitler did for me. After my second child was born, I knew I wanted to give my children a better life and a good education. We came to America in 1955, where we had our third child. I never felt German, and preferred to cook the Italian food my husband enjoyed. We were married 57 years and have three children, eight grandchildren and one great grandchild.

Ruth Orvieto's Risotto

While Ruth's background is German, her husband Vittorio, favored his familiar Italian dishes. Even when they lived in Ecuador, Ruth cooked in the Italian tradition. Risotto was one of her go-to dinners, studded with sweet onions, Porcini mushrooms and lots of freshly grated Parmesan cheese. No doubt, you need to baby-sit risotto a little, while the crunchy outer kernels of the Arborio rice slowly absorb the white wine and hot broth. Be sure to use a dry white that is wine-glass-worthy; never cook with wine that is not good enough to drink!

Yields: 4 servings, as a main course, 6 servings as a starter; Start to Finish: Under 1 hour

1 (1-ounce) dried Porcini mushrooms	2 cups uncooked Arborio rice
4 to 5 cups vegetable broth	½ cup white wine
3 tablespoons olive oil	½ cup grated Parmesan cheese
1 small onion, chopped (about ½ cup)	Kosher salt and pepper
3 tablespoons butter	Chopped fresh flat-leaf parsley, for garnish

Soak the dried mushrooms in 1 cup of hot water for 30 minutes, and then strain the mushrooms and their liquid, using a small piece of cheesecloth. You should have about ¾ cup of liquid reserved. In a medium saucepan, heat the vegetable broth and add the mushroom liquid. Cover and keep on a low simmer. Rinse, and then chop the mushrooms, pat dry and reserve.

Heat the olive oil in a large skillet, cook and stir the onions, over medium heat, until they are just softening and translucent, about 5 minutes. Stir 1 tablespoon of butter in the pan, and add the rice. Cook and stir the rice for several minutes (the rice will go from white to almost clear). Stir in the white wine and cook until the wine evaporates, this should only take a minute or two.

Using the back of the ladle spread the rice out in the pan so it is in one thin layer. Begin stirring in your first ladle (about ½ cup) of heated broth. Keep the heat low; you don't want to rush this process. When the liquid is almost completely absorbed, stir in your next ladle. Continue adding the broth and stirring until you have used about half the liquid. Stir the reserved Porcini mushrooms into the rice. Continue the ladling process until there are about 2 ladles of broth left in the pot. Stir the remaining 2 tablespoons of butter and grated cheese into the rice. Test the rice to see if it is *al dente* —you want it to be creamy but retain a little bite. Add the remaining broth, or hot water until you achieve your desired consistency. Season to taste with salt and pepper. Serve immediately with a sprinkling of grated cheese, a drizzle of olive oil and a pinch of freshly chopped parsley.

Variations: Ruth suggests adding 1 cup of thawed frozen peas when you add the mushrooms.

For Risotto Milanese, Ruth would flavor the dish with saffron. Saffron is very expensive, but a little goes a long way. Omit the mushrooms and their liquid; they would overwhelm the subtle flavor of the saffron. Use 5 cups of broth and add ½ teaspoon of saffron to the broth as it heats. When you stir the broth into the rice, you will see the color begin to change to a mellow yellow. Threads of saffron will remain in the finished dish.

Ruth Orvieto's *Gnocchi Alla Romana*–Semolina Gnocchi with Cheese

Ruth's version of gnocchi, crusty, pillowy rounds of baked semolina layered with butter and Parmesan cheese, makes a beautiful presentation and a rich alternative to polenta or baked noodles.

Yields: 4 to 6 servings; Start to Finish: Under 1 ½ hours

2½ cups whole milk

¾ cup semolina flour

4 tablespoons butter; 2 tablespoons cold, 2 tablespoons melted

1 egg yolk, beaten

1 teaspoon kosher salt

¼ cup Parmesan cheese

In a medium saucepan, heat the milk till scalding (the point right before boiling, you'll see a skin begin to form on the top of the milk). Lower the heat to a simmer and begin adding the semolina, ¼ cup at a time. Stir with a whisk to avoid clumping. Once the semolina is completely incorporated, begin stirring with a wooden spoon; the mixture will look like mashed potatoes. On the lowest simmer possible, cook the semolina for 15 to 20 minutes, it will continue to thicken and when you stir, it should pull away from the sides of the pot. It is done when it is very stiff and resembles wet dough.

Take off the heat and stir in 2 tablespoons of cold butter, the egg yolk, salt and half the cheese. The semolina will become very elastic and completely leave the sides of the pot. Clean and lightly dampen a large counter, or a marble slab. Turn the semolina mixture onto the cool, clean, damp surface and using a wet spatula or rolling pin, spread the semolina into a ½-inch layer. Let the mixture cool for at least 20 minutes. The dough should be cool to the touch before beginning the next step.

Preheat the oven to 425 degrees and lightly butter the bottom of an 11 x 7-inch rectangular baking dish.* In a separate small bowl, melt the remaining 2 tablespoons of butter and reserve.

Using a 1½-inch round cookie cutter, cut circles from the dough and begin layering them in the pan. Start with 24 rounds on the bottom (4 across, 6 down). Using a pastry brush, brush the rounds with the reserved melted butter and sprinkle a little of the remaining cheese on top. Cut 18 rounds for the next layer, and in a pyramid fashion, place those rounds on top of the first layer, (3 across, 6 down). Brush with butter and sprinkle with cheese. Your next layer will be 12 pieces, (2 across, 6 down) and the final layer will be 6 pieces, right down the center; brush with butter and sprinkle each layer with cheese. You will need to gather the scraps of dough and roll them out again in order to complete the layering. Pour any remaining butter on top and sprinkle with the rest of the cheese. Bake at 425 degrees for 20 to 25 minutes or until the top lightly browns.

You can also use an 8-inch round or 9-inch square pan, following the same layering patterns. You will need between 60-64 rounds.

David and Mary May Prussin

Judy's parents, David and Mary May Prussin, both immigrated to the United States from Germany, as living there became ominously dangerous. Her father arrived in 1937, her mother in 1939. David and Mary's two children, two grandchildren and six great grandchildren are happy they did.

Judy Prussin's Spiked *Mandel* Bread

Judy makes a traditional German cookie, *Mandelbrot*, from the German meaning "almond bread." Judy's derives its almond flavor from a nice dose of Amaretto, which she pairs with a variety of dried fruit and nuts. Judy's is a twice baked, stand-up-to-a-big-mug-of-coffee, crunchy, chocolaty delight.

Yields: 28 cookies; Start to Finish: Under 3 hours

1 stick (½ cup) butter, room temperature

¾ cup sugar

2 eggs

1 cup Amaretto

2½ cups all-purpose flour, plus more if needed

⅓ cup unsweetened cocoa powder

1½ teaspoons baking powder

¼ teaspoon salt

1½ to 2 cups assorted nuts and dried fruit; almonds, hazelnuts, pistachios, macadamia nuts, dried cranberries and dried cherries (break-up any large pieces)

1½ cups chopped white chocolate or 12 ounces white chocolate chips

Preheat the oven to 325 degrees and grease and flour a 20 x15-inch baking sheet.

Beat the butter and sugar in a large bowl, on medium speed, until light and creamy. Lower the speed and beat in the eggs and Amaretto.

In a separate bowl, combine the flour, cocoa powder, baking powder and salt. On low speed, stir the flour into the butter mixture and then blend on medium speed until well combined. The dough will be thick, pasty, and wet. If the dough is very wet, add a little more flour. Thoroughly stir in the nuts, dried fruit and white chocolate. Divide the dough in half. On the prepared baking sheet, shape each half of dough into a log about 14 inches long x 1 ½ inches wide x 1 ½ inches high (lightly wet your hands or use the spatula to help shape the logs). Space the logs several inches apart, as they will grow while baking.

Bake at 325 degrees for 30 to 45 minutes; the top of the cookie should be firm. Carefully transfer the logs from the baking sheet to a cooling tray and let them cool for 1 hour. You can turn the oven off and reheat it about 20 minutes before you need to bake the cookies for the second time. After an hour, using a serrated knife, slice the logs, on the diagonal, into pieces that are about 1–inch thick. Try not to use a rocking motion, which might break the cookies. Transfer the cut-cookies back onto the baking sheet, standing them upright, about ¼-inch apart. Bake at 325 degrees for an additional 30 to 45 minutes, depending on how crunchy you like them. Cool the cookies on a tray and store them in a sealed container.

Wolfgang "Wolfie" Rauner

A little Henny Youngman, a bit Master of Ceremonies and completely charming, that's how I would describe Wolfgang "Wolfie" "Johnny" Rauner. He loves to cook, write and kibbitz.

I was born in Trier, the oldest city in Germany. My early childhood was spent in the southwestern portion of the country, close to Alsace Lorraine. Our cooking techniques borrowed heavily from the French. My mother learned the domestic arts in France, so her food not only tasted delicious, but also was presented beautifully; a sandwich would look like a banquet. In 1935, my father anticipated the mounting turmoil in Germany and moved the family to nearby Luxemburg. It was easy for us to leave because we had very little in Germany so there was little to leave behind. For five years we lived peacefully, however, my father struggled to support us. We attended public schools, which were staffed by nuns in the early grades. In May of 1940, Hitler invaded Luxemburg, and we were now under German occupation. In 1941, we left Luxemburg for the United States.

I annually observe the anniversary of my arrival in this country, June 21, 1941 as a personal holiday, by proudly flying the Star Spangled Banner. It was then that we settled safely in Washington Heights, New York, or, as we liked to call it, "the fourth Reich." Both of my older brothers were drafted into the armed forces, one in 1942 and the second in 1943. My first brother was part of the "Ritchie Boys" who worked intelligence during the war. The second brother was in the Airborne Infantry and served as a translator. He was wounded landing in a glider while crossing the Rhine.

I always worked, often in sales. At one time, while working for Buitoni, a large supplier of Italian prepared foods, I was instrumental in bringing kosher supervision to the company. To this day, I love cooking Italian food; some of my most creative specialties are from that region.

Pesach in my home always included matzo balls. Not the usual preparation or serving style. In my mother's home growing up, they were boiled. In my father's they were fried. It's funny because my parents grew up in towns very near each other, but they each had a different way to serve the matzo balls. In my home growing up, my mother, the diplomat, made both. Boiled were served with soup, the fried ones with the main dish. For over 30 years this tradition has survived. These matzo balls are not like what we make today, they had their origin in the Alsatian kitchen. To this day, I'm still very much affected by the love my mother showed, through her cooking. My wife and I have two children and five grandchildren.

Top left: Wolfie (second from the left) with his two older brothers, Ludwig and Edgar and sister, Gertrude (Trudy)

Wolfie Rauner's *Matzo Kloesse*–Dumplings

Wolfie, with his usual witty style, describes in great detail the process for making this traditional Passover dish that he has eaten since he was a boy. When boiled they are a replacement for matzo balls, when fried they are a lot like falafel. "My grandfather on my father's side operated a small bakery in the town of Merzig and also owned the best–known matzo bakery in the entire region. Generations later, people asked me, on first meeting, if I was related to "the Matzo Baker of Merzig." Thus in my parent's home, every Pesach my mother made two kinds of "*Matzo Kloesse*." We called them "*Freudenburger*" and "*Merziger*." Essentially they were made of the same basic recipe, only *Freudenberger* were boiled and the *Merziger* were fried. When making these, I start by throwing everyone out of the kitchen. I end by cleaning up the mess, before my wife gets back in. Be sure they don't fall on the floor, because if they hit your foot, they could just break your toe! In my early-married years and when my children were growing up I remember standing the whole day before Erev Pesach and making huge quantities of both varieties. Usually having guests at our seder and two growing boys, we managed to put away quite a few. Even in later years when we went for seder to my son's house I still had to bring them along."

Yields: 20 to 24 Matzo Kloesse; Start to Finish: Step One: Under 30 minutes, then at least 2 hours or up to 24 hours in the fridge, Step Two: Under 30 minutes

2 large onions, chopped (about 2 cups)

2 tablespoons chicken fat or vegetable oil

4 sheets matzo, broken into small jigsaw puzzle-like pieces

3 eggs, beaten

¼ cup chopped curly parsley

⅛ to ¼ teaspoon ground ginger

2 teaspoons kosher salt

½ teaspoon pepper (white preferred)

Matzo meal

Oil for frying or broth or salted water for boiling

Step One: Heat the fat or oil in a large skillet, cook and stir the onions, over medium heat, until brown but not burnt, about 15 minutes. While the onions cook, soak the broken matzo in a bowl filled with cold water. After 10 minutes, squeeze all the water from the matzo and let them sit in between two pieces of paper towel to absorb any residual water. Stir the matzo into the cooked onions, and cook over low heat, until the mixture is dry, about 5 minutes.

Spoon the cooked matzo and onions into a bowl, let them cool down for 5 minutes, then stir in the eggs, parsley, ginger, salt and pepper. Using a wooden spoon, or your hands, combine the mixture thoroughly. The mixture might look liquidy, but it soaks up the eggs as it sits. Cover with a piece of plastic wrap and refrigerate for at least 2 hours or up to one day.

(Continued)

Step Two: *To Prepare "Freudenburger" –Boiled Matzo Kloesse*

Take the mixture out of the fridge and bring a large pot of salted water or broth to boil.

Add ½ cup of matzo meal to the matzo ball mixture. This should help firm the mixture and prevent the matzo balls from falling apart when boiled. Roll the matzo mixture into 1-inch balls (a little oil or Pam sprayed on your hands will help). Drop the matzo balls into the boiling liquid, reduce the heat to medium, and boil until the matzo balls fluff up and rise to the surface, about 15 minutes. Eat with the soup or serve with a helping of fried onions on top.

To Prepare "Merziger" –Fried Matzo Kloesse

Add ¼ cup of matzo meal to the matzo mixture. Sprinkle a little matzo meal on a flat plate. Roll the matzo mixture into 1-inch balls (a little oil or Pam sprayed on your hands will help), then roll the balls in the matzo meal crumbs for an extra crunch on the outside. Let them sit in the fridge while the oil heats.

Heat a skillet with ¼-inch of oil. When the oil is hot, carefully place the *Matzo Kloesse* in the pan and brown on all sides, over medium heat, for several minutes. They should be brown and crisp on the outside, soft inside. Drain on a paper towel and eat as a side dish.

Feedback

The matzo mixture, before it is boiled or fried, would make a terrific Passover stuffing. Try pairing it with Florence Edelstein's breast of veal (see page 291).

Mark Schachner

Professional contributor

Wolfie explains that according to tradition or interpretation of the Talmud, because the Pascal lamb was roasted, you are not supposed to have fire-roasted meat at the seder. His father interpreted it more strictly and did not permit anything even remotely roasted to be served. Their first seder night would always be boiled chicken, and their second night would always be boiled sweet and sour tongue. Mark Schachner, owner of the famous Mill Basin Deli, contributed a delicious and classic sweet and sour sauce that pairs with Wolfie's holiday recollections.

Tongue Polonaise

Contributed by Mark Schachner, owner of Mill Basin Deli, Brooklyn, New York

Tongue Polonaise takes the classic elements of sweet and sour to create a delicious sauce that complements the delicate flavor of pickled tongue.

Serves: A large family!

1 quart sauerkraut

2 teaspoons salt

½ teaspoon pepper

2 quarts tomato puree

Juice of 3 lemons

1 cup sugar

1 (16-ounce) can chunk pineapple

Mix all the ingredients in a large pot, bring to a boil, then simmer for about 45 minutes, or until thick. Boil a pickled tongue until cooked or buy sliced pickled tongue. When ready to serve, pour the sauce over the meat and enjoy. Any remaining sauce can be used for stuffed cabbage or brisket.

Feedback

Pickling tongue at home is time consuming, and requires brining and soaking the tongue in that brine for up to a week. However, most specialty butchers sell tongue already pickled. You simply boil the tongue, then reduce the heat to a low simmer for about 3 hours, or until the tongue is fork tender. Be sure to skim and discard the foam that rises to the surface. Slice thin and serve with the Polonaise sauce.

Irma and Martin Reich

As told by their daughter, Suzanne Schaps

Both of Suzanne's parents were Holocaust survivors; one endured internment, the other was a refugee. Suzanne remembers a home where food took on such an important role. She recalls a Hebrew expression that her Mom would use, that translated means, "food is my life." That was the overwhelming feeling growing up in her home. Suzanne provides us with a glimpse into their experiences and shares one of her favorite family recipes.

My mother, Irma was one of two surviving children of Henny and Alfred Hamburger. She lived in a small town near Hamburg; called Fürstenau, Germany. My mother was lucky enough to be a passenger on a *Kindertransport*, which in 1938 took children from Germany to England. She was 18 years old at the time. Her brother had left Germany earlier and was now living safely in Colombia, South America. To support herself, my mother first worked as a housekeeper in England. She had no language skills, but was very bright and able to adapt. She was very unnerved by the bombings that took place in England. It was then that she made the decision to leave England to live with her brother in South America. When she arrived, she was threatened with deportation, but ultimately was able to stay.

My father Martin's experience was very different. I know he survived internment in France, in four different camps. When he came to America, he and my mother made a life together. I was raised very American, and my mother's cooking was not strictly, "immigrant style." She was a phenomenal cook and always made delicious food and presented it with an elegant flair. As their only child I try to keep the traditions alive and share them with my two daughters, so they will hopefully live on.

Top left: Irma Hamburger Reich

Henny Bachrach's Almond and Apple Cake

Suzanne was effusive when describing her grandmother's holiday cake. "I particularly remember the delicious nut cake my mother would make for us every year at Passover. It was a recipe handed down to her, by her mother, my grandmother, Henny Bachrach. It had small coffee beans as decoration and a wonderful mocha filling. Because my grandmother Henny didn't have measuring utensils, she would use the broken eggshells to measure the matzo meal. We left that in as a nod to my grandma's resourcefulness. Be sure to prepare the cake one day ahead, it makes it easier to frost and allows the ingredients to set. I hope you enjoy it as much as I did as a child."

Yields: 10 to 12 servings; Start to Finish: Under 1 ½ hours

For the batter:

8 eggs, separated

1 cup sugar

8 ounces ground almonds (about 1 ¾ to 2 cups)

The zest of 1 lemon peel

Juice of half a lemon

(5 to 6) half eggshells matzo meal (a little less than 1 cup)

1 large red unpeeled apple, grated

Mocha Cream Frosting or Filling:

½ pint (1 cup) heavy cream

1½ teaspoons sugar

1 tablespoon brewed coffee, cooled

Raspberry jam for filling (optional)

Mocha coffee beans for garnish (optional)

Preheat the oven to 350 degrees and grease a 9-inch spring form pan.

To prepare the batter, beat the egg yolks and sugar, in a large bowl, on medium speed until pale yellow, about 4 minutes. Stir in the almonds, lemon zest, lemon juice, matzo meal and grated apple.

In a separate bowl, beat the egg whites to form stiff but not dry peaks. Gently fold the egg whites into the egg mixture. Pour the batter into the prepared pan and bake at 350 degrees for 1 hour. Cool well before removing from pan.

While the cake cools, prepare the mocha cream by combining all the frosting ingredients and beating on high speed until the cream is thick but not hard. To assemble the cake, carefully slice the cake in half, through the middle, creating two layers. Spread either a layer of mocha frosting, or a layer of raspberry jam in the middle. Place the second layer on top and frost the sides and top with the mocha frosting. Decorate with the mocha coffee beans, if using. The cake can be frozen in the spring form pan and frosted at a later time.

Melly Resnicow

In her own words

Melly is a very articulate woman who came to America following Kristallnacht. Her story talks about the quota system, which was a calculated method for controlling immigration to the United States. Your status was linked to the country in which you were born. Those born in Germany received a more favorable number than those born in Poland. This system was responsible for dividing her family when they immigrated to the United States.

I was born in the Saxony region of Germany. The family settled in Munich and experienced Kristallnacht there. My father was arrested and taken to Dachau, but after two weeks he was released and ordered to leave the country within 24 hours, which we happily did! My mother was able to obtain visas to Switzerland for herself, my father, my brother and me. That is where he waited for his quota number to come up. Because he had been born in Poland, he was listed on the Polish quota, while we were part of the German quota. We arrived in America in December, 1938, my father was able to join us in April, 1939.

I was comfortable being here, and after two years at PS16 in Williamsburg, I became editor of the school magazine. I had two teachers who worked with me to teach me English (I had some private lessons when I was in Munich but only learned a few words of what I call " British" English). In 1946, when I was twenty, I married my American-born husband; we were married for 52 years. Together we had four children and I am the proud grandmother of six grandchildren.

I learned to cook in Germany, when I was about seven or eight. We had a housekeeper who did the cleaning, but my mother always cooked. I started baking around that time, mostly "assisting" my mother when she was baking. Someone presented me with a cookbook for children and then I really got going. I remember making lots of cookies, which my younger brother gladly consumed; he still has a "sweet tooth." I continue to cook and bake at home for holiday meals and then I transport it to my children's homes; they refer to me as " the caterer" and are very appreciative!

Top left: Melly Resnicow (left) with her mother

Melly Resnicow's Chocolate Roll

Melly is a home baker with professional skills and knowledge that could put Martha Stewart to shame. This light and elegant confection is a flourless chocolate cake filled with sweet whipped cream. It is certain to impress company and satisfy anyone seeking a delicious chocolate dessert. Don't let the steps intimidate you, as Melly says, "it's practically foolproof."

Yields: 10 to 12 servings; Start to Finish: Under 2 hours

For the batter:

6 ounces semi-sweet chocolate chips

3 tablespoons water

¾ cup granulated sugar

5 eggs, separated

For the filling:

1 cup heavy cream

2 tablespoons confectioner's sugar

1 teaspoon vanilla

For dusting the cake:

Dutch cocoa powder

Confectioner's sugar (optional)

Preheat the oven to 375 degrees.

Begin the batter by melting the chocolate and 3 tablespoons of water in a double boiler over simmering water, stirring occasionally to keep the chocolate smooth. Remove from the heat, transfer the chocolate to a large bowl and cool slightly. In a separate bowl, beat the sugar and egg yolks, until light and fluffy. Stir the egg mixture into the cooled chocolate. In a medium bowl, beat the egg whites until stiff but not dry and gently fold them into the chocolate batter.

Grease a 15x11x2-inch jellyroll pan, then line with a piece of wax paper with the ends of the paper hanging over the edges of the pan. This will help lift the cake off when it is done. Grease the wax paper and spread the batter evenly in the pan. Bake at 375 degrees for 15 minutes.

Dampen a dishtowel and wring out the excess water so it is barely wet. Cover the cake with the towel until the cake is completely cooled, about 1 hour. Using a small knife, loosen the edges of the cake that might have attached to the sides of the pan, and gently lift the cake off the pan (using the extended side pieces of wax paper as handles). Sprinkle the cake with a dusting of cocoa powder (a small kitchen strainer works well). Cover the counter with 2 new overlapping pieces of wax paper, and then gently turn the cake over so that the bottom is now the top. Peel the wax paper from the cake.

To make the filling, whip the cream, sugar and vanilla until firm. Spread evenly over the entire cake. To create a log that is 15 inches long x 3 inches wide, using the wax paper as a guide, gently roll the cake away from you. After each turn, press down gently sliding your hands over the roll. The " seam" should be on the bottom. Take a small knife and cut off the paper along the sides of the roll, but leave the ends!! This will facilitate lifting the roll onto a platter. Cut a thin piece of cake from each end on the diagonal (Melly says, "these are for the baker"), additionally, cut off the paper "handles." For presentation you can leave the log whole or cut into slices. Confectioner's sugar can be sprinkled on top, and additional cocoa powder can be dusted on top if the cake has any small cracks.

Evelyn Pike Rubin

In her own words

Evelyn Pike Rubin is the author of *Ghetto Shanghai*, an amazing story of sanctuary and survival. She lives in Jericho, New York, with her husband, Leonard. The following is an edited excerpt from her book.

I was born in Breslau, Germany (now Wroczlaw, Poland) at the onset of the Nazi era to a religiously observant Jewish family. My parents owned and operated a wholesale paper and twine business, which had been founded by my mother during World War I. My parents were vacillating between leaving Germany immediately or "waiting it out" as Jews had been doing during the 2,000 years of the dispersion. In 1935 the Nuremberg Laws were promulgated. It was at that time that my parents were looking for countries we could immigrate to. They tried Brazil, Palestine (under British Mandate), Cuba, England, America, all to no avail. When it seemed there was no way out of Nazi-ruled Germany, we heard about one little glimmer of hope. The conquering Japanese, victors of the Sino-Japanese war of 1937, had established the port of Shanghai, China, as an "open" city. There was a good possibility one could go there without a visa, just for the price of a steamship ticket. My parents, however, decided to put the idea of going to Shanghai "on the back-burner," still hoping to get an American affidavit from a great-aunt of mine living in Brooklyn, New York in the near future. When we finally received the affidavit, to our consternation, we were informed by the American Consulate that we were assigned to the Polish quota because, under the Versailles Treaty, after World War I, my father's place of birth was integrated into Poland. In 1938 that quota was filled and we were assigned a high number.

Kristallnacht—November 9-10, 1938—of course, was the beginning of the end for European Jewry. My father had been among those arrested and sent to Buchenwald. During his incarceration, my mother purchased tickets for us to leave for Shanghai the following February. This was most fortuitous, for the Nazis had decided to release almost all those arrested during the Kristallnacht pogrom, with the proviso that they would leave Germany within two months. My father was released in December. On February 9, 1939, we took the train to Naples, Italy for the month-long voyage into the unknown—Shanghai, China.

We arrived in Shanghai on March 14, 1939. My mother sold the personal possessions we had brought with us to purchase an apartment and to establish a typewriter business with my father doing the repairs with a hired Chinese mechanic and my mother taking care of the business end. My father's mother joined us in Shanghai in June, 1940. The refugee population had reached approximately 18,000 by 1941. My father, whose war wound had acted up in Buchenwald and was left untreated, succumbed to these conditions at age 43, leaving my mother, my grandmother and me.

On February 18, 1943, the Japanese issued a proclamation to the refugee community stating that we had three months to "relocate to a designated area." In effect we were going to live in a ghetto. The area was Hongkew. My mother sold her apartment to a Japanese family and with three other families we moved into a four room hovel, one bathroom, cold running water, and no heat. A T'ung, Special Pass, could be

Top left: Evelyn with her parents

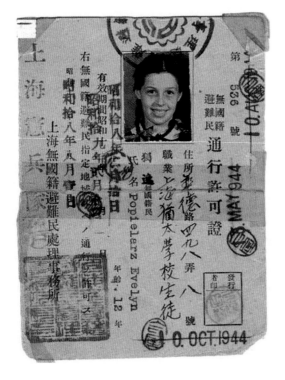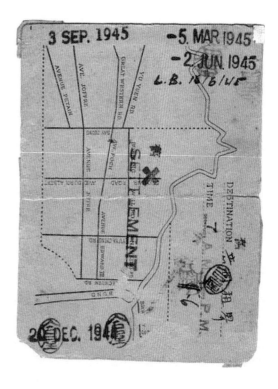

obtained from Mr. Goya, one of the Japanese ghetto administrators. Most, though not all of the Special Pass applicants who could demonstrate they needed a pass to make a living outside the ghetto, did receive such a pass. My mother also received one by applying as a typewriter mechanic, with customers in the French Concession. However, she used her pass for a different purpose. By visiting Chinese peddlers in parts of the city that westerners did not often frequent, she purchased sundries (i.e. scarves, sunglasses, belts, etc.), which she brought back to the ghetto peddlers who sold them on a consignment basis. That same year, my grandmother died at the age of 74.

On July 17, 1945, American fighter planes bombed the ghetto. Some thirty refugees were killed and hundreds more were wounded. Scores of Chinese inhabitants also were killed that day. Six weeks later, Major General Claire Chenault arrived in Shanghai from Chungking, with the American Liberation Forces. Now the war was over for us also. Thus ended another chapter of Holocaust survival. When the world closed their doors to the beleaguered Jews of Europe, Emperor Hirohito had left one door open through which approximately 18,000 refugees, fleeing the Nazi terrorism, entered!

My mother and I arrived in the United States in March, 1947, on an American troop transport, passing under the Golden Gate Bridge in San Francisco. I am the proud parent to six children and sixteen grandchildren.

Top: T'ung, Special Pass, Shanghai

Evelyn Pike Rubin's Sweet Summer Peach Cake

This easy to bake cake involves a rich batter layered with perfectly ripe fruit, capturing that just-picked summer fresh taste. Peaches are one of those fruits that jump out of the orchard bushel and into your grocery cart when they are at their peak. They should be firm to the touch, but smell sweet and ripe. In the fall, try making this with crisp apples. Follow the harvest and tailor this recipe to whichever fruits are in season.

Yields: 10 to 12 servings; Start to Finish: Under 2 hours

For the batter:

4 eggs

½ cup vegetable oil

1 cup apple juice

1 teaspoon vanilla extract

3 cups all-purpose flour

2 cups granulated sugar

1 teaspoon salt

3 teaspoons baking powder

For the filling:

1 pound peaches (about 3 to 4 medium), sliced

5 tablespoons sugar mixed with 3 teaspoons ground cinnamon

Preheat the oven to 375 degrees and grease and flour a 9-inch spring form tube pan. (There are cooking sprays that have a touch of flour in them, perfect for this application.)

Prepare the batter by beating the eggs, vegetable oil, juice and vanilla, in a large bowl, on medium speed, for several minutes. In a separate bowl, sift together the flour, sugar, salt and baking powder. A standard kitchen strainer makes a great sifter. On low speed, slowly add the flour mixture to the egg mixture, and then beat on medium speed, for several minutes, until smooth and thick. If you don't have an electric mixer, you can do it Evelyn's way, sifting together the sugar, flour, baking powder and salt then creating a well and using a wooden spoon, stirring in the juice, oil, vanilla and egg.

Start the filling by removing the pits from the peaches. A simple technique is to cut around the circumference of the peach and twist. The two halves should separate and the stone pit will be easy to remove. Cut the peaches into ¼ –inch thick slices. Sprinkle the cinnamon and sugar over the peaches and toss to coat. Don't let the peach mixture sit too long or it will become soggy.

Pour a third of the batter (about 1 to 1 ¼ cups) into the bottom of the prepared pan. Top the batter with half the peaches, trying not to let them touch the sides of the pan. Spoon in the next third of batter, and then the remaining peaches, finishing with the remaining batter. Bake at 375 degrees for 1½ hours.

After 1 hour, check the cake to be sure the top is not browning too quickly. If it is, cover loosely with foil and continue baking. After 1½ hours a bamboo skewer inserted into the center of the cake should come out clean, the cake should be golden brown and the texture firm to the touch. Allow the cake to cool completely before removing from the pan. Sliding a knife around the edges and underneath the cake will make transferring to a cake plate much easier.

Feedback

Cook any remaining peaches in a saucepan until they become very soft and the syrup thickens. Cool and enjoy as a topping for the cake. A dollop of whipped cream and a scoop of vanilla ice cream couldn't hurt. The cake has a dense texture, similar to coffee cake, which makes it wonderful for breakfast the next day.

Doris Schechter

Doris is a unique contributor to the book as she is both a survivor of the Holocaust and an accomplished baker, cookbook author and restaurateur. The following is an excerpt from her first book, *My Most Favorite Dessert Company Cookbook* (HarperCollins Publishers Inc., 2001).

"I was born the year Hitler marched into Austria. My parents were living in Vienna at the time. I never learned how my father obtained the visa that allowed him to leave Vienna for Italy not long after the Anschluss. He sent for my mother and me a short time later. Italy became our adopted homeland... In 1944, my family was among the 986 refugees invited by President Roosevelt to spend the duration of the war in the United States. We crossed the Atlantic in a perilous journey on an army transport ship called the "Henry Gibbons"... In 1946, my family started a brand-new life in the Bronx... Our life was very family oriented with Friday night dinners that my grandmother Leah always prepared."

Doris married, had children and discovered her love for cooking after having received a book on the cooking of Vienna. Her European background included baking with butter, but Doris was determined to "prove to myself that pareve baking could be delicious and elegant." It was from there that My Most Favorite Dessert Company was born. Her dream was for the company to have a Manhattan presence, "a little bit of Vienna uptown." "The traditions of my faith

and my heritage colored every aspect of my life and my family's lives... I have come full circle in my life. I am the sum total of my experiences. I came to this country as a Jewish refugee from Italy, having been born in Vienna. I became an American and have loved being an American. I started baking, with the aromas of Vienna filling my head... Tradition affects every aspect of my life and connects me to my background."

I have five children and sixteen beautiful grandchildren.

Aside from being decadently delicious, Doris' Blackout Cake has a great history with the Museum of Jewish Heritage. When famed journalist and champion of Jewish refugees, Dr. Ruth Gruber, was being honored at the Museum, Doris prepared and donated 500 chocolate chip loaves, based on this recipe, for the occasion. They were such a hit, that annually, Doris bakes these as a gift to the Museum. Doris calls it "an omen" that when she saw the photograph on the invitation for the event, she was stunned to see herself, as a six year old, in the group photo taken in Oswego, New York where she lived with her family after coming to America.

Top: Doris Schechter as a child with other refugee children in upstate New York

Doris Schechter's Blackout Cake

Reprinted with permission from *My Most Favorite Dessert Company Cookbook*
(HarperCollins Publishers Inc., 2001)

One chocolate cake, cooled (recipe below)

About ¾ cup orange-scented sugar syrup (optional) (recipe follows)

Chocolate Pudding (recipe follows)

Chocolate Cake

Makes one 10-inch cake

1 ½ cups all-purpose flour

½ cup unsweetened cocoa powder

1 teaspoon baking soda

¾ teaspoon salt

¼ teaspoon baking powder

2 teaspoons pure vanilla extract

1 cup strong, freshly brewed coffee, cooled

8 tablespoons (1 stick) unsalted margarine

1 ½ cups sugar

4 extra-large eggs

Preheat the oven to 350 degrees. Grease the bottom and sides of a 10-inch cake pan. Cut out a round of parchment paper to fit the bottom and line the pan with it. Do not grease the paper.

Onto a sheet of wax paper, sift together the flour, cocoa powder, baking soda, salt and baking powder.

Stir the vanilla into the cooled coffee.

In the bowl of a standing electric mixer fitted with the paddle attachment, cream the margarine with the sugar on medium speed until lightened and fluffy. Scrape down the sides of the bowl with a rubber spatula.

With the machine running, add the eggs, all at one time, and beat until incorporated.

Reduce the mixer speed to low, and start adding the dry ingredients, alternating with the coffee mixture, beating until the batter is smooth and the ingredients have been fully incorporated.

Pour the batter into the prepared cake pan and smooth the top with the spatula. Bake for 45 minutes, or until a cake tester inserted in the center comes out clean. Remove the pan from the oven and let it stand 5 minutes. Unmold the cake, remove the paper liner, and place the cake right side up on a wire rack to cool.

To freeze
Wrap the cooled layer securely in plastic wrap, place it in a freezer bag, and freeze for up to 1 month.

To defrost
Unwrap it completely and let it stand at room temperature. Trim and frost as directed in the recipe.

Orange-Scented Sugar Syrup

Brushed on cake layers, it helps prevent them from drying out and can keep them tasting fresh for several days. A good syrup can also impart flavor to the cake layers.

Makes about 2 ½ cups

2 cups water

1 cup sugar

Peel of ½ medium orange

In a medium heavy-bottomed saucepan, bring the water, sugar, and orange peel to a boil, stirring and washing down any sugar crystals on the sides of the pan with a pastry brush. Cook, stirring, until the sugar is dissolved. Then cook, without stirring, for about 5 minutes. Remove the pan from the heat and let the syrup cool. The syrup is ready to use.

Chocolate Pudding

Makes about 3 ½ cups

2 cups cold water, plus ½ cup

2 tablespoons unsalted margarine, cut into pieces

6 ounces bittersweet or semisweet chocolate, coarsely chopped

1 cup sugar

¾ cup unsweetened cocoa powder, sifted

⅓ cup cornstarch

In a medium saucepan, combine 2 cups cold water and the margarine over medium heat, stirring, until the margarine melts and the water comes to a boil. Add the chopped chocolate and the sugar, and cook, stirring constantly, until the chocolate has melted and the mixture is smooth.

Add the cocoa to the chocolate mixture and stir to combine.

In a bowl whisk together ½ cup water and the cornstarch until no lumps show.

Increase the heat under the chocolate mixture to medium-high and bring the mixture to a boil, whisking constantly. Add the cornstarch mixture and cook, whisking constantly and vigorously, until the pudding thickens and becomes shiny and smooth, 2 to 4 minutes. (Be sure to whisk the bottom and sides of the pan or the pudding will cook onto them.) Remove the pan from the heat.

Scrape the pudding into a large heatproof bowl and smooth the top. Press a piece of plastic wrap directly on the surface of the pudding to prevent a skim from forming and let the pudding cool. The pudding is ready to use as a filling or frosting, or chill and serve at another time as a pudding.

(Continued)

To assemble the cake:

With a long-bladed serrated knife, horizontally slice off the crown of the cake to make a level layer. Be sure to reserve the trimmings (they become the crumbs).

With the knife, slice the cake into 3 thin, even layers. Reassemble the layers on top of each other and trim the edges of any hardened crust all the way around. Add all the trimmings to the reserved crown and hold at room temperature.

Place one of the layers on a cake stand or cake plate. Brush the top lightly with some of the orange sugar syrup, if desired. Measure about ¾ cup of the chocolate pudding and spread it evenly over the layer.

Brush one of the remaining cake layers with sugar syrup, if using, then invert it onto the cake on top of the pudding. Brush with sugar syrup.

Take another ¾ cup pudding and spread it evenly over the cake. Brush the remaining cake layer with sugar syrup and invert it onto the pudding. Brush with sugar syrup.

With a metal spatula, spread the remaining chocolate pudding evenly over the sides and top of the cake, using it as frosting.

Over a piece of parchment paper or small baking sheet, rub the reserved cake trimmings gently between the palms of your hands, crushing them to make fine cake crumbs. (You should have about 1 ½ cups crumbs.)

Dust the top and sides of the cake with the crumbs, covering it completely. Store leftover cake, covered with a cake bell or lightly with plastic wrap, in the refrigerator for 5 days, or perhaps as long as 1 week.

Feedback

Room temperature butter can be substituted for margarine in the cake and pudding recipes.

Ruth Schloss

In her own words

Ruth was one of 130 children who received kindness and protection from France's Baron Edouard de Rothschild. As a child she went from Germany to France with a *Kindertransport*, ultimately arriving in America in 1947. She continues to press for recognition of Abbé Glasberg, the priest who saved her life.

I was an only child born in Höheinöd, Pfalz, Germany, a small town near the French border of Germany. We had a beautiful big house and I went to public school, everyone was my friend. In 1937 I was no longer allowed to go to school and I had no friends. However, I was one of the lucky ones when in 1939, the Baroness de Rothschild brought me and 130 other children to live in her castle, Chateau De la Guette, near Paris, France. She was very kind and tried to help us as best she could. In the interim, my parents were deported to Camp de Gurs, in France, near the Spanish border. When I was thirteen or fourteen, the Baroness arranged for me to see them. That was the last time I saw my parents, they were sent to Drancy, then Auschwitz. As a child I did not appreciate the importance of that visit.

The Baroness tried desperately to protect us during the war and to place us in safe houses. I was hidden in a foundling home where I cared for the babies there. When it became too dangerous to stay, I went into the woods with a friend named Danielle. For nearly three months, two lovely ladies from the French underground came and would care for us. One day one of the women came and told us we were going to Switzerland where we would be safe. We crossed the border for a new life carrying with us the name and address of the person we were to meet. That person said, "I will take you to a farm and you can work there." Unfortunately he took us instead, to the police station in Geneva and there the Swiss police gave us back to German authorities. They took us to prison and after four days I was sent to Camp Rivesaltes. Three months after arriving at Rivesaltes, an Abbé (a French secular name for a priest) came into the Camp to rescue us. He hid four of us under his coat. Outside the camp there was a wagon filled with hay and he hid us there. The German soldiers probed the wagon with pitchforks but could not find us. He took us to stay with a farmer in France. Once again, I ended up in the woods, and was eventually safely placed in St. Joseph's convent.

The priest's name was Abbé Glasberg. I was a nosy little girl and wondered how could he be an Abbé with that Jewish last name? We saw him after the war and he told us that he was born in Russia to a very religious Jewish family. He had visions of the Virgin Mary, left Russia, went to France, converted and became an Abbé. He checked up on us all the time, even when I was in the United States. When we asked him what we could do for him, he told us we must light candles every Friday night, and that the boys must be Bar Mitzvahed. In addition, we must continue to be proud Jews and marry in the Jewish faith. I continue to press for Yad Vashem to recognize him as a "Righteous Among the Nations" for his selfless acts. At this time, Jewish converts cannot be recognized with that honor.

I came to America in August, 1947. I spoke only French and German and worked as a domestic. I taught myself to read and write. When asked how I look at life, I would say don't ever, ever lose God, pray and think about the good things that were in your past as a child. I am married 59 years, and together we have two children and three grandchildren.

Top left: Ruth, age 13, with her parents

Ruth Schloss' *Spaetzle* with Cooked Dried Fruit

Spaetzle noodles are traditionally eaten as a main course or a side dish to soak up a buttery sauce or rich gravy. Ruth's *spaetzle* becomes the comforting foundation for gently cooked dried fruit. Literally translated, *spaetzle* means "tiny sparrow," which describes the way these light noodle-like dumplings look as they flutter in the boiling water.

Yields: 4 servings; Start to Finish: Under 2 hours

For the fruit:

2 cups dried fruit: dates, figs, prunes, apricots or any combination you choose.

1 tablespoon sugar (optional)

For the *spaetzle* batter-dough:

1¼ cups all-purpose flour

Pinch of ground nutmeg (freshly grated is best)

Pinch of salt (optional)

1 egg, beaten with 8 ounces of water

2 tablespoons butter or oil, for frying

Cinnamon-sugar for sprinkling (optional)

In a bowl combine the dried fruit and add enough water to completely cover the fruit. Let the fruit sit for at least 45 minutes or up to 1 hour to soften and plump up. Cook the fruit over a low heat till soft. When the fruit is done cooking, let it remain in the pot while preparing the *spaetzle*.

In a small bowl, combine the flour, nutmeg and salt. Stir in the egg and water and mix until you have a wet elastic batter-dough.

Bring a large pot of salted water to boil. When the water boils, place the *spaetzle* dough on a cutting board and using a knife, cut it into tiny pieces. Carefully push the pieces off the board into the pot of water. You might need to dip the knife in the water, to help slide the dough off the board. Do not overcrowd the pot or the *spaetzle* will stick together. Boil, uncovered, for 20 minutes. Drain the *spaetzle* in a colander.

To brown the *spaetzle*, heat the butter or oil in a skillet, cook and stir the *spaetzle*, over medium-low heat, until it is lightly browned and crisp on all sides, about 10 minutes. Spoon the *spaetzle* into a serving bowl and toss with the warm fruit. Ruth invites you to "enjoy with a good appetite."

Variation: Inge Auerbacher (see page 173) similarly loved preparing and eating *spaetzle*. Her version, is very unique. Inge would prepare a lentil soup, much like the recipe we feature on page 330. When ready to serve, Inge ladles the soup into a bowl, adding a splash of red wine or apple cider vinegar. She then tops the soup with a heaping spoonful of boiled or fried *spaetzle*, to create this traditional German dish.

Jules Wallerstein

As told by his wife, Helen

Jules was one of the 937 passengers who boarded the SS St. Louis, presumably for safe harbor in Cuba. The fate of this ship has been the subject of books and a Hollywood movie entitled *"Voyage of the Damned."* The story of the passengers and their circumstances are still debated today.

My husband, Jules was born in Fürth, Germany. His father owned a jewelry store in town, which on Kristallnacht was ransacked and burned. His father was taken away for two days. Miraculously he was returned. My husband's family had a very successful cousin who lived in America; he owned Bosco, the chocolate syrup company. It was this cousin, Leo Wallerstein, who provided visas for the family to escape Germany. When my husband was twelve years old, his family and a total of 937 people, boarded the SS St. Louis headed for Cuba. Although they had all filed for and received proper documents, only 37 people were allowed entry when the boat arrived on Cuba's shores.

When the bulk of passengers were not allowed to disembark, the ship's Captain Schroeder sailed the boat within sight of Miami. Despite his hopes and the efforts of some members of the American government, the passengers were not allowed to enter the U.S. The boat was ultimately turned away, and Captain Schroeder began desperately wiring other nations to see who would take these passengers. France, Holland, England and Belgium all agreed to take a portion of the people on board. My husband's family went to Belgium, and there he lived, and even became a Bar Mitzvah. They lived peacefully with the Belgian people, until the Germans invaded. Jules' father went to the bank to withdraw their money and unfortunately was stopped and arrested. He was sent to an internment camp in France. Once again, his family reached out to their cousin Leo, and in 1942, they joined his father in France and then came to America.

Three years later, now an American citizen, Jules was drafted into the army and sent overseas to serve as an interpreter and interrogator. He said it felt good this time, "to be the one with the gun." To my husband, this was another adventure in his life.

In the year 2000, we received an invitation from The Watchmen of the Nations. They invited us to Canada to be part of a ceremony where the Canadians apologized for not accepting any passengers from the SS St. Louis. This same group sent us to Florida in 2001 where over 600 people gathered at the site where the ship had been anchored off the coast of Florida. We all said Kaddish and it felt like the hands of the dead were reaching out. We then went with this group to Hamburg, to see where the voyage began. We set out on a boat, and re-enacted the ship's departure. On the edge of the coast there were Christian Germans waving Jewish flags to honor the survivors. It was unbelievably emotional and moving, we could never have imagined such a sight. Together we have two daughters and five grandchildren.

Since completing the book, I sadly learned that Jules passed away. We extend our sincerest condolences to his devoted family. May his memory be a blessing.

Top left: Jules and Helen Wallerstein on their wedding day, May 31, 1953

Helen Wallerstein's Potato *Latkes*

With Helen's recipe you achieve *latke* nirvana: a potato pancake that is light and crispy. Helen grates her potatoes on the finer side, but you can shred them if you prefer more texture. Make sure you have plenty of sour cream, applesauce or simply sugar on hand to dunk, cozy up to or sprinkle on top.

Yields: 24 Latkes; Start to Finish: Under 30 minutes

5 medium russet potatoes, peeled

1 medium onion, grated (use a large one if you like a strong onion flavor)

4 eggs, beaten

½ cup matzo meal

1 to 2 teaspoons salt

¼ to ½ teaspoon pepper

½ cup vegetable oil for frying

In a food processor using the metal blade, or using a box grater, finely grate the potatoes. Place them in a colander, and squeeze out all the liquid. Grate the onion, using the food processor pulse feature to capture any small chunks. Stir the onions, eggs, matzo meal, salt and pepper into the potato mixture.

Heat ½–inch of oil in a non-stick skillet, over medium heat, until very hot (a drop of water should dance in the pan). To test the seasonings before frying the entire batch (you wouldn't want to taste the raw potato and egg mixture), drop one tablespoon of the mixture into the hot oil, fry for several minutes on each side and drain on a paper towel. Taste the *latke* and add more salt or pepper if needed. Now you are ready to make the rest. Drop a generous tablespoon of *latke* batter into the skillet and flatten the pancake with the back of a spatula. Turn the *latkes* over when the underside is nicely brown, about 3 to 5 minutes. Fry until golden on both sides. Drain on waiting paper towels. Repeat this process adding more oil to the pan and a touch more matzo meal to the mixture if needed to absorb the excess liquid that will collect in the bowl. Serve hot.

Feedback

Latkes play nicely with a variety of vegetables. Grate or shred 2 carrots or 1 large zucchini into the *latke* mixture for a unique taste.

Helen Wallerstein's *Gesundheit Kuchen*–Chocolate Cake

Helen calls this cake the "God Bless You Cake," but you can call it a light chocolate "tea" cake, that is delicious and not too sweet. Drizzling the smooth chocolate ganache over the cake right before serving adds another layer of goodness.

Yields: About 8 slices; Start to Finish: Under 1 ½ hours

1 stick (½ cup) butter or margarine, room temperature

4 eggs, separated

¾ cup sugar

1 tablespoon zested lemon peel

½ cup whole milk

1 tablespoon cocoa powder, plus ½ teaspoon cocoa powder

1 ½ cups all-purpose flour

½ teaspoon baking powder

Preheat the oven to 350 degrees and lightly grease a 9-inch round cake pan.

Beat the butter, eggs and sugar several minutes, on medium speed, until light and fluffy. Add the lemon zest, milk and 1 tablespoon cocoa powder and continue mixing.

In a separate bowl, sift together the flour, baking powder and remaining ½ teaspoon cocoa powder. On low speed, add it to the egg mixture. Continue beating, on medium speed, for several minutes until all the ingredients are combined. Pour the batter into the prepared cake pan and bake at 350 degrees for 50 minutes or until the cake is firm and a toothpick inserted in the center comes out clean. Dust with confectioner's sugar or chocolate ganache (recipe follows).

Chocolate Ganache

What sounds like such a complicated culinary confection is a simple two-ingredient wonder.

Yields: About 2 cups; Start to Finish: Under 15 minutes

8 ounces heavy cream

8 ounces semisweet chocolate or chocolate chips

Heat the heavy cream in a small saucepan, just until it is hot, but not scalding, you do not want a skin to develop. Take the pot off the stove and pour the warm cream over the chocolate, whisking to combine. Let the sauce sit and cool for a few minutes. The ganache will be thin enough to drizzle. If you prefer a thicker consistency, reheat and add more chocolate. Cooled thicker ganache can be used as a frosting or filling.

JFH

Dr. Ruth Westheimer

In her own words

While you know that Dr. Ruth is an expert in her field, what you might not know is that she survived a traumatic childhood and fought in the Israeli Hagganah! She is known for her strength and moxy; after reading the story she shared with us, you will better understand why.

Cooking is important to every culture, but in cultures that always had a homeland, like the French or Italian or Chinese, cooking was only one aspect as there was also the land, the great rivers, the mountains, the architecture. When you're French and surrounded by France, cooking is only a small part of who you are. But when you're a Jew and for thousands of years you didn't have a homeland, the food you ate became so much more integral to your identity.

While I can guarantee that the "Celebration Cake" recipe described below will produce a delicious cake, I must also admit that the recipe isn't mine and no such dessert would ever be made by my hands. Let me explain to you why...

I was born in Frankfurt, Germany. In November of 1938, when I was ten years old, the SS came to take away my father. Because of that, I met the qualifications to be sent with 100 other children from Frankfurt to safety in Switzerland. In early January, 1939, my mother and grandmother put me on a train, and the last time I would see them was as they were running alongside the train waving goodbye.

We were sent to a Swiss school for Orthodox children. We German Jewish children spent hours cleaning everything from top to bottom. During the first few years, we were given a rudimentary education, but when we were old enough to go to high school, only the boys were sent. We girls continued with our cleaning and so, as a result, when I left that school it was with a Swiss diploma in housekeeping! Needless to say, it's not a diploma that I ever hung up on my wall.

As a result of my educational experience during that time period, I don't have any fondness for domestic duties. I had a husband and two children (and four grandchildren) and did what I had to do, but not with any joy, enthusiasm or much skill. My family was never hungry, but one can't say that they have fond memories of all those meals I made. And as soon as my fortunes changed (I was a college professor and then became Dr. Ruth), I gave up anything that even hinted that I was putting my Swiss diploma to use.

Top left: Dr. Ruth Westheimer

Dr. Ruth's Celebration Cake

Ruth explains the origin of this delicious cake. "I have a friend, Marga, who is a wonderful cook, especially when it comes to desserts. She is a cousin of my late husband, Fred, and for many years we were neighbors in Washington Heights. As often as Marga was willing to send over a care package of some of her delicious culinary skills, we gladly accepted. And later, when my grandchildren were born, Marga would always bake them birthday cakes; when they were older, she would bake with them. (While this recipe is from another cousin, Rose Westheimer, it's the one Marga has always used and I love.) Since Marga never had children, my grandchildren became her adopted grandchildren. If you follow this recipe, I'm sure that you're going to be rewarded with a lot of compliments from your friends and family. And rather than go through this whole story, go ahead and take credit for it. After all, you got it from me, and now that you know my background, you also know that the last thing I want credit for is as a baker!"

Yields: 10 to 12 servings; Start to Finish: Under 2 hours

The batter:

12 large eggs, separated

1 ½ cups plus 2 tablespoons sugar

2 tablespoons fresh squeezed lemon juice

3 cups (about 12 ounces) finely ground walnuts

Frosting 1:

16 ounces heavy cream

4 teaspoons sugar

Frosting 2:

8 ounces heavy cream

2 tablespoons sugar

2 tablespoons cocoa powder, sifted

1 teaspoon instant coffee granules

For garnish:

Chocolate curls (optional)

Preheat the oven to 325 degrees.

Grease three 9-inch round cake pans, line them with parchment paper, and grease the paper and dust with potato starch. (Flour can be used for a non-Passover version.)

Beat the yolks, in a large bowl, on high speed with an electric mixer until thick. Add the sugar and lemon juice and continue beating until the mixture is a light yellow. Turn the beater off and stir in the nuts.

In a separate bowl, beat the egg whites, on high speed, until stiff peaks form. Fold the egg whites gently into yolk mixture.

Spoon a third of the batter into each prepared pan (using a measuring cup will help insure that you evenly distribute the batter). Bake at 325 degrees for about 45 to 60 minutes, until golden brown. A tester inserted in center will come out slightly wet, as the cake will retain a moist pudding texture. Loosen the edges with a knife immediately after removing the pans from oven. Cool completely. Remove from pans and peel off parchment.

While the cakes cool, prepare the two frostings in separate bowls. Combine all the ingredients for each frosting and whip each at high speed until stiff peaks form. When the cakes are completely cooled, assemble the cake, by placing the first cake layer on a plate. Top with a little less than half of Frosting # 1. Place the second layer on top and spread Frosting # 2. Top with the third layer, and frost the top and sides with remaining Frosting # 1. Using a vegetable peeler, shave small chocolate curls from a block of milk or dark chocolate. Decorate the top of the cake with the curls. Chill before serving.

Belgium and France

In addition to their beautiful accents and gracious manners, the contributors from these two countries display a flair for haute cuisine. Classic French and Belgium ingredients such as flavorful herbs, crisp white wine and stout are commonplace elements for our cooks from this region.

We are fortunate to have several survivors representing these two countries. Their foods are indicative of the passion for cooking for which this region is known. We hope you will welcome into your repertoire the recipes remembered by our spirited French and Belgian survivors.

RECIPES

Arlette Levy Baker: *Poisson en Cocotte*–Fish in a Small Dish

Arlette Levy Baker: *Dinde Braiseé avec Choucroute*–Braised Turkey with Sauerkraut

Sonia Jeruchim: *Eingebrente*–Potato Soup

Cecile Jeruchim: Belgian Endives

Cecile Jeruchim: *Hachis Parmentier*–Cottage Pie

Arlette Levy Baker

In her own words

Arlette, an elegant and articulate woman, was very much affected by the Holocaust throughout her young life growing up in Paris. She maintains a strong French identity and her home and cooking reflect that heritage.

I was very young when on December 30, 1942 the French police, who were working with the Nazis, came to our home. My father bought my life by bribing these men and insisted that our housekeeper be allowed to bring me to my grandparent's home. My father and my mother were taken to Drancy (a transit camp not far from Paris) and on February 13, 1943 I later learned they were sent to Auschwitz. I went to live with my grandparents in Paris. My grandmother had died but my grandfather's, second wife, a Catholic woman, raised me. I have always felt like a true Jew, even though my grandparents were very secular. Although I felt safe with my grandparents, they had my suitcase as well as theirs, packed, just in case. As an adult, I came to America to marry my husband, William Baker, we raised two children who gave us three grandchildren.

Top left: Arlette Baker, photo from her French Identity Card

Arlette Baker's *Poisson En Cocotte*–Fish in a Small Dish

Arlette's fish with herbs is classically prepared in a *cocotte*, a small crock designed for cooking individual portions. You can use a Dutch oven or covered skillet and achieve the same result, a moist, flaky fish with a hint of herbs, lemon and wine. The potatoes gently cook in the sauce and provide a provincial element to the dish.

Yields: 4 servings; Start to Finish: Under 45 minutes

1½ pounds (about 10 to 12) small Red Bliss potatoes, washed and quartered

4 thick-cut slices (about 6 ounces each) of fresh cod or halibut

4 tablespoons of butter

1 medium onion, sliced

Juice of 1 lemon (about 2 to 3 tablespoons)

½ cup white wine or cognac

Pinch dried thyme

1 bay leaf

Kosher salt and pepper

1 tablespoon chopped fresh flat-leaf parsley, for garnish

Bring a medium size pot of salted water to boil and cook the potatoes until tender but not mushy, about 15 minutes. Drain and reserve.

Melt the butter, over medium heat, in a large skillet and lightly brown the fish (on both sides), and onions, for 5 to 10 minutes. Stir in the lemon juice, white wine or cognac, reserved potatoes, thyme and bay leaf. Season with salt and pepper. Cover and cook until the potatoes are very tender and lightly browned, about 10 minutes longer. Sprinkle with chopped parsley and remove bay leaves before serving.

Arlette Baker's *Dinde Braiseé avec Choucroute*–Turkey with Sauerkraut

Arlette clearly remembers her grandmother's Alsatian specialties simmering away in Le Creuset pots in their kitchen outside of Paris. In true Alsatian cooking *choucroute* (French for sauerkraut) is a popular ingredient in slow simmering meat dishes. When braised, sauerkraut serves as the vegetable in the dish while cutting the grease and lending a sweet note.

Yields: 4 servings; Start to Finish: Under 1 ½ hours

2 to 3 pounds of turkey (wing, thigh, leg or breast)

7 tablespoons of margarine or vegetable oil

2 medium onions, quartered

1 pound sauerkraut, washed and drained

½ cup cognac or brandy

1 carrot, peeled and diced (about ½ cup)

Kosher salt and pepper

Melt 5 tablespoons of the margarine or oil in a heavy pot or Dutch oven, and brown the turkey and onions over medium heat, for 20 minutes. (If cooking wings, separate at the joint for faster cooking and easier presentation.) In a separate skillet, lightly brown the sauerkraut in the remaining 2 tablespoons of margarine or oil. When the turkey and onions are brown, stir in the cognac, carrots, and sautéed sauerkraut. Pour in 2 cups of water and season with salt and pepper. Cover and cook on the stove over medium-low heat for 1 hour, or until the turkey is fork tender and the sauerkraut is nicely brown.

Alternate Preparation: Arlette is a devotee of the pressure cooker. Not only does she feel it cuts her cooking time dramatically, but she loves the intense flavor it develops. For this dish she uses a 6-quart pressure cooker. Arlette suggests browning the turkey and onions in the pressure cooker. She adds the cognac or brandy and then the balance of ingredients. Cover the cooker securely and place pressure regulator on vent pipe and let it cook for 15 minutes with pressure regulator rocking slowly (stove switch at "low"). Let the pressure drop of its own accord. Arlette uses a 12-quart cooker to make a whole turkey in the same manner.

Cecile and Simon Jeruchim

In their own words

Cecile Rojer Jeruchim and Simon Jeruchim are a very multi-talented couple. Both are published authors and both speak before children at schools and synagogues about their experiences during the war. But, as their stories will show you, what they share most prominently is that they both survived the Holocaust as hidden children. Cecile benefited from the kindness of the Belgian people, and Simon from the French. Their stories are important reminders that even in the harshest times, there were good people who did good deeds.

Cecile

I was born in Brussels, Belgium in 1931. I lived in Woluwe St. Pierre, a suburb of Brussels with my Polish-Russian immigrant parents, Abraham and Sheva Rojer, and my two siblings, my older sister, Anny, and my younger brother, Charly. I had a wonderful childhood prior to the Nazi occupation, but the war changed everything. I will never forget a particular day in January, 1943. I was sitting at the kitchen table eating my lunch, which had been prepared by my mother: steak, mashed potatoes and Belgian endives. I hated Belgian endives! Yet, my mother, like

most Belgian housewives, prepared and served them several times a week. I was about to finish my meal when my gentile girlfriend came to my house asking if I wanted to accompany her to voice lessons, which I also used to take. Since Jews were restricted from going to school, I could only accompany my friend but was not allowed to participate. I asked my mother if I could go. She responded, "Not before you finish your endives, or I will save them for your dinner." I decided to leave with my friend, expecting the endives to be waiting for me when I returned home. While I was away the Nazis came to my house and arrested my parents. They were deported to Auschwitz where they perished. That afternoon was the last time I ever saw my mother. My decision to go with my girlfriend separated me from my mother forever, but also saved my life.

Today I often eat Belgian endives as their subtle flavor gently brings me closer to my mother and reminds me of my lost childhood. Through the intervention of compassionate and courageous gentiles my sister Anny and I were hidden in a Catholic convent in Louvain, Belgium, where we were baptized and stayed until the war ended. My brother Charly, who was hidden in the countryside, also survived. After spending the postwar years in homes for Jewish children, my sister, my brother and I immigrated to the United States in 1948 to live with relatives. I was always a talented dancer. My first job in the U.S. was as a ballroom dancing instructor. I also love writing. I am the author of *Hello do you know my name?* an educational

Top left: Cecile (center) with her brother, Charly and sister, Anny. Brussels, 1941

children's book and of several short stories about my childhood. I have been married for the past 53 years to Simon Jeruchim, also a "hidden child" from France. We are the proud parents of two wonderful daughters and six beautiful grandchildren.

Simon

I was born in Paris, France in 1929. My parents were Polish-Jewish immigrants who settled in a Paris suburb where I lived happily with my two siblings, my older sister, Alice, and my younger brother, Michel. My father, Samuel, was a watchmaker and my mother, Sonia, a homemaker. I adored them and to this day they still inspire me as role models. My mother was a free spirit, generous and optimistic, a lover of art and music. My father instilled in me the love of books and his strong set of ethics. We lived comfortably in a middle-class neighborhood. My parents were not religious Jews and I grew up with gentile friends, not thinking that I was any different than they were. However, World War II shattered such a belief and also our lives when the Nazis invaded and occupied France in 1940.

Soon, anti-Semitic persecutions began with the wearing of the Jewish star and culminated in round-ups and deportation. The defining moment of my life was July 16, 1942 when the French police, who collaborated with the Nazis, rounded-up the Jews from Paris and its suburbs. By sheer luck, my mother had an appointment on that very day with her dentist who confided that one of his patients, a police officer, told him of this impending major

round-up. I remember vividly my mother relaying the news to my father who dismissed it as just another rumor. But my mother persuaded my father for us to spend the night at our cleaning woman's home and thus we escaped arrest. For the following week we hid in the back rooms of stores, and the people in our mostly non-Jewish neighborhood allowed us to stay a night at a time. Another miracle occurred with the intervention of a compassionate gentile couple who, upon hearing of our plight, arranged for us children to go into hiding. We said goodbye to our parents, not realizing that it was the last time we would ever see them. My parents were arrested only a month later and were deported to Auschwitz where they perished.

My siblings and I were placed with farmers in Normandy. We pretended to be Christians by praying and going to church. Life was harsh and lonely. While in hiding, I met the village schoolteacher who gave me a watercolor set and a sketchpad. I loved to draw. It was one of the most treasured gifts I ever received. I filled the pad with watercolors of people and places where I lived and luckily kept them for posterity. I was at the crossroads of the invasion when my village was liberated in August, 1944 by American troops. Following the liberation, my siblings and I were placed in a series of Jewish children's homes by an uncle who had become our guardian. For the first time, I was taught about Jewish traditions. In one orphanage I was asked to paint Hebrew letters on the dining room wall. That was the first time I felt some pride in being Jewish. When I was fifteen, I became a Bar Mitzvah, in a simple ceremony.

My siblings and I immigrated to the United States in 1949 to live with relatives, hoping for a better life. However, my hopes were dashed when I was drafted in 1951 into the American army and sent to combat in Korea. Luckily I survived this conflict and found happiness when I met and married my wife, Cecile, and started a family of our own. I was also fortunate to fulfill my dreams of becoming a professional artist, as an award-winning package designer, graphic artist and book illustrator. My childhood watercolors are now in

Top left: Simon, Alice and Michel taken 1947-1948 in an orphanage near Paris

the permanent collection of the U.S. Holocaust Museum and my Korean drawings in the Korean War National Museum. Through my writings and talks, I keep alive the memory of my parents and all of the victims of the Holocaust. I wrote about my childhood in a book titled *Hidden in France–A Boy's Journey Under the Nazi Occupation* and a sequel, *Frenchy–A Young Jewish-French Immigrant Discovers Love and Art in America–and War in Korea.*

Sonia Jeruchim's *Eingebrente*–Potato Soup

Simon's sister Alice remembers fondly calling this family favorite, *Farbrente* soup, but what we believe she meant was *eingebrente*, which in Yiddish loosely translates to mean "sautéed, almost burnt." The name derives from the classic lightly browned roux that is added in the last few minutes, amplifying the soup's simple flavors.

Yields: About 6 servings; Start to Finish: Under 30 minutes

4 russet potatoes, peeled and diced (about 4 cups)

Kosher salt and pepper

1 teaspoon onion powder

2 tablespoons cold butter

¾ cup all-purpose flour

Croutons and fresh-snipped chives, for garnish (optional)

In a medium soup pot, boil the diced potatoes with 6 cups of water. Season with salt, pepper and 1 teaspoon of onion powder. While the potatoes cook, combine the butter and flour in a small bowl and use a fork to blend and break-up the mixture into tiny crumbs. Cook the flour and butter, in a small skillet, over low heat, stirring constantly, until the crumbs are a light brown, being careful not to burn them. Let them cool while the potatoes continue to cook.

When the potatoes are cooked fork tender, about 20 minutes, stir the slightly cooled browned crumbs into the potato soup. Cook for an additional 5 minutes. Season to taste with salt and pepper. If the soup is too thick, add some boiling water until you reach the desired consistency. Serve with croutons and fresh-snipped chives.

Feedback

In this recipe, a classic roux is incorporated to thicken the soup and intensify the flavor. To create a roux, flour and butter or oil are combined (usually in equal parts) and cooked over a low heat and lightly browned. For most dishes, you'll want to achieve a light blonde color. The lighter the roux, the more subtle its flavor, and the more it will thicken your liquid. Dark roux imparts more of a nutty flavor, but thickens less, watch the pan closely as burnt roux needs to be discarded. Let the roux cool slightly before adding to hot soup, gravy or sauce and cook for several minutes to let it do its thing and lose its floury taste. Two tablespoons butter or oil to 2 tablespoons of flour will lightly thicken 1 cup of liquid. Roux can be made in advance and kept refrigerated until ready to use.

Cecile Jeruchim's Belgian Endives

Cecile credits this very Belgian vegetable for saving her life. As a child, she felt endives were bitter, but as an adult, she loves the flavor of lightly sautéed, curiously sweet endives.

Yields : 4 to 6 servings; Start to Finish: Under 30 minutes

3 large firm Belgian endives, split down the middle lengthwise

1 tablespoon butter

½ teaspoon sugar, or more to taste

2 to 3 tablespoons beer

To clean the endives, wipe them with a paper towel, do not rinse. Heat the butter in a medium skillet and sprinkle in the sugar, add the endives and cook, over medium heat, until brown on all sides, for several minutes. When the endives are nicely brown, stir in the beer. Cover and continue to cook over low heat for about 3 to 5 minutes, or until the endives are just beginning to soften, adding a touch more beer or sugar to taste.

Cecile Jeruchim's *Hachis Parmentier*–Cottage Pie

Every year, on June 13th, Cecile prepares this dish that she remembers from her childhood. She invites her brother Charly over and together they celebrate the day they arrived in America. 2008 marked their 60th anniversary! This is the French version of cottage or shepherd's pie, with a fresh veggie mixed in for color and flavor. *Hachis* derives from the French, "to chop," and Parmentier is the last name of the French man credited for having brought potatoes to France.

Yields: 4 servings; Start to Finish: Under 1 hour

1½ pounds Yukon Gold potatoes, peeled and quartered

2 to 3 tablespoons margarine (for mashing the potatoes)

1 pound fresh spinach leaves, carefully washed and stems trimmed

3 tablespoons vegetable oil

1 pound lean ground beef

1 medium onion, chopped (about ¾ cup)

2 cloves garlic, chopped

Kosher salt and pepper

Bring a medium pot of salted water to boil, cook the potatoes until fork tender, about 15 to 20 minutes. Drain, and then mash the potatoes, adding enough margarine to make them smooth and creamy. Using the same pot, steam the spinach leaves in about 3 inches of water, just until wilted, about 5 minutes. Remove from the water, and then drain and chop the spinach. Stir the spinach into the mashed potatoes.

Heat 1 tablespoon of oil in a skillet and cook the ground beef, over medium heat, until brown, about 10 minutes. Remove the meat with a slotted spoon and drain the fat from the pan. Stir the meat into the potato and spinach mixture. Add the remaining 2 tablespoons of oil to the skillet, cook and stir the onion and garlic, over medium heat, until lightly brown, about 10 minutes. Combine the onions and garlic with the meat and potato mixture. Season to taste with salt and pepper. The dish can be served just as is, or spooned into a lightly greased casserole and baked at 325 degrees just until the top is crisp, or browned under the broiler for a crispy finish.

Hungary and Czechoslovakia

These two countries share borders, which help define their shared cuisine. Their cooking highlights big flavors—handfuls of dill, potfuls of meat—and bellyfuls of rustic home cooking. Hungarian and Czech cuisine was very much influenced by the area's natural resources. Because this region is truly land-locked, fish preparations took a back seat to game, poultry and beef. There is a rich tradition of inventive vegetable preparations, hearty soups, rich goulash and everything paprikash!

Hungary is forever linked to the small red pepper plant from which paprika is harvested. Many American cooks add paprika for the color it imbues rather than the flavor it imparts. But Hungarians have known for centuries that paprika's spicy and potent properties help other foods unlock their flavor. In an ironic and most interesting twist of fate, in 1937, Dr. Szent Gyorgyi, a Hungarian national, won the Nobel Prize for his work with paprika pepper pods. As the political climate began to change in Hungary, Dr. Gyorgyi facilitated the escape of his Jewish friends, worked with the underground resistance and even used his notoriety as a scientist to secretly negotiate with the allies on behalf of his government.

Our Hungarian and Czech survivors are a living reminder of staunch fortitude. It is with spirited abandon that we present the piquant recipes remembered by these intrepid survivors.

RECIPES

Joan Ferencz: Beef Goulash

Ethel Feuerstein: *Bab Leves*—Hungarian Bean Soup

Ida Frankfurter: Potato *Kugel*

Judita Hruza: Poached Carp in Aspic

Lilly Kaplan: Chicken Paprikash

Lilly Kaplan: Hungarian Butter Cookies

George Lang: Caraway-Seed Soup with Poached Eggs

George Lang: *Húsvéti töltött csirke*—Stuffed Chicken for Passover

George Lang: Asparagus Pudding

George Lang: *Anyám cseresznyés lepénye*—My Mother's Cherry Cake

Freda Lederer: Passover Stuffed Cabbage

Greta Margolis: *Nockedly*—Hungarian Dumplings

Mary Mayer: Veal Paprikash

Mary Mayer: Cucumber Salad

Mary Mayer: Raspberry Linzer Tarts

Katherine Noir: Mushroom Barley Soup

Katherine Noir: Apricot Preserves

Matilda Winkler: "Mama's" Crunchy Beans

PROFESSIONAL CONTRIBUTORS

Gale Gand: Cabbage Strudel

Gale Gand: Myrna's Beef Short Ribs

JFH: *Granatos Kocka* (Grenadier March)—Potatoes and Pasta

Joan Ferencz

In her own words

Joan greets me with a broad smile that almost never left her face during our conversation. Her positive attitude comes from what she calls her philosophy of life. "I mourned for what I lost, but I knew I needed to make a life for myself and I try very hard not to be bitter, nobody likes a bitter person."

I will never forget my childhood in Sziget, Hungary. I was the sixth child in a family of eight born to a father who was a small businessman and a mother who was a homemaker. What stands out for me were the holidays. Every holiday was observed and every holiday was really very festive and social. Passover was my favorite because it was so exciting in my house. The Passover dishes were kept in the attic and I remember running up the stairs to bring down the dishes, scrubbing and cleaning everything for the week ahead. At our seder we would invite so many guests and my father would sit at the head of the table, dressed in his white robe, I can just see it now. I was mesmerized by Elijah's cup and when I was asked to open the door for Elijah, I remember being so scared that he might actually be standing there.

Our lives changed in 1944 when I was just a teenager, when Eichmann came to Hungary and hurried to finish the Final Solution. By spring, Hungary was occupied, and we were relocated to the ghetto. Within a month we were ordered to pack our bags and report to the train station. I really didn't know what our fate would be. When you are a young girl, you listen but the facts don't really penetrate. We made the trip to Auschwitz as a family, but once in the camp, only my two sisters and I remained together. I clearly remember a day when we were separated on two different lines, and I knew that one sister's line to the left would not survive. Slowly I crept toward my sister and stretched out my hand for her to take hold. I pulled her over to my line, to safety.

She became a mother and a grandmother; that was my reward. The three of us were sent to several German towns where we worked at oil refineries, repaired railroad tracks and ultimately on an assembly line inspecting bullets. The Allies were continually dropping bombs, as our work camp looked very much like a military base. While sleeping in our barrack, a bomb dropped a mere half a yard away from me. Miraculously it did not explode. The soft ground absorbed the bomb and we were spared. I came out of the war without a scratch; others who worked beside me were not as lucky.

The Russians liberated me, after a six-week march that ended in Czechoslovakia. I returned to my hometown where I went to a soup kitchen that some valiant Jewish men had stocked. These returning prisoners of forced labor gathered linens and supplies from townspeople; all items had formerly been in Jewish households. I am proud to say I married one of those men. It didn't happen right away, and our story is pretty funny. I went to Prague to be with my sister, and then from Prague to Paris to await the voyage to go to America. It was in Paris that once again, I bumped into my future husband, Michael. After we spent some time together he proposed by saying the following, "If nobody marries you in America, I would like to." I left that January in 1947 and in August we reunited in America. He asked if I was married yet and I told him, "You are out of luck, you have to marry me." We were married 52 years and have two children and four grandchildren.

Joan Ferencz' Beef Goulash

Joan's cooking style was not very Hungarian as she embraced an American lifestyle, always cooking wholesome food, nothing from a can. However, one dish she remembers from her childhood was a very pure and authentic Hungarian goulash made simply with seasoned beef in slow simmered broth and thinly sliced potatoes that soften as they cook away in the robust sauce. When slow cooking, don't be tempted to use a higher quality cut of meat, the cheaper cuts work better as their extra fat helps the meat melt into assertive flavorful bites.

Yields: 4 servings, Start to Finish: Under 2 hours

2 pounds beef chuck or shank, cut into 2-inch pieces

Kosher salt and pepper

2 tablespoons sweet Hungarian paprika

All-purpose flour, for dredging

3 tablespoons vegetable oil

2 large onions, sliced

2 cups beef broth

4 russet potatoes (about 1½ pounds), peeled and cut into ½-inch thick slices

1 teaspoon hot paprika (optional)

Pat the meat dry with a paper towel and season with salt, pepper and sweet paprika. Dredge the beef in the flour, shaking off the excess. Heat the oil in a medium size Dutch oven or deep covered sauté pan and brown the beef (in batches if necessary) over medium heat, for several minutes. When the meat begins to brown, add the sliced onions, continue to cook and stir, over medium heat, until the beef and onions are nicely brown, about 10 minutes longer. Stir in the broth, cover and cook over low heat, for one hour. After one hour, add the sliced potatoes and season to taste with salt and pepper. For an extra kick, add hot paprika. Cover and continue to cook until the potatoes and beef are tender, about 30 minutes. If the sauce is too thick, add additional broth or water.

Feedback

When a recipe calls for dredging meat in flour, it accomplishes two things. First it coats and dries the meat so it can brown better and develop a crust. Second, it serves as a thickening agent for the sauce. Fill a brown paper bag with the flour, season as the recipe suggests, and drop the meat into the bag (this is my Dad's technique). A vigorous shake should do it. Be sure to shake the excess flour off before placing the meat in the pot. And never crowd the pan when browning; doing so steams the meat. Always pat dry and brown the meat in batches for a better result.

George and Ethel Feuerstein

In their own words

George Feuerstein and Ethel Duranter Feuerstein know all too well how life can change in an instant. They both know the power of love and the role fate and luck play in your life.

George

I remember March 19, 1944 as the Germans came into Hungary. Weeks later, I was arrested and put in a Hungarian work camp, a type of jail. After a few months, on October 6, 1944, all the Jews were collected and sent to Germany. I was a barber and the Germans recruited me to shave and provide haircuts for the SS guards. I did that for six weeks. I was on many work details and always managed to get food to share with others. As the war was drawing to a close we were moved from the camp and forced to walk 25km. It was on that march that the Americans liberated us. I was not in good shape and was sent to a hospital to recuperate. I looked out the window and saw a shining star. I knew it was my mother watching over me, I think that's why I survived. After recovering, I went to Israel where I was met by kibbutzim and sent directly into the army as part of the elite guard. Although my siblings and I were separated during the war, we all survived. In 1962, I came to America to visit New York City. I met a woman and we shared Friday night dinner. She showed me around her city, and on my next visit, just after knowing her 36 hours, I proposed.

Ethel

I was from the town of Ungvár in Hungary. My sister was a seamstress of great talent and renown. Although I was not permitted to attend school, I learned to sew from her. Together we were sent to Auschwitz and left not knowing what had become of our mother. One day, my sister went to a bathroom in the camp and as fate would have it, bumped into our mother. Because the barracks needed to account for each and every prisoner, you could not add someone to your barrack without sending someone in exchange. Luckily for us, our mother was able to switch with another prisoner, and we were reunited. My mother told us that when she arrived, Josef Mengele was deciding who should live and who

should die. He would point to one line for the sick and elderly, and another for the young and healthy. He directed my mother to the line that would perish. She spoke up in German and told him that she was willing to work. He then pointed to the other line, and she was spared.

In another twist of fate, my sister had, prior to the war, met a very handsome man while she was on vacation. They fell in love and communicated through the mail. The letters abruptly stopped and my sister did not expect to ever see this man again. Unbelievably, she found him in Auschwitz. While he still looked dashing, my sister was wearing ill-fitting clothing, and certainly did not look her best. Although he did not recognize her, he recognized her voice. He was now engaged to a woman who had some clout in the camp, and at his request that woman watched over our family. Her protection, and the coincidence of meeting this man, helped us survive.

As the camp was liquidated, we were sent into the woods where many were killed. Fate stepped in again, and we were saved by liberators who came through the woods on motorcycles. I spent time in a Swedish hospital, where I recuperated fully. While there, my abilities as a seamstress came into play. I met a woman from my hometown who I also knew from Auschwitz. I made a special dress for her that impressed the woman she worked for, who happened to be the Italian consul's wife. The diplomat's wife came to me in her chauffeur-driven limousine to ask me to design and sew clothing for her, explaining, "why would I travel to Paris, when I could have custom made clothing right in my own town?" This led to a string of jobs where I was designing and making clothing for some of Europe's most elegant and well-connected women. I was only twenty years old at the time.

Years later, now living in New York, I went on a blind date. George and I fell in love and were married soon after. Together we have three children and four grandchildren.

Ethel Feuerstein's *Bab Leves*–Hungarian Bean Soup

This melting pot Hungarian bean soup is inspired by Ethel's recollection of the flavorful soup she ate in Hungary and still prepares today. Hungarian soups are bountiful, incorporating a variety of vegetables, legumes and meat.

Yields: 8 to 10 servings, Start to Finish: Under 4 hours

2 cups dried beans; kidney, black-eyed, navy or mixed

5 tablespoons vegetable oil

2 large onions, diced (about 2 cups)

5 tablespoons all-purpose flour

4 carrots, peeled and diced (about 2 cups)

1-pound smoked turkey (if smoked turkey is not available, use smoked chicken, or any meat of your choice. If the meat is not smoked, add a splash of liquid smoke to give the dish a smoky flavor)

4 teaspoons kosher salt

1 teaspoon black pepper

2 tablespoons sweet paprika

2 tablespoons finely chopped fresh flat-leaf parsley

2 teaspoons garlic powder

In a medium pot, boil the beans for several minutes, drain, then soak them in fresh cold water for 1 hour. Drain and reserve the soaked beans. While the beans soak, prepare the remaining ingredients.

Heat the oil in a large soup pot, cook and stir the onion, over medium-low heat, until soft and translucent, about 10 minutes. Stir in the flour being sure to coat all the onions. Cook several minutes, allowing the onions to brown to a golden color before adding the beans, carrots, turkey, salt, pepper, paprika, parsley and garlic powder. Add 8 cups of water, or enough water to cover all the ingredients. Bring to a boil, then reduce the heat to low, cover and cook for 1 ½ to 2 hours or until the beans are tender, adding boiling water as needed if the soup becomes too thick. Cut the meat into bite-size pieces and blend into the soup, or serve on the side.

Feedback

Ever hear the expression, *you don't know beans?* It means you don't know anything. While we won't go that far, I can say that knowing a little about beans, will help you "digest" the true meaning of this expression. Many maintain that beans need to be soaked overnight to help them split and release their natural gas (so you don't). Others suggest adding vinegar to help the fermentation process. But, Ethel uses a simpler and faster method outlined above, as she says, "all to prevent gas." It accomplishes the same thing in less time. Conduct your own test with some of our recipes that call for beans; see which method you agree with and more importantly, which agrees with you. Additionally, don't be fooled by what seems to be a small amount of beans in a recipe. 1 cup dry becomes 2 ½ cups cooked.

Ida Frankfurter

In her own words

Ida has a war "souvenir" that few others would dare to keep. It became a focal point in her home as part of her Passover table.

I see my surviving as a double miracle, not just because I am alive, but also because I was on the line that was selected to die. We were marching and two SS officers came to my line. One SS officer pointed to another woman, but the other said in German *andere*, which means the other— which was me. Because they miscounted when selecting the initial group, they needed two more people and I was saved.

I was eighteen when I was transferred from Auschwitz to Peterswaldau in Ober Silesia, to work in a grenade factory. Right before I was liberated the guard took two of us back to the factory and instructed us to throw the grenades into a swimming pool that the guards audaciously used at the camp. They foolishly thought this would prevent the liberators from discovering what they had been doing. I kept one grenade, the whole thing, but apparently the timer was not set, and thankfully never went off. I kept it in my home in Hungary, carefully placing it in a china closet in my little apartment. When we left Hungary quickly, I didn't think about it and left it behind. An aunt of mine went into the apartment and thought it was valuable silver, so she took it for me. I still have it today. Every Pesach, I put it on the table as a reminder that we were slaves, like when we were slaves in Egypt. We are connected with that kind of idea.

I have been married for 62 years to my husband, George, also a survivor. I have two adopted children and seven grandchildren.

Ida Frankfurter's Potato *Kugel*

Like many cooks, Ida prepares familiar dishes with a little of this and a little of that. However, her potato *kugel* recipe was carefully written for her granddaughter who wanted to duplicate her grandma's traditional dish. It can stand alone, but makes a perfect foundation to soak up a hearty sauce.

Yields: 12 servings, Start to Finish: 1½ hours

5 pounds russet potatoes, peeled and grated

2 medium onions, grated (about 1 ½ cups)

5 egg whites or 3 whole eggs, beaten

1 cup vegetable oil

1 ½ to 2 cups all-purpose flour (matzo meal can be substituted at Passover)

2 teaspoons kosher salt

½ teaspoon black pepper

Preheat the oven to 350 degrees and lightly grease a 13x9x2-inch baking dish.

Grate the potatoes and onions, in batches, using the metal blade or fine shredding disc of the food processor, or a box grater. Use the pulse feature to capture and process the small chunks. Spoon the mixture into a bowl. Add the eggs, oil and enough flour to absorb the liquid. The mixture should resemble thin rice pudding and a spoon should fall from side to side if placed in the mixture. Season with salt and pepper (see Feedback).

Pour the batter into the prepared baking dish. Fill to 1-inch below the rim of the dish. (If you have any remaining potato mixture, refrigerate to make latkes at another time.) Bake at 350 degrees, uncovered, for 1¼ hours, or until the *kugel* is a medium brown on top and set in the middle.

Feedback

Once a *kugel* is baked, it is impossible to adjust the salt and pepper. It is also hard to taste before cooking, because raw egg is added to the raw potato mixture. A simple solution is to fry a small amount of the mixture in hot oil, adjust the seasonings, and then proceed with the remainder of the recipe.

Dr. Judita Hruza

In her own words

Judita grew up on the Hungarian border, and like many Hungarian Jews, lived a restricted, but relatively safe life in Hungary, even as the war progressed. That was until 1944, when the Germans came and deported her parents. It was then that she was sent to a little town on the Hungarian-Austrian border where she worked digging trenches to buffer against Soviet army attacks. Her memories prior to the war were happy and typical. However, one memory, related to food, has an almost ironic meaning for Judita.

I was a laborer in a work camp in Austria, when one day I was sent to clean a house on the grounds of the camp. I was very grateful for the assignment as it was a break from the heavy work of digging trenches and I felt fortunate to be working indoors. While cleaning the house, I needed to get hot water, so I took my bucket and went to fill it, when I smelled something cooking in the kitchen. There was an old lady in there making something that smelled so wonderful. I recognized the aroma of sweet fried onions. The woman took pity on me, asking me if I was hungry. I, of course, said yes. She filled a little box for me, with the food she was preparing. When I returned to the barrack, I hid it under my jacket because I was fearful that there was not enough to share with everyone. My mother's best friend was with me in the camp and together we ate the dish in secrecy. Although it was now cold, I don't think I ever enjoyed any food as much as that. I had never eaten a dish like this at home as my mother was very health conscious and we ate lots of vegetables. This dish, which was a combination of pasta, potatoes and fried onions, I later learned is called, Grenadier March. Although this is a dish I associate with a terrible part of my life, I continued to make it after the war, because I have such a strong memory of enjoying it that day.

After the war, I went to a DP camp and then back to Hungary. I discovered my brother, who had obtained false papers, had also survived, but that most of my extended family, twelve members, had perished in Auschwitz. Eventually I went to Sweden where I earned my medical license and was a practicing pediatrician for 20 years. When I arrived in America, in 1970, I became a psychiatrist. I have two children and four beautiful grandchildren.

Granatos Kocka (Grenadier March)—Potatoes and Pasta

If it is true that armies march on their stomachs, then it is understandable how this dish evolved. This nutritious, carb-loving concoction was a favorite of Hungarian foot soldiers because it provided energy from potatoes, pasta and onions. It's really a deconstructed pierogi, with the potato and onion filling keeping company with the noodle, rather than being tucked inside it.

Yields: About 8 servings, Start to Finish: Under 45 minutes

1½ pounds potatoes (red bliss, Yukon gold or russet), peeled and quartered

6 ounces uncooked pasta, can be broad noodles, bow tie, broken lasagna noodles; your choice

1 large onion, chopped (about 1 cup)

½ cup chicken fat or vegetable oil

Kosher salt and pepper

Bring a large pot of salted water to boil. Cook the potatoes until very tender, about 20 minutes. While the potatoes cook, bring another pot of water to boil and cook the noodles according to package directions, drain and reserve.

Heat the fat or oil, in a large skillet, cook and stir the onions, over medium heat, until nicely browned, about 15 minutes. When the potatoes are ready, remove them from the pot with a slotted spoon and place them directly into the skillet with the cooked onions. Let them settle in, and then lightly mash.

Season to taste with salt and pepper. Stir the pasta into the potato and onion mixture. Serve as is, or spoon into a lightly greased casserole and bake at 350 degrees for 20 minutes, until the top is lightly browned.

JFH

Judita Hruza's Poached Carp in Aspic

Judita explains, "This dish has an extra special meaning for me. As a child I was a very poor eater, every meal was a cumbersome chore for me. I had a few favorites like this carp, which was on the top of my list. My grandmother used to make it for Passover dinner. One time she made it for me at a casual visit. Since we came between meal times, my grandma served my food to me on a tray and left me alone. I began to eat and suddenly I felt very sad and started to cry. My grandma came running from the kitchen, alarmed: "What's wrong? Don't you like it?" "No," I replied, "It's not the same." I was five and I couldn't put into words what I was feeling. Looking back years later I realized what had made me so sad. Sitting there alone I was desperately missing the faces around the table, my extended family who had gathered here from all parts of the country for this one occasion, all in their fancy clothes, happy to see each other, me saying my *ma nishtana*, the ceremonies, my little finger dipping in the wine, my grandfather telling the story that I never got tired of hearing again and again. The fish didn't taste the same eating it by myself in the big dining room. Luckily, we had several more Passover seders before the start of the war. Here is the dish I remember so vividly."

Yields: 6 to 8 servings, Start to Finish: 2 to 3 hours to salt the fish, then under 2 hours cooking time. The fish then chills for at least 4 and up to 24 hours.

1 whole carp* (about 5 pounds), cleaned, head and tail removed and reserved

Kosher salt

3 medium onions, sliced

2 parsley roots (parsnips), peeled and sliced ½-inch thick

3 carrots, peeled and sliced ½-inch thick

1 teaspoon paprika

1 package unflavored gelatin

Have your fishmonger clean and cut the fish for you. Liberally salt the fish and let it sit covered in the fridge for 2 to 3 hours. Place the vegetables in the bottom of a pot designed for poaching or use a shallow pot large enough to hold the fish submerged in water. Place the salted carp, head and tail on top of the vegetables, season with paprika and cover with cold water. Simmer on the stove, over low heat for 1 hour, or until the carp is moist and flaky and fully cooked.

Remove the carp and continue to let the vegetables, head and tail cook until the vegetables are very tender and the broth begins to thicken. Strain the broth, discarding the solids. Sprinkle a little of the gelatin into the broth and stir to dissolve. (Although the broth should gel on its own, the gelatin gives it a little extra help.) Put the carp in a dish deep enough to hold both the fish and the reserved liquid. Pour the liquid over the fish, cover and refrigerate several hours or overnight to allow the broth to set. Serve the fish with the jelly.

*Carp was a very popular fish in Eastern Europe and while still eaten today, especially at Passover where it is a common component in gefilte fish, carp is not always readily available. It is also a very bony fish and difficult to filet. Pike or whitefish are easy substitutes for carp.

Feedback
Judita's recipe reflects the Hungarian style of poaching fish. For many Polish cooks, it would be unthinkable not to put sugar in the water, much as they do with gefilte fish. For a sweeter taste, you can add up to ½ cup sugar to the water when poaching the fish. If cooking the entire fish is intimidating or uninviting, you can have your fishmonger cut the fish into steaks. You will still need the head and tail as the thickening agents are in the bones of the fish and are needed to create the aspic (savory jelly).

Lilly Schwarcz Kaplan

In her own words

Lilly Kaplan was always considered to be one of the most reputable and active realtors in New Rochelle, New York, my hometown. In addition to being a successful businesswoman, she was a wonderful homemaker, wife and mother to her two daughters. Her home always smelled of delicious home-cooked meals, which she loved to share with extended family and friends. In addition to her love of good food, Lilly instilled in her family a love of Israel, Jewish customs and values and the importance of *tikkun olam* (repairing the world) and *tzedakah* (charity).

I was born in Ungvár, the oldest child, having a younger sister and three younger brothers. Before the war, my family ran a wholesale bakery business. As a young teenager, I often worked alongside my parents. I was good in math and helped with the recordkeeping. On Fridays, people in town would bring us their pots filled with *cholent* so we could slow roast the *cholent* overnight in our commercial ovens. After Shabbos services everyone would come to the bakery and collect their pots. I have to admit that on rare occasions a few people were given someone else's pot, which got them upset. It struck me as funny that people would always know their own *cholent* from the dozens in the oven. I remember my

mother inviting Yeshiva students who were coming through town to our Shabbos table.

The war came to our area in 1944. Everyone in the family (except my father who was forced to serve in a labor battalion) was deported to Auschwitz. On our arrival I was separated from my family and chosen for work detail. My mother, grandmother and siblings were sent to the other group and perished. After I was liberated from Auschwitz, I was very ill with tuberculosis and typhus. I was fortunate to be sent to a hospital in Sweden. I received word in the hospital that my father had also survived but I was hesitant about contacting him right away because I thought I was dying and wanted to spare him additional heartache. I did make a full recovery, and made contact with my father. In Sweden, I received an education and got a job. I later reunited with my father in New York after trying for several years to get him out of a DP camp in Germany. I married my husband, Lew Kaplan, an American from the Bronx, shortly after I came to New York and we were married for 47 years, until he passed away in 1998.

I didn't talk about the war very much when my children were growing up. I didn't want to burden them. I loved cooking and baking and felt it was one way that I was caring for my husband and girls. I always made everything myself. I relied on my instincts and educated guesswork to create meals for my family. My motto was "If you can read, you can cook." After losing so many of my own family members in the war, I feel blessed that I have such a loving family, especially my two wonderful daughters (and their husbands) and my four beautiful grandchildren.

Top left: Lily Kaplan, late 1940s-1950, Sweden

Lilly Kaplan's Chicken Paprikash

This authentic Hungarian specialty features plenty of paprika, which lends a rich red color and subtle spicy flavor to this popular chicken dish. While Lilly uses sweet paprika, for an extra jolt of flavor, add a teaspoon of cayenne or smoked paprika.

Yields: 4 servings, Start to Finish: Under 2 hours

2 medium onions, sliced

4 garlic cloves, chopped

3 tablespoons olive oil

4 pounds chicken parts, on the bone, skin removed

1 (14-ounce) can chopped tomatoes

1 cup chicken broth

¼ cup white wine

2 teaspoons sweet paprika

Kosher salt and pepper

1 green pepper, cored, seeded and sliced

Heat the olive oil in a large sauté pan, cook and stir the onions and garlic, over medium heat, until lightly browned, about 15 minutes. Remove with a slotted spoon and reserve. In the same pan (adding more oil if needed), brown the chicken pieces in batches and set aside on a plate. When all the chicken is browned, add the chicken (not the juice that has collected), onions and garlic back into the pan. Stir in the tomatoes, chicken broth, white wine, paprika, salt and pepper to taste. Top with the green pepper slices.

Simmer, covered, for 45 to 60 minutes, or until the chicken is tender and cooked through. Remove the chicken to a serving platter and bring the sauce to a slow boil. If the sauce is too thin, thicken it by creating a *roux*. In a skillet, heat 2 teaspoons of oil and then blend in 2 teaspoons of flour, stirring constantly to avoid burning the roux. You'll want it to be a light blonde color. Let the *roux* cool a bit, and then stir it into the sauce, cook for several minutes to let it do its thing. If the sauce is still not thick enough, repeat the above process. Pour the sauce over the chicken and serve with noodles or dumplings. See Greta Margolis' dumpling recipe (see page 274) or homemade noodles (see page 30).

Feedback

Paprika can be hot, sweet, and several degrees in between. Look for pure Hungarian paprika, it's worth the difference. And be sure never to add paprika directly into a dry pan, it will burn quickly as it releases its natural sugar.

Lilly Kaplan's Hungarian Butter Cookies

Lilly maintains that it is easier to bake than to go to the bakery. Pretty funny when you consider her family was in the commercial bakery business. Her daughter adds, "We never had a bakery box in the house!" Lilly shares with us her simple, foolproof light and crisp butter cookie recipe. The dough is delicate, so work quickly.

Yields: about 3 to 4 dozen cookies; Start to Finish: Under 30 minutes

1 stick (½ cup) butter, room temperature

¼ cup confectioner's sugar

½ teaspoon almond extract

1 cup all-purpose flour plus 2 tablespoons

Confectioner's sugar for dusting

Beat the butter, sugar and almond extract, on medium speed, until creamy. Lower the speed and slowly add the flour until a dough forms. Divide the dough into two pieces, flatten each into a disc and wrap in wax paper. Chill the dough in the fridge while the oven heats.

Preheat the oven to 400 degrees and lightly grease a large baking sheet or line it with parchment paper or a non-stick silicone mat. When the oven is heated, remove the first piece of dough from the fridge.

Generously flour your work surface and the rolling pin, and roll the dough to ¼-inch thick. Cut the dough with a cookie cutter, any size and shape you choose. Lilly would use the rim of a glass and overlap it to create half moon shapes. Gently lift the cookies with a cookie spatula, and place them on the prepared cookie sheet.

Bake at 400 degrees for 10 minutes or until the cookies are a very light golden color. Do not over bake. The cookies will develop a burnt taste if they are too brown. When cool, sprinkle with confectioner's sugar.

Feedback

The grocery shelves are now lined with specialty extracts. The flavors in these extracts are very concentrated and impart a real burst of flavor. In this recipe, you might try substituting lemon or orange extract for the almond, it adds a refreshing note.

George Lang

Based on our conversation and excerpts from his memoir

Stepping into the legendary restaurateur George Lang's office on New York's Upper West Side is like stepping into a perfect culinary library. I was surrounded by thousands of cookbooks, some dating back to the 19th century. The cover of his memoir, *Nobody knows the Truffles I've Seen*, terms him a restaurateur-raconteur extraordinaire. It didn't take long for me to realize that was not hyperbole, but fact. We talked about his transformation from Hungarian violin virtuoso to American iconic restaurant consultant. Here is just a glimpse into his remarkable journey.

George remembers much about his childhood in Hungary, explaining, "I was brought up in an unusual Jewish home. My father was a genius in 200 different ways, but he could barely read or write. He didn't believe in religion. My mother was very religious; her father was a Rabbi. Our kitchen was about as kosher as you could get. At Pesach I particularly loved the after dinner stories, but we practiced a particular Jewish, non-Jewish, Jewish. I felt ashamed of being a weak minority, but then I turned around. Every five seconds there was anti-Semitism in Hungary. I was an alien in my own hometown. Anti-Semitism was not institutionalized, though, like other Hungarian national sports, it enjoyed great popularity."

Life changed dramatically for George on February 6, 1944, the day he boarded the train to report to a forced labor camp. Prior to going, he and his father hid his prized violin and his mother's jewelry at a family friend's farm. Through a series of events, all orchestrated by George, he escaped the camp by obtaining false documents. He assumed the last name, Hegedüs, which in Hungarian meant "violinist." He made his way to Budapest, which was in upheaval. The ruthless Arrowcross party had taken over the city, while the Russians were encroaching on the city's borders. George made the daring decision to join the Arrowcross, not only to keep himself alive, but also to facilitate lending a helping hand to other Jews caught in the turmoil. "During the next three weeks, we organized rescue missions in a number of safe-houses and yellow star ghetto buildings, and our little group succeeded in bringing out a couple of dozen people without a shot being fired."

As the war came to a close, and the Russians took control of the city, George was charged with war crimes related to his brief service with the Arrowcross. After being incarcerated and standing trial, the judges of the People's Court weighed the evidence and concluded the following: "Based on all the facts, however, the activities of the accused were directed exclusively toward helping his despondent fellow humans living under abject conditions, bringing medicine, doctors and food to them, and these activities certainly did not help in the continuation of the power of the Arrowcross movement—which was the main point of the charges. Furthermore, his activities were actually instrumental in the cessation of Arrowcross power."

It was now September 1945, and having been acquitted of all charges, George moved on with his life. He learned that both his parents were deported and perished in Auschwitz. He discovered few family members survived the war, but was able to reunite with a cousin, Evi, and her new husband, Victor. Both remained close to George over the next sixty years. George knew he needed to leave Hungary so he connected with a group that smuggled people across the border into Austria. At the time, he didn't realize it would entail his hiding in a black coffin and traveling over the border in the back of a hearse. George remained in Austria, saving money and working with the Hebrew Immigrant Aid Society (HIAS) for passage to America.

In July of 1946, George left Vienna and boarded the SS Marine Flasher. He movingly describes the moment he entered New York harbor. "Hundreds of my fellow refugees were crammed together into a single cheering crowd. With a few of them, I climbed to a small platform on the deck, and there she was, the Statue of Liberty, seemingly within touching distance. I had my trusty violin and my paper-mache valise (tied with a piece of string), and I was wearing a tie, since I felt I should be properly dressed for the occasion. I like to believe that everybody is entitled to one miracle in a lifetime. My allotment was the miracle of my survival between February 6, 1944, the first day of my life in the labor camp, and July 15, 1946, when I first saw Lady Liberty." Lang continued his musical aspirations, playing with such orchestras as The Dallas Symphony, but after hearing Jascha Heifetz play his beloved Mendelssohn, George realized he was never going to be the best violinist. Luckily, for the food world, he directed his attention to the culinary arts.

He started modestly, cleaning vegetables, and then working at a banquet facility on the Lower East Side. George found his true talent, organizing and arranging the most lavish affairs. He had seamlessly made the leap from Hungarian Holocaust survivor to New York's premier restaurateur, bon vivant, and master of fabulous fetes.

He elevated dining to a new level and developed the concept of food as entertainment. He planned events for such dignitaries as Khrushchev and Queen Elizabeth. Possibly his crowning culinary glory was resurrecting Hungary's national treasure, *Gundel*, in Budapest. His pride and joy for nearly 35 years was New York's legendary Cafe des Artistes, which he bought in 1975. The Cafe, as he liked to call it, was run by his wife Jenifer, whose cooking he touts as being "the best in the city."

In turning his attention to food, George has some very strong beliefs. "What is important is to find out why the Jews took certain dishes from other countries. I can't think of a Jewish food that doesn't taste good. I've tasted every food on earth. I could live nicely without broiled steak, but

not without fried chicken. I love dishes presented beautifully. I like the kind of dessert that if your mother is a very good baker, you would get the dessert you deserve." As for Hungarian food, George maintains, "Even Hungarians don't agree on it. I discovered that cooking is influenced by the nature of your country. Every age of Hungarian cooking is defined not only by whom they conquered, but also by who conquered them. And I love paprika!"

At the Cafe, George would feature a Hungarian tasting menu, and offer one dish daily that he called "poor people's good food." George confessed that sometimes that was his favorite dish of the day. "If I am inventive enough, I can come up with dishes, cooking methods, service, everything which has individual power and character that even though it doesn't have caviar and truffles, it becomes rich man's food."

When I asked what he has learned from his experiences during the Holocaust and what he wants his legacy to be, he answers quickly and assuredly. "I define myself in a number of ways, but I want to create things that are wonderful, beautiful and useful. I consider life fabulous and wonderful and it depends on what you do to it, not what people do to you. I have learned that no condition is so bad that you cannot survive it or on rare occasion, even change it." George and Jenifer have two children.

With his gracious permission, I pored over George Lang's remarkable books to select the recipes to be included with his equally remarkable story. This was like letting a botanist loose in the Botanical Gardens and telling him to pick the most fragrant flower. The history of Hungarian cuisine is poetically detailed in his eponymous *George Lang's Cuisine of Hungary* (Wings Books, 1994). It reads like a culinary journey, and reveals how his love and respect for Hungarian cooking holds a deep-rooted meaning in his life. The journey begins, aptly, with soup and ends with a dessert that has special significance to George—as they say in Hungarian, *Elvéz*! Enjoy!

George maintains, "It is most probable that Hungarian housewives and cooks are either born with, or develop, a keen *soup sense*. He goes on to write, "The simple methods of Hungarian soup making (no stocks generally, no fancy spices, no cognac or sherry or other taste crutches) produced soups as good as those from any nation's kitchen, because of the fine vegetables of the land and the foolproof methods faithfully followed." George feels the following soup "is a perfect example of the Hungarian talent for making a delicious dish out of meager ingredients."

George Lang's Caraway Seed Soup with Poached Eggs

*Excerpted from George Lang's memoir, Nobody Knows the Truffles I've Seen
(Alfred A. Knopf New York, 1998)*

Without the egg it's called "Poor People's Soup" in Hungary and is usually served with chunks of toasted bread. My happy recollection is that my mother, knowing my father's and my predilection for marrying soup and bread, served it with her economy-size croutons. The soup becomes a "Rich Man's Soup" when quail eggs are used instead of the regular chicken variety. In either case, you should use a strong meat broth (even though my mother was able to make a satisfying caraway soup using only water).

Serves 4

2 tablespoons vegetable oil

1 tablespoon caraway seeds

2 tablespoons flour

½ teaspoon sweet Hungarian paprika

3 cups water

2 cups beef or chicken broth

Salt

4 eggs

1. Heat the oil in a medium soup pot over medium heat. Sprinkle the caraway seeds into the oil, stir, and sauté until the seeds begin to jump around. Sprinkle on the flour and stir continually until it turns light golden brown. Off the heat, stir in the paprika (if you add it over the heat, you'll burn out its sugar content).

2. Add the water and broth, and season with salt to taste. Bring to a boil, then lower the heat immediately to a simmer, and cook, uncovered, 25 minutes.

3. Strain the soup through a cheesecloth (if you use a regular strainer, you will end up with caraway seeds in the soup and eventually in your teeth).

4. Just before serving, bring the soup to a simmer and very carefully break in the eggs one by one, making sure that they remain whole and separate. Simmer 2 minutes, so that the yolks remain soft.

5. To serve, carefully spoon an egg into a warm soup plate and ladle the soup around it.

George Lang's *Húsvéti töltött csirke*–Stuffed Chicken for Passover

Excerpted from George Lang's Cuisine of Hungary (Wings Books, New York 1994)

This matzo-stuffed chicken is Jewish family fare during Passover holidays. The stuffing is so different from the usual bread-based kind that regardless of religion or time of year, you should try it. If you are able, put some of the stuffing under the skin of the bird.

6 to 8 servings

1 fat fowl, 4 to 4½ pounds	Salt and pepper
3 whole pieces of matzo	2 eggs
½ small onion, chopped fine	2 tablespoons crushed matzo
¾ cup rendered chicken fat*	1 medium-sized very ripe tomato, cut into pieces
4 chicken livers, very carefully cleaned**	1 medium-sized onion, sliced
1 tablespoon chopped parsley	1 green pepper, sliced
¼ pound mushrooms, chopped	1 garlic clove, mashed

1. Soak the chicken in salted ice-cold water for 1 hour. Soak matzo in lukewarm water till soft, then squeeze until dry.

2. Cook chopped onion, covered, in 2 tablespoons of the chicken fat; do not brown. After 5 minutes add chicken livers, parsley and mushrooms. Cook, covered, for another 5 minutes. Let the mixture cool.

3. Add squeezed matzo and put the whole mixture through the grinder. Add salt and pepper to taste. Add eggs and bread crumbs and mix well. Let the stuffing rest for a couple of hours.

4. Mix in 6 tablespoons chicken fat.

5. Remove chicken from ice-cold water, wipe it well inside and outside and salt it. Fill with the stuffing. Sew up the opening.

6. Spread 2 tablespoons of chicken fat on the bottom of a baking pan. Put in tomato, sliced onion and green pepper. Add garlic, a sprinkle of salt and ¼ cup water. Spread remaining 2 tablespoons fat on top of the chicken, put the chicken in the pan, cover the pan, and cook the chicken on top of the stove over low heat. Baste often.

7. Preheat the oven to 475 degrees F. When the chicken is done, take it out of the pan and keep it warm. Put vegetables through a sieve or blender to make sauce.

8. Put chicken back in the pan and place it in the preheated oven for about 10 minutes to make it brown and crisp.

9. Serve the sauce separately. Accompany with egg noodles, boiled and then sautéed in chicken fat for a few minutes, or rice.

*You can buy chicken fat at almost any market, or render your own (see recipe on page 40).
** For kosher preparation, broil the livers before adding them to the pan.

In his chapter on vegetables, Mr. Lang writes, "In Hungary, vegetables are not just *cooked*, they are *prepared*. The difference between an American vegetable dish and a Hungarian one is similar to the difference between plain boiled meat and a meat stew." You only need to visit his New York office to experience his love affair with asparagus. "I love single ideas, like asparagus," he explained as I gazed at the hundreds of asparagus inspired objects that fill his office shelves. The following recipe is George's tribute to the simple stalk.

Asparagus Pudding

Excerpted from George Lang's Cuisine of Hungary (Wings Books, New York 1994)

6 servings

1 pound fresh young asparagus	**4 tablespoons butter**
Salt	**4 eggs separated**
1 roll	**4 tablespoons sour cream**
½ cup milk	

1. Peel the asparagus and cut slantwise into 1-inch pieces. Place in a saucepan with 1 cup water and 1 teaspoon salt. Cook until done, but it should be almost crunchy and not soft. Drain.

2. Soak the roll in the milk, then squeeze. Thoroughly butter a pudding mold with 2 tablespoons of the butter.

3. Whip the rest of the butter till foamy. Add the roll, egg yolks, sour cream and 1 teaspoon salt. Whip till well mixed and fluffy.

4. Whip egg whites stiff and fold them in gently with a rubber spatula. Combine the mixture with the cooked asparagus; do it very carefully so as not to break the egg-white foam.

5. Pour the mixture into the buttered pudding mold. Do not fill mold more than three-quarters full. Put on a tight-fitting top.

6. Fill a 4-quart pot half full of hot water. Set pudding mold into the pot and cook, with the cover on, for 1 hour.

Variation: To serve this as an appetizer, sauté 1 cup bread crumbs in ¼ pound butter until golden brown; pour crumbs on top of pudding or spoon a little over each slice. You may also combine the bread crumb mixture with grated cheese.

George Lang's *Anyám cseresznyés lepénye*
My Mother's Cherry Cake

Excerpted from George Lang's Cuisine of Hungary (Wings Books, New York 1994)

Summer luncheons of my childhood often ended with this dessert. This cherry cake is all that a cake should be.

10 to 12 pieces

1 pound fresh cherries	**1 cup flour**
⅜ pound sweet butter	**Pinch of salt**
¾ cup granulated sugar	**¼ cup bread crumbs**
3 eggs, separated	**Vanilla sugar**

1. Pit cherries, taking care not to split them. Set aside. Preheat oven to 375 degrees F.

2. Mix butter well with half of the granulated sugar. After a few minutes of vigorous whipping add egg yolks and continue whipping. Finally add flour and salt.

3. Beat egg whites with remaining granulated sugar till the mixture is stiff and forms peaks. With a rubber spatula, gently fold it into the butter mixture.

4. Butter a baking pan 10 X 6 inches and sprinkle it with bread crumbs. Put dough in pan, and top with cherries.

5. Bake in the preheated oven for 30 minutes. Before serving, sprinkle with vanilla sugar.

Freda Lederer

In her own words

Freda Lederer is soft-spoken, warm, friendly and full of positive energy. She credits her survival as "a combination of luck and perseverance." She is quick to point out, "You roll with the punches, instead of being bitter and complaining. Everyday you have a new opportunity to make the best of this life and take the challenges that come your way."

Although I was born in Mukaevo (Mukacheve), Czechoslovakia, my new passport, which I renewed a few years ago, said I was born in the Ukraine, because the borders have changed. I was the only girl in a family of five children. We were a religious family and my father was a small businessman. I was the only one who had gone through high school. At the time, it wasn't acceptable for a girl to be educated, but I was very adamant. I went to a public school and graduated in May, 1944. After the school year was over, the graduates had to take oral and written tests to officially pass your graduation. At the time I had to take these exams, I was in the ghetto. I had a wonderful teacher who arranged for me to come and go out of the ghetto so I could take these tests. I was so naive; I didn't realize what was waiting for me. In June, 1944, after I graduated, the entire ghetto was liquidated and we were taken to Auschwitz. From the first minute on I was separated from my family. I was only nineteen.

My first stroke of luck was that a German industrialist needed 300 young people to work in his factory making radar parts. He pointed to me and asked if I spoke German, I answered him in German saying that I graduated from high school. He pushed me to the side where he was gathering people for work. After I was there for a few months they needed people to work in a town near Hamburg. The Allies were bombing Hamburg day and night. The Germans marched us to the nearest camp, which was Bergen-Belsen. I think someone up in heaven was looking out for me because after three weeks, in April, 1945, the British army liberated the camp. The British went out of their way, if not for them I would not be alive. I was very sick and they requisitioned private German homes and made them into makeshift hospitals. A Swedish doctor came by and asked if I would like to go to Sweden to recuperate. I said yes, and went to Sweden where I stayed with a Jewish family for one year. Through the Red Cross I found that three of my brothers survived as well and were in a DP camp in Germany. I left Sweden and we were reunited. At that time, President Truman mandated that 90,000 refugees were permitted to enter the United States without a direct sponsor. I was sponsored by the Harrisburg community; that's where I settled, that's where I stayed. The Rabbi there has said, "It was a good marriage." It takes time to become an American. At first I saw myself as a refugee; you don't become an American instantaneously. I was married 28 years and have three children, five grandchildren, and two great grandchildren.

Freda Lederer's Passover Stuffed Cabbage

Every year Freda hosts both seders at her house with her entire extended family. She cooks everything, but is famous for her stuffed cabbage. Freda says, "This is the original recipe" she ate as a child, but notes, "I had no idea how to make it then, and I really didn't care." Lucky for us, she does now. Freda's version is clean and simple with a definite sweet and sour tug of war. She prefers using a small head of cabbage, feeling the leaves are a better size to stuff, and the head of cabbage is easier to handle.

Yields: 15 to 18 rolls, Start to Finish: Under 2 hours

1 small green cabbage (about 1½ pounds), boiled

For the filling:

1 pound ground beef

1 large onion, chopped (about 1 cup)

3 tablespoons vegetable oil

1 piece matzo, soaked until soft, then squeezed dry

2 eggs, beaten

½ cup water

¾ teaspoon kosher salt

¼ teaspoon black pepper

For the sauce:

1 (15-ounce) can tomato sauce

15 ounces water (fill the tomato sauce can)

2 to 3 tablespoons sugar

Juice of 2 lemons or a pinch of sour salt

Bring a large pot of salted water to boil. Prepare the cabbage by removing the center core. Cook the whole cabbage until the leaves begin to wilt, at least 15 minutes. Carefully remove the cabbage from the water (pierce the cabbage with a large serving fork to lift out of the water, support the cabbage underneath with a large slotted spoon). Place the cabbage on a dish and let it cool so you can easily begin removing the outer leaves. Keep the water on a low boil, in case you need to place the cabbage back in to help loosen the inner leaves. Begin peeling the cabbage, you will need 15 to 18 leaves. Cut a small V-shape in each leaf to remove the hard white rib. Let the leaves hang out on a paper towel to help absorb any remaining water.

Prepare the filling by heating 1 tablespoon of the oil in a skillet, cook and stir the beef, over medium heat, until nicely browned, about 10 minutes, breaking up any large pieces. Remove the meat with a slotted spoon. Discard the liquid from the pan and heat the remaining 2 tablespoons of oil, cook and stir the onions, over medium heat, until lightly browned, about 10 minutes. Combine the onions and meat and let them cool for a few minutes.

While the meat mixture cools, soak the matzo in cold water, until it is soft, but not mushy; it should resemble wet cardboard. Remove from the water and squeeze out as much liquid as possible. Add the matzo to the meat and onions and then stir in the eggs, water, salt and pepper.

In a Dutch oven or covered pot, combine the sauce ingredients. Bring to a boil, and then lower the heat to a slow simmer.

To stuff the cabbage, take a generous spoonful of meat filling and place it in the cabbage leaf, use more for the larger leaves, less for the smaller. Roll the leaf to cover the meat, tuck in the sides, and then continue rolling. You should have a nice, neat package. Place the stuffed cabbage rolls in the sauce, close together, layering if necessary. Cover and cook for 1 to 1½ hours, checking occasionally to see if water needs to be added to the sauce to prevent it from drying out. Serve family style with the sauce spooned over the cabbage rolls.

Variations: Lilly Kaplan also makes a delicious stuffed cabbage featuring two ingredients that you might want to try adding next time. Lilly lines the pot with sauerkraut—1 large can, rinsed and drained, before filling the pot with the cabbage rolls. Additionally, she chops the small inner leaves and adds those to the pot. When the pot is full, she dots the cabbage rolls with about 1 cup of dried Turkish apricots to add a layer of sweetness. If you don't have apricots, you could stir 1 cup of apricot preserves into the sauce instead.

Ruth Stromer also makes a wonderful stuffed cabbage, and uses a different method to prepare the cabbage leaves (see page 136 for her recipe and technique).

Gale Gand

Professional contributor

While we have you thinking about cabbage and how it gathers a sweet mellow flavor when slow simmered, you might want to try premier pastry chef Gale Gand's family recipe, which takes cabbage from a main course to a sweet dessert.

Cabbage Strudel

Contributed by Gale Gand, executive pastry chef and owner of Tru restaurant, Chicago

This recipe came from my Hungarian great grandmother, Rose (Frankel) Simon, which she passed down to my grandma, Elsie (Simon) Grossman. The story I was told was that my family was poor... so poor they couldn't afford apples for their apple strudel, so they used cabbage as a cheaper substitute and with enough sugar and cinnamon apparently it tastes practically like apples.

Makes 1 log or 8 servings

Filling:

¼ cup butter

½ green cabbage, shredded

¼ teaspoon salt

½ cup sugar

½ cup raisins

¼ cup walnut pieces, toasted

3 sheets phyllo pastry, thawed overnight in the refrigerator, if frozen kept moist

8 tablespoons (1 stick) butter, melted

½ cup sugar

1 cup walnuts, lightly toasted and finely chopped

Filling: In a sauté pan, melt the butter. Heat it to medium high heat and sauté the cabbage until tender. Add the salt and sugar and stir to dissolve. Add the raisins and cook a few minutes to reduce and thicken any juices. Stir in the walnuts and spread on a sheet pan to cool.

Preheat the oven to 375 degrees.

Line a sheet pan with parchment paper. Transfer 1 sheet of phyllo to the sheet pan. Using a pastry brush, brush the phyllo with butter. Sprinkle with a third of the sugar and a third of the chopped walnuts. Repeat with the two remaining sheets of phyllo. Reserve the remaining melted butter and sugar. Turn the sheet pan so that the phyllo is horizontal to your body. Spoon the cooled cabbage filling 2 inches in from the left hand edge of the phyllo, working from top to bottom, leaving 2 inches bare at the top and bottom. Turn the sheet pan ¼-turn and roll up the pastry to encase the filling, forming a log. Move the log to the center of the sheet pan and tuck the ends under to keep the filling from oozing out. Brush the surface with melted butter and sprinkle with sugar. Bake until golden brown, about 30 minutes. Let cool 10 to 15 minutes on the pan. Using a serrated knife cut carefully into sections and serve warm.

Greta Margolis

In her own words

Greta had to assume many different personas to survive the war. First blending in as an Aryan peasant, then a partisan in the woods. Her sharp intellect certainly helped her understand the need to adapt.

I was born in 1937 in Czechoslovakia, and was an only child. I remember my childhood very clearly. My father had a lot of friends in the government and we did receive some protection for a while. My father was a government official, and we left only when his friends advised him it was no longer safe for us to stay. At that time, in 1943, many people had already been taken by trucks and trains and disappeared forever. We had papers with false names, and leaving everything behind, we traveled west to the capital of Slovakia. My parents felt that in a big city we could get lost. We stayed in a hotel for a while, and then decided to move again to another town. We stayed there until the Germans invaded, and then we ran for our lives. We wound up in a tiny farming village. Our being Jewish was always an issue, even though we had papers stating we were Aryan. However, we looked different, our demeanor was different and we did not blend in well. My father had money and paid a family so that we could live in their home. I didn't go to the school, which was in another village, but I helped my mother and the farmer's wife with the cooking, while my father did chores. I never felt like I was home. I didn't play with the neighbor's children and I always understood the danger of being found. I stayed close to my parents.

Every so often, we would have to flee into the woods and join the partisans. We would stay in a bunker until it was safe to return. In 1945, the Russian troops came through the woods and liberated us. Trucks ran through the village, filled with Russian soldiers. It was on such a truck that I was returned to my home. The soldiers were friendly and nice; they knew we had been through a very traumatic period. I do remember that they took my father's watch. Some of the soldiers had their arms lined up and down with watches. We felt it was a small price to pay for our freedom. We returned home and found my grandparents who lived in our same small town. Their house was intact and they had survived, having been hidden by an uncle. I always knew we would come to America. My mother's entire family was here, but our papers had not come through in time to avoid the war. Right after we were liberated, my father began the process again. Three and a half years later, in 1948, we came to the Bronx, New York.

I was only eleven, and spoke not a word of English. I started school right after Christmas, and by June, I was fluent. I skipped several grades and graduated from the 6th grade that summer. I enjoy the holidays and try to cook like my mom, who made many Hungarian dishes, even though we weren't Hungarian. My mother never taught me to cook, but I enjoy it and love incorporating all styles of cooking. I am married to my husband, Martin, almost 52 years. Together we have two sons and five wonderful grandchildren.

Top left: Greta, age 10, at a ballet recital in 1947

Greta Margolis' Nockedly—Hungarian Dumplings

Greta remembers her mother making these dumplings. "She would put the dough on a flat plate and with the side of a tablespoon, push little pieces into the pot of boiling water. These are excellent with any gravy or sauce."

Yields: 4 servings, Start to Finish: Under 30 minutes

2 eggs, beaten

1 cup all-purpose flour

1 tablespoon water

Kosher salt and pepper

Bring a large pot of salted water to boil.

Stir the flour into the beaten eggs, season with a pinch of salt and pepper and add 1 tablespoon of water to create the dough. Knead the dough for a couple of minutes; it should be smooth, elastic and not too sticky. If you need additional water or flour, feel free to add it to achieve the right consistency. When the water boils, place the dough on a plate, and using a tablespoon, cut the dough into 1-inch pieces, pushing the dough into the boiling water with the spoon. You might need to dip the spoon into the water to help slide the dumplings off the spoon. Cover and cook until the water returns to a rapid boil. When the water boils, lower the temperature and gently boil, covered, for 15 minutes. Drain and rinse quickly in cold water. Serve with gravy, sauce or lightly fried onions. These dumplings are an authentic addition to many Hungarian dishes. Try serving them with Lilly Kaplan's Chicken Paprikash (see page 261).

Mary Fenyes Mayer

In her own words

I met Mary at her home, and she greeted me at the door with an apology. She was sorry that she felt she had no story to tell. Three hours later, I left Mary's impeccable home with a remarkable story, some terrific Hungarian recipes and a care package of *mandel* bread for my husband.

I was born into a privileged family in Budapest, Hungary. My father was the president of an oil company and my mother was a homemaker, who had five servants to do much of the work. I sometimes compare my mother to the lead character in *A Streetcar Named Desire*. She was a good and loving mother who had an unusual view of the world. On September 1, 1939 after having spent the summer in Switzerland, one of my governesses came to take me home on a Red Cross train. My family felt there was little danger for us in Hungary, as my father was a decorated soldier and revered in our mostly non-Jewish community. Everything changed on May 23, 1944 when my father was first saluted, then arrested by the Gestapo. He was taken as a hostage, along with several Gentile executives, and held in a nearby hotel for ransom.

Unbelievable amounts of money were paid for their freedom, however, they were taken away and never seen again.

At that time, my mother and I were given fifteen minutes to vacate our beautiful home, which had a wonderful rose garden. My mother remained in a "safe house" under the protection of Raoul Wallenberg. I was forced to work on a farm and then in a factory, where I worked very hard. A daily roll call stopped me from trying to escape as we were told that if you we were not accounted for, your family would be punished or shot. The first of several fortunate circumstances that changed my destiny occurred on a quiet July day. The factory I worked in was severely bombed on July 2, 1944. I was not in my usual bunker, but in the Gentile section, which was off limits during the week. I took the opportunity and the distraction the explosions created to escape. I remember calmly walking the 20km to my German governess' home and removing the yellow star from my clothing so people would not know I was Jewish. The next day she arranged for me to have legal papers that had been secured by the daughter of my French governess. I assumed that young girl's identity. The risk these two loyal and loving women took by helping me was tantamount to being a Jew, since harboring or helping a Jew was punishable by death.

Circumstances continued to unravel as Hungary became more and more dangerous. I evaded arrest and capture several times, once because a stranger advised me not to return home. To this day, I believe that stranger was the angel Gabriel, sent to save me. I boarded a train to St. Endre, a village located north of Budapest on the Danube River. Upon arriving at the train station, I took a help wanted ad that was posted

Top left: Mary Mayer

on a wall and decided to answer it. When I knocked on the door of the couple seeking help, they laughed that I certainly was not fit for the job. They were looking for a handyman, and I did not look the part. They did, however, provide me lodging for the night. When they awoke the next day, I had chopped the wood, built a fire and fetched buckets of water. The couple reconsidered, and I was safe once again. Fortunately, I carried the fake documents that concealed my Jewish identity. It seemed ironic that I had grown up in a household where others did the cooking and cleaning for me and now I was doing the same for strangers.

Months passed and on December 26, 1944, when I was working in the attic, I saw a very typical sight. A large black sedan driven by German soldiers sped through the town. That day something was different. A Russian tank almost collided with them coming from the opposite direction, killing the Germans. We had been liberated.

Once again, a stranger guided me to safety. This time, it was an important Russian high-ranking officer who was billeted with the couple I worked for. At first I spoke to him in German, but quickly realized that was offending him. I then spoke to him in French, explaining my circumstances. Miraculously, this Russian officer spoke French as well, and after hearing my story provided me with a cadre of soldiers to escort me home to find my mother. He gave me a letter that would open every door; I called it a passport to safety. Unfortunately, when we got to the river, the Germans had blown up the bridges connecting the two sides of Budapest. I returned to St. Endre, crossed the frozen Danube and walked the 20km home! I finally made it and was reunited with my mother. I have gone from Hungary to America, where I built a life. I often question why I was spared, how I came to be so lucky. Maybe it was because my destiny was to give life to my wonderful son and daughter and enjoy my five grandchildren.

Mary Mayer's Cucumber Salad

Mary's perfect dinner would be rounded off with this simple cucumber salad. The longer you let it sit, the softer the cucumbers become and the more pickled the flavor. If you don't mind the seeds and peel, go for the low maintenance prep, just thinly slice the cucumbers. Not a fan of the seeds? Cut the cucumbers in half lengthwise and scoop out the seeds with a spoon. For you higher maintenance eaters, do all the above and peel the cucumbers.

Yields: about 2 cups, Start to Finish: Under 15 minutes, then time to marinate

1 large cucumber (about ¾ pound), thinly sliced

1 teaspoon kosher salt

1 tablespoon white vinegar to taste

1 teaspoon sweet paprika (optional)

Toss the sliced cucumber and salt in a colander. Let the cucumber slices drain for 10 minutes, and then gently squeeze the cucumbers to release their liquid. Spoon the cucumbers into a bowl and toss with the white vinegar. If the flavor is too strong, add a little water, not strong enough, add more vinegar. You can sprinkle the cucumbers with paprika for color and flavor. Cover and refrigerate until nice and cold and the cucumbers take on a pickled taste. Serve as is as a side dish, or toss with red onion and tomatoes for a refreshing salad.

Mary Mayer's Veal Paprikash

As a child Mary recalls eating everything paprikash. Veal was a luxurious change from chicken or beef. In her home, goose fat was used to brown the meat imparting a rich gamy flavor. Today's cooks tend to use olive oil, but chicken fat or goose fat will add an extra element to the sauce. Slow cook the dish for the most intense flavor, and to insure tender, juicy veal.

Yields: 4 to 6 servings, Start to finish: Under 2 hours

3 to 4 tablespoons vegetable oil

2 to 3 large onions rough chopped (about 2 ½ to 3 cups)

2 green peppers, cored, seeded and cut into chunks

2 pounds veal cut into 1-to-2 inch pieces

Flour for dredging, seasoned with kosher salt and pepper

1 (15-ounce) can tomato sauce

1 teaspoon sweet paprika

Kosher salt and pepper

Heat the oil in a large sauté pan or Dutch oven, cook and stir the onions and peppers, over medium heat, until lightly browned, about 10 to 15 minutes. Remove the vegetables from the pan with a slotted spoon and reserve.

Pat the veal dry, and then dredge the pieces in the seasoned flour. Add oil if needed to the sauté pan and brown the veal on all sides, about 3 minutes per side. If necessary, cook the veal in batches, do not over crowd the pan or the pieces will steam, not brown. Have a plate standing by to hold the cooked meat. When all the meat is browned, add it back to the pan with the cooked vegetables. Stir in the tomato sauce and paprika. Season to taste with salt and pepper. Cover and cook on the stove, over low heat for 1 ½ hours, or until the veal is fork tender and the sauce has taken on a burnt sienna color. The vegetables will have all but melted into the sauce.

Spoon the Paprikash over a bed of noodles or potato dumplings. (See Regina Finer's recipe on page 29, or for traditional Hungarian dumplings, see Greta Margolis' recipe on page 274).

Mary Mayer's Raspberry Linzer Tarts

Linzer tarts come in all shapes and sizes and Mary's are usually flavored with vanilla for a subtle sweet taste. For a nutty, marzipan flavor add almond extract in place of vanilla. The cookies are delicate to handle, but look so inviting with the preserves peeking out from the center. Only the shape of your cookie cutter and choice of filling limit your creativity.

Yields: 20 to 24 (1-inch cookies), 16 to 18 (2-inch cookies), 10 to 12 (3-inch cookies); Start to Finish: Step One: Under 30 minutes, then chill several hours or overnight, Step Two: Under 30 minutes

For the dough:

1 stick (½ cup) butter, room temperature

½ cup sugar

2 egg yolks

1 teaspoon vanilla extract or ½ teaspoon almond extract

1½ cups all-purpose flour

Confectioner's sugar, for dusting

1 cup preserves, any flavor

Step One: Prepare the dough by beating the butter and sugar, on medium speed, until light and creamy, in a standing mixer, or you can use a food processor, fitted with the metal blade. Add the egg yolks, vanilla or almond extract and 1 ¼ cups flour. Mix the ingredients on low speed, until they are completely incorporated. Work the dough with your hands, on a lightly floured surface, slowly adding up to ¼ cup of the remaining flour to form a firm, non-sticky dough. Wrap the dough in plastic wrap and flatten into a thick disc. Refrigerate several hours or overnight.

Step Two: When ready to bake, preheat the oven to 350 degrees and line a cookie sheet with parchment paper.

Remove the dough from the refrigerator and let it sit for about 10 minutes. Divide the dough into several pieces to make rolling easier. Generously sprinkle your work area with flour. Roll the dough to ¼-inch thick and using a cookie cutter, cut into the desired size and shape. Create a small hole in the center of one half of the pieces by pressing a thimble or bottle cap into the dough; these pieces will be the tops of the finished cookie. Using a cookie spatula, place the cookies on the prepared cookie sheet.

Bake at 350 degrees for 12-15 minutes or until they are a very light golden color. Gently lift the cookies off the baking sheet and allow them to cool before assembling. When the cookies are cool, spread a thin layer of your favorite preserve on the bottom pieces (the ones without the hole). Cover with the top piece, and press gently allowing the filling to spill out of the hole, and then add an extra dollop of preserves right in the center. Sprinkle lightly with confectioner's sugar.

Katherine Wassermann Noir and Robert (Bela Schwartz) Noir

In Katherine's words

Katherine Noir is a genuinely lovely woman who welcomed me into her home on a crisp, clear winter day. There was hot coffee waiting and three types of Hungarian home baked pastries—all made even more remarkable by the fact that Katherine is legally blind. My wonderful visit began with the retelling of her story.

We were three children in my home, my grandmother lived with us and she was very strict around the kitchen, like a sergeant. My mother worked with my father, and they would close their beauty salon at lunchtime when we had our big meal. I was a lousy eater. The cuisine, we didn't call it that, was a mixture of Hungarian, Slovak and kosher Jewish. My father was a very bright man, he learned English by listening to the BBC on the radio. He taught us what was going on in the world. We learned Hebrew and Judaic studies from a private tutor that my parents hired. My parents felt I should learn a trade, so I went to beauty school and learned to be a hairdresser. After two years, I graduated with honors and even today have my original certificate!

In 1938, when I was thirteen, Czechoslovakia was dismembered. My father was sent to a slave labor camp where they were used on the front lines as buffers—expendable slave laborers, as most Jewish men were. One day, we were given two hours notice to move into the ghetto. We were told we could take one change of clothing. My mother, who was very clever, advised us to layer and we wore several pairs of socks and panties. We stayed in the ghetto only a short time, maybe six weeks and worked as hairdressers. We were moved to Auschwitz, where my mother and brother perished. My sister, Suzi, and I worked in a munitions factory where, on an assembly line, I made the clocks for the grenades. We were eventually sent to Bergen-Belsen, and I became very ill. One day, I thought I was delirious, because I was certain I heard British voices. I wasn't dreaming. That was the day we were liberated. My sister Suzi and the British liberators saved me by taking me to the hospital. While recuperating in the hospital, we were invited by the King of Sweden to come to his country to receive medical attention and build a new life. We boarded an old ship and left for Sweden where we stayed for two years. The Red Cross located an uncle of ours, in New York, and he sponsored our trip to America.

I found work as a hairdresser in the Bronx. I made $15.00 a week and 25 cents in tips. I was so happy. My husband, who I was married to for 50 years, was also a hairdresser and a survivor. He was born in Hungary and lived in the same town as my cousin. Before the war, he actually had dinner at my home in Ungvár, Czechoslovakia. When the war started, he was sent to Auschwitz. While he was there, he overheard two SS guards discussing their wives. One was complaining that his wife needed a good haircut. My husband quickly spoke up. From then on, he became this woman's hairdresser. This connection earned him a spot in the kitchen where he received extra bread that he shared with others in the barracks. It assuredly helped save his life.

When he came to America, he changed his name from Bela Schwartz to Robert Noir. He felt you needed a fancy name to own a hair salon in New York. He owned that salon, on 57th Street, for many years. I am not a big stomach person, who loves to eat. In our home I cooked Hungarian food for my husband and two children. I brought my traditions to this country.

Katherine Noir's Mushroom Barley Soup

Katherine's basic soup starter of onions, garlic, carrots and celery creates the perfect foundation for so many soups and inspired this mushroom barley. Katherine's husband used to joke, "Your soup is not edible." When Katherine would ask why, he would answer, "Because you didn't give me a spoon!" A spoon is all you'll need to enjoy this flavorful soup. For those who prefer to chew their mushroom barley soup, feel free to increase the amount of barley.

Yields: 8 servings, Start to Finish: Under 1 ½ hours

1 large onion, chopped (about 1 cup)

3 to 4 cloves garlic, chopped

2 celery ribs, chopped (about 1 cup)

1 large carrot, peeled and chopped (about ½ cup)

3 tablespoons olive oil

2 quarts beef broth or water

2 bay leaves

1 pound Cremini mushrooms, cleaned and chopped

1 cup pearl barley

Kosher salt and pepper

¼ cup chopped fresh dill leaves

Heat the olive oil in a large soup pot, cook and stir the onions, garlic, celery and carrots, over medium heat, until they begin to soften, about 15 minutes. Add the water or broth, bay leaves, mushrooms and barley. Season with salt and pepper. Bring to a boil then reduce the heat and cover and simmer for 50 minutes, adding boiling water if the soup becomes too thick. After 50 minutes, season to taste with salt and pepper. If you used water instead of broth, now would be the time to add one or two bouillon cubes to enhance the flavor. Stir in the chopped dill, and then continue cooking for 10 minutes. Discard the bay leaf before serving.

Feedback

Mushrooms are like little sponges, they soak up liquid, so when cleaning them, resist the urge to soak them. Wipe them with a damp cloth to remove surface dirt, or rinse them quickly under cold running water and pat dry. When buying fresh mushrooms, look for tightly closed mushrooms, that are heavy and have short stems, they are the freshest. And while on the topic of mushrooms, when frying them in a skillet, do not salt them right away. The salt will cause them to release their liquid and you will be left with soggy, chewy mushrooms.

Katherine Noir's Apricot Preserves

This recipe is simple and fresh, pure and delicious.

Yields: 1½ to 2 cups preserves, Start to Finish: Under 45 minutes

1 pound dried preserved Turkish apricots   **1 to 2 tablespoons sugar, to taste**

In a small saucepan, slowly simmer the apricots, 1 cup of water and the sugar. Check the pot regularly to make sure the apricots are not scorching, add water if needed. Cook until the apricots have absorbed all the water, and are very plump, soft and mushy, about 30 to 45 minutes.

Let the apricots cool slightly and then puree them in a food processor. You can add additional sugar or sugar substitute if you prefer a sweeter taste. Refrigerate the preserves until ready to use. Because they are already preserved with sulfur, they hold for a very long time in the fridge.

Feedback
The same method can be used to make preserves from dried plums (prunes).

Matilda Winkler

As told by her daughter, Susan Erem

Susan and I spoke while she was north of the border in neighboring Canada, visiting her mother who had settled there after the war. Even as a child, her mom was incredibly responsible, acquiring her cooking talents at a very young age. With a lot of pride, Susan explains, "Whatever she did, she always did to the best of her ability."

My mother was born in a small town in eastern Hungary on March 10, 1921. Her father died when she was very young and her Mom became a single working mother. My grandmother ran a tavern, and it became my 10-year-old mother's job to look after her brother who was two years younger than she. That's how my mother learned to cook at such an early age; she took care of the household. Attached to the tavern was a general store and she remembers making paper cones that she would fold and make into cups to fill with barley and grains. Cooking was always her thing. A lot of her self worth was locked up in her cooking ability.

When the war broke out and the Nazis came to Hungary, her family first went into a ghetto then were deported to Auschwitz. My mother remembers very well when she was separated from her mother at the train station. She naturally ran after her mother, but an SS guard pushed my mother aside, essentially saving her life. In Auschwitz, my mother was selected to work in the kitchen; she was about 23 at the time. Even the Germans were able to see that she was very capable. My mother would cook for her fellow prisoners and she remembers that in order to wash the very large pots, she would have to climb inside them. After the war, women would often tell me how my mother had tried to grab extra food for them in Auschwitz.

After being liberated, she wanted to come to America. First, she returned to Hungary to see her brother who she learned had also survived. In 1948 she met and married my father, Miklos; I was born 3 years later. During the Hungarian Revolution in 1956, my parents decided to make their way to America. Once we made it to the DP camp in Austria, the International Red Cross processed us. They asked my father where he wanted to go... "America" he said...He was told that there was a 3 month wait for America, but if Canada was ok, we could leave immediately. So in February, 1957, we arrived in Toronto. Our home was Hungarian with a Yiddish twist. There was always something good to eat; my mother was the best cook ever! I try to keep those traditions going for my two children and two grandchildren.

Top left: Matilda and Miklos (Mendel) Winkler, 1948

Matilda Winkler's "Mama's" Crunchy Beans

Susan's mom developed a unique way to prepare vegetarian *cholent*, which her granddaughter, Adina, lovingly dubbed crunchy beans. She would cook beans and barley; each with onions, garlic and seasonings, then combine and roast them in a hot oven until they were crunchy and their distinctive nutty flavor was released. This prep is unlike conventional *cholent*, which slow bakes and becomes soft and mushy. You gotta be a bean lover to love this dish, but if you are, this is the recipe for you.

Yields: about 6 to 8 servings (8 cups), Start to finish: 5 to 6 hours

1 pound dried kidney beans, combination of dried beans or a bag of "*cholent*" beans, rinsed, boiled and soaked

3 large onions, diced (about 3 cups)

6 garlic cloves, crushed

1 tablespoon paprika

½ cup olive oil, additional oil for baking

1 teaspoon kosher salt

½ teaspoon black pepper

1 cup dried pearl barley, rinsed

Matilda would use the overnight soak method for the beans, but the quick soak method works well for this dish. Boil the beans in a large pot of water, for several minutes. Drain then spoon into a bowl and cover with fresh cold water. Let the beans soak for about 1 hour. Drain and reserve.

In a large pot combine the beans, 2 cups of diced onions, 4 garlic cloves, all the paprika and half the oil, salt and pepper. Cook the beans, over medium-low heat, for about 1½ hours or until the beans are very soft, (they will not absorb all the liquid). Try not to over stir the mixture while it cooks, you don't want to break up the beans.

In a separate pot, combine the barley, the remaining 1 cup of diced onions, the remaining 2 cloves of garlic, ½ teaspoon salt, ¼ teaspoon of pepper and 2 cups of boiling water. Cover and cook on medium-low heat, for about 30 minutes, or until the barley and onions are very soft. If the water cooks out, add a little more hot water to the pot and continue cooking. Take the barley off the heat and wait for the beans to finish.

After the beans have been cooking for 1 hour, preheat the oven to 400 degrees and coat the bottom of a large roasting pan with the remaining ¼ cup of oil.

When the beans are ready, gently stir the barley into the beans, until they are completely combined. Spoon the entire mixture into the prepared roasting pan. Bake at 400 degrees for 1 to 3 hours, stirring every 30 minutes, and drizzling the top with olive oil after each stir. The dish is ready when the liquid is gone and the beans and barley have the desired crunch. For soft beans, figure 1 hour; crunchy beans 2 hours; and super crunchy 2 ½ to 3 hours. Serve as a side dish for meat or poultry.

Gale Gand

Professional contributor

Beans and barley make a fabulous side dish as they can stand up to a rich stew that has a robust sauce and bold flavor. Gale Gand's family short ribs recipe is just the thing to hold its own alongside Matilda's crunchy beans. The following recipe suggests using potatoes, with a variation for parsnips. If serving with Matilda's crunchy beans, parsnips would be the way to go.

Myrna's Beef Short Ribs

Contributed by Gale Gand, executive pastry chef and owner of Tru restaurant, Chicago

This is my mother's recipe, which I remember her making as a child but never learned from her first hand. My mother died when I was 36 and so later in my life when I was having a craving for this dish, the only way to learn it was to slowly but anxiously hunt through her recipe card file and try to find it. You could always rely on my mother and sure enough, there was the recipe, as if it were waiting for me to resurrect it. Complete with sidebars written in her distinct handwriting, with comments like "try this with parsnips next time." I felt like she was right there in the kitchen with me as I methodically worked my way through her instructions. It was like she was still with me...true eternal life!

Serves: 6 to 8

3 pounds beef short ribs, cut up

Salt

Fresh ground black pepper

Flour

2 tablespoons vegetable oil (we'd probably use Canola oil now)

1 medium onion, sliced

½ cup celery leaves

2 sprigs of parsley

1 ½ cups beef stock or broth

2 cups canned tomato chunks

6 medium carrots, peeled and cut into chunks

8 small onions, peeled

4 medium potatoes or 2 parsnips, peeled and cut into chunks

1 teaspoon paprika

Remove any excess fat from the ribs. Sprinkle them with salt and pepper then roll them in flour. In a Dutch oven heat the vegetable oil and brown the short ribs on all sides. Add the sliced onions, celery leaves, parsley and beef stock. Cover and simmer on low heat for 2 hours or until the meat is very tender adding more stock if needed. Add the canned tomato, carrots, onions and potatoes or parsnips, paprika, and season with a little salt and pepper and continue cooking, covered, another 30 minutes or until the vegetables are tender. Serve family style on a very large platter.

Romania, Russia and the Ukraine

We would need an atlas and a geography lesson to fully understand the relationship between Romania, Russia and the Ukraine. So many hands have touched this area that their customs and foods absorbed flavors and traditions from every culture, all of which played a role in shaping the region.

From Romania we got spicy, saucy, vibrant food that reflected a cosmopolitan bent. Czernowitz, where many of our contributors were from, was known as "Little Vienna," and was the home to intellectuals, poets, and artists and can even lay claim to the melodic folk song, Hava Nagilah. Their cooking was affected by its proximity to Bulgaria, Turkey and Greece, imparting a Mediterranean note, which harmonized beautifully with their traditional fare.

Ukrainian and Russian cooking packs bold soups with garlic and dill, laden with vegetables, and dishes featuring jewel red beets were abundant. Filling, substantial and nourishing were the trademarks of foods from this region, while the influences from neighboring Eastern European countries lent a Yiddish flavor to many preparations.

Several of our contributors from this area found refuge in other parts of Europe or across the ocean. However, even in their new homeland, they flexed their Romanian and Slavic muscles and incorporated the cooking styles from home. Open your kitchen to the bold flavors of our recipes remembered from these hardy survivors.

RECIPES

Florence Edelstein: Robust Mushroom Soup

Florence Edelstein: Breast of Veal

Mila Ginzburg Fishman: Cabbage Pie

Nella Frendel: Beef Bourguignon

Nella Frendel: Chocolate Mousse Cake

Elly Berkovits Gross: Baby's Biscuits

Peri Hirsch: Rugelach

Peri Hirsch: Walnut Cookies

Sara "Hannah" Rigler: Romanian Eggplant

Sara "Hannah" Rigler: Spinach Soufflé

Sara "Hannah" Rigler: Chocolate Thinsies

Olga Paverman Schaerf: Romanian *Karnatzlach*–Spicy Grilled Meat

Olga Paverman Schaerf: *Salade De Bouef*–Beef Salami Salad

Fira Stukelman: Summer *Borscht*

Berta Kiesler Vaisman: *Malai*–Corn Bread

Berta Kiesler Vaisman: *Barenikes–Pierogis*

Chana Wiesenfeld: *Kasha Varnishkes*

Chana Wiesenfeld: Ukrainian Winter *Borscht*

PROFESSIONAL CONTRIBUTORS

Michelle Bernstein: Duck Breasts with Jerez, Oranges and Spanish Almonds

JFH: Carrot and Prune *Tsimmes*

JFH: Toasted Garlic-Rubbed Rounds

JFH: *Schi*–Russian Cabbage Soup

Michael and Florence Edelstein

In their own words

I talked to Michael and Florence in the heart of their home, the kitchen as it filled with the early aromas of the approaching Passover holiday. Michael quipped, "We are married 53 years and in the end I agree with whatever she says." They share a positive outlook, a close-knit family and a legacy of philanthropy.

Michael

In 1999, fifty-four years after I was forced from my hometown of Skala in the Ukraine, I went back and retraced the steps of my escape from the ghetto. If you ask me what I had for dinner last night, I would have to ask the boss (he points to Florence), but I remembered everything about what happened fifty-four years earlier. My town had 2,000 Jews before the war; I was one of only 80 that survived. Nikola Gitman was one reason we survived as he helped smuggle my father and me out of the Borshchiv ghetto. We hid in the back of his wagon, shielded by hay as he drove us out of the ghetto and toward town. From there we were able to remain hidden and eventually make our way to the woods.

I remember knocking on doors, hoping someone would help us. These were former neighbors, people who knew us, but they didn't help. In one case, a woman told us to come back the next day when she would give us a loaf of bread. Instead, she called the police and tried to turn us in. In the summer, we hid in the woods, but when winter came, we knew that if we left deep footprints in the freshly fallen snow it would be too easy to track and discover us. I recalled hearing a woman in the woods describe a bunker in town that her husband had dug. We went into the town and hid in that cellar. The bunker was so small that when my father turned in one direction, I would have to turn in the other. Our second angel was Olenka Kowaleszen, who treated us with kindness and humanity. Once or twice a week she would make soup for us, or even polenta with onions. After liberation, this same woman helped me recuperate. I can still hear my father telling me,"Every day you gain, is one more day."

Years later, we retold the story of these two courageous people, and they were fittingly honored as "Righteous Among the Nations" at Yad Vashem. Florence and I believe that when you do good, it comes back to you. When I reconnected with Olenka, I wanted to do something for her as a way of saying thank you. We helped her family establish a business, and I was happy to repay my gratitude by sending her grandchildren and great granddaughters to college and medical school.

Florence

I was born in Zamosc, Poland. My family were members of the Belzer sect of Hasidic Jews. When I was three years old, we left Poland for Russia. At the time, in 1939, Poland was divided between the Germans and the Russians. We chose the Russians and decided to run with the Russian army. My entire family survived because we made this choice. We lived in many parts of Russia, and finally settled in Siberia. We were hungry and tired, but we did not fear for our lives. After the war, we went back to Poland and stayed in a DP camp in Germany. We wanted to go to Israel and applied for passage, but instead the HIAS was able to arrange our travel to the United States. We joined the Macabee Club, for new Americans; that's where I met Michael. Shortly after we met, he was drafted into the U.S. army. Michael served two years in Korea, and when he returned, we were married. My life has been built on my firm belief that 90% of what you do is luck and the other 10% is guts. When you see a situation, grab it. In my wildest dreams, I could never imagine that we would accomplish for ourselves and for our three children and eleven grandchildren, what we have. It's a dream come true.

Florence Edelstein's Robust Mushroom Soup

Florence told me how her grandmother, while they were barely surviving as refugees in Siberia, would scrounge up scraps of potatoes to nourish her family. Florence quickly learned that delicious soup can be built around any ingredient. The focus in this soup comes from the variety of mushrooms, concentrated Porcini liquid and the array of fresh vegetables that Florence adds to the earthy mushroom base. Puree the soup for a creamy finish and indulge in a swirl of crème fraîche to lend a tangy, silky note.

Yields: 12 cups; Start to Finish: Under 2 hours

1 (1-ounce) package dried Porcini mushrooms, soaked in 1 cup hot water

6 tablespoons olive oil

2 medium-large onions, chopped (about 1 ½ to 2 cups)

1 large or 2 medium leeks, white part only, chopped and thoroughly rinsed (about 1 cup)

2 large carrots, peeled and diced (about 1 cup)

3 ribs of celery, diced (about 1 ½ cups)

1 pound white mushrooms, coarsely chopped

½ pound Shitake mushrooms, chopped (remove the stems and save them to flavor stock)

½ pound Cremini mushrooms, chopped

2 medium russet potatoes, peeled and diced

Kosher salt and pepper

1 cup crème fraîche or light sweet cream

Freshly chopped dill leaves and crème fraîche, for garnish (optional)

Soak the dried mushrooms in 1 cup of hot water for 30 minutes.

Heat 3 tablespoons of the olive oil, in a large sauté pan, cook and stir the onions, leeks, carrots and celery, over medium-low heat, until they begin to soften, about 15 minutes. While the vegetables cook, chop the fresh mushrooms. When the vegetables are done, begin adding the mushrooms in batches. You don't want to overwhelm the pan, so allow each batch to cook down before adding the next. Once all the mushrooms are in the pan, let them cook with the onions, over low heat, for 15 minutes.

Spoon the cooked vegetables and the diced potatoes into a very large soup pot. By this time, the dried mushrooms should be done soaking. Using a small piece of cheesecloth (a strainer lined with a piece of lightly dampened paper towel or a coffee filter makes an adequate substitute), strain the dried mushrooms, reserving the liquid (you should have about ¾ cup). Add the reserved Porcini liquid to the soup pot. Rinse then chop the Porcini mushrooms and add them to the pot. Lastly, add 6 cups of water, or enough to cover all the vegetables. Season with salt and pepper, cover and cook, on low heat until all the vegetables are soft, about 1 hour. If the soup becomes too thick, add boiling water to achieve the desired consistency.

Puree about three-quarters of the soup. Pour the pureed soup back into the pot and stir in 1 cup crème fraîche or sweet cream. Season to taste with salt and pepper, and heat through. Serve with a dollop of crème fraîche and a sprinkling of fresh chopped dill.

Feedback

Crème fraîche is a cross between heavy cream and sour cream. It has a slightly sour, nutty taste, which plays nicely against the sweet flavors of many stews and soups that contain slow-cooked root vegetables and onions. The beauty of crème fraîche is that its smooth texture won't curdle or separate when heated.

Florence Edelstein's Breast of Veal

Florence loves this cut of meat as an elegant alternative to brisket. There are several options when buying breast of veal: your butcher can cut it on or off the bone, and with or without a pocket for stuffing, the choice is yours. Because the veal does not yield lots of meat, stuffing is a good option and creates a festive dish. Whichever you choose, allow the veal to marinate so it can soak up the tangy sweet and sour flavor. Because the veal can rest in the fridge after being roasted, this is a great dish to make in advance when expecting company. Florence recommends you try this same preparation if making a delicious French roast beef.

Yields: 4 to 6 servings; Start to Finish: Step One: Under 30 minutes, then at least 2 and up to 24 hours to marinate, Step Two: Under 2 ½ hours

For the marinade:

1 large onion, diced (about 1 cup)

2 tablespoons olive oil

5 cloves garlic, chopped

½ cup brown sugar

¼ cup vinegar

1 ½ cups ketchup

1 teaspoon kosher salt

½ teaspoon black pepper

1 (3 to 4 pound) boneless breast of veal, (5 to 6 pounds) if bone-in

Step One: Heat the olive oil in large sauté pan, cook and stir the onions, over medium heat, until lightly browned, about 10 minutes. Stir in the garlic and cook an additional 5 minutes. Stir in 1 ½ cups water, brown sugar, vinegar, ketchup, salt and pepper and bring to a boil. Simmer for 5 minutes. Pour the marinade into a shallow dish, large enough to hold the veal, and allow the marinade to cool. Place the veal in the dish, cover and let it rest in the fridge for at least 2 hours and up to 24 hours (the longer it sits the better the flavor develops). Do not stuff the veal at this time.

Step Two: When ready to roast, preheat the oven to 400 degrees. If you are stuffing the veal, loosely fill the pocket and close the pocket with skewers, kitchen twine or reusable bands at 2-inch intervals, to prevent the stuffing from falling out while roasting. (See page 184 for Ruth Eggener's or page 266 for George Lang's stuffing recipes). Roast the veal until tender, about 1 ½ to 2 hours, basting after 1 hour and adding water if needed to prevent the sauce from drying out.

When the veal is done, remove it from the roasting pan and allow it to cool, before cutting it into thin slices. If the veal is on the bone, slice between the bones. You can serve at once, or place the sliced veal back in the sauce and let it rest for several hours or overnight in the fridge. When reheating, cover and heat, at 300 degrees, until warmed through, adding water to the sauce if needed. The sweet and sour flavor of the roast partners perfectly with carrot and prune tsimmes (recipe follows).

Carrot and Prune *Tsimmes*

Florence's holiday *tsimmes* inspired this recipe which features prunes lightly sautéed with sweet onions. The unexpected pairing melds perfectly with the carrots, apricots and raisins.

Yields: About 10 servings (6 cups); Start to Finish: Under 1 ½ hours

10 to 12 carrots, peeled and sliced into ½ -inch thick rounds

4 sweet potatoes, peeled and quartered, then quartered again

2 tablespoons vegetable oil

1 medium onion, chopped (about ¾ cup)

1 pound pitted prunes

½ cup dried apricots or ½ cup apricot preserves

1½ cups orange juice

¼ teaspoon ground cinnamon

½ cup honey

¼ cup brown sugar

¼ cup granulated white sugar

½ cup golden raisins

Preheat the oven to 350 degrees.

Bring a pot of salted water to boil, and cook the carrots and sweet potatoes, until just tender, about 15 minutes. Drain and reserve. Heat the oil in a skillet, cook and stir the onions, over medium heat, until lightly browned, about 10 minutes. Stir in the prunes and apricots (if using preserves add them later, along with the orange juice); and continue cooking for 10 minutes longer. Stir in 1 cup of orange juice, (preserves), cinnamon, honey, brown sugar, granulated sugar and raisins.

Place the carrots and sweet potatoes in a 13x9x2-inch Pyrex baking dish. Stir in the prune mixture. Bake at 350 degrees for 30 minutes. After 30 minutes add the remaining ½ cup orange juice. Continue baking until the potatoes and carrots are tender, but not mushy, about 15 minutes longer.

JFH

Mila Ginzburg Fishman

As told by her granddaughter Anna Moskovich

We're a family of women!! My great grandmother and her two daughters (my grandma and great aunt) literally ran from the siege of Stalingrad as the German planes were shooting at people. They were from a small city near Moscow and fled to Siberia. After the war, when there was nothing left, my great grandfather found a job and an apartment in Czernowitz, in the Ukraine. They shared this apartment with a non-Jewish family. Years later, when my father was twelve, he and his family actually wound up in the same apartment building, maybe even the very same apartment. It was then that my parents met; together they had two daughters who between the two of them, had four more girls.

The recipe I've provided, translated from Russian by my mother, is yummy. Just thinking of it, I can taste it! My memories are of my mother making it... her memories are of her mother and even grandmother making it. They had a small corner of a kitchen in the Ukraine where they made everything from scratch. She remembers her grandmother rolling the dough with her little hands, the smell of the dough rising...

Top left: Mila Fishman, 1940s

Mila Ginzburg Fishman's Cabbage Pie

Yields: 15 to 20 pieces, Start to Finish: Step One: Under 1½ hours, Step Two: Under 1½ hours

For the dough:

1 glass (8 ounces) whole milk

1 (¼-ounce) package or 2¼ teaspoons dry yeast

2 tablespoons sugar

½ teaspoon salt

1 tablespoon vegetable oil

4 to 5 cups all-purpose flour

1 egg, lightly beaten

1 stick (8 tablespoons) butter, cut into 8 pieces

For the filling:

3 eggs, hard-boiled

1 head of green cabbage (about 2 pounds), cored and shredded

½ stick (4 tablespoons) butter or margarine

Kosher salt and pepper

Egg wash glaze:

1 egg plus 1 teaspoon of water, beaten

Step One: Begin the dough by warming the milk, in a small saucepan, a little hotter than lukewarm (if you have a thermometer, it should read between 105 to 115 degrees). If microwaving, about 1 minute will do. Whisk in the yeast, sugar, salt and oil.

Pour 4 cups of flour into a large bowl, food processor with the metal blade, or the bowl of a standing mixer, fitted with the paddle attachment. Slowly pour in the milk, beaten egg and 4 tablespoons of butter. Mix until the dough begins to form a ball. Remove from the mixer or bowl and work with your hands on a lightly floured surface for several minutes. If using a standing mixer, change from the paddle attachment to the dough hook and knead for several minutes. If the dough is sticky, add more flour, a little at a time. Cover the dough with a towel and let it rest for 1 hour. Leave the remaining butter out to soften.

While the dough rests, prepare the cabbage filling. Start by placing the eggs in a small saucepan and covering them with cold water. Bring to a rapid boil, reduce the heat to medium-low and cook for 10 minutes. Remove the eggs from the water and place them in ice cold water until ready to peel. The ice water will help prevent that telltale green ring that sometimes develops on a hard boiled egg yolk.

Heat the butter, in a large skillet, cook and stir the shredded cabbage, over medium heat, for 10 minutes. Season to taste with salt and pepper. Spoon the cabbage into a bowl to cool. Peel the eggs, cut them into small pieces and add to the cooled cabbage. Cover the cabbage and refrigerate overnight.

Once the dough has risen, generously flour a work surface and roll the dough into a rectangle about ½ -inch thick. Spread 2 tablespoons of the remaining butter or margarine on the dough. Fold the dough like an envelope, roll out again and spread the last 2 tablespoons of butter on top. Fold and roll twice more. Finally, fold the dough like an envelope, wrap in a plastic wrap and refrigerate overnight.

Step Two: Preheat the oven to 375 degrees and grease a 15 ½ x10 ½ -inch jellyroll pan.

Take the dough from the fridge and cut the dough in two pieces; making one piece slightly bigger than the other. Roll out the bigger one to about ¼-inch thick to fit the baking pan. Lay the dough in the prepared pan, bringing the dough up the sides. Spread the cabbage filling on top. Roll out the second piece of dough. Lay the second piece on top of the cabbage and pinch the edges to seal the pie. Brush the top with the egg glaze and then with a knife make 3 slits in the dough for the steam to escape. Bake at 375 degrees for about 1 hour or until the top is golden brown. Serve the pie straight from the oven.

Feedback

Folding like an envelope, as described above, was a technique I didn't master at first; I tried, but mine looked more like origami. And you know what? It didn't matter in the end. Roll the dough the best you can, fold it as evenly as possible. For Step Two, when rolling out the dough, use the pan as a guide for gauging the size. Lay the dough in the pan and use your hands to stretch it to fit. Cut any overhanging pieces and use them to patch where your dough falls short. If you can achieve that perfect rectangular shape - more power to you, if you don't; only your ego will suffer, the recipe will not.

Robert and Nella Frendel

As told by their daughter Paulette Mondschein

Paulette comes by her cosmopolitan elegance naturally. Both her parents were lovers of the arts and made sure they imbued their only child with a sense of security and an appreciation for culture.

My father and mother were both from Czernowitz, Romania, "Little Vienna." They were married in Romania when my mother was nineteen and my father was twenty-five. My father was a very smart man, and I adored him. My mother was also very bright, but my father was exceptional in his intellect. When the war broke out, they left their town and went to Bucharest where they obtained fake documents. My father had light hair and baby-baby blue eyes, my mother had red hair and green eyes; they did not look Jewish. They stayed in people's homes, and because they had money were able to evade arrest. They crossed the border from Hungary to Vienna. From Vienna they went to Paris with the help of the underground. They remained in Paris for seven years.

When they lived in Paris, my mother was a designer. Knowing how persuasive she could be, she probably talked her way into her job as Christian Dior's apprentice. When I was two years old, my parents, my grandfather and I immigrated to the United States. We traveled on a boat from Marseilles to New York. When we arrived here, a photographer for the *New York Herald Tribune* snapped my picture. I was wearing a French beret, with my curly hair peeking out. The headline the next day read "New American." My parents loved this country, and they became very American. I never felt we had a Romanian identity; they spoke French, German or English. Every Friday night we would have a traditional Shabbos meal. My mother was a phenomenal cook. She would also make delicious, classically French dishes like chocolate mousse and beef bourguignon. As a child, I wanted to be an American, I didn't want parents who spoke different languages or cooked European foods. Looking back now, I know I should have felt differently.

What defined my parents was their ability to always make me feel safe and secure. They were wonderful parents, and we were a beautiful little family unit. My parents were extraordinarily elegant, exuding that old European charm and culture. I was always in Carnegie Hall or taking piano lessons (even though I wasn't very good.) When they came here, the first thing they bought was a piano. I think that it was very important for Jewish people to expose themselves whenever they could to culture, books and learning because it was something no one could take away. They were married 30 years, I was the only child, and they have two grandchildren and three great grandchildren.

Top left: Nella and Robert Frendel, with Paulette, on the boat to America

Nella Frendel's Beef Bourguignon

While Friday night dinners featured the traditional Jewish fare, Nella would wake up a weekday with a rendition of this classic and beautifully fragrant dish. Slow braised beef mingles with carrots, onions and potatoes in a rich wine sauce. Be sure to use a good deep red wine from the Burgundy region of France - it is the basis for the sauce and will infuse the beef and vegetables with an earthy flavor. If you can exhibit some self-control, let the finished dish sit overnight in the fridge, it intensifies the flavor and thickens the sauce.

Yields: 4 to 6 servings, Start to Finish: Under 5 hours

2½ pounds beef chuck, cut into 1-inch pieces, and patted dry

2 tablespoons olive oil

2 cloves garlic, chopped

2 cups frozen pearl onions, thawed

2 large carrots, peeled and cut into 1- inch pieces (about 1 cup)

1 medium russet potato, peeled and cubed (about 1 cup)

1 generous tablespoon tomato paste

1 cup beef broth

3 cups red wine

1 teaspoon Herbs de Provence

2 teaspoons kosher salt

Black pepper, to taste

2 bay leaves

Preheat the oven to 250 degrees.

Heat the oil in a large Dutch oven and brown the beef, over medium-high heat, for several minutes on all sides. You might need to brown the meat in batches. Do not over crowd the pot or the beef will steam not brown. Remove the browned beef to a plate. In the same pot, cook and stir the garlic and pearl onions, over medium heat, for 2 to 3 minutes, add oil if needed. Stir in the beef, and its collected drippings, and the remaining ingredients. Place the covered pot in the oven and slow roast for at least 4 hours. Remove from the oven and check the sauce to see if it is thick enough. If not, create a slurry by mixing 1 tablespoon cornstarch with 2 tablespoons of water, stir into the sauce and cook 15 minutes longer. The dish can be refrigerated overnight and reheated the next day on the stove, over a low heat.

Feedback
Herbs de Provence is a unique blend of floral herbs containing dried basil, rosemary, tarragon, marjoram, thyme and parsley. Some preparations also contain lavender. If you do not have Herbs de Provence, use a teaspoon of any of the above-mentioned herbs, alone or in combination.

Nella Frendel's Chocolate Mousse Cake

Light, airy and just sweet enough describes this luscious French cake that Paulette's mother made for special occasions. The very proper ladyfingers serve as a foundation for this classic preparation. Ladyfingers hide in the market and can usually be found in the fresh fruit section alongside the berries. If ladyfingers are not available, or you want to simplify the preparation, prepare only the mousse and serve it from a large dessert bowl or in individual ramekins. The mousse is so decadently delicious that it can stand alone.

Yields: 10 to 12 servings, Start to Finish: Step One: Under 1 hour, then chill 4 hours (if preparing the mousse only) or overnight (for the cake), Step Two: Under 15 minutes

For the mousse:

2 (3-ounce) packages, ladyfingers

12 ounces good semisweet chocolate or semisweet chocolate chips

2 whole eggs

4 eggs separated

2 cups heavy cream

For the topping:

1 cup heavy cream

2 teaspoons sugar

Chocolate shavings or mini chocolate chips (optional)

Step One: If preparing as a cake, arrange the ladyfingers vertically around the sides of un-greased 9 x3-inch spring form pan with the rounded, finished sides against the pan, these will face out when you un-mold the cake. Line the bottom with ladyfingers and set the pan aside. Save the remaining ladyfingers for another time. If making only the mousse, skip to the next step.

Prepare the mousse by melting the chocolate in a double boiler, over a simmering heat, stirring occasionally, until completely melted and smooth. Once melted, pour the chocolate into a large bowl and allow it to cool completely. Beat the 2 whole eggs and stir in to the chocolate. The texture of the chocolate will change immediately. Keep stirring vigorously until the chocolate is thick and has a deep, shiny, chocolaty color. Whisk in the 4 egg yolks, one at a time, stirring hard, after each addition.

In a separate bowl, beat the 4 egg whites until stiff but not dry. Gently fold the egg whites into the chocolate mixture. Stir until the egg whites are completely blended, being sure to spoon the chocolate up from the bottom of the bowl in large but gentle circular motions. The mixture will be fluffy.

In a separate bowl, whip 2 cups of the heavy cream until very thick but not hard. Stir the whipped cream into the chocolate mixture. When completely incorporated, the color should resemble milk chocolate. Spoon into the prepared spring form pan and chill overnight. If foregoing the cake presentation, spoon into one large dessert bowl or individual ramekins and chill for at least 4 hours.

Step Two: Prepare the topping by whipping the remaining 1 cup of heavy cream with the sugar. Beat until thick and shiny. Using a vegetable peeler, curl chocolate shavings. Spoon the whipped cream over the top of the cake and garnish with the chocolate shavings or chips. For the dessert bowl presentation, spoon a dollop of whipped cream over each serving and dot with the shaved chocolate or chips.

Elly Berkovits Gross

In her own words

Elly is a woman on a mission. Through her talks at local schools and her five books, she feels she has "a commitment to remind the world that the tragedy that happened should never happen again." Thousands of children have heard and read her story, and as she explains, "They sometimes look at me like I'm from the moon, but if I can change the mind of one or two of them, then it's worth it." Apparently Elly has done a wonderful job of doing just that, as one child wrote to her after reading her story, "you are an inspiration to all my friends...Your story makes me want to grow up and do everything I can to prevent anything like this from ever happening again."

I was born Elly Berkovits on February 14, 1929, in Simileu-Silvaniei, Romania. In March 16, 1939 my brother, Adalbert, was born. I loved the handsome little boy. That spring Nazis invaded Czechoslovakia, and, in 1942, my father, age 36, was drafted into forced labor and forever disappeared from our lives.

Beginning early in the winter of 1944 we Jews had to wear the Yellow Star. My mother tried to comfort me, saying, "Elly, you have to learn not to complain and take life as it comes." After Passover, we were ordered to leave our house. We were escorted to the ghetto, which was in a former brick factory at Ceheiu. In the ghetto four females were ordered to peel potatoes, and by blind luck, at age 15, I was one of them. At night, I was allowed to take my mother and brother one or two potatoes. As long as I live, I'll never forget my little brother, who waited to see me, not for the potato, but because we loved each other. His handsome face got smaller day-by-day, my heart breaks when I think of him. In his short life few good days he had.

On Saturday May 27, 1944, Erev Shavuos, we began our five day journey to Auschwitz-Birkenau where my mother and brother perished. I was put to work carrying water. In the end of August 1944 a group of us were transferred to Fallersleben, Germany, to work in a forced labor camp.

Top left: Elly Gross (back row, third from the left), school photo, 1936

Although I got a respiratory infection with fever, for some reason I was spared. The German officer in charge of our group ordered that I should not work in the factory, but instead wash the living quarters' floor.

In early April, 1945, we were shipped to Salzwedel where I was reunited with my two cousins. On April 14, 1945 the Allies liberated us. Later we were moved to Hillersleben and, in a few months, returned home. In 1946 at the age of 17, I married Ernest Gross, a survivor of forced labor. We lived under the communist regime in Romania for 20 years and raised two children. In 1966 we moved to the United States. My husband and I worked long hours to support our family while our children focused on their education and we were able to reach the American dream. God Bless America.

In 1998 I served as plaintiff on the case for reparations for all former slaves, Gentiles and Jews alike. That same year I took part in the "March of the Living" tour of Holocaust sites. While walking through Auschwitz-Birkenau, I found my mother and brother's picture in front of a boxcar taken when we had just arrived, on the morning of June 2, 1944. There I made a commitment that as long as I am able, I will remind everyone who will listen of our tragic past. In May of 2005, I was invited to Germany and participated in one of their ceremonies. I also was invited to Fallersleben where I had worked as a slave laborer at the age of 15. One part of the ceremony was especially emotional for me. From among all of the Holocaust victims, 15 families were selected for the permanent exhibition in the new Museum of Murdered European Jews in Berlin. My parents and brother were among the few selected for this high post mortem honor. It is a small, but nice, piece of closure of my struggle to leave a lasting memory for my family, which includes my husband of 63 years, one daughter, one son and five grandchildren.

Since our last printing, I sadly learned that Elly's husband, Ernest, passed away. We extend our sincerest condolences to his devoted family. May his memory be a blessing.

Elly Gross' Baby's Biscuits

Reminiscent of the cookie we all gave our little ones, Elly's uncomplicated biscuits are great to make for children or with children. All they need is a quick dunk in a tall glass of milk or a soothing cup of tea.

Yields: About 3 dozen biscuits; Start to Finish: Step One: 15 minutes then 6 to 8 hours or overnight, Step Two: Under 30 minutes

2 eggs

4 ounces (about 1 cup) confectioner's sugar

1 teaspoon vanilla extract

½ teaspoon baking powder

2 cups all-purpose flour

Step One: Whisk together the eggs and confectioner's sugar, until the sugar is completely dissolved and no longer visible. Whisk in the vanilla and baking powder. Slowly begin adding the flour. You'll need to use a wooden spoon to stir the mixture as it thickens, the dough will be sticky. Scoop the dough onto a piece of wax paper and tightly wrap the dough. Refrigerate for 6 to 8 hours or overnight.

Step Two: Preheat the oven to 325 degrees and lightly grease a baking sheet

Take the dough out of the fridge, and divide it in half. Keep one half refrigerated while you work with the other. Very generously flour a work surface, and roll the dough to ¼-inch thick. Cut with a 2-inch cookie cutter. Use a cookie spatula to place the rounds on the prepared baking sheet. Bake at 325 degrees for 10 minutes; the cookies will remain a pale color with lightly browned edges. They harden as they sit, so do not over-bake.

Peri Hirsch

In her own words

My husband and I traveled to Florida to speak to Peri. Her husband, Felix, who could have worked the Borscht Belt, contributed one liners and insights into the character and cooking talents of this wonderful, vibrant woman. While we savored her sweet rugelach and delicious walnut cookies, we listened to Peri retell her story and a remarkable ending that occurred more than fifty years later.

I was born in Transylvania, Romania, as one of nine children, and lived in an extended family with my parents and grandparents. I remember a very traditional home, where I loved watching my mother and grandmother prepare for Shabbos. My job on Friday was to shine all the shoes in the house and, if I was lucky, I would wash the dairy dishes as well. My father was in the meat business, so we ate well and my mother, who was very good-natured, would share what we had with the neighbors who didn't have as much. My last Passover at home was in 1944, when the Germans officially came into our town. Within a few weeks, we were taken to the ghetto and then to Auschwitz-Birkenau. At first, my entire family stayed together. I remember when they took us off the train in Birkenau and my mother was sent

to a different line than me. I wanted so badly to go with her, but a Jewish man who was working the lines, threw me to the other side, saving my life. I was lucky to still have my two sisters with me at that time. We were sent to a forced labor camp where we worked in factories located near the oil refineries and coal mines, which were targets for the Allied forces. I clearly remember September 11, 1944, the day a bomb exploded; it was like an atomic bomb. The SS cut the fence wires and everyone scattered into the fields. One of my sisters was immediately killed by the blast, while my other sister was badly wounded. I had hidden under a bridge with a few other girls. A priest who saw us cowering under the bridge signaled us to run quickly into his house, and moments after we did, the bridge I was hiding under was destroyed.

I knew that a German doctor had taken my sister into a hospital, but I knew little else. I had actually visited her once, but was not allowed to again. It was not until more than fifty years later that I would learn of the incredible compassion of this doctor, and the fate of my sister. As for me, I found some family members and after being recaptured and marched through the woods, I eventually found safety in a farmer's home. I hid there, with seven other girls, until the Americans liberated us on April 14th, 1945. Using cigarettes that we had collected, we bribed a German and hired a truck to take us to the DP camp. My hope was to go to Paris and then Israel. Instead, in 1946, I came to America aboard the SS Marine Perch.

More than half a century later, I returned to Germany, hoping to discover what happened to my sister. I connected with a wonderful woman, Dr. Marianne Kaiser, who was able to fill in the blanks for me. She told me that Dr. Rudolf

Top left: Peri Hirsch

Bertram was the German doctor who had established St. Joseph's Hospital near the factory where we were forced to work. He heroically rescued and treated 18 Jewish girls in the basement of the hospital; my sister, Blanka, was one of those girls. I was told that when the Gestapo came to Dr. Bertram and demanded he release the girls, insisting they were strong enough to return to work, Dr. Bertram took a hard line. He told the SS that if he were forced to release even one girl, he would never treat another German soldier again. His defiance saved many of these girls; unfortunately my sister was not among them. After a second bomb attack, she was sent to Bottrop where she died of her injuries. In an act of unparalleled compassion, Dr. Bertram created a small plot where my sister and others were buried. On my trip to Germany, I was able to erect a proper headstone and honor my sister's memory. I have photos from a simple ceremony in Bottrop where a Rabbi led us in saying Kaddish and unbelievably, where German citizens, out of respect for my sister, placed symbolic stones on her headstone. I wrote to Dr. Bertram to thank him for what he did for my sister; we corresponded until he died in 1975. His family became part of my family and I will always be grateful to him for his kindness. For his heroism and humanity, Dr. Rudolf Bertram posthumously received the title of "Righteous Among the Nations" at Yad Vashem. Felix and I are married 60 years; we have three children, and three grandchildren.

Peri Hirsch's Rugelach

Peri's rugelach are jam-packed morsels, tender and flaky, with a subtle sweetness. Felix, Peri's husband, credits the family rolling pin for the perfection of these little bites of heaven. He says, "It has worked magic for generations." The beauty of this recipe is you can increase the sweet factor or nutty texture by adjusting the filling to your taste.

Yields: 32 pieces (recipe can easily be doubled to make 64 pieces); Start to Finish: Step One: Under 30 minutes then chill at least 4 hours or overnight, Step Two: Under 1 hour

For the dough:

1 stick (½ cup) butter, room temperature

2 tablespoons sugar

1 (4-ounce) package cream cheese, softened at room temperature

1 tablespoon orange juice

1 egg

1 cup all-purpose flour

1 teaspoon baking powder

For the filling:

½ cup apricot preserves, room temperature

½ cup sugar plus 1 to 2 teaspoons ground cinnamon, more to taste

½ cup raisins

1 cup (4 ounces) chopped nuts, more to taste

For the topping:

1 lightly beaten egg plus 1 tablespoon of water, egg wash

Sanding sugar (optional)

Step One: Prepare the dough by beating the butter, sugar and cream cheese, just till soft and combined. Stir in the orange juice and egg. In a separate bowl, combine the flour and baking powder. Stir the flour mixture into the cream cheese mixture and combine, creating a soft slightly sticky dough. Divide the dough into 2 pieces, flatten each into a disc and wrap in plastic wrap. Refrigerate at least 4 hours or overnight.

Step Two: Take one package of dough out of the fridge and let it rest for 10 minutes. Keep the remaining dough chilled. Flour a work surface, and roll the dough out into a 12-inch circle. With a spatula, spread half the preserves over the entire circle, and then sprinkle with half the sugar, raisins and nuts. Use the spatula to gently press the filling into the dough. Using a pizza wheel, cut the dough into fourths, then cut each fourth into fourths. You should have 16 pieces. Some might be larger than others, no worries; it will give your cookies personality. Roll the wedges up starting at the widest end. When rolled, you should have a nice crescent shape.

Chill the rugelach while you preheat the oven to 350 degrees.

Remove the rugelach from the fridge and brush lightly with the egg wash. You can sprinkle with sanding sugar for a nice shine and sweet crunch, or sprinkle additional cinnamon-sugar on top. Bake at 350 degrees for 25 minutes or until they are light brown. Repeat with the remaining dough.

Feedback

A good way to chop nuts is to use a serrated knife. Try rocking the knife back and forth over softer nuts like walnuts. Harder nuts, like almonds, might need the oomph that only a grinder or food processor can provide. Do not over-process or you will have crumbs. 2 ounces of shelled nuts = 1/2 cup chopped nuts.

Peri Hirsch's Walnut Cookies

Sweet butter and crunchy walnuts combine with sugar and cinnamon for a crispy, light cookie.

Yields: About 4 dozen cookies; Start to Finish: Under 1 hour

½ pound (2 sticks) butter, room temperature

1 cup sugar

2 eggs

1 teaspoon vanilla extract

1 ½ teaspoons baking powder

2½ cups all-purpose flour

1 cup (about 4 ounces) finely ground walnuts

Topping:

Whole walnuts

3 tablespoons sugar mixed with ½ teaspoon ground cinnamon

Beat the butter, sugar, eggs and vanilla for several minutes, on medium speed, until light and fluffy. In a separate bowl, combine the baking powder and flour. Stir the flour mixture into the butter mixture and mix thoroughly. Pour in the walnuts, and mix by hand until evenly distributed. Wet your hands with a touch of water and divide the dough into 4 parts. On a lightly floured surface, roll each part into a log about 2 inches in diameter, wrap in plastic wrap and freeze.

When ready to bake, preheat the oven to 350 degrees.

Remove the dough from the freezer and cut it into ½ -inch slices. Place on an un-greased baking sheet about 2 inches apart. Sprinkle the cinnamon sugar over each cookie and bake at 350 degrees for about 15 minutes, or until light brown. When they come out of the oven, gently press a whole walnut in the center of each cookie.

Sara "Hannah" Rigler

Based on her memoir

Hannah was born Sara Matuson, in Shavli, Lithuania, thirteen years before the Nazis invaded her town in 1941. Years later, she took the name Hannah to honor the memory of her sister, who perished along with the rest of her immediate family. Hannah is a doer. From the time she arrived in the United States in 1947, until today, she has been involved in health services, community politics, Holocaust studies and is presently a guest lecturer at the Museum. Her life story is chronicled in her profound book, *10 British Prisoners-of-War Saved My Life*. Her story here is excerpted from that remarkable accounting of her childhood and experiences during the war. We have placed Hannah's story in the Russian section, as she was our sole contributor from Lithuania. Make no mistake, Hannah is proud of her Lithuanian roots and heritage.

"We lived in a Jewish world. Our holidays were celebrated as a community, and each celebration was an event. My mother use to prepare for Passover weeks before the holiday. I went with Maryte, our live-in help, to the public baths to

kosher the utensils for Passover. Today I think of the holidays as a time that brought us closeness and reverence to our family and bound us forever, a generation to generation with our people. The charmed life of my childhood came to a close in 1940; my family and I did not know the worst. The Russians invaded Lithuania and within a few weeks nationalized our factory. We were forced to share our home with a Russian pilot and his wife. They lived with us for a year when on June 22, 1941 the war started between Russia and Germany. Within a week, the Germans occupied Lithuania."

Through a series of events, her father was arrested and jailed, and she, her mother and sister were ghettoized. They remained in the ghetto for three years, and then they were moved by the Germans, first to Stutthof and then to several work camps. In December, 1944, they were taken on a "death march" at which time Hannah made a life-changing decision. "My mother had hidden my father's diamond ring and I asked her to give it to me so that I could trade it for bread. I slipped out of line, eluding the guards and ran to the nearest barn. In the barn, I tried to trade the ring for bread, but a Polish man who was working there called the police, who chased me back to the line. I was a filthy, starving bundle of rags and yet I did not want to die and so I was running for my life. I ran and hid in another barn. After a few hours, a man entered the barn; he told me he was a British prisoner of war - Stan Wells. He told me the Germans had given up the

Top left: Mother, Father, Hannah, Sara and Liuba, in Shavel, 1937

search for me. He brought me something to eat, and then tried to figure out a way to save me. As he left he said, "May God watch over you." Stan showed me there was still some decency in the world. Stan did return in the morning and told me the English POWs had decided to bring me back to their camp. On top of the barn was a hayloft and they had a plan to make a hole in the straw close to the chimney where I would lie, hidden all day. Late at night, Willy Fisher, one of the POWs, took me to his comrades. Neither Willy nor Stan came to see me again, but they did send me a kind and gentle substitute, Alan Edwards."

"In the morning I waited for Alan and my breakfast...in the afternoon I waited for Alan and supper. Alan stole a maroon coat, stockings, a pair of shoes and a sweater to go over my dress. My dress had a large Mogen David on the back that no amount of washing could take out, so the sweater was designed to be my disguise. Alan went to look for my mother and sister in Praust, but he could not get into the camp. One day, Alan decided to have me meet the other nine POWs. Each of the men gave me a small gift. After three weeks, Alan told me the Russians were close...he and the others were evacuated immediately. He offered to take me with them in place of Stan who had opted to stay behind. By shaving my head and disguising me as a boy, they hoped to save me. I stayed behind and was lucky to find a job working for a farmer named Heinrich Binder. He realized I was the Jewish girl that had escaped the Nazis several weeks earlier. He agreed not to turn me in, in return for my writing a note in Yiddish stating that he helped save my life. He felt this would help him as the liberating army was fast approaching. He saw me as a way of saving himself."

Hannah's story did not end there, at one point she was arrested as a German spy, as she spoke both German and Russian so well. They believed her dress, with the Jewish star on the back, was part of her disguise. When she was finally vindicated, the interrogator suggested she write fiction as he felt, "nobody could go through what I experienced and live!" Months later, Hannah arrived in Bialystok, where she waited for news of her mother and sister. Hannah met a girl from her hometown of Shavli who broke the news to her that her mother and sister had perished. She, however, remained in Bialystok, awaiting passage to Palestine or America.

Hannah came to America in 1947 and in 1952 married Bill, the love of her life. They have been married 56 years. For years, Hannah searched for the British men who had saved her life, writing letters to every Edwards in the London phone book. Through a series of lucky encounters, Hannah made contact with Willy Fisher, one of the British POWs whose diary verified Hannah's amazing but true story. And despite impossible odds, in 1972, after 24 years of searching, Hannah was eventually reunited with the men who saved her life. They met at the Portman Hotel in London.

"My ten angels came with their wives to see a woman who was no longer a bag of bones but had a productive and satisfying life. They toasted their little sister who had found a special place in their hearts - and the stoic British cried. In 1989, they were honored at Yad Vashem...all of them designated as "Righteous Among the Nations." The message of my story is a simple one- never give up. The message of my book is to use the uniquely human trait of memory to connect the generations and to work unceasingly to leave this world a better place than when we entered it. This is a message I have tried to imbue in my two children and two grandchildren."

Hannah Rigler's Romanian Eggplant

Although Hannah's heritage is Lithuanian, she recalls this classic Romanian dish featuring roasted eggplant, sweet red onions, crisp peppers and ripe tomatoes, that her Romanian mother-in-law taught her to make. Hannah advises buying medium size eggplants, which feel light in your hands; their meat is less seedy and sweeter. Make the salad your own by adding lemon juice or vinegar for a sour note or garlic for a sharper taste. It makes a terrific side dish or pureed as a flavorful dip or spread, served on garlic rounds (recipe follows).

Yields: 2 cups, Start to Finish: Under 1 hour

2 medium eggplants (about 2 pounds), sliced lengthwise in half

1 medium yellow pepper (about ½ pound), cored, seeded and finely diced

1 small red onion, finely diced

2 plum tomatoes, seeded and cut into small chunks

2 tablespoons canola oil

Kosher salt and pepper

Olive oil for drizzling

Preheat the broiler. Place the eggplants, cut side down on a sheet of aluminum foil that has been sprayed with a non-stick cooking spray. Broil the eggplants for 30 minutes. Remove them from the oven and let the eggplants cool and drain in a colander, you want them to release their liquid. Meanwhile, prepare the remaining ingredients.

When the eggplants are cool enough to handle, scoop out the meat. Try to discard any large seeds, they are bitter. Transfer the eggplants to a chopping bowl, and chop the meat very fine. Stir in chopped vegetables and oil. Season to taste with salt and pepper. Cover and refrigerate for several hours. Drizzle with olive oil before serving as a salad. Puree the mixture to make a spread or dip.

Toasted Garlic-Rubbed Rounds

This is the basic foundation for bruschetta and makes a good vehicle for serving Hannah's tangy Romanian eggplant spread.

Yields: Depends on the loaf, Start to Finish: Under 15 minutes

1 French baguette-style loaf of bread

Several garlic cloves, peeled and cut in half

Fresh parsley or sliced grape tomatoes for garnish (optional)

Preheat the broiler.

Cut a thin loaf of baguette-style bread, on the diagonal, into slices about ½-inch thick. Broil on both sides until just lightly browned. Remove from the oven and rub the cut garlic clove across the top of the toasted bread. The garlic oil will infuse the bread with a subtle flavor. Spoon the eggplant spread on each round, drizzle with a touch of olive oil and garnish with parsley or tomatoes for color.

JFH

Hannah Rigler's Spinach Soufflé

Hannah recommends this simple and flavorful soufflé as a delicious side dish, filling lunch or nice alternative to a breakfast quiche.

Yields: 4 servings, Start to Finish: Under 1 ½ hours

1 (10-ounce) package frozen chopped spinach, thawed and drained

⅔ cup half and half

1 tablespoon dried minced onion

3 eggs, lightly beaten

2 cups shredded cheese (can be Swiss, cheddar or a combination)

Preheat the oven to 400 degrees and grease a 6-cup Pyrex dish.

After thawing the spinach, squeeze out all the liquid. In a bowl combine the drained spinach, half and half, onion, eggs and 1¼ cups of cheese. Spoon the spinach mixture into the prepared Pyrex dish. Top with the remaining ¾ cup of cheese. Bake at 400 degrees for 15 minutes, then reduce the heat to 350 degrees and continue to bake for another 45 minutes or until the top has formed a nice, brown crust and the soufflé is cooked through.

Hannah Rigler's Chocolate Thinsies

While living in Europe, after the war, Hannah would receive care packages from her Aunt Mary in the States. One of her favorite treats were these wafer-like chocolate cookies, which taste like miniature ultra-thin brownies. They can be prepared in a snap with flour for anytime, or with matzo cake meal for Passover.

Yields: About 60 cookies, Start to Finish: Under 30 minutes

3 tablespoons cocoa powder

½ cup sugar

¼ cup flour (or a little less matzo cake meal)

¼ cup vegetable oil

1 whole egg, or 2 egg whites

½ teaspoon vanilla extract

⅓ cup (about 1.5 ounces) finely chopped nuts

Toppings:

Sprinkles, chocolate chips, chopped nuts, (optional)

Preheat the oven to 400 degrees and line a 15 ½ x 10 ½ -inch baking sheet with parchment paper.

Stir together the cocoa, sugar and flour. Pour in the oil and stir. Stir in the egg and vanilla until all the ingredients are combined. Stir in the finely chopped nuts.

Spread the batter onto the prepared pan, the thinner you spread the batter, the crisper the cookies will be. Bake at 400 degrees for 10 minutes. Allow the cookie to cool, before cutting it into bite-size pieces (a pizza wheel works great). If any of the cookies are not crisp enough, pop them back into the oven for a minute or two. Remove them from the parchment paper when cool.

Olga Paverman Schaerf and Henry Schaerf

In Olga's words

Olga sits across the table from me, stark white hair perfectly coiffed, movie star eyes and a personality that screams, 'I have some amazing stories to share'. Fortunately for Olga and her America-born husband, Henry, they escaped the brunt of Nazi oppression having found refuge in France during the war. Olga tells, with remarkable clarity, her story of how she came to France.

My husband Henry and I left Czernowitz, "Little Vienna," and went to Bucharest in the early 1930s because it was bigger, easier and there we did not stand out as Jews. Prior to the war, although my husband was born in Europe, he and his family had been living in the United States. His family remembered the life they had in

Europe and longed for it, so they went back. Now he had to leave, again. We stayed in Bucharest for many years until the Russians were getting close. At that time, you could pay to obtain a visa. We were able to secure one to South America, even though we knew that we did not want to settle there. It was a way for us to get out quickly. The visa was good for only a week or two.

Fortunately we were able to change our plans, and we made the decision to take a boat to France as my brother lived in Paris and it seemed natural for us to move there. On the boat, I remember we had a very large suite, called the Royal Suite; it was the only room available. We took it, and shared it with an unknown passenger. One day, my husband leaned across our balcony and saw that the man sharing our suite was a priest. That same day my husband went downstairs to the bar to buy an orange juice. He had only Romanian money, which the bartender would not take. The man sitting next to my husband at the bar said "put it on my tab." As it turned out, that man was the priest sharing our suite. We came to know him well. Monsignor Kirk was an emissary to the Pope and was planning to disembark when the boat made its first stop in Naples. One day, the priest asked my husband to watch his two suitcases. He would not tell us what was inside, but we suspected they were war-related secret documents he was carrying to the Vatican. We tried many times to locate him, to thank him for his kindness and tell him we were safe, but at the time were unsuccessful.

We arrived in Marseilles and as was very typical, France was enduring a strike. We were

Top left: Henry and Olga Schaerf, Italy, 1950s

unable to travel to Paris and reach my brother. My brother was very resourceful and had a plan. He rented an ambulance, knowing it would get through the snarled traffic, and made the trip from Paris to Marseilles. Together we remained in Marseilles for about one month, before moving to Paris. Once there we lived well, as the people I came in contact with treated the refugees beautifully. I always felt that the French hated each other but they liked us. Even when it came to rations, I felt we got more than our mandated share.

We came to America in 1949, but kept our Romanian traditions. Remarkably, years later, in an unbelievable coincidence, my son, Ray, who is a cardiothoracic surgeon, operated on a young priest. My son told his patient about our encounter with the Monsignor. Not only did his patient know the priest, he had studied with him and knew that Monsignor Kirk had recently died. We thought it was very special that our son saved the life of this young man who was so personally connected to the man who helped us. If you ask me who I am, I would answer I am first a Jew, then an American. I try to look at things brightly and enjoy what I am doing. I am very happy with what I have. I have one son and four grandchildren.

Olga Schaerf's Romanian *Karnatzlach*–Spicy Grilled Meat

Olga remembers devouring these garlicky little bites of beef for dinner or as a filling appetizer. Today in Romania they are called *Mititei*, and they have become trendy street food. They are crowd pleasers at a summer barbecue hot off the grill and served on long bamboo skewers, or as finger food broiled in the oven and served like sliders or with the accompanying dipping sauce.

Yields: 12 pieces, Start to Finish: Step One: 15 minutes, then refrigerate for at least 4 or up to 24 hours, Step Two: Under 30 minutes

1 pound ground beef

4 to 5 cloves of garlic, grated

1 teaspoon kosher salt

1 teaspoon sweet paprika

½ teaspoon ground black pepper

1 generous splash Worcestershire sauce

1 tablespoon ketchup

¼ cup finely chopped fresh flat-leaf parsley

Dipping sauce:

Yields: about ¼ cup

4 tablespoons ketchup

2 tablespoons Dijon mustard

¼ teaspoon ground cumin

Splash of Worcestershire sauce

Combine all the ingredients and serve on the side for dipping.

Step One: In a medium bowl combine the ground beef, garlic (grated over the meat so the garlic juice is incorporated) salt, paprika, pepper, Worcestershire sauce, ketchup and parsley. Combine with your hands to thoroughly blend. Cover and refrigerate at least 4 hours or up to one day.

Step Two: Light the grill or preheat the broiler.

Wet your hands and form the meat into rounds the size of a golf ball, then elongate them into a thumb-like shape, about 3 inches long. Grill/broil, 5 inches from the heat source, for 4 to 5 minutes, turn over and continue to cook for 3 to 4 minutes longer. Serve as is or with the dipping sauce.

Feedback

You can experiment with ground veal, lamb or turkey or a combination of meat. For the turkey, add a little extra Worcestershire and salt, as the turkey tends to be more dry and bland. You can spice these bites up even more by adding ½ teaspoon of cumin to the meat, or replacing the sweet paprika with hot. Some prefer a spongier texture, which can be achieved by adding ¼ cup of seltzer and ¼ teaspoon of baking soda to the meat. This causes them to fluff up a bit when cooking.

Olga Schaerf's *Salade De Bouef* - Beef Salami Salad

Both Olga and her dear friend Nella Frendel regularly made this provincial salad with a Jewish twist. It's a picnic in a bowl, with a French accent.

Yields: 6 to 8 servings (about 6 cups), Start to Finish: Under 15 minutes

1 (8.5- ounce) can Le Sueur early peas, drained

1 (8.25- ounce) can diced or sliced carrots, drained

1 (12- ounce) whole beef salami, cut into bite size pieces

1 pound mayo-based potato salad

5 teaspoons Dijon mustard

1 cup chopped sour pickles

Chopped fresh flat-leaf parsley and olive oil, for garnish

In a medium-size bowl, combine all the ingredients and gently stir to combine, you don't want to mash the peas when mixing. Chill in the fridge and serve as a side dish or lunch salad. Garnish with chopped parsley and a drizzle of olive oil.

Cantor Gershon Sirota

Based on my family history

In 1943, one of the greatest voices in Cantorial music was silenced forever. That voice belonged to Gershon Sirota, a close relative of my great grandfather, Rabbi Aaron Sirota. Hazzan Sirota, who was often referred to as "The Jewish Caruso" was a leading Cantor in Europe at a time when Cantorial music was as its height. He was born in the Odessa region of what is now the Ukraine, but traveled extensively and unfortunately found himself in Poland during the war. He was one of the first Cantors to ever record his music, and sang throughout Europe and the United States in the early 1900s. In 1902 he honored the Zionist pioneer, Theodore Herzl, with his rich tenor voice. In New York City, a sold-out crowd at Carnegie Hall was treated to his haunting melodies.

Cantor Sirota fatefully returned to Europe and assumed the position as Cantor at the prestigious Tlomackie Street Synagogue in Warsaw. He later relinquished that position as his travels took him away from the Temple for prolonged periods of time. His final years were spent with his wife and children, in the Warsaw Ghetto, where they all perished.

As a child, I recall my parents playing on the phonograph the groundbreaking recordings my distant relative had made. At the time, I didn't appreciate the depth of his voice or the impact of his music. When my Hebrew schoolteachers, or choir directors, heard that I was related to the great Hazzan Sirota, they were awed and I beamed proudly. However, I knew little of his life story and nothing of his tragic death. My great grandfather's Jewish roots ran deep, but once he arrived here in the U.S. his connections to "the old country" were replaced by his Rabbinical obligations. He tended to small communities, where Rabbis were rare and sorely needed. In Moodus, Connecticut, he was not only the Rabbi, but he was the *shoichet* and a gentleman farmer. When I would visit my great grandfather, we never talked about his family that remained in Russia, or those who did not survive the Holocaust. We did talk about Jewish traditions, one of which was blowing the Shofar. He was a born teacher, and he taught me how to sound the Shofar that he brought with him from Russia. Today, I replicate the ancient calls at my synagogue on Rosh Hashanah. I feel it is a fitting way to honor my great grandfather and the family I never had the chance to meet.

Top left: Cantor Gershon Sirota, archival photo

Schi-Russian Cabbage Soup

My grandma, Rose Sirota Feiss, kept many of the Russian traditions alive through her ethnic cooking. One of those dishes, *schi*, Russian cabbage soup, is a dish my grandmother taught me to make and it has become a mainstay in my repertoire of family favorites. It is a dish they ate in Minsk, where she was born, and was popular throughout Russia. To honor Cantor Sirota, I have included my grandmother's version of Russian cabbage soup. *Schi* is a robust and rich soup with lots of cabbage and sauerkraut, mingling with beef short ribs and ultimately jumbo franks. It is a meal in itself; all you need is a chunk of crusty bread and a big spoon.

Yields: 10 servings, Start to Finish: Under 2 hours

1 large head of green cabbage, cored and shredded

1 (28-ounce) can whole tomatoes, with ½ cup of its juice

3 to 4 pounds of flanken/short ribs, cut into 2 to 3-inch pieces

1 (15-ounce) can sauerkraut, drained

2 quarts beef broth

8 jumbo hotdogs

The juice of 1 to 2 lemons

Kosher salt and pepper

Place the shredded cabbage in a very large soup pot. Add the tomatoes, crushing them over the pot with your hands, allowing the juices to stream in. Add ½ cup of the juice from the can. Tuck the ribs into the cabbage and top with the sauerkraut. Pour the broth into the pot and bring to a boil. Reduce the heat to low, cover and cook for 1½ to 2 hours. If the meat is not falling off the bone, cook an additional 30 minutes.

When the meat is cooked, remove it from the pot, so you can trim the meat from the bones to make serving easier. Cut the meat into large chunks and reserve. Add the hotdogs and the juice from one lemon and cook for 15 minutes. Season to taste with salt and pepper.

If time allows, refrigerate the soup overnight so the fat rises to the top and solidifies. Remove this layer of fat, reheat and serve. Serve the soup with a piece of short rib in each bowl and extra lemon to squeeze for a more sour taste.

JFH

Fira Stukelman

In her own words

Talking to Fira is like speaking to a college professor. She has a unique perspective, profound insights and a genuine respect for education. She remains strong willed and fierce. Fira is a community leader, and has worked with Congressmen and Senators and proudly calls Mayor Bloomberg a friend. In 1993, Fira founded the New York Holocaust Association, which is an active association of Holocaust survivors.

I was born on March 25, 1933 in Vinnytsya, Ukraine. In Russia I never knew we were Jewish, because in Russia, everyone was Russian. It was not until the war broke out that we became more observant. A pogrom occurred in September, 1941 and another in November, when German soldiers arrived on my street. My mother was taken away while I hid under the bed. I never saw my family again. I survived because a Christian woman came into the room and took me into her

Top left: Fira Stukelman, age 5, 1938

apartment. She put a scarf on my head, and took me to live with my grandmother. During the day we stayed in the woods, at night we hid in broken and destroyed homes. One terrible night, my grandmother died in her sleep. I was eight years old and truly alone.

I spent the rest of the war in a camp and then the ghetto, until March of 1944 when the Soviet army liberated us. I was sent to Chernovtsy, which was in Romania. I was sent to study in a trade school designed for young orphaned women. At sixteen I graduated and worked in a sewing factory. I married and had a family, while working two shifts and attending night school. I graduated from Moscow Textile Institute in 1961. At that time I could feel an undercurrent of anti-Semitism. Life in Russia was not good, there was no freedom, and so, in 1979, we applied for documents to come to America. It took ten years for the gates to open. I always had the attitude that I would work and I would care about my family. I studied English and began a new life here in America. I would try and learn English everywhere I went. I paid attention at the store, at the bus stop, listening and learning always. In 1991 I went to Touro College, where I earned a degree in social work.

One thing that I miss about Russia is how the family all stays together. I try to keep our family, my two children and three grandchildren, together with the cooking traditions. I make mostly Jewish food, and I bake a lot. It wasn't until I married that I had parents (in-laws) who could teach me how to keep a Jewish home. I learned so much from my mother-in-law. She was really something. My husband and I were married for 35 years. The best of my life is here; everyday I stand up and say God Bless America.

Fira Stukelman's Summer *Borscht*

While hot *borscht* with vegetables and flanken warmed the cold nights, Fira's blazing red cold *borscht* turned vibrant fuchsia from a dollop of swirled sour cream, cooled the hot summer days. Fira skips the middleman and boils the potatoes with the beets so they not only pick up the sweet flavor, but they become a colorful addition when served. For an authentic experience, have a chilled shot of *Horilka* (Ukrainian vodka) standing by.

Yields: 8 to 10 servings, Start to Finish: Under 2 hours, then time to chill in the fridge

3 to 4 large beets (about 2 pounds), washed and scrubbed clean

2 medium red bliss potatoes, peeled and cut into eighths

3 carrots, peeled and grated on the large hole of a box grater

2 teaspoons kosher salt

½ teaspoon black pepper

2 tablespoons sugar (more or less to taste)

½ teaspoon sour salt or 3 tablespoons lemon juice (more or less to taste)

Suggested garnish:

Sour cream, fresh chopped dill leaves, hard boiled eggs, chopped garlic, chopped sour pickles, grated carrot fried in a little butter

In a large pot bring 8 cups of water to boil and cook the scrubbed beets, over medium heat, for 45 minutes. Remove the beets with a slotted spoon and allow them to cool for 30 minutes, do not discard the water. While they cool, cook the potatoes and grated carrots, in the beet water. When the beets are cool enough to handle, trim the ends and peel the beets using a paper towel to gently rub off the outer skin. Hold the end of the beet with the towel (or a tined gripper) and grate the beets, on the largest hole of a box grater, directly into the soup pot. Cook, uncovered, over low heat for 1 hour. Stir in the sugar and sour salt or lemon juice and additional salt and pepper, adjusting to your taste. Transfer the soup to a large container and chill in the fridge until nice and cold.

Top the *borscht* with any or all of the suggested garnishes. If you prefer to serve the potatoes as a side dish, prepare the soup as directed above, and boil the potatoes separately before serving.

Feedback
There's no need to waste the vibrant green leaves from the beets. They have a similar taste to Swiss chard. Rinse them in cold water and place in a small pot. Steam, in a few inches of water, for about 4 minutes, until they wilt but do not lose their bright green color. The greens can then be chilled and tossed in a salad or sautéed in a skillet with olive oil and garlic and served as a side dish.

Berta Kiesler Vaisman

As told by her daughter Juanita Siebenberg

Juanita comes by her cooking talent and warm South American ways naturally, as her mother, a Romanian refugee who found safe haven in Venezuela, brought all her traditions together in their home and in the kitchen.

My mother was born on the 12th of March 1919 in Czernowitz, Romania. She was married at the age of twenty, and soon found herself living under Soviet occupation. In June of 1941, her husband was taken prisoner by the Romanian army and was turned over to the Russian army where he died serving on the front line. During this time, my mother was in the ghetto in Czernowitz. She was considered a valuable worker and therefore was not immediately deported to Transnistria, a part of the Ukraine that was conquered by the Germans and Romanians. On June 19, 1942 all that changed. She and her parents were sent by the Romanian government across the Dreister River to Transnistria. They stayed on the Romanian side of the river for a short time, before being transferred to a concentration camp. For more than a year, my mother worked on road construction. Learning that her parents had not survived the camp, she made the decision to return to Czernowitz, as repatriation was still legal. She returned to Czernowitz on March 22, 1944, crossing the border back into Romania. She eventually gained passage to South America where one surviving brother lived.

My father had gone to Venezuela years earlier and my parents met and married in 1947. My sister, Melita, was born in 1949 and I followed two years later. We came to America in 1980 and settled in New York. I was raised in Venezuela and I am the first generation of my family to live in America. My mother was a terrific cook and loved to make Latin dishes. I try to carry on many of her traditions, both those from Eastern Europe and Venezuela. My parents were married a short 15 years when my father died. My parents had two children, five grandchildren and one great grandchild.

Top left: Berta Kiesler in Romania

Berta Vaisman's *Malai*–Corn Bread

While black bread or challah was the natural choice in Berta's native Romania, as an immigrant in Venezuela, Berta learned the regional specialties of her new home. Venezuelan cooking leans heavily on Caribbean influences as evidenced in her creamy and subtle corn bread, with a grainy texture and smooth filling.

Yields: 9 squares, Start to Finish: Under 1 ¼ hours

1 cup all-purpose flour

1 cup ground yellow corn meal

2 cups whole milk

2 eggs

1 teaspoon baking powder

2 tablespoons vegetable oil

¼ teaspoon salt

½ cup (4 ounces) small-curd cottage cheese (optional)

Preheat the oven to 350 degrees and grease an 8 x8 -inch baking dish.

Combine all the ingredients, except the cottage cheese, and mix by hand with a wooden spoon. Pour half of the mixture into the prepared baking dish. Spread a layer of cottage cheese, and then top with the remaining batter. Bake at 350 degrees for 1 hour or until the bread is firm and lightly brown.

Michelle Bernstein

Professional contributor

As a refugee in Venezuela, Berta adopted cooking techniques consistent with Spanish culinary influences in her South American home. The very talented and warmly expressive Chef Michelle Bernstein infuses many of her dishes with ingredients that give a nod to Spain as well as her South American heritage. As a Jewish American-Argentinean chef, she uses these flavors to bring "luxurious comfort food" to the table. The following recipe is a prime example of her culinary point of view.

Duck Breasts with Jerez, Oranges and Spanish Almonds

Contributed by Michelle Bernstein, chef/co-owner of Michy's, Miami

I wrote this recipe just for the book. It mixes old world with new, a hint of Jerez from Spain with the old French classic flavor of duck a l'orange. The duck is topped with Marcona Almonds, my very favorite. The sauce is a delicious balance that just cuts through the fat of the duck. My Mom always made whole roast duck for many of the holidays; I find the duck breasts in this presentation much easier on the home cook.

Serves 4

4 Peking or Maple Leaf Duck Breasts (2 whole breasts halved), scored in crosshatches

2 cups duck or chicken broth

2 shallots, minced

¼ teaspoon ground coriander seeds

Pinch of ground cinnamon

1 star anise

The juice and zest of 3 oranges

2 tablespoons orange marmalade

2 ounces Dry Jerez (Spanish sherry, I prefer Amontillado for this recipe)

1 tablespoon sherry vinegar

2 tablespoons cornstarch mixed with 2 tablespoons water (slurry)

2 tablespoons finely chopped cilantro

1 tablespoon finely chopped Italian parsley

¼ cup Marcona Almonds, chopped

Season the breasts with salt and pepper, set aside.

In a small saucepan, heat the orange juice. Reduce three-quarters of the way down. Add the duck stock and reduce by about three-quarters.

Heat a sauté pan over medium low heat; cook the duck breasts skin side down for 8-10 minutes or until golden brown. Remove the duck from the pan, set aside skin side up. Remove all but 1 tablespoon of duck fat from the pan. Add the shallots, spices, orange zest, marmalade, Jerez, and vinegar and simmer for about 4 minutes. Add the orange-duck reduction. Place the duck breast into the pan. Heat the duck for 2 minutes (longer if you prefer the duck medium to medium-well done). Add the cornstarch slurry, whisking the sauce for 2 minutes. Remove the star anise. Add the cilantro and parsley. Season to taste with salt and pepper. Slice the duck, spoon the sauce over each and top with the almonds.

Berta Kiesler Vaisman's *Barenikes*–Pierogis

Did you hear the one about the child who set sixteen places at the table for Shabbos dinner. When her mother asked her why there were sixteen place settings, when there were only four of them eating, the child replied, "because grandma said she was bringing a dozen pierogis!" Every culture has their version of a pierogi. The Eastern European variety are usually filled with a flavorful potato and onion mixture that wants to burst out of its sealed pocket and dive right into a bowl of cold sour cream. You can finish them in the oven topped with fried onions or toss them into a hot skillet and brown them on the stove. Either way, make plenty, they disappear quickly.

Yields: About 30 pierogi, Start to Finish: Under 1½ hours

For the filling:

3 large Yukon gold potatoes, peeled and quartered

3 medium onions, chopped (about 2 ¼ cups)

½ cup (8 tablespoons) vegetable, Canola oil or olive oil

Kosher salt and pepper

For the dough:

3 cups all-purpose flour

1 stick (½ cup) butter or margarine at room temperature

1 egg plus 1 egg yolk

1 teaspoon salt

½ cup of the reserved potato water

To prepare the filling, bring 3 quarts of salted water to boil, and cook the potatoes until very tender, about 20 minutes. While the potatoes boil, heat 4 tablespoons of oil in a large skillet, cook and stir the onions, over medium heat, until lightly browned, about 15 minutes. Reserve the onions. Remove the cooked potatoes from the pot and reserve ½ cup of the potato liquid. Drain and reserve the potatoes.

Mash the potatoes and stir in half of the browned onions and 2 tablespoons oil. Season to taste with salt and pepper. Reserve the remaining onions and the remaining 2 tablespoons of oil for baking.

Preheat the oven to 325 degrees and bring a fresh large pot of salted water to boil.

For the dough
In a large mixing bowl, or the bowl of a food processor, fitted with the metal blade, combine the flour, butter, egg, egg yolk, salt and reserved potato water. When a ball forms, remove the dough from the bowl and knead with your hands for a couple of minutes. The dough should be smooth and elastic.

Divide the dough into two halves. Flour a work surface, and roll the dough to a little less than ¼-inch thick (don't try to stretch, it will only tug back). Cut the dough into rounds using a 3-inch cookie cutter or the rim of a glass. Have a small bowl of water standing by to dip your fingers into. Place 1 teaspoon of filling in each round and seal by dipping your fingers in the water, running them along the rim of the dough, folding the circle into a half moon and pinching the edges closed. Drop the pierogis one at a time into the boiling water, and boil for about 5 minutes, do not overcrowd the pot, they will float to the surface when they are done. Drain on paper towels. Repeat with the remaining pierogis. When all the pierogis have been boiled, place them in a large Pyrex dish and cover them with the remaining onions and oil. Bake at 325 degrees for 30 minutes. If you prefer a crisper pierogi, do not bake them. Fry them in a large skillet, heated with the remaining olive oil. Drain on paper towels, and serve with the remaining onions.

Chana Wiesenfeld

In her own words

Chana credits her willpower and drive for getting her through a very tough life. Her Romanian and Ukrainian roots show in her cooking style, which definitely reflects her rich heritage.

I was born in Buchovina, which has changed hands many times, but is now considered the Ukraine. My father was a manager of sorts, supervising the forest workers, and my mother stayed at home. 1941, when I was just a child, we went to the ghetto. My father had been taken away earlier, and managed to escape through the woods and found us months later. We stayed there in the woods for 3½ years, at which point the partisans, and then the Russians, liberated us.

After being liberated, we returned to Czernowitz, but found the Russians had plans for us and we did not want to go along with their idea. We escaped from Romania, hoping to go to Palestine. I enlisted in a Zionist organization and boarded a train, which took thousands of children through Transylvania and then Bulgaria, Turkey and Greece. In 1946, I spent a year living in Cyprus before leaving for Palestine. We eventually traveled by boat to Palestine where we lived in bunkers, because of the war. I was too young to enlist in the army, so I existed in limbo until I turned eighteen.

I then served in the Israeli army, and in 1956 I was called up to serve again as a reservist. At that time, I met my husband and he had proposed. He returned to the States and after eight months passed, he came back to Israel and we were married. Together we came to the United States. I missed my family, I missed Israel, but I stayed here and made a life with my husband and two children. We were married nearly twenty-five years when he passed away. I was lucky to meet and marry a second wonderful man, who I was married to for twenty-two years.

I have five beautiful grandchildren and from them I *shepn* so much *naches*. I would love to transmit to the younger generation there should be something leftover from their grandparents, when they start a conversation, there will be Jewishness so it wouldn't fade away. It is also good to bring up what happened. Let them know, let them teach, let them have an idea. They are starting to forget a little bit, I feel it in the air, and they shovel it away. Everyone will become better people by knowing what we went through.

Chana Wiesenfeld's *Kasha Varnishkes*

If we called this dish pasta with toasted grains and sautéed onions, it could easily appear on the menu of a trendy restaurant. But long before we realized whole grains were nourishing, filling, inexpensive and healthful, Eastern European cooks discovered their goodness. Chana says her grandchildren "go bananas" for this dish, which works well as a side for stews, braised meat or a light lunch.

Yields: 6 to 8 servings, Start to Finish: Under 1 hour

1 (12-ounce) bag or box uncooked bow-tie pasta

2 large onions, chopped (about 2 cups)

3 tablespoons vegetable oil or butter

1 egg, beaten

1 cup Kasha (buckwheat groats)

2 cups chicken or beef broth or water (broth will make the dish more flavorful)

Kosher salt and pepper

Bring a large pot of salted water to boil, and cook the bow-tie noodles according to package directions, drain and reserve.

While the pasta cooks, heat the oil or butter, in a large skillet, cook and stir the onions, over medium heat, until they are very brown but not burnt, about 20 minutes. Using a slotted spoon, remove them from the pan and reserve. In a small bowl, mix the egg and kasha. Using the same pan you used for the onions, spread the kasha and egg mixture in a thin layer and cook, over medium heat, until the egg has cooked out and the kasha lightly browns, about 3 minutes. This step will help develop the kasha's nutty, toasted flavor.

In a small saucepan, bring 2 cups of broth or water to boil. Slowly pour the liquid into the skillet with the kasha and simmer, covered, for 15 minutes. Stir to completely break up any hardened bits of kasha. When the kasha is tender, combine the noodles and onions with the kasha. Generously season to taste with salt and pepper. If the mixture is too firm, add a touch more fat or liquid to loosen the mixture. Serve hot or cold.

Chana Wiesenfeld's Ukrainian Winter *Borscht*

Chana makes this wonderfully colorful and flavorful soup, chock-full of beets, vegetables and beef to warm even the coldest Russian night. While long considered peasant food by many, beets have been rediscovered for their amazing nutritional quality and sweet buttery taste. Beets have a high sugar content yet surprisingly low caloric count. They are rich in nutrients and vitamins and can be eaten cold in a salad or hot as in this authentic Ukrainian soup. Be sure to follow Chana's advice, "a good cook is the one that watches the pot."

Yields: 12 cups, Start to Finish: Under 2½ hours

1 pound beef flanken

4 large purple-red beets (about 2½ pounds), washed, peeled and halved

1 pound carrots (about 5 to 6), peeled and grated

1 small green cabbage (about 1 pound), shredded in long strips

1 whole onion, peeled

4 (8-ounce) cans tomato sauce

Kosher salt and pepper

2 garlic cloves, chopped

¼ to ½ cup freshly chopped dill leaves

2 tablespoons Telma chicken flavor powder, (optional)

Boiled new potatoes, for garnish, (optional)

In a very large pot, bring 6 cups of water to boil and cook the flanken, skimming off and discarding any foam that rises to the surface. While the flanken cooks, prepare the vegetables for the soup. Take a spoon or small melon baller and scoop out the center of each cleaned and peeled beet half. Chana warns the centers are tough and sometimes bitter; discard them. Using a large box grater, grate the beets and carrots on the largest hole. Shred the cabbage into long strips and peel the onion, but leave it whole. By this time, the flanken should be cooked.

Remove the flanken from the pot, rinse and pat dry. You can remove the meat from the bone and cut it into small chunks, or leave it on the bone. Rinse out the pot and fill it with 8 cups of fresh water or broth. Stir in the beets, carrots, cabbage, onion, tomato sauce and flanken. Cover and cook on medium heat for about 1½ hours, skimming off and discarding any foam that rises to the surface. After 1½ hours, stir in the Telma powder (if needed to boost the flavor), garlic, and dill and season to taste with salt and plenty of pepper. Cook an additional 5 to 10 minutes. Serve the soup hot with the traditional garnish of boiled potatoes.

Feedback

Chana makes another version, called *Knubble* (garlic) *borscht*. Eliminate the tomato sauce and add 4 tablespoons lemon juice (or a little sour salt) and 2 tablespoons of sugar in the last few minutes of cooking. This sweet and sour version also features lots of fresh dill tossed in at the end and plenty of garlic, 8 to 10 cloves, stirred into the soup before serving. Additionally, you can take thick slices of crusty black bread and coat them with the juice of freshly halved garlic cloves, by rubbing the cut side of the garlic clove on the bread. This makes a delicious accompaniment.

Greece

I began interviewing survivors from Greece just as I finished testing recipes from my Eastern European Ashkenazi contributors. My kitchen was transformed; no chicken soup simmering, gefilte fish poaching or kugels baking. Instead it was filled with the aroma of fragrant oregano, dark sweet honey and salty feta cheese. Olive oil replaced chicken fat as the recipes from Sephardic survivors relate more to the Mediterranean style of eating than what we classically consider "Yiddish" cooking.

Despite tremendous losses during the war, or maybe because of them, the American Sephardic community remains strong and vibrant with a robust enjoyment of family, friends and food. With great respect for their Sephardic traditions and Greek roots, we present the flavorful recipes remembered by our gutsy Greek survivors.

RECIPES

Luna Cohen: *Fakee*–Greek Lentil Soup

Luna Cohen: *Tourlo*–Greek Ratatouille

Luna Cohen: *Loukoumades*–Greek Doughnuts

Koula Kofinas: *Fasülye*–Braised Marrow Bones with White Beans

Koula Kofinas: *Papoutsakia*- Stuffed Eggplant Skins

Solomon Kofinas: Roasted Baby Eggplant

Stella Levi: *Bamya*–Okra Stew with Chicken

Stella Levi: *Sevoyas Reynadas*- Stuffed Onions

Rachel Angelou Mosios: Roasted Lamb with Lemon Potatoes

Rachel Angelou Mosios: Spinach Pie

Mathilde Turiel: *Boyos*–Cheese and Potato Turnovers

PROFESSIONAL CONTRIBUTORS

Jennifer Abadi: *Leban m'Naa'na*-Yogurt Cucumber Mint Dressing

Jennifer Abadi: *M'jedrah*–Rice and Lentils

Samuel Capsuto: *Bimuelos de Patata*-Potato Pancakes

Joe Dobias: Horseradish Hanger Steak and *Harosset*

Jill Schulster: The Drunken Pharaoh

Luna and Haim Cohen

As told by their daughter Rachel Cohen

The Greek *Sephardic* community is a strong, proud group with very different cooking styles than the *Ashkenazi*. Rachel is a product of that distinct culture, and shared her family's story and treasured recipes with me.

My parents lived in Larissa, Greece, where my five siblings were born. My father was a broom-maker, my mother a homemaker. In 1942, when the Germans came into their town, they felt they would not be bothered. However, there came a time when Germans ordered the head of each household to report to the synagogue on a daily basis. My mother refused to let my father go. She felt it was very suspicious that only the Jews needed to report and that the other religious groups were not singled out. My parents felt it was obvious that they had to leave. Because of my father's occupation he had many contacts with peasants who lived outside of the city; after all he bought straw from them for his brooms. He felt the family would be able to blend in with the peasant community. Additionally, because my parents were simple people and not wealthy, they had little to leave behind by way of tangible items. They had not acquired an expensive home, or other goods that they might regret leaving. They left with little, except their children, and my teenage aunt and uncle.

Through the underground, my parents obtained documents saying they were a Christian family, whose surname was Chiliakos. My parents fit the profile of this family, so it seemed like a safe solution. For years, my parents moved from town to town where they were known as the Chiliakos family. In one town, my brother was a student in a Christian run school. He attended church services and he recalls when he was held up by the priest as an exemplary Christian student.

Although I was not born during this period, my parents always talked openly about the war. I find there is a thread that runs through children of survivors. We worry about things other children might not even think about. My childhood was very influenced by our Greek roots. I married an American man, but my cooking style is very Greek. I grew up eating what is now the trendy Mediterranean diet: for me, eating lentil soup, legumes, lots of salad and meat only once a week was a way of life. My parents were married 61 years and have six children and nine grandchildren.

Top left: The Cohen family arriving at South Station, Boston, May 1956. Left to right, front row: Luna Maisis Cohen, Rachel, Rosa, Haim Cohen (shaking hands with HIAS representative; 2nd row: Nissim, Solomon; 3rd row: Isaac, Pinkhas

Luna Cohen's *Fakee*-Greek Lentil Soup

This traditional lentil soup is a perfect example of bringing good, healthful ingredients together. What makes this soup Greek is the acidic "zing" that Rachel suggests you add right before serving.

Yields: 6 to 8 servings; Start to Finish: 1½ hours

1 medium onion, chopped (about ¾ cup)

2 cloves garlic, chopped

2 tablespoons olive oil

1 pound lentils, rinsed

2 celery ribs, diced (about 1 cup)

2 carrots, peeled and diced (about 1 cup)

2 bay leaves

Kosher salt and pepper

1 (6-ounce) can tomato paste

6 to 8 tablespoons balsamic vinegar, for serving

Heat the olive oil in a large soup pot, cook and stir the onions and garlic, over medium heat, until lightly browned, about 10 minutes. Add the lentils, celery, carrots, bay leaves and 6 cups of water. Season with salt and pepper. Cook, covered, on low heat for 50 minutes. Check the soup from time to time, adding boiling water as needed if the soup becomes too thick. After 50 minutes, stir in 1 can of tomato paste and cook for an additional 10 minutes. Don't overcook the soup, the lentils will become mushy and lose their nutty bite. Remove the bay leaves and drizzle 1 tablespoon of balsamic vinegar into each soup bowl right before serving.

Feedback
Lentils come in a variety of colors, but the brown and green lentils tend to hold their shape better. These legumes are rich in fiber and have been eaten since Biblical times. It is written that Jacob used lentils to buy his birthright from his brother Esau.

Jennifer Abadi

Professional contributor

Once you become familiar with lentils, you will cook with them often. They are flavorful, filling and inexpensive. Lentils are terrific cold in a salad, or comforting and nourishing hot as a side dish. They partner perfectly with rice as in Jennifer Abadi's Middle Eastern preparation, a favorite of Syrian cooks who shared many of the same cooking techniques as the *Sephardim* of Greece. It makes a filling foundation for the Cohen family's ratatouille (recipe follows) or when topped with lots of fried onions and yogurt mint dressing, it becomes a stand on its own, healthy and hardy meal.

M'jedrah–Rice and Lentils

Excerpted from A Fistful of Lentils: Syrian-Jewish Recipes From Grandma Fritzie's Kitchen, by Jennifer Abadi. (© 2002, used by permission from The Harvard Common Press)

A staple in the Syrian-Jewish community, this is as close to Syrian comfort food as you will get. In fact one time while my cousin was temporarily living in Montana he felt so homesick for rice and lentils he had my grandmother literally FedEx it to him! When I first went to my Grandma Fritzie's to learn how to make this dish for my cookbook, *A Fistful of Lentils*, she walked out with a big old banged up pot that she had used to produce the best rice and lentils for more than 40 years. I now own this pot and keep it as a memory of my Grandma Fritzie and all the great times we shared Syrian cooking together.

Yields: 4 servings

For Rice and Lentils:

1 cup dried brown lentils

1 teaspoon salt

1 cup long-grain white rice

For Serving:

3 tablespoons vegetable oil

1 cup thinly sliced yellow onions

1 to 2 tablespoons salted or butter, cut into tiny bits

Yogurt-Cucumber-Mint Dressing

Place the rice in a medium-size bowl, add cold water to cover, and let soak for 10 minutes. Drain through fine-mesh strainer and set aside.

In a heavy medium-size saucepan, combine 2 cups of water with the lentils and bring to a boil. Reduce the heat to medium-low and simmer, uncovered, until the lentils are al dente in texture (tender enough to bite through, but still firm–do not overcook!), 15 to 20 minutes. Remove from the heat.

(Continued)

Pour any excess liquid from the cooked lentils into a measuring cup. Add enough water to this to equal 2 ½ cups of liquid. Return the liquid to the saucepan with the cooked lentils. Add the salt, cover, and bring to a brisk boil over high heat.

Once the lentils are boiling, add the drained rice. Stir twice gently so as not to mush the lentils. Boil, uncovered, until the water reaches the level of the surface of the rice and lentils, about 5 minutes. Cover tightly, reduce the heat to its lowest possible level, and steam. After 7 minutes, mix by gently folding the rice and lentils from the bottom of the pan to the top with a spoon. With the back of a spoon, scrape gently along the side of the saucepan and push the contents toward the center to create a mound. Cook until the water is cooked off, about another 15 minutes, repeating the folding and scraping several times. (May be prepared in advance at this point. To reheat, place in a preheated 350 degree oven until very hot, about 20 minutes.

To fry the onions, heat the 3 tablespoons of oil in a small skillet over medium-high heat and fry until very brown and crispy (even black), about 30 minutes.

Arrange the rice and lentils on a serving platter or in a large serving bowl and pour the fried onions and their oil over the top. Do not mix. Dot the top with the butter and serve with yogurt-cucumber-mint dressing on the side.

Leban m'Naa'na–Yogurt-Cucumber Mint Dressing

Excerpted from A Fistful of Lentils: Syrian-Jewish Recipes From Grandma Fritzie's Kitchen, by Jennifer Abadi. (© 2002, used by permission from The Harvard Common Press)

This dressing is very easy to make and traditionally what Syrians serve on top of rice and lentils. If you add a little water and adjust the seasonings it also makes a refreshing cold soup for the hot summer months.

Yields: 2¼ cups

2 cups plain whole milk yogurt (low fat or nonfat yogurt can be substituted)

1 heaping tablespoon dried mint leaves

Few dashes of garlic powder

About ¼ teaspoon salt to taste

1 cup peeled and finely chopped or coarsely grated Kirby cucumbers, excess water drained

Place the yogurt in a small bowl and stir until creamy. Add the dried mint by crushing it between the palms of your hands. Add the garlic powder and salt and mix well.

Fold the cucumber into the mixture, cover, and chill until serving time; it will keep, refrigerated, for up to 2 days.

Luna Cohen's *Tourlo*–Greek Ratatouille

Rachel makes this summer-fresh dish in the height of the season when the vegetables are abundant. *Soujouk*, authentic Mediterranean beef sausage, revs up the colorful and flavorful combination of peppers, zucchini and eggplant. The dried salted beef is spiced with garlic, pepper, cumin and a Turkish seven-spice mixture. Middle Eastern stores feature this variety, but it might be difficult to find a kosher version. If you cannot, substitute chicken, turkey or veal sausage, and then add a pinch of cumin or red pepper flakes to enliven the dish.

Yields: 4 to 6 servings; Start to Finish: Under 2 hours

1 eggplant, cut into chunks, salted and drained

3 to 4 tablespoons olive oil

1 medium onion, chopped (about ¾ cup)

4 cloves garlic, chopped

2 zucchini, cut into bite-size chunks

2 tomatoes, cut into bite-size chunks

1 green pepper, cored, seeded and cut into chunks

1 red pepper, cored, seeded and cut into chunks

Kosher salt and pepper

½ teaspoon dried oregano

½ pound beef, turkey, chicken or veal sausage, chunked

Place the chunks of eggplant in a colander and sprinkle liberally with kosher salt. Place a plate on top of the eggplant to help weigh it down. Let the eggplant drain for 30 minutes. Rinse, dry and reserve. While the eggplant drains, prepare the remaining vegetables. Heat the olive oil in a large skillet, cook and stir the onion and garlic, over medium heat, until lightly browned, about 10 minutes. Stir in the zucchini, tomatoes, eggplant, green and red pepper. Cover and cook over low heat for 30 minutes. While the vegetables cook, preheat the oven to 350 degrees.

Spoon the vegetables into a baking dish and season to taste with salt, pepper and oregano. Stir in the sausage and bake at 350 degrees, uncovered, for 30 minutes.

Feedback

Eggplants are 95% water and if not handled properly can soak up your sauce or cause it to be watery. Whenever possible, drain the eggplant as described above before adding it to the rest of your ingredients. If roasting the eggplant, this step is not necessary.

Luna Cohen's *Loukoumades*–Greek Doughnuts

Few desserts have as rich a history as these small, sweet bites that are free-formed doughnuts. As early as the first Olympics, "honey tokens" were given to the victorious Olympians. Throughout Greece, *loukoumades* are sold at street fairs, pastry shops and served in *Sephardic* households as a celebratory treat anytime and especially at Chanukah. Rachel's recipe is pure and simple, with just the right ingredients to create these puffy delights. If you can find Greek honey, which is darker than most, it makes a wonderful finish to the dish.

Yields: 40 to 50 "doughnuts", about 10 to 12 servings; Start to Finish: Under 2 hours

For the dough:

1 package (¼-ounce) or 2¼ teaspoons active dry yeast

1 teaspoon sugar

2 cups warm water

3 to 4 cups all-purpose flour

Oil for deep frying

Toppings:

Golden Greek honey, confectioner's sugar, ground nuts or ground cinnamon (optional)

To prepare the dough you will need a large bowl, as the dough will rise to more than double its size. Dissolve the yeast, sugar and 1 cup of warm water (water temperature should be between 105 to 115 degrees). Allow the yeast to bubble for 5 to 10 minutes. (If it does not, either your water was not the correct temperature, or your yeast was not fresh. Discard and start again, as the dough will not rise or puff up properly). Stir in 3 cups of flour and the remaining 1 cup of warm water. Mix until the dough is a cross between a very thick batter and sticky dough. It will resemble thick oatmeal, and when you tug on the dough, it will resist and pull back. You can add up to 1 more cup of flour to achieve this consistency. Cover the bowl with plastic wrap and let it double in size, about 1 to 1 ½ hours. The dough is ready when it has doubled and its craggy bumps resemble the surface of the moon.

In a saucepan or deep fryer, heat 3 to 4 inches of vegetable oil to about 375 degrees (if you have a thermometer to test the oil temperature, it is helpful). It is important to maintain that temperature to prevent the doughnuts from absorbing the oil. Have a bowl of warm water, 2 tablespoons, and a plate with a paper towel ready. Dip the spoons in the warm water. Scoop out some dough onto one spoon and use the second spoon to push it into the hot oil. If the dough does not sizzle and immediately float and become golden brown, your oil is not hot enough. Begin dropping the dough into the oil, being careful not to let water from the spoons drip into the pot. Do not overcrowd the pot, it lowers the temperature and the doughnuts will be greasy. The dough should quickly puff up and float to the top. They will become golden brown and many will turn themselves over; nudge those that don't, so all sides become golden. When they are done, remove them with tongs, shake off the excess oil back into the pot and drain on the waiting paper towel. Continue frying until all the doughnuts are cooked. Drizzle honey over the fried dough and have plenty of napkins standing by! You can also sprinkle them with confectioner's sugar, roll them in chopped nuts or cinnamon. They are best when eaten right away.

Solomon and Koula Koen Kofinas

In their own words

I met Solomon and Koula at the Kehila Kedosha Janina Synagogue, a small New York land-marked temple that is nestled between Asian food stores and the trendy new establishments dotting New York's famed Lower East Side. This synagogue is the center of their lives and the pride and respect they have for their Romaniote traditions permeated our conversation. Solomon is a human dictionary for Koula and together they tell me about their family history, lives in America and joy of cooking their Greek specialties.

Koula

My family originally came from Ionannina, in the northwest part of Greece, but eventually settled in Larissa. I had one brother and two sisters. My father sold dry goods, traveling from bazaar to bazaar selling and trading his wares. In Greece, it was difficult for Jews to have regular jobs, so we created our own work and peddled to make a living. When I was about six, we began hearing how the Nazis were making life difficult for the Jews in Athens. My father moved us to a very small village, maybe only a few hundred people, where no one bothered anyone. We took non-Jewish Greek names, and spent the war years living there. Before that time, my parents had very lucky names: my Dad was called Siman Tov and my mother Mazel Tov; maybe the luck from their names brought us luck in surviving. I can still see my father and brother fishing out back and using the fish to barter for other food. When the war ended we went back to Larissa, and started from the beginning all over again. That's where I stayed until I came here in 1956.

Solomon

I was born in Athens and when the war came to Greece, my brother and I ran away from our home and lived outside the city until the war ended. I lost the rest of my family in Auschwitz. After the war, we returned to our home and found out that German soldiers had lived there. We gained our house back by asking the Greek police to return it to us. I met Koula here in America and we have been married for 51 years, we have two sons and two grandsons. I am proud to say that I married a Cohen, which is spelled Koen in Greek, because we do not have the letter C in our language. Our son now leads the service in the Temple and he is teaching our grandsons the same traditions.

Top left: Koula Kofinas and her wedding party

Koula Kofinas' *Fasülye*–Braised Marrow Bones with White Beans

Koula recalls, "Friday nights we always had meat. Meat was reserved for celebrations like Passover and Rosh Hashanah, and of course, Shabbos. It's not the law, it's tradition. Some years we only had bones, this is why we made *fasülye* (beans) and we would make believe we were eating meat. We would eat the marrow from the bones, it was better than caviar." While this dish showcases the rich, buttery marrow, some prefer to have some meat on their bones. If that's the case, you can substitute short ribs.

Yields: 4 servings (about 2 bones per person); Start to Finish: Under 3 hours

½ pound (about 1 cup) giant lima beans or any dried white bean

4 tablespoons olive oil

2 large onions, diced (about 2 cups)

2 carrots, peeled and finely chopped (about 1 cup)

2 celery ribs, finely chopped (about 1 cup)

4 cloves garlic, chopped

1 (28-ounce) can chopped tomatoes, with its juice

2 pounds (about 8-thick cut) round marrowbones

2 teaspoons kosher salt

½ teaspoon black pepper

Bring a medium pot of water to boil and cook the beans for several minutes, drain and let the beans sit in a bowl of cold water for 1 hour. Drain and reserve. While the beans soak, prepare the remaining ingredients.

Heat the olive oil, in a Dutch oven or covered pot, cook and stir the onions, carrots and celery, over medium heat until just beginning to soften, about 10 minutes. Stir in the garlic and continue cooking for 5 minutes. Pour in the tomatoes with their juice, and add the drained beans. Tuck the marrowbones in the sauce and add enough water to cover the bones by 3 inches (about 2 cups of water). Season with salt and pepper. Cover and cook, over low heat, for 2 hours or until the vegetables, beans and marrow are soft. Check the pot occasionally to see if additional water needs to be added. If the center marrow begins to ooze from the bones, remove them from the pot and allow the beans to cook until tender. You don't want to lose the marrow in the sauce. In the end, if you find the sauce is too watery, Koula suggests you leave the lid off the pot for the last 15 minutes. Serve with plenty of crisp bread for dunking.

Feedback

Mirepoix is the French term for the classic combination of sautéed onions, carrots and celery. This trio of aromatic vegetables makes a wonderful foundation for hundreds of preparations. Slow simmered stews, such as Koula's *fasülye*, benefit from this "holy trinity" of ingredients. Generally, the ratio is 2 parts onion, 1 part carrot, 1 part celery, but it can be adjusted to your taste.

Koula Kofinas' *Papoutsakia*—Stuffed Eggplant Skins

Koula explains, "When we grew up we made everything from scratch, it took me twenty years to buy anything from outside." Her ingredients represent the best of Greek cooking: fragrant parsley, flavorful oregano, good olive oil and fresh vegetables. Her stuffed eggplant brings in the salty addition of crumbled feta cheese, which melts into the meaty eggplant stuffing.

Yields: 4 servings; Start to Finish: Under 1½ hours

2 large eggplants, halved lengthwise (do not peel)

1 pound feta or farmer's cheese, crumbled (about 4 cups)

2 tablespoons finely chopped fresh flat-leaf parsley

½ cup seasoned bread crumbs

Kosher salt and pepper

1 egg

2 to 3 tablespoons olive oil

Preheat the oven to 375 degrees and coat the bottom of a baking dish with olive oil.

Bring a large pot of salted water to boil and cook the eggplants until they just start to soften. Do not let them fully cook or become too soft. Remove the eggplants from the pot and allow them to cool.

In a medium size bowl combine the feta, parsley, bread crumbs, salt (go light, the feta is salty) and pepper. When the eggplants are cool enough to handle, scoop out the meat, being careful not to scrape too deep or tear the skins, they need to be intact to stuff. As you are scooping out the meat, discard the large seeds, they are bitter. Chop the eggplant meat into small pieces and combine with the feta mixture. Crack the egg into the eggplant and feta and mix thoroughly. Fill each eggplant skin with one-quarter of the eggplant and feta stuffing.

Place the eggplants, skin side down in the prepared baking dish. Drizzle the tops with a little olive oil. Bake at 375 degrees for 45 minutes or until golden brown. Serve with a drizzle of olive oil.

Solomon Kofinas' Roasted Baby Eggplant

Solomon credits his longevity to Koula's culinary talents, "I'm here after so many years because of her good cooking." But Koula is not the only chef in the house. Solomon enjoys preparing eggplant his way. He prefers the sweeter Japanese eggplant, which is much more like what they ate in Greece, small with few if any seeds. If you cannot locate Japanese eggplant, substitute small baby eggplant.

Yields: 4 servings; Start to Finish: Under 1 hour

1 pound Japanese eggplant or baby eggplant, quartered lengthwise

1 tablespoon finely chopped fresh flat-leaf parsley

Kosher salt and pepper

1 teaspoon dried oregano

3 tablespoons olive oil

Preheat the oven to 400 degrees. Toss the eggplant slices with the parsley, salt, pepper and oregano. Pour ½ cup water into a baking dish large enough to comfortably hold the eggplant. Place the eggplants in the dish. Bake at 400 degrees for 45 minutes, or until the eggplants are soft. Periodically, check to see if water is needed to prevent the eggplant from scorching. Sprinkle with grated cheese and a drizzle of olive oil before serving.

Feedback
While fresh herbs are almost always preferred, I actually recommend dried oregano in place of fresh. The flavor is a little less pungent and will not overwhelm the other ingredients. When adding dried oregano, or any dried herb to a dish, gently rub it between your fingers to release its full flavor.

Stella Levi

In her own words

Stella is just one of those women. If you passed her on the street you would marvel at her stature and elegance. If you spoke to her you would be enthralled by her intellect and humor. Much of her time is devoted to New York's Centro Primo Levi, which "seeks to broaden the historical perspective of contemporary Jewish life and encourage understanding among different peoples." Her story is unfortunately typical for Greek Jews during the Holocaust, but her attitude is amazingly strong and positive.

I was born on the island of Rhodes and as far as I know so were many generations of my family before me. The Jewish community was considered *Sephardic*. I had a good childhood living in the "Juderia," the Jewish district of the walled city of the island. The other inhabitants within the walls were the Muslims of Turkish nationality. Rhodes and the other 11 smaller islands called Dodecanese were part of the Italian territory from 1912 till the end of the Second World War, when they were ceded to Greece.

Yes, I had a very pleasant childhood: summers at the beach nearby and mild winters that allowed the young people to go for long excursions outside the town to visit the recently excavated Greek classical monuments, an amphitheater and temple. To remember the weekly celebration of Shabbos brings still a pleasant feeling mixed with a strong sense of loss, the same that I have also for the many festivals that were always concluded with my mother and aunts and neighboring women singing beautiful songs in Ladino and Hebrew.

After the elementary Jewish school, I went to the Italian school run by Catholic nuns. It was an excellent school but unfortunately the gates were to be closed to us (Jewish girls, and the same for the school for the boys) in September, 1938 following the laws of "racial discrimination" against the Jews issued by the fascist government of Benito Mussolini. True, we at Rhodes did not experience the ferocious anti-Semitism and persecutions that plagued many Jewish communities in other European countries, but nonetheless we definitely bore material suffering and the emotional alienation and stigma of second-class citizens.

The community saw a big emigration of young people, especially young men, going either to the then Belgian Congo and/or Rhodesia (today Zimbabwe). My brother left with them. The war years were painful, what with shortages of food and the constant bombardments by the British and American air forces: the Juderia, being next to the commercial port, one of the main targets of the air raids, suffered much destruction and loss of lives. But the beginning of the end of the Jewish community of Rhodes and of the town of Rhodes as I knew it, came in September, 1943, when the Italian government surrendered. The country split in two: pro-Mussolini and the Germans against the rest who went with the King and General Badoglio. For reasons that I cannot still fathom, the government in Rhodes surrendered the island with some tens of thousand of Italian soldiers to the cunning Germans.

The small Jewish community, unaware of the atrocities and mass killings already happening to their coreligionists in Poland and other countries under the Nazi regime, waited with dread nonetheless for the end of the war. But the end came in a manner so barbarous, so cruel, and so inhuman that I still do not like to talk about or to think about it. Suffice to say that we all ended up in Auschwitz-Birkenau where most perished. A very small percentage of Jews from this region survived—among them were my sister and I. In 1947 we arrived in New York to join some members of my family who had immigrated to the U.S.A. before the war. A few years later I got married and had a son, who lives in New Jersey and gave me the joy of having three good grandchildren.

Stella Levi's *Bamya*–Okra Stew with Chicken

One of Stella's favorite Greek specialties is *Bamya*, Greek for okra, which inspired this recipe. Chicken and okra stew is much like a New Orleans gumbo. Spicy cumin and aromatic coriander wake up the chicken and okra as they slow simmer with tomatoes, onions and garlic. Stella feels lamb or beef marries well with the sauce, so experiment with your favorite. A fresh squeeze of lemon adds a refreshing note at the end.

Yields: 4 servings; Start to Finish: Under 2 hours

1½ to 2 pounds chicken thighs	2 cloves garlic, chopped
Kosher salt and pepper	2 cups chopped canned tomatoes, with their juice
¼ cup olive oil	
1 pound fresh okra, rinsed, and cut into 1-inch slices (remove the ends, they are tough)	1 teaspoon ground cumin
	1 teaspoon ground coriander
2 medium onions, diced (about 1½ cups)	Juice of 1 lemon (about 2 to 3 tablespoons)

Pat the chicken dry, and then generously season the chicken with kosher salt and pepper. Heat the olive oil in a Dutch oven, and brown the chicken in batches, on all sides, over medium heat. While they brown, prepare the okra, onions and garlic. When the chicken is browned, remove it to a waiting plate. Don't worry about the little pieces stuck to the bottom of the pot; you'll be cooking the dish in this pot, so they'll join in the fun later.

In the same pot, add a little olive oil if needed, cook and stir the onions, over medium heat, until lightly browned, about 10 minutes. Stir in the garlic, and cook for an additional minute or two. Add the tomatoes, cumin, coriander, 2 cups of water and the juice of half the lemon. Add the chicken into the pot (not the liquid that has collected on the plate). Season with salt and pepper. Turn the heat to low, cover and cook for 45 minutes. After 30 minutes, preheat the oven to 350 degrees; the *bamya* will finish cooking in the oven.

When 45 minutes is up, transfer the pot to the oven and bake, covered, at 350 degrees, for 30 minutes. Add water if the sauce is too thick: the okra is gummy and is a great natural thickener. If the sauce is thin, uncover the pot for the final 15 minutes. Squeeze the rest of the lemon juice over the finished dish just before serving.

Stella Levi's *Sevoyas Reynadas*–Stuffed Onions

While Eastern Europeans prefer to stuff cabbage leaves, Greek cooks favor grape leaves and these delicious slow simmered stuffed sweet onions. We've added Stella's variation, which involves frying the stuffed onions. Either way you prepare this dish, it is a creative and bold way to serve this established favorite.

Yields: 25 rolls; Start to Finish: Under 2½ hours

5 Large (about 5-inch diameter) onions, peeled, stem and root removed

For the filling:

1 pound ground beef or veal

3 tablespoons uncooked rice

1 tablespoon olive oil

1 tablespoon finely chopped fresh flat-leaf parsley

1 tablespoon tomato sauce, with pulp

1 tablespoon water

Kosher salt and pepper

For the sauce:

3 tablespoons olive oil

4 plum tomatoes, peeled and chopped into 1-inch pieces

Kosher salt and pepper

1 teaspoon oregano

Toothpicks to help close the rolls

Bring a very large pot (one that can hold all 5 onions submerged at one time) of salted water to boil. Gently place the onions in the water and boil for at least 20-25 minutes. While the onions boil, mix all the filling ingredients and reserve.

With a slotted spoon, carefully remove the onions from the pot, but keep the water on a slow boil, you might need to drop the onions back in if the layers need additional coaxing. Let the onions cool, covered with a towel, this will help them steam, making them easier to peel. When the onions are cool enough to handle cut a slit in the onion vertically, from stem to root. (Imagine the onion is a globe of the earth, cut the onion from the North Pole to the South Pole, not around the equator!) Peel the onion, layer by layer, they should easily fall away and feel soft and pliable. You will need to continually trim the root and stem to help the layers fall off. Try to remove the thin film that you will find between the layers. Each onion should yield about 5 pieces, large enough to fill. Reserve the small inside portions to chop for the sauce.

Take an onion layer and fill it with a teaspoon of the meat filling. Roll the onion up: the onion will actually curl and form a tight roll on its own. Use a toothpick to close if needed.

To prepare the sauce, you will need to peel the tomatoes. Remove the small stem and then with a sharp paring knife, carefully remove the skin. If you are not confident with that method, bring a medium pot of water to boil. Prepare a bowl with ice water. Make a small X in the bottom of each tomato. Drop the tomatoes, one at a time, into the boiling water. After 30 seconds, remove with a slotted spoon. Plunge the tomato into the ice bath, the skin should begin to fall away. Chop the tomatoes into 1-inch chunks and reserve.

(Continued)

Roughly chop the small inner onion portions that you reserved. Heat the oil in a large sauté pan, cook and stir the chopped onions, over medium heat, until lightly browned, about 10 minutes. Stir in the chopped tomatoes, and allow them to simmer with the onion. Pour 1 cup of water into the pan and then gently place the filled onions in the pot, nestling them in the sauce close together, layering them if necessary. Season to taste with salt, pepper and oregano. Cover and cook on medium-low heat for 45 minutes. After that time, add water if needed (you don't want the sauce too dry or diluted) and turn the onions over. Cover and continue to cook an additional 45 minutes. Serve by spooning the sauce over the onions, remembering to remove the toothpicks before eating.

Variation: Sometimes Stella fries the onion rolls before placing them in the sauce. Simply beat 2 eggs and dip the filled rolls into the beaten egg, then dredge lightly in flour. Fry, in a large skillet, coated with olive oil, for several minutes on all sides, until lightly browned. Place the rolls in the sauce and continue as directed above.

Rachel Angelou Mosios

In her own words

Rachel has a warm Greek accent and a personality to match. She is an Athenian Jew who, like many from her area, survived the war by living as Christians in the Greek mountains. Both she and her husband came to America after the war where they met in New York and built a home centered on Jewish traditions and wonderful Greek flavors.

I am very proud of where I came from, which is Athens, Greece. I was the oldest child, having no sisters and three brothers. The people in Athens were very close to the Jewish people. When things got bad, they gave us IDs with Christian names. The police tried to help other Greek Jewish people. We lived a very festive life. I remember very clearly a night where our family was at a great big party. Everyone was dancing and celebrating; yet they knew the war was approaching. From 1943 until 1944, we were okay. We had to hide occasionally from the Germans, but because my father was a very good businessman, we always had materials to trade with the farmers for food. My father had heard from his business partner, a man from Salonika, that it was unsafe to stay in Athens. My mother did not want to leave, but my father convinced her. On the last Passover that I spent in our hometown, I got very drunk! I was only nine but I remember being so tipsy. Soon after that holiday we went into hiding. We went to a city called Pedely, a place that people would go to when they were ill. At first we lived in a small cabin at the top of the mountains. One day, we found other members of our family and we went crazy with joy! We moved into a "villa" that we shared with them for the duration of the war. My father was always on the lookout, and fortunately for us the Communists in the area hated the Germans more than they hated the Jews. When the Germans would approach, they would use a megaphone to warn us. I really believe they saved us many times.

After the war, we returned to our home, which was such a mess. The house was part of my mother's trousseau, and we were not going to leave it until we had to. When I was twenty, in 1954, my favorite aunt brought us to Astoria, Queens, which was a very Greek section of New York. I met my husband, Victor, who I am married to for 51 years. Together we have two children and six grandchildren. I was proud to learn that recently one of my granddaughters stood up at her school and told her classmates the importance of never forgetting the Holocaust. That is a lesson I am very happy to know she learned and is strong enough to pass on.

Rachel Mosios' Roasted Lamb with Lemon Potatoes

Sunday night meant leg of lamb for Rachel's family. She made the traditional roasted lamb and studded it with garlic, seasoned it with oregano, and treated it to a splash of lemon, which adds an acidic note to the dish. The roasted potatoes linger in the oven after the lamb is cooked and pick up all the flavors of the zesty sauce. In America, you might not be able to find a kosher leg of lamb; feel free to substitute rolled and tied shoulder in its place.

Yields: 6 servings; Start to Finish: Under 2½ hours

1 (3 pound) leg of lamb

3 to 5 cloves garlic, peeled and halved

Kosher salt and pepper

1 teaspoon oregano

Juice of 1 lemon

8 red potatoes (about 2 pounds), peeled and cut into quarters or chunks

Preheat the oven to 350 degrees. With the tip of a sharp knife, pierce the lamb every 2 inches and insert the garlic. While the knife holds the slit open, sprinkle salt and cracked pepper into the roast. Season the entire lamb with additional salt, pepper, oregano and the juice of 1 lemon. Place the squeezed lemon in the bottom of the roasting pan and add ½ cup of water. Roast the lamb for 25 minutes per pound, or until a meat thermometer inserted in the roast reads 150 to 155 degrees. Remove the lamb from the roasting pan and cover with foil; it will gain 5 to 10 degrees while it rests.

Raise the oven temperature to 400 degrees and add the potatoes and ½ cup water to the roasting pan. Cook for 45 to 60 minutes, checking the pan every 20 minutes to see if additional water is needed to prevent the potatoes from scorching and to create the sauce. When the potatoes are crisp on the outside and fork tender on the inside, they are done. Slice the lamb and place in the pan juices and reheat if necessary until warmed through. You can squeeze additional lemon juice into the pan if you prefer a more tart flavor.

Rachel Mosios' Spinach Pie

One of the reasons Rachel loves making this dish is because it boldly features dill, and as Rachel explains, "Greek Jewish people love dill!" While many spinach pies also pile on the parsley, Rachel feels it overwhelms the spinach and cheese and should be used in moderation. Resist the urge to cut this flaky pie into cute triangles; Rachel says they are not traditional. While her mother would make her own phyllo dough, we suggest store bought frozen phyllo, which is readily available in most supermarkets. Phyllo is temperamental, so you might want to have an extra box on hand in case you need additional sheets.

Yields: 30 pieces; Start to Finish: 5 hours to thaw the phyllo, then under 1½ hours

1 box phyllo dough (large sheets), thawed

For the filling:

4 boxes chopped spinach, thawed and drained

1 medium onion, chopped (about ¾ cup)

1 tablespoon olive oil for frying

6 eggs, beaten

2 bunches of scallions (about 12), white and light green portion only, chopped (about ⅔ cup)

1 pound feta cheese, crumbled (about 4 cups)

4 ounces (½ cup) small-curd cottage cheese or Farmer's cheese

2 ounces (¼ cup) cream cheese, softened at room temperature

Kosher salt and pepper

1 large bunch of dill, leaves chopped (about 1 cup)

¼ cup finely chopped fresh flat-leaf parsley

For assembly:

1 cup olive oil

3 tablespoons freshly grated Parmesan cheese

Thaw the phyllo according to package directions, about 5 hours at room temperature or overnight in the fridge. At the same time, thaw and drain the spinach. Remove the liquid from the spinach by squeezing the spinach with your hands, placing it in an old dish towel and squeezing out the liquid, or putting it in your salad spinner.

Heat 1 tablespoon of olive oil, in a large skillet, over medium heat, cook and stir the onions until lightly browned, about 10 minutes. When the onions are translucent, add the spinach to the pan and continue cooking and stirring for several minutes. Place the spinach and onions into a large bowl, stir in the eggs, scallions, feta, cottage cheese, cream cheese, salt (go lightly, feta is a salty cheese) and pepper. Stir to combine all the ingredients, breaking up any large clumps of cheese. Add the chopped dill and parsley. Refrigerate until ready to bake.

Preheat the oven to 375 degrees and prepare a large 15 ½ x 10 ½ -inch jellyroll pan, by coating the bottom with olive oil. A pastry brush is very helpful for this and for the phyllo layering. Open the phyllo dough and cover the sheets with a piece of waxed paper then a damp towel, this is to prevent the phyllo from drying out while you assemble the pie.

Place one sheet of dough on the bottom and brush with oil. Place the next two sheets in the pan so they meet in the middle and hang over the opposite sides. Brush with oil, lay two more sheets in the pan draping those ends over the opposite side, and brush with oil. Continue layering the sheets in the

(Continued)

center of the pan, brushing each sheet with oil. Do not be concerned if some of the sheets tear, there will be many layers and it will not matter in the end. Once you have used half the package (about 10 sheets), spread the spinach mixture in the pan, smoothing it out with an offset spatula, a piece of greased wax paper, or your lightly greased hands. Sprinkle the spinach with the grated Parmesan cheese. Fold the over-hanging sheets over the mixture and begin layering the top sheets, by brushing each with oil and layering them in the center of the pan. When you are done layering, tuck in any straggling edges and brush liberally with the olive oil. Score the pie (cut through the top layers, but not piercing the bottom) into 30 pieces and sprinkle a touch of water on top.

Bake at 375 degrees for 1 hour. If the top browns too quickly, cover loosely with foil and continue baking. Serve warm or cold.

Feedback
Rachel's spinach filling is delicious and versatile and can be used in so many ways. It makes a terrific ingredient for stuffing or layering pasta or filling a pre-baked pie shell to create a quick and easy quiche. If handling the phyllo seems daunting, a wonderful variation is to buy puff pastry shells. Bake them according to the package directions. When fully cooked, spoon the spinach filling into the shells and heat through. They make an elegant appetizer or a delectably light lunch.

The Turiel Family

As told by Bernie Turiel

Bernie Turiel is a very articulate gentleman who credits Selahattin Ülkümen for having saved his family and dozens of other Rhodes Jews. It is interesting to note that Ülkümen, a Muslim, was the reason the term "Righteous Christians" was changed. He was the first Muslim to be honored by Yad Vashem, and from that time on, those courageous men and women who risked their lives to save Jewish people were known as "Righteous Among the Nations."

I was born on the island of Rhodes in November, 1934. At that time Rhodes was an Italian possession. My immediate family consisted of my father, Daniel, mother, Mathilde Nahum, and younger brother, Elliot. My mother was born in Izmir, Turkey. When she married my father in 1933, she came to live in Rhodes. Because of her closeness with her family in Turkey, my mother made sure that she registered with the Turkish Consul in order to remain a citizen of Turkey. This turned out to be very fortunate for our family and the others who also registered.

In early September, 1943, the Germans took possession of Rhodes. The adult male Jews were asked to report and register periodically with the German authorities. On the first day of Passover in 1944, after we had come home from synagogue, a severe air raid took place. While we were sitting having our lunch at home, a bomb dropped down the street from us and we saw the home that was hit go up in flames. My father became greatly alarmed as to what was happening in the city. He decided that it was time for us to move out of our home and move to a nearby village.

Our family had an old farm in a village outside the city, but it had no adequate living facilities. Abidin, a Turkish farmer who lived in the same village, was the caretaker of our farm and was a good friend of the family. Without announcement, we showed up at his doorstep after we left the city. He and his family welcomed us, and even though they had meager living facilities in their home, they emptied out one room, laid out mattresses on the floor and we were welcomed to spend as much time as we needed with his family. We continued to live on the farm until July of 1944. Living with this Turkish family was one of the happiest events

of my life. Even though we did not live in comfort, we were welcomed into their home. I remember learning to ride horses on the farm, cultivate the fields, do the farming, pick fruits and nuts from the trees, and join the sons of Abidin in work and play. We had become part of his family and they had become part of ours.

In January of 1943 a young Turkish diplomat, Selahattin Ülkümen, was appointed as the Consul General to the island of Rhodes. On July 19, 1944 after the arrival of SS officers in Rhodes, a leader of the Jewish community was informed by a German officer that all Jewish males over the age of 16 years had to report to a designated spot the following day. This time, when the adult male Jews were gathered, they were immediately placed in a detention center by a group of SS officers. Wives and children of all the men detained were ordered to report within 48 hours. Mr. Ülkümen was aware of what was going on in Europe, just as we all were aware of the existence of the concentration and extermination camps. He immediately went to confront the German Commander on the island, General von Kleemann. Mr. Ülkümen demanded that all Turkish citizens and their families be protected since the Turkish Republic was a neutral country and not involved in the war. With his determination and energy, he got the German authorities to concede to the release of the Jews holding Turkish passports and their families. With his energetic and determined intervention on behalf of the Turkish Jews, he was also able to procure the release of my father and other heads of families from the detention center who were married to women who maintained their Turkish citizenship, even though there was no basis for this contention. He also made a valiant effort to seek the release of other Jews who had abandoned their Turkish citizenship.

Through his efforts he was able to rescue 42 persons who were either Turkish citizens or married to Turkish citizens. Within days, the Jewish community of Rhodes was placed on three small cargo boats and shipped to the Greek port of Piraeus near Athens, and from Athens they were transported to Auschwitz.

In January of 1945, we were given permission to leave Rhodes, and 26 of us embarked on a sailboat for a prolonged trip that started at dawn. We arrived at Marmaris, Turkey, at about 11:00 p.m. It was a treacherous and hard trip, but we were all happy to land on the shores of Turkey. After a short stay in Marmaris, we were able to travel to Izmir, Turkey, where we lived with my mother's family until we left for the United States in July, 1946. When we came to New York, and until she was in her 90s, my mother continued to make her delicious *Sephardic* dishes: *ojaldres*, (baked phyllo triangles), *ooscas* (delicious sweetened rolls), *bimuelos* (potato pancakes), homemade *harosset* and so many more. I'm hungry now after just describing these dishes, but although I've made some of them, I think Mom had a secret ingredient because hers were always so much better.

In June, 1990, Mr. Ülkümen was honored at Yad Vashem in Jerusalem and his name was placed in the Avenue of the "Righteous Among the Nations" for his efforts in rescuing Jews from deportation from the island of Rhodes. My mother had the honor to be present at the ceremony. He will always be remembered in history as a kind, compassionate and righteous person. My parents had two sons, my brother and me, three grandchildren, and six great grandchildren.

Mathilde Turiel's *Boyos*–Cheese and Potato Turnovers

Mathilde's son Elliot and grandson Josh are the guardians of her potato and cheese stuffed *boyos* recipe. *Boyos*, from the Spanish for bun, are small "oil-dough" filled turnovers, which can be stuffed with a variety of savory fillings. Elliot recalls a close-knit community of Rhodes immigrants gathering on Saturday nights in New York to play endless poker and feast on *Sephardic* specialties such as these.

Yields: 20 to 24 pieces; Start to Finish: Step One: 15 minutes, then refrigerate 6 to 8 hours or overnight; Step Two: Under 45 minutes

For the dough:

1 cup lukewarm water

1 tablespoon salt

2 tablespoons vegetable oil

2 tablespoons vinegar

3 cups all-purpose flour

Vegetable oil to soak the dough

For the filling:

½ russet potato, peeled and boiled

½ pound (or 7.5- ounce package) farmer's cheese

2 eggs

¼ cup grated Parmesan cheese

¼ teaspoon baking powder

½ teaspoon salt

For assembling:

½ cup Parmesan cheese

Step One: In a medium bowl prepare the dough by mixing the water, salt, oil, and vinegar. Slowly sift in the flour and continue mixing until you have smooth, elastic dough. Cover the bowl with a damp cloth and let it sit for 30 minutes. After the dough has rested, form it into small 1 ½-inch diameter balls (size of a golf ball). Place the dough balls in a shallow pan and cover generously with vegetable oil. Refrigerate, covered, for 6 to 8 hours or overnight.

Prepare the filling by bringing a pot of salted water to boil. Cook the potato until fork tender, about 20 minutes. Mash the potato and then stir in the farmer's cheese, eggs, grated cheese, baking powder and salt. Cover tightly with plastic wrap and refrigerate until ready to use.

Step Two: Preheat the oven to 375 degrees, lightly grease a baking sheet and take the dough and filling out of the fridge.

Fill a bowl with ½ cup of grated Parmesan cheese. Place a ball of dough on a flat surface and begin stretching it, being sure not to tear it; the oily dough is not very elastic. Try to create a flat shape resembling a 4 or 5-inch square. Even though the dough is extremely oily, use a pastry brush to spread a little additional oil in the center of each piece (you can use the remaining oil from the pan that the dough rested in overnight). Sprinkle the center of the dough with a pinch of Parmesan cheese. Drop a generous teaspoon of filling in the center. Fold the opposite corners into the middle, making a neat package, being sure there are no openings in the dough. Sprinkle the top with additional Parmesan cheese and place, seam side down, on the prepared baking sheet. Continue this process until you have used all the dough. Bake at 375 degrees for about 30 minutes or until the *boyos* are a lightly browned.

Variations: There are many fillings that can be used for the *boyos*. Why not try our spinach filling (see page 345) or potato and onion filling (see page 322).

Samuel Capsuto

Professional contributor

The Capsuto family and the Turiel's have much in common. They both have their family roots imbedded in the Turkish culture and both enjoy *bimuelos*, a *Sephardic* take on the classic potato pancake. The following is a personal recipe from Samuel Capsuto's family, which brings a regional element and surprisingly yummy flavor to the dish. If you are ever in New York during Passover, visit Capsuto Freres, which features uniquely personal Passover dishes.

Bimuelos de Patata–Potato pancakes

Contributed by Samuel Capsuto, owner of Capsuto Freres, New York

Yields: 14 pancakes; Start to Finish: Under 45 minutes

3 russet potatoes, peeled, boiled and mashed

5 eggs, beaten

1 cup sharp grated cheese

½ teaspoon salt

Vegetable oil for frying

Bring a medium pot of water to boil and cook the potatoes until very soft, about 20 minutes. Drain then mash the potatoes. Add the eggs, cheese and salt. The mixture should be thick. In a large skillet, heat about 1-inch of vegetable oil. When the oil is about 375 degrees, drop the potato mixture, by generous tablespoons, into the oil. Cook until golden on each side, about 3 to 5 minutes per side. If you prefer to bake the pancakes, grease a baking sheet and bake at 375 degrees for 30 minutes.

Raisin Syrup

1 pound raisins

4 cups water

Lemon juice to taste

Bring all the ingredients to boil in a saucepan. Reduce the heat and cook until the liquid is reduced by one- third. Strain the sauce and serve the syrup on the side or drizzled on the potato pancakes.